THE CUBAN ECONOMY AT THE START OF THE TWENTY-FIRST CENTURY

Edited by
Jorge I. Domínguez
Omar Everleny Pérez Villanueva
Lorena Barberia

Published by Harvard University
David Rockefeller Center for Latin American Studies

Distributed by Harvard University Press
Cambridge, Massachusetts
London, England
2004

Library of Congress Cataloging-in-Publication Data

The Cuban economy at the start of the twenty-first century / edited
by Jorge I. Domínguez, Omar Everleny Pérez Villanueva and Lorena
Barberia.
    p. cm.
  Includes bibliographical references.
  ISBN 0-674-01798-6
  1. Cuba—Economic conditions—1990– 2. Cuba—Economic policy. 3.
Cuba—Social conditions—1959– 4. Cuba—Foreign economic relations.
5. Cuba—Foreign relations. 6. Globalization. I. Domínguez, Jorge
I., 1945– II. Pérez Villanueva, Omar Everleny, 1960– III. Barberia,
Lorena, 1971–   .
  HC152.5.C8116 2004
  330.97291—dc22
                        2004021019

May the future of U.S.–Cuban relations be as friendly, collegial, and constructive as has been our work together for this book.

Contents

Introduction

Part I: Macroeconomic Issues

Part II: The International Economic Context

Part III: Social Policy and Welfare

Part IV: Transnational Networks and Government Responses

Tables and Figures

Tables

Tables (continued)

Figures

Boxes

Appendix

Contributors

Lorena Barberia is a Program Associate at the David Rockefeller Center for Latin American Studies at Harvard University. For the last four years, she has directed the Center's efforts to strengthen academic exchanges and deepen collaboration between Cuba and Harvard through initiatives in the social and natural sciences and medicine. With a research focus on economic policy, she is currently working on various articles related to Cuba's development challenges in the 1990s, including work aimed at examining remittance flows and their impact. Prior to joining the David Rockefeller Center for Latin American Studies, she worked in Ecuador and Panama as a junior economist and on research projects at the Harvard Institute for International Development that focused on developing and transition economies. She obtained her Master in Public Policy from the John F. Kennedy School of Government at Harvard University, where she received a Woodrow Wilson Fellowship, after earning her Bachelor of Arts in Economics and Spanish from the University of California, Berkeley.

Xavier de Souza Briggs is Associate Professor of Public Policy at the John F. Kennedy School of Government at Harvard University. His work focuses on poverty, urban policy and collective problem-solving. He is a former Deputy Assistant Secretary for Policy Development and Research at the U.S. Department of Housing and Urban Development. Beyond his nationally-awarded research on young people, cities, segregation and opportunity, he has been a community planner in the South Bronx and other inner-city communities, a senior advisor to The White House and Congress while in the federal government and a consultant to leading national and international organizations. Currently, he is at work on a major book and teaching project—*The Art and Science of Community Problem-Solving*—focusing on what shapes local, collective problem-solving efforts and their impact worldwide, as well as further research on segregation, social capital, and urban neighborhoods. His recent publications include "Reshaping the Geography of Opportunity: Place Effects in Global Perspective" (*Housing Studies*, November 2003) and the introductory chapter "More Pluribus, Less Unum? Changing the Geography of Race and Opportunity" in *The Geography of Opportunity: Race and Community Choice in Metropolitan America* (edited by Xavier de Souza Briggs, forthcoming).

Jorge I. Domínguez is the Clarence Dillon Professor of International Affairs and Director of the Weatherhead Center for International Affairs at Harvard University. He is a past President of the Latin American Studies Association and past Chairman of the Board of the Latin American Scholarship Program of American Universities. He has published *Cuba: Order and Revolution* (1978) and *To Make A World Safe for Revolution: Cuba's Foreign Policy* (1989), both from Harvard University Press, and co-edited with Rafael Hernández, *U.S.–Cuban Relations in the 1990s* (Westview, 1989). His most recent book (with Chappell Lawson and others) is *Mexico's Pivotal Democratic Election: Candidates, Voters, and the Presidential Campaign of 2000* (Stanford, 2003).

Susan Eckstein is Professor of Sociology at Boston University and a past president of the Latin American Studies Association. She is author of *Back from the Future: Cuba under Castro* (Princeton University Press, 1994 and Routledge, 2001), *The Poverty of Revolution: The State and Urban Poor in Mexico* (Princeton University Press 1977, 1988), *The Impact of Revolution: A Comparative Analysis of Mexico and Bolivia* (SAGE, 1976) and some six dozen articles. She is also editor of *Power and Popular Protest: Latin American Social Movements* (University of California 1989, 2001) and co-editor of *Struggles for Social Justice in Latin America* (Routledge, 2002) and *What Justice? Whose Justice: Fighting for Fairness in Latin America* (University of California Press, 2003). She is currently writing about Cuban-American/Cuban transnational ties and their cross-border effects.

Mayra Espina Prieto is a Researcher at the Centro de Investigaciones Psicológicas y Sociológicas (CIPS) and an Adjunct Professor (Titular) at the University of Havana's Department of Sociology. She is a member of the research board of CIPS and the Centro de Antropología and of the editorial board of the journal *TEMAS* and the journal *Cuadernos* (Universidad ARCIS, Santiago de Chile). She is president of the National Commission for Enlace MOST /UNESCO in Cuba. Her recent publications include: "Cuba: reforma económica y reestratificación social" in *Cuba: Sociedad y Trabajo* (edited by J. Busquets) (Fundación Comaposada, 2000), "Transición y dinámica de los procesos socioestructurales" in *Cuba: Construyendo Futuro* (edited by M. Monereo, M. Riera, and J. Valdés) (Viejo Topo, 2000) and "The effects of the Reform on Cuba's Social Structure: An Overview" (*Socialism and Democracy,* Summer 2001*)*. In 2003, she received a grant from the Consejo Latinoamericano de Ciencias Sociales (CLACSO) as part of the CLACSO/CROP Program for Poverty Research in Latin America and the Caribbean.

Anicia García Álvarez is a Professor in the Economics Department and a Researcher at the Centro de Estudios de la Economía Cubana (CEEC) at the University of Havana. Holding a Ph.D. in International Economics from the University of Havana's Department of Economics, her research focuses on the competitiveness of Cuban industry, agricultural markets, economic policies and their impact on agricultural exports. García received her Master's Degree in International Economics from the Universidad de la Republica de Uruguay in 2001. Prior to joining the CEEC, she was an economist at the Instituto Nacional de Investigaciones Económicas at the Ministry of Economics and Planning. Recent publications include "Productividad y factores de producción en la agricultura cubana" in *Cuba, reflexiones sobre su economía* (Editorial Félix Varela, 2002); "Eficiencia técnica y producto potencial en el agro cubano" in *La economía cubana en el 2001* (CEEC, 2002), and "Sustitución de importaciones de alimentos en Cuba: necesidad vs. posibilidad" in *CD 8vo Seminario de Economía Cubana* (CEEC, 2003).

Pedro Monreal González is Senior Researcher and Professor at the Centro de Investigaciones de Economía Internacional (CIEI) at the University of Havana and Foreign Professor at the School of International Studies at Utsunomiya University in Japan. He received the Ph.D. in Economics from the University of Havana. A development economist, he has published *Cuba: Restructuring the Economy. A Contribution to the Debate* (with Julio Carranza and Luis Gutiérrez) (Institute of Latin American Studies, University of London, 1996) and edited *Development Prospects in Cuba: Issues of an Agenda* (Institute of Latin American Studies, University of London, 2001). He received the 2003 international award "Caribbean Thought" for the book *Dilemas de la globalización en el Caribe: Hacia una nueva agenda de desarrollo en Cuba* (with Julio Carranza) (Siglo XXI Editores, forthcoming). He currently serves as consultant to UNESCO's Regional Office of Culture for Latin America and the Caribbean.

Omar Everleny Pérez Villanueva is a Researcher at the Centro de Estudios de la Economía Cubana (CEEC) and a Professor in the Economics Department at the University of Havana. He received his Ph.D. in Economics from the University of Havana and a Master's in Economics and International Political Economy from the Centro de Investigaciones y Docencias Económicas in Mexico City. A macroeconomist, his recent publications include *La realidad de lo imposible: La salud pública en Cuba* with Miguel Figueras (Editorial Ciencias Sociales, 1998), "Foreign Direct Investment in Cuba: Recent Experience and Prospects" in *Development Prospects in Cuba: An Agenda in the Making* (edited by Pedro Monreal González, Institute of Latin American Studies, 2002). He served as an advisor to the City of Havana from 2000 to 2002.

Dwight H. Perkins is the Harold Hitchings Burbank Professor of Political Economy of Harvard University and Director of the Harvard University Asia Center. He is past Chairman of the Department of Economics, 1977–1980 and the former Director of the Harvard Institute for International Development (HIID), 1980–1995. He has authored or edited twelve books and over one hundred articles on economic history and economic development, with special references to the economies of China, Korea, Vietnam and the other nations of East and Southeast Asia. His most recent books include *Innovative East Asia: The Future of Growth* (with Shahid Yusuf and others) (Oxford University Press, 2003) and *Industrialization and the State: The Changing Role of Government in Taiwan's Economy, 1945–1998* (with Chen Kuo Hsu and Li-Min Hsueh) (Harvard University Press, 2001).

Jorge Mario Sánchez Egozcue is an Assistant Professor in the Department of Economics and a Researcher at Centro de Estudios de los Estados Unidos (CESEU) at the University of Havana. A Ph.D. candidate in a joint program in International Economics of the University of Barcelona, Spain, and the University of Havana, his doctoral dissertation is on the challenges in Cuba's reinsertion within Caribbean-U.S. trade. He received a Master's Degree from Carleton University Ottawa in international economics in 1995. His most recent publications include "Cuba, estabilización y tipo de cambio" (*Revista comercio exterior,* 2000) and *El conflicto Estados Unidos–Cuba* (Editorial Félix Varela, 1998).

Viviana Togores González is an Assistant Professor in the Department of Economics and a Researcher at the Centro de Estudios de la Economía Cubana (CEEC). A Ph.D. candidate in a joint program in International Economics of the University of Barcelona, Spain, and the University of Havana, her research focuses on poverty, the informal sector, labor markets, cooperatives, and the development of small and medium enterprises in Cuba. She has published numerous articles including: "Una mirada al gasto social en Cuba a partir de la crisis de los noventa" in *Seguridad social en Cuba: Diagnóstico, retos y perspectivas* (Nueva Sociedad, 2003); "La Organización Mundial del Comercio y Convenio de Lomé, posible inserción de Cuba" (with Tania García) in *La última reforma agraria del siglo: La agricultura cubana entre el cambio y el estancamiento* (Nueva Sociedad, 2000); "Cuba: efectos sociales de la crisis y el ajuste económico de los 90's" in *Balance de la economía cubana a finales de los 90's* (CEEC, 1999); and "Consideración sobre el sector informal de la economía: un estudio de su comportamiento en Cuba" (mimeo, CEEC, 1997).

Miren Uriarte is an Associate Professor of Human Services and Community Planning in the College of Public and Community Services at the University of Massachusetts Boston. She is a senior research associate at the Mauricio Gastón Institute for Latino Community Development and Public Policy, where she served as founding director from 1989 to 1993. She is a sociologist, specializing in applied sociology and race and ethnic relations. Her most recent publications include "The High Stakes of High Stakes Testing" in *The Power of Culture* (edited by Zeynep Beykont, Harvard Education Publishing Group, 2002); *Latinos in Rhode Island: A Scan of Issues Affecting the Latino Population in Rhode Island (2002)*, a monograph published by the Rhode Island Foundation, and *Cuban Social Policy at a Crossroads: Maintaining Priorities, Transforming Practice*, a monograph published by Oxfam America (2002).

Preface

by John H. Coatsworth

Only two economies in Latin America managed to grow in the 1980s, ending the decade with higher per capita incomes than at the beginning. One of the two was Cuba.[1] Cuba grew its economy, in part, through careful management of its economic relations with the Socialist Bloc led by the Soviet Union. The benefits of this strategy were impressive: rising standards of living in a society characterized by a high degree of equality and universal access to employment, basic nutrition, housing, education and medical care. When the Soviet Union fell apart and the Socialist Bloc disintegrated, Cuba confronted an economic catastrophe roughly equivalent to what would occur in the rest of Latin America if the U.S. government were suddenly to impose an economic embargo on trade and investment on the Western Hemisphere.

More than a decade has passed since Cuba's so-called "Special Period" began. This book analyzes the extraordinary shock of 1990 and its impact on Cuban productivity and welfare, how the Cuban economy survived and began to recover from this shock, and the implications of this experience for Cuba's economic strategy and social development.

The Cuban Economy at the Start of the Twenty-First Century is the product of discussion and debate among U.S. and Cuban scholars with diverse interests and perspectives. Its primary goal is to make information and analysis on the contemporary Cuban economy available to students, scholars and the public. Like every work of history or social science, it seeks to advance understanding of important events and processes, focus attention on key issues and contribute to improving the quality of future discussion and debate.

Since its founding in December 1994, the David Rockefeller Center has assigned a high priority to overcoming the many obstacles that impede scholarly collaboration and exchange between individuals and institutions in Cuba and the United States. Guiding these efforts has been the conviction that restoring and enhancing cooperation between the U.S. and Cuban academic communities can play a significant role in promoting peaceful changes within and between our two countries. In the past ten years, the Center has played host to 50 Cuban visiting scholars for extended periods of work and collaboration in fields as diverse as archival preservation and indexing, economics, history, tropical medicine, political science, public administration and public health. An even larger number of Harvard faculty and students have traveled to Cuban for research or to engage in other educational activities.

The Center has also sponsored six academic conferences focusing on Cuba, including such topics as the history of U.S.-Cuban cultural relations, the impact of recent health reforms on public health systems in Latin America and the lessons derived from Cuba's public health model, the history of the former Harvard Botanical Garden—now the beautifully maintained Jardín Botánico de Cienfuegos, the lessons to be learned from Cuba's dengue control program; the current and future prospects for U.S. business in Cuba, and issues relating to poverty and social policy in Cuba in the context of recent work in developing countries and the United States. The first of these conferences resulted in the joint publication, with the Centro Juan Marinello, of a volume of papers entitled *Culturas Encontradas: Cuba y los Estados Unidos* (Havana, 2001) edited by John H. Coatsworth and Rafael Hernández.

The Cuban academic and scientific institutions with which the Center has cooperated, including the Centro Juan Marinello, the research institutes of the University of Havana, the Instituto de Medicina Tropical Pedro Kourí, the Jardín Botánico de Cienfuegos and the Academia de Ciencias, have demonstrated a high level of professionalism and commitment to international scientific and scholarly standards.

Harvard faculty and students have benefited from these exchanges and collaborations, as have so many at other institutions throughout the United States. We have learned from our Cuban colleagues, from their knowledge of their fields and their passion for truth, from their resilience in the face of the hardships their country has faced, from their patriotism, and from their extraordinary warmth and humanity.

The David Rockefeller Center's program of scholarly collaboration and exchanges with Cuba has received generous support from the John D. and Catherine MacArthur Foundation, the Ford Foundation, and the Christopher Reynolds Foundation. Early versions of many of the chapters in this volume were written by Cuban scholars who visited Harvard University on research visits made possible by the MacArthur Foundation's support. The Ford Foundation provided crucial support for the April 2003 and January 2004 workshops on poverty and social policy jointly organized by Xavier de Souza Briggs of Harvard University and Miren Uriarte at the University of Massachusetts-Boston with Cuba's Centro de Investigaciones Psicológicas y Sociológicas (CIPS).

Discussions among participants at this meeting led to two of the chapters and the Barberia, Briggs and Uriarte commentary contained in this volume. The translation and publication of this volume was supported by a grant from the Christopher Reynolds Foundation, which for over a decade has been a crucial supporter of policy research on the lessons learned from Cuba's economic reforms.

On behalf of the editors, I also want to thank the anonymous reviewers of this volume whose comments greatly improved the final product, June Carolyn Erlick for her careful editorial assistance in the final stages of the manuscript preparation, and Yadira Rivera for administrative support. The authors in this volume are also grateful to the University of Havana and its research centers, namely the Centro de Estudios de la Economía Cubana (CEEC), the Centro de Investigaciones sobre la Economía Internacional (CIEI), and the Centro de Estudios de los Estados Unidos (CESEU) for many valuable academic exchanges in the social sciences over the years. Finally, thanks are due to those policy makers and officials in both governments who have helped to advance bilateral scholarly cooperation, and to the staff in both countries who provided the logistical support that permits projects such as this to take place and come to fruition.

Notes

1   The other was Colombia, whose economic "success" was due, in part, to the export of illegal substances to the United States and came at a high price—homicide rates from drug wars that made it one of the most dangerous countries on earth. Maddison's estimates, adjusted for purchasing power parity, would push Chile and the Dominican Republic onto this list by small margins. See Angus Maddison, *The World Economy: Historical Statistics* (Paris: OECD, 2003), pp. 144, 147.

Acronyms

ACS	Association of Caribbean States
ATM	Automatic Teller Machine
BCC	*Banco Central de Cuba* (Central Bank of Cuba)
BFI	*Banco Financiero Internacional*
BNC	*Banco Nacional de Cuba*
CACR	Cuban Assets Control Regulations
CADECA	*Casas de Cambio S.A.* (currency exchange bureaus)
CANF	Cuban-American National Foundation
CARICOM	Caribbean Community and Common Market
CARIFTA	Caribbean Free Trade Area
CCC	Commodity Credit Corporation
CCS	*Cooperativas de Crédito y Servicio* (Credit and Service Cooperatives)
CEA	*Centro de Estudios sobre América* (Center for the Study of the Americas)
CEE	*Comite Estatal de Estadísticas* (predecessor to ONE, State Statistics Committee)
CEEC	*Centro para el Estudio de la Economía Cubana* (Center for the Study of the Cuban Economy)
CEPAL	*Comisión Económica para América Latina y el Caribe* (known by its English acronym as ECLAC)
CESEU	*Centro de Estudios sobre Estados Unidos* (Center for the Study of the United States at the University of Havana)
CIEM	*Centro de Investigaciónes de la Economía Mundial* (Center for the Study of the International Economy at the University of Havana)
CIMEX	*Corporación Importadora y Exportadora, S.A.* (state import-export company)
CIPS	*Centro de Investigaciones Psicológicas y Sociológicas* (the Center for Psychological and Sociological Studies)
CLACSO	*Consejo Latinoamericano de Ciencias Sociales*
CMEA	Council for Mutual Economic Assistance (also COMECON)
COMECON	Council for Mutual Economic Assistance (also CMEA)
CPA	Agricultural Production Cooperatives
CROP	Comparative Research Programme on Poverty

CSME   Caribbean Single Market Economy
DACRE   *Dirección de Asuntos de Cubanos Residentes en el Exterior* (government agency in Ministry of Foreign Affairs that handles the affairs of Cubans residing abroad)
ECLAC   Economic Commission on Latin America and the Caribbean, known by its Spanish acronym as CEPAL
EIU   Economic Intelligence Unit
EJT   *Ejército Juvenil de Trabajo* (Army of the Working Youth)
ETECSA   *Empresa de Telecomunicaciones de Cuba S.A.* (joint venture telephone company)
FAO   United Nations Food and Agriculture Organization
FDI   Foreign Direct Investment
GDP   Gross Domestic Product
HDI   Human Development Index
ILO   International Labor Organization
IMF   International Monetary Fund
INIE   *Instituto Nacional de Investigaciones Económicas* (National Institute of Economic Studies)
ITC   International Trade Commission
JUCEPLAN   *Junta Central de Planificación* (Central Planning Board)
LASA   Latin American Studies Association
LIBOR   London Interbank Offered Rate
MERCOSUR   *Mercado Común del Sur* (Southern Cone Common Market)
MFP   *Ministerio de Finanzas y Precios* (Ministry of Finances and Planning)
MINAG   *Ministerio de Agricultura* (Ministry of Agriculture)
MINAL   *Ministerio de la Industria Alimenticia* (Food Industry Ministry)
MINCIN   *Ministerio de Comercio Interior* (Ministry of Domestic Commerce)
MINFAR   *Ministerio de las Fuerzas Armadas* (Ministry of the Armed Revolutionary Forces)
MINREX   *Ministerio de Relaciones Exteriores* (Ministry of Foreign Relations)
MINTUR   *Ministerio de Turismo* (Ministry of Tourism)

MINVEC *Ministerio de Inversión Extranjera y Colaboración Económica* (Ministry of Foreign Investment and Economic Cooperation)
NAFTA North American Free Trade Agreement
OFAC U.S. Treasury Office of Foreign Assets Control
ONE *Oficina Nacional de Estadísticas* (National Statistics Office)
OPIC Overseas Private Investment Corporation
S.W.I.F.T. Society for Worldwide Interbank Financial Telecommunication
TDA U.S. Trade and Development Agency
TRD *Tiendas de Recaudación de Divisas* (sometimes known as *Tiendas de Recuperación de Divisas*) (government "dollar stores")
UBPC *Unidades Básicas de Producción Cooperativa* (semi-private cooperatives: Basic Cooperative Production Units)
UNCTAD United Nations Conference on Trade and Development
USAID U.S. Agency for International Development
U.S. SBA Small Business Administration
WTO World Trade Organization

1

The Cuban Economy at the Start of the Twenty-First Century: An Introductory Analysis

by Jorge I. Domínguez

- Approximately two million tourists visit every year.
- The diaspora sends a billion dollars every year.
- Sugar exports rank fourth among sources of foreign exchange.
- Foreign firms operate in nearly all sectors of the economy.
- Music compact disks and works of art are newly significant exports.

Cuba's economic future has already begun. An extraterrestrial visitor that might land on Cuban territory only once every fifteen years would not recognize today's Cuban economy from what it had been on the previous visit. One constant that connects Cuba's past to its future is the profound dependence of its economy's prospects on the international economy. Yet Cuba is well on its way toward substantial and comprehensive economic change. Today the dynamic sectors in Cuba's economy operate increasingly on market principles, even if the state enterprise sector still employs the largest number of people. The service sector—not agriculture, not manufacturing—leads the economic recovery. Cubans face a choice as they prepare for the future, however. They can continue to rely, as in the past and still today, on the labor-intensive exploitation of the country's soil and subsoil resources. Or they can build on the large investment from the past several decades in the development of the nation's human capital. The work that Cubans do with their brains—knowledge-intensive services, manufacturing, and agribusiness—would better generate future prosperity.

Macroeconomic and Societal Issues

Until the end of the 1980s, Cuba had a centrally owned and operated economy closely tied to the Soviet Union and its other economic partners in the Council for Mutual Economic Assistance. Agreed-upon officially-set prices governed a large fraction of Cuba's international trade and domestic economic transactions. No international private firms invested in Cuba. The tourism industry was miniscule. Relations between Cubans at home and Cubans abroad were usually tense, at times hostile. Sugar was at the very heart of the economy and was by far the leading source of foreign exchange, as it had been for much of the country's history. Agro-industrial enterprises anchored the economy at home and in its international relations.

Cuba's economic and social performance had worked reasonably well from the start of the 1970s until the mid-1980s. The economy grew substantially, recovering from the troubled performance in the decade following the January 1959 revolutionary victory. By the mid-1980s, the standard of living of ordinary Cubans had become comfortable, albeit not prosperous. Soviet international price supports and other inter-state economic arrangements bolstered Cuba's external resources. Massive investments in education and health care created a highly skilled labor force that enjoyed the health standards of the North Atlantic countries. Economic inequality was extremely low. Politics had stabilized in the aftermath of the revolutionary 1960s. The Communist Party of Cuba held its First Congress in 1975. A new Constitution went into effect in 1976, and that same year the new National Assembly (parliament) held its first meeting. In this single-party political system, multi-candidate local elections were held to fill municipal offices under the new Constitution. Also in 1975, the Organization of American States lifted collective economic sanctions on Cuba and, in 1977, the United States and Cuba agreed to post diplomats to "Interests Sections" in their respective capital cities.

There were many problems but they seemed manageable. The very high economic dependence on the Soviet Union and its allies pointed to a vulnerability that would hurt after 1990. However, in the 1970s, many believed, not unreasonably, that surely the Soviet Union would last forever. In addition, since the early 1960s Cuba had re-fashioned its economy almost as if it were on a war footing with the United States. This "war economy" produced many items but at very high cost and frequently poor quality, as is often the case worldwide under such circumstances. One of the many consequences of this war economy was

Cuba's inability to export much other than primary commodities (including milled sugar). Similarly, highly trained Cubans were skilled in administration but not business management. They were highly knowledgeable about engineering but not economics. Cuba's internationalism was displayed heroically on the battlefields of Angola and the Horn of Africa but not in the meeting rooms of Davos or the boardrooms of the City of London.

The collapse of the Soviet Union and all European communist regimes between 1989 and 1991 contributed to a sudden and dramatic shrinkage of the size of Cuba's economy and the value of its international trade. Omar Everleny Pérez Villanueva's first chapter reports the loss of 35 percent of gross domestic product between 1989 and 1993 but also notes the start of an economic recovery during the second half of the 1990s. However, the worldwide recession that opened the first decade of the twenty-first century slowed down the pace of the economic recovery.

In the meantime, the economy's structure was transformed. The service sector came to predominate. The number of tourists increased nearly six fold from 1990 to 2000. The volume of milled sugar output dropped from 8.1 million metric tons in 1990 to 2.2 million metric tons in 2003. As the new century opened, the government shut down nearly half of the country's sugar mills. Outside the service sector, the principal success was the exploitation of Cuba's petroleum and natural gas. Cuba produced no natural gas as the 1980s ended but, with a boom beginning in 1997, production reached 586.7 billion cubic meters by 2002. Economic efficiency remained problematic, however. After a significant reduction of government subsidies to enterprises from a peak in 1993, overall subsidies, in one form or another, remained high— some three billion pesos per year from 1996 through 2003. Real salaries, and personal domestic consumption more generally, also dropped substantially in the early 1990s. They recovered in the years that followed, albeit more slowly than the economy as a whole, as Viviana Togores and Anicia García demonstrate in their chapter. Salaries had accounted for approximately three-quarters of household income from the 1960s to the 1980s but barely more than half in the 1990s. International remittances, officially licensed self-employment, and informal sources of income have become more important. In 1993, decriminalization of dollar holding and use also created a differentiated domestic consumer market. Access to dollars became a key for household consumption.

In the 1970s and 1980s, rationed markets accounted for more than half of all consumer goods; since 1990, they have accounted for less than half. The principal change in the structure of domestic consumer markets in the 1990s was the boom in illegal or "black" market between 1990 and 1993 (when it supplied about half of all consumer goods) and its sharp contraction thereafter, replaced by various forms of lawful markets in which prices are set principally by supply and demand. One of those markets operated in hard currency, mainly U.S. dollars. In 2000, there were already 5500 retail units serving the domestic market operating in hard currency. Also in 2000, U.S. dollars accounted for more than half of all currency in circulation.

During the 1990s, calorie and protein consumption fell below the nutritional standards recommended by the United Nations Food and Agriculture Organization (FAO), though those standards were met again as the new century opened. The consumption of vitamins and fats remained below FAO standards at the start of the century's first decade, however. In this new decade, consumers must resort far more than in the past to food markets where prices are freely set by supply and demand. For example, in metropolitan Havana adults aged 14–64 could obtain only two-fifths of their calorie needs and a third of their protein needs through the rationed food outlets. Access to hard currency, therefore, made the difference between an adequate and a deficient diet. Imports accounted for about half of human food consumption and energy use. The situation regarding non-food consumer items was and remained much more severe, however, and household circumstances depended much more on access to hard currency to make significant non-food consumer purchases.

The social effects of economic difficulties were dramatic. Before 1990, Cubans had come to expect that inequality would be modest and all instances of poverty eradicated. In her chapter, Mayra Espina Prieto calls those expectations the outcome of the creation of "spaces of equality," that is, the means of distribution were in the hands of, and guaranteed by, the state, encompassed the entire population, made goods and services available free of charge or easy to obtain as a matter of right and according to universalistic criteria, and sought to ensure approximately equal results for all. There was extensive societal participation, in principle open to all citizens, privileging collective over individual problem solving.

After 1990, however, the decline of the role of the state and the delinking of household incomes from the salaries of its members—as transnational dollar remittances and self-employment made other sources of income available—opened the doors to social re-stratification and wider inequality. Higher-income households were more likely to receive remittances than low-income households. The Gini index of income inequality rose from 0.24 in 1986 to 0.38 in 2002. By worldwide standards, that makes Cuba still rather egalitarian, but not in terms of its own history from the 1960s to the 1980s. Inequalities also widened among Cuban provinces—the eastern provinces and the rural areas being poorer—because of the uneven distribution of new dynamic sectors of the economy throughout the national territory. Poverty increasingly reappeared. In urban Cuba where most Cubans live, poverty had fallen to just above 6 percent of the urban population in 1985, rising to about 15 percent in 1995, and about 20 percent in 2002.

To face the economic debacle of the early 1990s and address the continuing hard times for many Cubans, the government adopted a new strategic framework for the economy. Several key components are evident in the previous paragraphs: the welcoming of foreign direct investment, the development of tourism, and the decriminalization of U.S. dollar possession and use. Each chapter in this book attests to the considerable success of this economic strategy and salutes Cuba's strong and consistent dedication to sustain a high commitment to education, health care and other social sectors, notwithstanding the problems just described.

What might be, however, an optimal economic strategy for Cuba to address this cluster of macroeconomic and societal problems, instead of continued reliance on a strategy improvised in the early 1990s to respond to the emergency circumstances of that moment? Cuba's economy, Pedro Monreal notes in his chapter, has long emphasized labor-intensive relatively low value-added economic activities depending on the exploitation of natural resources. The sugar economy and nickel mine exploitation are examples. The way the new tourism industry developed since the 1990s is another, for its emphasis on beach tourism channels most Cuban workers to jobs as maids, waiters, and chauffeurs. And yet, an important Cuban accomplishment during the last four decades of the twentieth century had been a massive and successful investment in education. For example, UNESCO's first international comparative study of school achievement standardized country median scores to a regional Latin American mean of 250. The median score in mathematics for Cuban fourth graders was 353; the next highest scoring Latin American country was Argentina at 269.[1] Cubans today have a long life expectancy and are likely to die from the same diseases as people who live in the most economically developed countries.

Cuba's human capital is potentially its single most important resource. A more effective long-term economic strategy ought to harness and re-train such human capital because it promises more remunerative activities and a higher standard of living in the long run. The investment in and of human capital argues for a strategy of export substitution across sectors that would change the mix of factors of production, Monreal notes. Cuba has begun to develop the export of medical services and some biotechnology products. Its musicians and artists have found a new international demand for their work. Its software engineers and its skilled mechanics make the country's computers and the 1950s Chevrolets run, notwithstanding continuing U.S. economic sanctions. Freeing the creativity and providing incentives to increase the productivity of Cubans is a desirable path to the future.

A better economic strategy should also pay greater attention to microeconomic issues whose salience arose as a result of policy implementation during the 1990s. Domínguez's chapter highlights several concerns. Cuban government statistics show that economic results in agriculture improve depending on the extent of the producer's autonomy as a market participant: the greater market autonomy, the better the economic results. Similarly, fiscal revenues have risen most rapidly from the taxation of joint ventures and quasi-private firms, not from state enterprises; excessively high taxes have reduced the revenue stream from private self-employment activities. Better incentives for private producers are likely to yield better economic results.

Cuba's system of multiple exchange rates severely distorts relative prices, enterprise profitability, and incentives to labor. It is one factor in the sugar industry's *de facto* bankruptcy. Exchange rate unification would establish a sounder long-term basis for economic growth. Moreover, the government's approach to license foreign firms that enter joint ventures with Cuban state enterprises in the tourism sector has created oligopolies that reduce the gains that Cuba would otherwise accrue from high competition among international tourism firms. Cuba would also save on those oligopoly rents and improve its economic performance if it were to liberalize self-employment regulations to permit the growth of small businesses. Finally, official rules allow practices that act as barriers to more substantial international investment flows; the tolerance for the "chain of non-payment"—firms that fail to pay their suppliers promptly—undermines the country's development capacity.

The International and Transnational Context

Cuba's economic strategy for the 1990s constructed the foundation for its evolving economic strategy thanks to its opening to the world beyond the country's borders. This element of national strategy will remain a key component for the future. Its building blocks were a welcome to foreign direct investment, a search to reactivate and diversify its international trade, a defensive management of the country's international financing, and a stimulus to transnational remittances.

By 2002, more than four hundred international firms operated in association with Cuban state enterprises. As Pérez Villanueva shows in his second chapter, the number of such joint ventures has increased steadily since 1990; the annual flow of foreign direct investment, on the contrary, was highly erratic. By 2002, joint ventures operating in Cuba accounted for nearly half of the country's goods exports. Such firms were especially important in mining, petroleum, natural gas, telecommunications, rum and tourism. Sherritt International alone produced forty percent of Cuba's petroleum.

From 1989 to 1992, Cuban goods exports plummeted from well over US$5 billion to below US$2 billion. For the next ten years, as Pérez Villanueva shows in his first chapter, exports oscillated within a narrow range, remaining typically below the US$2 billion mark. That masked a restructuring of Cuban exports, however. The worth of sugar exports declined markedly while nickel exports increased sharply after 1995; the export of tobacco products also increased. New goods export product lines appeared but their overall contribution to the value of exports remained modest. Imports grew much faster than exports in response in part to the economic reactivation of the second half of the 1990s, and the trade deficit widened as a result.

Tourism, remittances and some international donations thus become particularly important in the light of the trade deficit in goods. The balance of payments current account remained in deficit in the years since 1990; this deficit has tended to worsen, as Pérez Villanueva also notes in his first chapter. The financing of this deficit is very difficult because Cuba stopped servicing its international hard currency debt in 1986. As a result, it was shut out of medium- and long-term international credit markets, depending heavily on suppliers' short-term credits.

The future of Cuba's international trade, Jorge Mario Sánchez Egozcue demonstrates in his chapter, displays features common throughout the Caribbean. Domestic markets are small, to the detriment of enterprises focused exclusively on such markets, thus making import-substitution strategies unlikely to be efficient. Agriculture is on the decline and manufacturing and services have become more important. International trade is heavily oriented toward North America throughout the Caribbean; even Cuba's trade with the United States and Canada rose since 1990. In the early twenty-first century, the United States became Cuba's principal international food supplier. The external sector is at the core of the Caribbean's prospects for economic growth.

In two respects, Sánchez Egozcue shows, Cuba is already well positioned to develop its external sector. It relies hardly at all on customs revenues to fund the central government; it reduced its customs duties systematically during the 1990s. And, as noted, it possesses impressive human capital resources. Cuba is adversely positioned to participate in international markets, however, because it is shut out of medium- and long-term international credit markets, continues to rely on intrusive economic regulations including non-tariff barriers, exhibits low labor productivity, relies disproportionately on obsolete manufacturing technologies, exports products whose quality is below median by international standards, and lacks appropriate marketing expertise. For these reasons, his analysis shows, Cuba's overall international trade might not grow much even if the United States were to lift its trade embargo; a likely outcome might be trade diversion toward the United States rather than net trade creation. On the other hand, the performance of the Cuban economy since the mid-1990s has improved somewhat across all of these dimensions except access to international capital markets.

The future of the financing of Cuba's development prospects may be less grim than the preceding paragraphs suggest, however, thanks to the marked increase in transnational people-to-people ties between Cubans at home and abroad. At the start of the century, the Cuban diaspora remitted approximately US$1 billion per year (the median estimate in the Togores-García chapter), most of it from Cuban-Americans—Cuba's second (behind tourism) most important source of hard currency. This fact highlights three important changes.

First, interpersonal relations between those who call themselves Cubans but live at opposite ends of the Florida Straits have improved, in some instances dramatically. Susan Eckstein's chapter calls attention to the strong formal and informal sanctions that had once constrained ordinary Cubans in Cuba and the United States from sustaining the ties that have only recently become widespread and she documents the extraordinary sociological transformation that has been under way to widen and deepen transnational interpersonal relations. This implies that a very important social and political change is under way, which in the long run may also facilitate a more peaceful and prosperous Cuban future. Second, remittances stimulate a demand-based consumer-driven decentralized market economy, contrasting sharply with the centralized command economy and consumption austerity that had marked Cuba in the past. Eckstein also shows the spread of consumerist norms in contemporary Cuba as an inherent dimension of this transnational social process. The effect of the flow of funds and the change in norms affects patterns of social stratification in Cuba, widens inequalities—including those along racial lines because non-whites are much less likely to receive remittances—and provides incentives for new market-shaped behavior. In the longer term, the financing of consumption and eventually investment do and increasingly will require mobilizing these private monetary resources.

Third, the remittances boom could only have developed thanks to the authorization and active support of the governments of Cuba and the United States, which cooperate indirectly to bring it about and sustain it. The changes in Cuban and U.S. policy toward remittances have been impressive, as Lorena Barberia shows in her chapter. In 1979, the Cuban government changed its policy and began to allow Cuban-Americans to return to Cuba to visit their families. Remittances followed, though limited during the 1980s by stiff Cuban government control requirements. In the context of severe economic hardship suffered by the country and its citizens, however, the Cuban government's 1993 decision to de-criminalize the holding and use of hard currency unleashed a torrent of remittances. State banks created interest-bearing dollar savings accounts. State enterprises and joint-venture firms opened thousands of retail stores operating in dollars. Government foreign exchange offices facilitated peso-dollar trades. The government authorized self-employment, the capital for which often came from diaspora dollars. Remittances remain untaxed and excludable from income tax filings.

For its part, as Barberia also shows, starting in 1977 the U.S. government exempted remittances from its ban on economic transactions in Cuba (though the ban was reimposed between 1994 and 1998) and sought, instead, to regulate the flow. U.S. policy on remittances remained for the most part highly restrictive, however, until 1998. The Bush administration confirmed U.S. remittances policies. It slightly liberalized U.S. policies on remittances to Cuba in 2001, and somewhat tightened those policies in 2004, but the fundamental U.S. government tolerance of remittances has persisted. The U.S. government has also authorized various financial intermediaries—most notably Western Union—to participate in this business. In short, though the motivations differ, the Cuban and U.S. governments cooperated to facilitate the flow of private remittances, thereby opening an important chapter for the present and future of consumption and investment in Cuba and the prospects for a more cooperative future.

The Book's Task

This book explores four broad themes. Its first part focuses on the salient macroeconomic questions. Domínguez provides an overview of important successes in economic and social policy even during the crisis of the early 1990s. Then, he analyzes the adverse consequences of lingering problems from the past, the unresolved effects of the shock of the collapse of Soviet support, and especially the undesired negative side effects of some of the very policies that were otherwise successful. Occasionally, he suggests how policy changes may address some of these challenges.

The first of Omar Everleny Pérez Villanueva's two chapters in this book provides a comprehensive empirical account of Cuba's salient macroeconomic characteristics. He assesses the evolution of the key macroeconomic indicators, investment, consumption, personal income, and budget revenues and expenditures, the performance of the agriculture and services sectors, and trends in international exports, imports, financing and debt. This highly informative chapter lays the groundwork for all the following chapters.

The book's second section analyzes the international economic context. Pedro Monreal dissects Cuba's economic development strategy as it has changed over time, noting its historic focus on commodity exports and, during the second half of the twentieth century, also on import substitution. He assesses Cuba's adaptation to its economic crisis in the 1990s, noting that it continues to export low value-added items, with continuing promotion of import substitution industrialization. He argues that Cuba should adopt a strategy of reindustrialization with export substitution, that is, transform and invest its human capital to generate high value-added exports.

Jorge Mario Sánchez Egozcue compares Cuba to the economies of the Caribbean basin and assesses Cuba's international trade prospects. He analyzes factors common to all Caribbean economies to understand their shared opportunities and constraints in international economic relations. He assesses Cuba's comparative advantages and disadvantages in this specific international context. He shows that Cuba may be able to follow the strategy that Monreal recommends but that it remains quite far from being able to implement it. His conclusions regarding the prospects for the growth of Cuba's international trade are sobering because he shows the serious impediments to such growth within the Cuban economy, even if the United States were to lift its trade embargo.

Omar Everleny Pérez Villanueva's second chapter in this book examines the impact of foreign direct investment on the Cuban economy. He describes the international and comparative empirical context to understand the role of such investment in economic development. He explores patterns of foreign direct investment in Cuba, including the number of firms, the impact of the investment on gross capital formation and exports, and the incidence of such investment across a wide array of different economic sectors.

Dwight Perkins closes this segment commenting on possible lessons for Cuba of economic reforms implemented in two other Communist countries, namely, China and Vietnam. He calls attention to Vietnam's successful response to the collapse of the Soviet Union, which had hitherto heavily subsidized Vietnamese imports, notwithstanding a continuing U.S. trade embargo. Perkins notes the salutary effect of freeing rural markets for most agricultural crops as well as freeing the foreign exchange market and letting the currency float until Vietnam's exports became internationally competitive. Perkins summarizes the lesson of China and Vietnam for Cuba succinctly: "If you are going to build a modern competitive industrial and service sector economy, one cannot do it with half way measures or gimmicks."

The book's third section studies social policy and welfare issues. Mayra Espina explores the Cuban approach to social policy and poverty reduction, alluded to earlier, indicating its noteworthy success and effectiveness for many years and the difficulties encountered in the 1990s. She describes the widening of income inequality; a fifth of Cuba's population has plunged into poverty. She also examines the impact of Cuba's new economic policies, launched in the 1990s, on income and social welfare differences among Cuban provinces, finding that the eastern provinces are the most disadvantaged. Such territorial differences are not new in Cuban history but they have reemerged with new force: the prospects are high for a further widening of territorial inequalities. Finally, Espina studies the manifold transformations of Cuba's social class structure over time, concluding with an assessment of the new forms of stratification associated with the reintroduction on a larger scale of various forms of non-state property since 1990.

Viviana Togores and Anicia García document trends in personal income and consumption, presenting a rich array of data. Their work highlights vividly the impact of macroeconomic phenomena on ordinary human beings. They describe thoroughly the hardship resulting from the decline of food consumption and the reappearance of a significant nutritional deficit while also examining the supply of other goods. They analyze in detail the forms and consequences of market segmentation—illegal, rationed, self-employed, parallel, farmers', dollar, agricultural, industrial, and state markets—since the start of the 1980s, indicating dramatic changes in composition over a relatively brief period of time as households adjust to changing circumstances.

This section closes with a comment from Lorena Barberia, Xavier de Souza Briggs, and Miren Uriarte who argue that Cuba should change its model for social policy. They emphasize that social policy can remain universalistic—everyone in need would receive assistance—without providing standardized assistance to every person. High-income Cubans need not receive subsidized food; the resources that subsidize Cuba's new rich should be reallocated through a targeting strategy to focus on helping Cuba's new poor. Targeting social assistance may be particularly cost effective in addressing the problems of poverty and territorial disparities that Espina's and Togores-García's chapters bring out so well.

The book's final segment addresses the study of transnational networks and the respective responses of the U.S. and Cuban governments. In addition to major changes in its economy and society during the 1990s, Cuba also witnessed a transformation of the relations between many of its people and many of those in the Cuban diaspora. Susan Eckstein's chapter traces the past formal and informal constraints on transnational relations between peoples of Cuban origin across the Straits of Florida and the breakdown of those barriers since the start of the 1990s. She describes the dramatic changes in both Cuba and the Cuban diaspora in the United States as members of these two communities adjust their behavior to engage with each other as normally as the respective governments will allow. She describes the normative shift on both sides and the transnationalization and transformation of Cuba's social stratification.

Lorena Barberia looks at changes in Cuban and U.S. government policy that affect Cuban diaspora remittances to Cuba. She provides a comprehensive history of Cuban and U.S. government mutual prohibition and more recent partial authorization of those remittances. She explores the growth of a new financial architecture in Cuba that has come to depend on the flow of remittances as well as the effect of such flows on Cuban domestic policy, such as consumer market liberalization, banking reforms, investment opportunities, and tax policy changes. And she describes the varied and often futile U.S. government attempts to regulate the flow of remittances. One tribute to the political power of remittances is that neither the U.S. nor the Cuban governments prohibited remittances as their political relations deteriorated sharply in 2003–2004.

All of these chapters focus on the Cuba that actually exists. This is not a book about what may happen to bring about a change of Cuba's political regime, nor a fantasy about what may occur if such a political change were to take place. There are sound scholarly grounds for focusing on the study of the world as we know it. That is what this book seeks to do, albeit allowing those authors who so wish to make suggestions about possible policy changes within the context of Cuba's existing political arrangements.

Conclusions

Cuba faces daunting challenges in the years ahead. Not until the end of this century's first decade is Cuba likely to have recovered its 1985 level of gross domestic product capita—the last time its economy had experienced a relatively long period of sustained economic growth. Cuba's macroeconomic strategy must move beyond economic recovery to sustained growth, harnessing more effectively its people's human capital. Cuba's economic returns on its huge investments in education, health care, and other components of human capital remain surprisingly meager. On the basis of the resources of its people, Cuba should fashion a knowledge-based economic strategy that substitutes brains for brawn as the key factor of production and export.

Economic difficulties, in turn, generate social hardships and make it more difficult to address them. The Cuban government has, in some respects, adapted well to the country's changed circumstances; particularly impressive has been its effort to sustain a social safety net for most Cubans. Ordinary Cubans have been even more adaptive, reinventing their skills and their economic activities, and in growing numbers constructing or reconstructing their ties with their friends and relatives in the Cuban diaspora as a means to build their financial and social capital. But Cuba's egalitarian social policies face the closely related challenges that Lorena Barberia, Xavier de Souza Briggs and Miren Uriarte identify in their chapter: how to sustain the comprehensive social policies in the relative absence of economic growth and how to shift away from the universalistic one-size-fits-all standardized set of social programs toward still universalistic-in-access but more targeted social programs that recognize the salience and legitimacy of needs-based differences in the delivery of social services.

Cubans have begun also to rebuild the bonds that had rendered the Cuban nation apart as growing numbers of diaspora Cubans rally to assist their relatives in Cuba not just to survive but also to build more productive lives. Government policies will have to change further, however, for the full potential benefits of these new transnational ties to be realized.

Cuba's economic future has already begun, however, and with it has come important change to its society. Perhaps the single most noteworthy trait of the change that has already taken place is that there are many more diverse ways than before 1990 for Cubans to engage in their economy and their society. From such diversity come both creativity and growth but also inequality. How these gains and losses are weighed, mixed, shaped and misshaped is a key to the future yet to be known.

Notes

1   Task Force on Education, Equity, and Economic Competitiveness in Latin America and the Caribbean, *Lagging Behind: A Report Card on Education in Latin America* (Washington, D.C.: Partnership for Educational Revitalization in the Americas [PREAL], 2001), 33.

PART

I

Macroeconomic Issues

2

Cuba's Economic Transition: Successes, Deficiencies, and Challenges

by Jorge I. Domínguez

Cuba's economic transition began formally on June 23, 1990 when the Political Bureau of the Cuban Communist Party declared: "The solid stability of the country, together with intelligent policies, attract the confidence of foreign investors and open the way for cooperation in the form of joint ventures. This does not clash with our socialist system; rather it means speedier use of potential resources."[1] Days earlier, on Cuba's premier beach, Varadero, President Fidel Castro publicly inaugurated the first hotel built jointly between a foreign investor and a Cuban state enterprise since the Cuban government seized all foreign-owned tourist enterprises in 1960. The foreign partners had the funds, management expertise and marketing skills that Cuban enterprises lacked, he said. Somewhat hesitantly, he added: "We do not know how to run a hotel, how to handle tourism and—I don't know if I should use the word or not—how to make the most money from tourism, how to exploit tourism."[2]

The decision to welcome foreign direct investment cast aside one of the foundation stones of Cuban socialism's political economy, built on the expropriation of foreign property. The promotion of international tourism was another shift. Despite some new or lingering tourism from Soviet bloc countries, Canada and other international sources between 1960 and 1990, part of the moral claim of revolutionaries in power in 1959 and 1960 was the extirpation of the image of Cuba as the whorehouse of the Caribbean. International tourism plummeted in the decades that followed.

The 1990 economic reform decisions were smart and necessary.

They were essential to ensure the political survival of the socialist regime. They were the prelude to other economic reforms that the Cuban government enacted in the years that followed. They responded to the vast changes already under way in the Soviet Union and the collapse of hitherto communist Eastern Europe; they anticipated the collapse of the Soviet Union itself eighteen months later. They signaled a public change in economic strategy while reaffirming fidelity to the socialist political system and to a set of values associated with it—public ownership and operation of most of the means of production, centralized planning and decision making, single-party rule, the public provision of free education and health care services, and the public provision of highly subsidized food, transportation, housing, and pensions, among other objectives.

The economic reform package that Cuba would have in place by the mid-1990s distinguished the path that its government followed from the package of policies that had brought down ruling communist parties in Europe at the end of the 1980s. In contrast to the European experiences, the Cuban Communist Party and its leaders succeeded: they remained in power. They reactivated the country's economy after a recession, shorter (four years) than in former Soviet Central Asia (six years), and sustained key aspects of social welfare. On the other hand, the Cuban Communist Party and its leaders under-performed in comparison with their peers in China and Vietnam; neither of these two still-communist countries suffered a deep recession.

Cuba's economic changes of the 1990s need reforming to set Cuba on a sustainable growth path. This chapter focuses on this question in the light of the comparative experiences of other communist or post-communist countries. The starting premise is that the initial stages of the Cuban economic transition were successful in many ways. Financial calamity compelled the government to undertake a series of pragmatic reforms to accommodate economic distress. But the policies adopted created new problems and failed to address others. The first wave of economic reforms was insufficient to set the economy on a sustainable growth path within the framework of Cuba's current political system.

The Crisis

The crisis was severe (Table 2.1). During the second half of the 1980s, the economy had been stagnant. Gross domestic product (GDP) failed to grow while exports and imports weakened. Between 1990 and 1993, trade collapsed. The plunge was sudden and dramatic. GDP lost nearly 30 percent of its value in that short time span. In 1994, the economy bottomed out, growing modestly for the remainder of the decade. In the second half of the 1990s, imports recovered to some extent but exports actually declined (Tables 2.1 and 2.2). A trade deficit appeared that—though not large by international standards—was problematic because Cuba's access to international capital markets for new funds is basically limited to suppliers' credits. Inflation was negligible in the second half of the 1980s and moderate from 1990 to 1993. There was an inflationary spike between 1993 and 1994, however, with inflation accelerating less rapidly though still fast in 1995 when the GDP price deflator (1985=100) reached 157.2. The economy stabilized then; the GDP price deflator remained basically unchanged through the end of the 1990s.[3]

Table 2.1 The Cuban Economy's Collapse and Recovery, 1985-2000
(1985=100)

	1990	1993	1994	2000
GDP[a]	99.9	70.4	70.9	81.4
GDP per capita	95.0	65.0	66.0	74.0
Imports[b]	92.3	25.0	29.3	60.5
Exports[b]	90.4	19.3	23.1	28.2
GDP Deflator	103.5	117.0	142.6	157.9[c]

a. GDP is gross domestic product in 1981 constant pesos.
b. Imports and exports are in current pesos.
c. Deflator statistic in column for 2000 is actually for 1998.

Source: Computed from Comisión Económica para América Latina y el Caribe, *La economía cubana: Reformas estructurales y desempeño en los noventa* (Mexico: Fondo de Cultura Económica, 2000), Tables A.2 for GDP 1985-95, A.12 for GDP price deflator 1985–98, and A.32 for exports and imports 1985-93. Computed from Oficina Nacional de Estadísticas, *Anuario estadístico de Cuba, 2000* (Havana: 2000), page 94 for GDP 2000 and page 128 for exports and imports for 1994 and 2000. Population data from Oficina Nacional de Estadísticas, *Anuario estadístico de Cuba, 2001* (Havana: 2002), Table II-1

Table 2.2 The Cuban Economy's Recent Performance, 1997–2002
(2000=100)

	1997	2002
GDP[a]	89	105
GDP per capita	89	104
Imports[b]	83	86
Exports[b]	109	84

a. GDP is gross domestic product in 1997 prices
b. Imports and exports are in current pesos.

Source: Oficina Nacional de Estadísticas (ONE), *Anuario estadístico de Cuba, 2002* (Havana: 2003), Tables III-1, III-3, and III-4

The detonator of the crisis was, for the most part, external. The Soviet Union had subsidized the price it paid for Cuban sugar by several multiples of the prevailing international sugar price and the price that Cuba paid for Soviet sales of petroleum. These subsidies amounted to outright grants to the Cuban economy. The Soviet Union supplied all weapons free of charge to the Cuban Armed Forces. It provided loans at low interest rates to cover the bilateral trade deficits that emerged notwithstanding those very high trade subsidies. The Soviets awarded low-interest-bearing loans for major economic development projects, such as the construction of a nickel ore processing plant and a nuclear power plant, among others, as well as many scholarships to train Cubans in the USSR in various professional endeavors. Most of these assistance programs were ending late in the Soviet period; they all ended with the dissolution of the Soviet Union.[4]

There were also fundamental flaws in the Cuban economy. Despite these massive Soviet subsidies, Cuba's GDP did not grow at all during the second half of the 1980s. Any economy would have been hurt by large adverse exogenous shocks but Cuba's stagnant and inefficient economy was devastated. A better economic future for Cuba requires a better functioning economy. Except for three years (1996, 1999, and 2000), GDP growth rates have been anemic since 1985. The economy fell in six of those eighteen years and registered growth rates below three percent in seven other of those years (including 2002 and 2003).[5] GDP per capita trends were poorer still.

And yet, in the 1990s Cuba's social performance was noteworthy especially when compared to that of several former communist countries. At the end of the 1990s, Cuba's social indicators remained good in various respects. In 2002, the infant mortality rate per thousand live births was 6.5. Fewer infants died at birth in the City of Havana than in Washington, D.C. The number of inhabitants per medical doctor was 168.[6] More than 97 percent of children ages six to fourteen were enrolled in school. Retention rates in primary, junior high school, senior high school, and vocational and technical schools exceeded 95 percent. (The adult illiteracy rate had already dropped below four percent in the 1981 census). In addition, the quality of much of Cuban education is quite good. For example, UNESCO's first international comparative study of school achievement standardized country median scores to a regional Latin American mean of 250. The median score in mathematics for Cuban fourth graders was 353; the next highest scoring Latin American country was Argentina at 269.[7]

The economic decline affected the population adversely, however. Calorie intake fell by 27 percent from 1990 to 1996. It became very difficult to obtain medicines and, for a few years, food. New diseases appeared and those that had seemed eradicated reappeared. The quality of medical services deteriorated as well.[8] In 2002, the working age population (ages 14 to 64) still had a caloric intake 57 percent below recommended nutritional standards and a protein intake 68 percent below the pertinent standards.[9] Schools suffered from lack of books, lab equipment, and other pedagogical materials. School cafeterias served less and lower-quality food. The government cut enrollments in higher education by 45 percent from 1991 to 1995.[10] By 1996, twelve percent of urban Cubans (in 2002, three-quarters of Cubans lived in urban areas[11]) earned less than 100 pesos per month (less than US$5 per month at the prevailing legal exchange rate), had no access to dollars, grew no food, and received no food subsidies.[12] They suffered extreme poverty.

In 1996, the Communist Party's top school for cadres published a book for the educated general public to explain what had happened to Cuba's economy and what measures had been adopted to address this crisis. The book's opening says that Cuba's key victory in the 1990s was to have resisted. The political system was sustained and economic recovery policies were enacted.[13] And yet, those are surely insufficient goals.

In 2000, on the eve of the Cuban economy's new slowdown, GDP per capita in constant prices remained still 26 percent below its 1985 level (Table 2.1). Exports in current prices plummeted between 1997 and 2002; imports contracted sharply after 2000 (Table 2.2). During the world recession in 2001–2002, the prices of Cuba's main export products declined but dollar revenues from international tourism also dropped six percent between 2000 and 2002—the first time since the start of the economic reforms.[14] To restore and sustain the social safety net and improve the quality of life, to enable the Communist Party to govern and remain politically competitive in Cuba's future, and to serve the public interest no matter who or which party is in power, the economy must recover fully and grow again.

The Repertoire of Successful Policies in 1990–93

At the January 1990 meeting of the Council for Mutual Economic Assistance (often known by its initials as CMEA or COMECON), the Soviet Union proposed that all trade among member communist countries be conducted on the basis of market prices and convertible currencies. The motion was approved. In effect, Cuba was given one year's notice to prepare for an economic shock.

During 1990–93, the Cuban government adopted three kinds of policies to address this challenge: elements of economic liberalization to provide avenues for economic recovery, some institutional reforms to facilitate the economic liberalization, and deferral of economic stabilization in order to maintain a basis of political support. All three would accomplish their goals in the short to medium term. There was an obvious short-term trade off between political and economic stabilization. In the Cuban leadership's estimation, success at political stabilization required deferring economic stabilization. The deferral of economic stabilization was just that—deferring the moment of reckoning, as it turned out for three years.

Economic liberalization first. As noted, the sign that much was about to change in Cuban economic policy was the June 1990 Political Bureau statement welcoming foreign direct investment and specifically the development of international tourism. Those two economic reforms alone account for much of the economy's recovery. These economic liberalization measures preceded the adoption of economic stabilization measures.

Institutional reforms second. Some institutional reforms were adopted also in advance of economic stabilization measures. The 1991 Fourth Party Congress authorized amending the 1976 Constitution to provide for some private property rights. Article 15 of the 1992 Constitution authorized the executive committee of the Council of Ministers, at its discretion, to grant property rights for various economic activities. Article 15 asserts that all productive property belongs to the state (except for a fraction of agriculture that has always been and remains in private hands). Such property cannot be privatized "except in those unusual cases where the full or partial transfer of some entity to natural or legal persons would advance the country's development and is not adverse to the political, social, and economic foundations of the State, provided the Council of Ministers or its Executive Committee approve in advance." This change was enacted because foreigners wanted some property protection before investing.

Article 15 obviously provides a weak constitutional protection for property rights. Nonetheless, it would be the foundation stone for the expansion of foreign direct investment in Cuba in the years ahead. However, no privately owned Cuban businesses big enough to hire non-relatives were authorized during the following dozen years.

Economic stabilization deferred. Economic stabilization was deliberately deferred in the early 1990s. Instead, the government ran a budget deficit to buy political stability. Fiscal revenues plummeted by 22 percent while budget expenditures increased 2.5 percent (both in current prices) from 1990 to 1993. During those critical years the government cut its expenditures for defense and internal security (38 percent) and administration (8 percent) to make room for an 83 percent increase in subsidies to cover losses in state enterprises. Subsidies as a percentage of budget expenditures rose from 26 to 42 percent between 1990 and 1993. Public health expenditures rose 15 percent, too, as the government struggled to sustain a key sector. The budget deficit reached 10 percent of GDP in 1990; it ballooned to 33 percent of GDP in 1993.[15] Economists may tear their vestments at these policies and their results, but they served the party leadership's main goal: buying political time and helping to keep the communist party in power. (In this respect, Cuban policies resemble those also pursued in Bulgaria and Uzbekistan to sustain the legacies of communist parties in power.)[16]

In May 1990, the Communist Party polled the population as one element to design this strategy. Its pollsters found that only 20 percent believed that the food supply was good, only 10 percent thought that public transportation was good, and only 10 percent believed that the housing supply was good. But 77 percent averred that public health services were good and 83 percent affirmed the same regarding the schools.[17] These findings on the high regard for the health care services and the schools are believable because they come from the same poll that uncovered highly critical information. Accordingly, the government invested its resources to sustain its strengths.

Economic stabilization at last. In the early 1990s, Cuba's fiscal policies led inevitably to high inflation rates, posing a different threat to political stability. Cuba had experienced rather stable prices up to the end of the 1980s (Table 2.1) but inflation accelerated after 1990. Monetary liquidity leapt 121 percent from 1990 to 1993.[18] The inflation spike in 1993–94 galvanized the government into action. During these years, official prices mainly remained fixed, but a vast illegal market developed with skyrocketing prices. (The early 1990s fiscal imbalance and accelerating inflation correspond also to the Russian and Central Asian experiences.)

The specific shock that finally compelled the government to change was the disastrous 1993 sugar harvest in which output was about half that of the previous year (and the lowest in thirty years). At last the government enacted reforms to stabilize public finances. The fiscal adjustment was dramatic. From 1993 to 1994, revenues jumped by 34 percent; expenditures fell 3 percent across nearly all categories of the budget. Subsidies as a percent of the budget dropped to 28 percent, roughly returning to the 1990 level. The deficit as a percent of GDP fell to 7.4 percent. Monetary liquidity fell by 10 percent.[19] The exchange rate stabilized. From the respective first semester in 1989 to 1993, the exchange rate rose in the illegal market from 7 to 120 pesos per dollar. In August 1994, it fell abruptly to 80 pesos per dollar, reaching 25 pesos per dollar a year later.[20] Cuba's fiscal balance continued to improve during the remainder of the 1990s. In 2002, the deficit was 3.2 percent of GDP while subsidies still accounted for a rather high 19 percent of the budget.[21] (Unlike Russia or Bulgaria, Cuba did not have financial meltdowns or hyperinflationary episodes in the remainder of the 1990s.)

More economic liberalization. In Summer 1993, the government enacted three other liberalizing economic reforms. First, it authorized Cubans to hold and use hard currencies, including U.S. dollars remitted by the Cuban diaspora; it expanded travel opportunities for Cuban-Americans to the island. Second, it increased opportunities for self-employment significantly beyond previously authorized practice. A newly licensed self-employed person still could not hire non-relatives, however, thereby limiting the opportunities for small-business development. Third, it transformed most agricultural state enterprises into semi-private cooperatives—*Unidades Básicas de Producción Cooperativa* (UBPC). These new cooperatives could use the land they tilled but ownership remained in state hands. Substantial regulatory burdens, including price controls, limited the autonomy of UBPCs.[22] In Fall 1994, the government adopted a fourth pair of liberalizing economic reforms, namely, authorizing private agricultural and handicraft markets for the first time since 1986. Producers could sell the remaining surplus of their output, after they had met their obligations to the state.

The architect of these successful policies of economic adjustment and continuing economic liberalization was the new Finance Minister José Luis Rodríguez, promoted shortly thereafter to Economy Minister. Vice President Carlos Lage backed him. President Fidel Castro authorized the changes. The three deserve credit for a remarkable feat of economic and political stabilization over a short time. Armed Forces Minister Raúl Castro played a key role advocating the authorization of free agricultural markets to increase food output.

The Repertoire of Successful Policies in 1994–2001

The liberalizing economic reforms adopted in 1993–94 had mixed effects in the years ahead but, on balance, improved economic efficiency and growth.

One standard is their impact on the income of ordinary Cubans. In current pesos, the salaries of state employees increased 27 percent during the years of recovery (1994–2000). However, the income of the UBPC semi-private cooperatives increased only 19 percent. Sugar cane UBPCs were the most important of these cooperatives and also the ones that performed least well. In harvest year 1994–95, their first in operation, only 23 percent of the UBPCs were profitable, a proportion that dropped below 8 percent in the next two harvests. The government eventually increased prices paid to sugar cane producers so that the proportion of profitable UBPCs reached 63 percent in 2000.[23]

Yet, although the UBPCs were not all that good for their members, they were the most efficient units of sugar cane production in Cuba and, in these terms, the UBPC reforms succeeded. The government, perhaps inadvertently, ran an experiment in agricultural organization in the late 1990s when six different kinds of entities operated in Cuban agriculture. In addition to the UBPCs, the Interior Ministry, the Armed Forces, and the Sugar Industry Ministry ran their own sugar cane state farms. Moreover, two kinds of private agricultural cooperatives also grew sugar cane. In Agricultural Production Cooperatives (CPAs), farmers pooled their land and worked it jointly. Credit and Service

Cooperatives (CCS) were formed by private farmers who owned and tilled their own land but joined to obtain credit, purchase equipment, and market their products. Table 2.3 summarizes agricultural output per worker in the six types of organizations, with harvest year 1993–1994 set to equal 100.

Table 2.3 Agricultural Output per Worker: Private, Cooperative, and State Sugar Farms, 1999–2000
(1993–1994=100)

UBPC	CCS	CPA	Sugar Ministry	Interior Ministry	Armed Forces
90	83	83	69	59	48

Source: Computed from Armando Nova González, "El cooperativismo en la agricultura cañera en Cuba de 1993 a 2000," *Economía y desarrollo*, no. 129 (June-December 2001), page 58

The late 1990s were a sad time for Cuba's sugar cane agriculture in terms of output, efficiency and prices but the evidence in Table 2.3 suggests that efficiency plummeted the most in state enterprises run by the Armed Forces, Interior, and Sugar Ministries. All three kinds of private or semi-private cooperatives performed better than the state farms, yet the Cuban government did not enact new reforms to grant greater autonomy to the cooperatives and to shift more productive activities from the state to the cooperative sector. The UBPCs, in particular, suffered from sustained and intrusive interference from state agencies.[24] The most likely reason for the failure to deepen these reforms is President Castro's publicly stated aversion to market-oriented policies in agriculture.[25] (In contrast, China's spectacularly successful agricultural reforms transferred ownership of land back to the families living and working on farms and deregulated controls over family farms.)

From 1994 to 2000 income increased fastest for Cuban private producers who suffered from fewer regulatory burdens. Farmers in private cooperatives saw their income rise by 50 percent (2.5 times the rate of increase in UBPCs) while farmers who owned and tilled their land on their own witnessed a spectacular increase of 423 percent, thanks principally to their ability to sell their products in free agricultural markets. Private non-agricultural producers saw their income jump by 180 percent, benefiting from the reform that authorized free handicraft markets and self-employment.[26] Sociological field research in several

Cuban localities provides convergent evidence: private farmer cooperatives were typically better and more profitable performers than state farms in comparable lines of production.[27]

The liberalizing economic reforms and these effects on income changed Cuba's occupational profile. At the time of the 1981 census, the state employed 92 percent of the labor force. By 2002, that proportion had fallen to below 77 percent. In contrast, the proportion of private farmers (including those who tilled on their own or joined in credit and services cooperatives) in the labor force rose from seven to eleven percent; the share of cooperative members rose from one to almost eight percent. Employment in joint ventures did not exist in 1981 but represented less than one percent of the workforce in 2002. Self-employment accounted for 1.6 percent of all workers in 1981, rising to 3.8 percent in 2002.[28]

Self-employment reforms have also succeeded, but their impact was limited because the government imposed very high license fees, taxes, and other regulations. Thus in the 1990s the proportion of self-employed persons in the labor force grew slowly, peaking at 4.1 in 1999, but falling slightly thereafter. Taxes paid by the self-employed to the government fell from 206 million pesos in 1997 to 123 million pesos in 2001, though tax evasion may also have avoided nearly confiscatory fees and taxes.[29]

The policies that fostered dollar remittances from the Cuban diaspora succeeded, though the exact magnitude of those remittances is difficult to measure. Cuba reports that international transfers accounted for US$470 million in 1994 and US$813 million in 2002. Most but not all of that entire sum is remittances (some of it is donations). The United Nations Economic Commission for Latin America and the Caribbean estimates that remittances amounted to US$537 million in 1995 and US$700 million in 1999. For comparison, the worth of sugar exports fell from US$760 million in 1994 to US$447.4 million in 2002.[30] The liberalization of remittances was, therefore, crucial to Cuba's balance of payments.

The original liberalizing economic reforms adopted in 1990—foreign direct investment and international tourism—were the most successful of all. Gross revenues from international tourism more than doubled from 1994 to 2000, when they exceeded US$1.7 billion, dropping 6 percent by 2002. Given the 16 percent plunge in the value of Cuba's goods exports since 2000, however, international tourism revenue has become the economy's mainstay. International visitors leapt from 619 thousand in 1994 to 1744 thousand in 2000 (dropping 5 percent by 2002). Foreign direct investment in the telephone system and the Cuban government's efforts to reach out to parts of the Cuban diaspora—whose members, once called "worms," had become "butterflies," officially re-labeled as the "Cuban community abroad"—doubled international telephone toll traffic from 1994 to 2000, when it reached 5.4 million hours (dropping to 4.8 million hours in 2002).[31]

Foreign direct investment also lifted Cuban mining exports from US$201 million in 1994 to US$599 million in 2000 and, because of lower prices, US$432 million in 2002. Foreign direct investment in Cuba's petroleum and natural gas reserves yielded impressive results. Cuba produced 274,000 tons of crude petroleum in 1980, 671,000 in 1990 and, thanks to foreign direct investment, 3.6 million tons in 2002. It produced less than 20 million cubic meters of natural gas in 1996, rising to 585 million cubic meters in 2002.[32] Thus, Cuba advanced toward energy self-sufficiency. Credit for the development of these enterprises goes to Basic Industries Minister Marcos Portal.

Table 2.4 Foreign Direct Investment Flows, 1994–2001
(US$ million)

1994	1995	1996	1997	1998	1999	2000	2001
563	5	82	442	207	178	448	39

Source: ONE, *Anuario estadístico de Cuba, 2000,* 128; ONE, *Anuario estadístico de Cuba, 2002,* Table VI-1

These results are remarkable because there has been so little foreign direct investment and its flow has been so unstable (Table 2.4). (More than half of the joint ventures launched between 1990 and 1993 have already been dissolved.[33]) Note that the enactment of the U.S. Democratic Liberty and Solidarity Act of 1996 (better known as Helms-Burton) had little observable effect on foreign direct investment in Cuba. Cuba received more such investment in 1997 and 1998 than in 1995 and 1996. The drop in 2001 can best be attributed to the international recession. Investment might have increased more rapidly in the absence of Helms-Burton, however. Helms-Burton may also have had other opportunity costs. The international firms that might have invested in Cuba could have been larger, generated better financial terms, own better technological processes, and possessed better access to international markets. Still, it is remarkable that the direct effects of Helms-Burton on foreign direct investment were so modest.

More institutional reforms. In the mid-1990s, the government adopted two additional institutional reforms. In response in part to lower foreign direct investment in 1995, the government enacted a new law to promote and regulate foreign direct investment beyond the narrow confines set in the 1992 Constitution. Law 77 establishes the terms for investment, provides rights and means to settle disputes including expropriation, and describes the government's discretion in accepting or rejecting investments. As a practical matter, the government emphasizes joint ventures between equal partners instead of permitting the development of wholly owned foreign firms, which Law 77 also permits.

Another institutional reform transformed some "plain" state enterprises into quasi-private state firms. The state remains their sole shareholder, approves the international firms with which they can partner, sets the prices that they must charge for their products and taxes their profit. As in all Cuban enterprises, the state also controls the allocation of labor and incentives systems. However, managers of quasi-private enterprises exercise wider discretion to make decisions than is the case in "plain" state enterprises. They allocate their own resources and generate efficiencies. Most of these enterprises are profitable. Quasi-private firms engage in international economic transactions because a parallel institutional change abolished the state's centralized approach to international trade. Decree-Law 187 promotes managerial capacities throughout the economy,[34] a daunting task. In 1993, 69 percent of all state enterprises were unprofitable and received state subsidies.[35] Some state enterprises in agriculture began to sell their surpluses in the free agricultural markets after meeting their obligations to the Ministry of Agriculture; by 1996 state enterprises already accounted for one-fifth of the value of agricultural sales in these free markets.[36]

The combination of joint ventures with international partners and the new entrepreneurial behavior of a number of state enterprises that had come to act like private firms generated a new environment of enterprise profitability that began to transform the government's fiscal accounts. Overall government revenues have increased moderately as a result of the new economic reforms (Table 2.5). However, government revenues rose dramatically from the taxation of enterprise profits (joint ventures and quasi-private state firms); these grow at a rate nearly three times faster than total state revenues. Table 2.5 also shows an even faster increase in taxation on the utilization of the labor force in these kinds of enterprises—a growth rate 3.5 times faster than total state revenues. In contrast, contributions from state enterprises that have yet to be transformed into semi-private firms declined. Revenues from taxation of self-employment show the limited fiscal impact of this reform.

Table 2.5   State Revenues in 2000–2002
(1996=100)

Year	Total State Revenues	Taxes on Enterprise Profits	Taxes on Labor Force Use	Taxes on Self-Employed	Payments from State Enterprises
2000	122	328	390	71	58
2002	132	360	462	64[a]	74

a. This statistic refers to 2001.

Source: Computed from ONE, *Anuario estadístico de Cuba, 2000*, page 105, and ONE, *Anuario estadístico de Cuba*, 2002, Table IV-4

In short, the policies of economic and political stabilization and economic liberalization that the Cuban government adopted in the first half of the 1990s succeeded. The economic collapse was stopped. An economic recovery commenced. Some fiscal balance was re-established. Sufficient political support for the regime was obtained. Nevertheless, the economic recovery has yet to return GDP to its level in the mid-1980s. The welfare effects on the population remain severe. Political support is much less substantial than before 1990. In the mid-1990s, the government no longer faced an economic and political abyss. The economic reform process slowed down and the government allowed new problems to fester as a result of inappropriately designed economic liberalization policies.

Problems Generated by Some of the New Economic Policies

Some of the economy's problems in the early twenty-first century arose from the unintended consequences of economic policies adopted in the 1990s. Cuba will need to reform these reforms to generate sustained growth. This section highlights three problems: multiple exchange rates, formation of oligopolies, and a contradictory approach to foreign direct investment. The first problem stems from partial dollarization, which created severe price distortions and market segmentation.

The two others come out of flawed institutional reforms. One bears on how the government reorganized the economy to create partial privatization, leading to the formation of oligopolies, while the other stems from Cuba's weak institutional foundation to attract effective and efficient foreign firms. A partial reform equilibrium—Cuba's circumstance in these three problematic areas—unfairly empowers insiders to exploit the nation's assets and creates opportunities for the corrupt exercise of arbitrage.

Multiple exchange rates. The Cuban economy's partial dollarization, resulting from measures adopted between 1990 and 1993, created a system of multiple exchange rates and set up structurally semi-independent coexisting economies. Partial dollarization occurred through the legalization of holding and using dollars remitted by Cuban-Americans but it results mainly from the government's structural choices. It segregated product markets operating in dollars from those that operate in pesos: International tourism operates in dollars, sugar in pesos, and the two do not meet through the financial system.

The segmented markets created through partial dollarization prevent the development of more normal means to finance enterprises, distort relative prices, make it virtually impossible to measure the true profitability of enterprises, and even to assess the state budget. The official exchange rate, fixed parity between the peso and the dollar, generates large, hidden subsidies.[37] As George Carriazo, Minister Rodríguez's successor as the Deputy Director of the *Centro de Investigaciones de la Economía Mundial*, put it already in 1996, Cuba must move to unify its exchange rate regime and, thus, the segments of its economy.[38] (Cuba's multiple exchange rate regime has already lasted much longer than Russia's did, and thus may have caused worse damage.)

The multiple exchange rate regime helped to decapitalize the sugar industry, leading to its *de facto* bankruptcy. On April 10, 2002, the government announced that it would shut down 45 percent of Cuba's 155 sugar mills.[39] Sugar exports are paid for in dollars but the government insisted that state enterprises in the sugar sector be paid in pesos at a parity exchange rate between the peso and the dollar. For example, in 2000 the international price that Cuba received for a pound of sugar was approximately US$0.10. At the prevailing exchange rate available to those Cubans who received remittances, the producer would receive two pesos but, at the official exchange rate, that producer received only 0.10 pesos or one-twentieth of the real worth of the products. On the other hand, the sugar industry had to purchase some imported supplies in dollars. No wonder state industrial and agricultural enterprises in the sugar sector performed poorly, given that its revenues remained in pesos while some of its inputs switched to dollars.[40] It did not help that between 1997 and 2002 the government cut back peso investments in the sugar sector by 54 percent while its peso investments in all sectors grew 8 percent.[41]

The multiple exchange rate regime also transferred subsidies to those Cuban consumers who could purchase imported petroleum or food products in pesos and thus have little incentive to constrain their consumption.[42] A beneficiary of remittances can lawfully import such goods at will to satisfy personal tastes at the same time that severe energy and food shortages plague consumers in the peso economy.

To capture the dollars from tourists and those remitted from abroad, the government created dollar stores. In 1996, dollar stores already sold goods worth US$640 million; by 1997, half of all Cubans had some access to hard currencies.[43] In fact, most of the shoppers at these dollar stores are Cubans who obtain dollars in various ways, legally and illegally. Some products are then re-sold in illegal markets. These stores are well supplied with products, often imported from abroad, in stark contrast with peso stores whose shelves are nearly bare. Access to dollars has become the principal determinant of inequality between Cubans today. Partial dollarization also generates powerful incentives to Cuban enterprises to obtain dollar resources, typically by selling their products to the dollar stores or to enterprises that operate in dollars even if the result is an inefficient allocation of national resources.[44]

Partial dollarization distorts the labor market as well. Workers have a strong incentive to shift from peso-generating to dollar-generating occupations such as those in the international tourism sector. It is common to find university graduates working in menial jobs to serve international tourists. Workers in international tourism receive part of their compensation in dollars. The result de-values education. Another effect on the labor market results from dollar remittances: people who do no or little work live well if they receive remittances.

Long-term sustained reliance on remittances may further weaken Cuba's already battered work ethic. Karl Marx wrote about the communist principle in the *Critique of the Gotha* Program: "From each according to his ability, to each according to his needs." That same text indicates that Marx would write the socialist principle, that is, the standard for work incentives in the transition away from capitalism, as: From each according to his ability, to each according to his effort.[45]

Since the early 1990s, Cuba has discovered a different principle: From each according to his connections, to each according to his luck.

The remedy to some of these distortions is to gradually unify the exchange rate through progressive devaluations. The objective would make the already existing "convertible peso" Cuba's currency. The value of this peso would float subject to central bank intervention. The long-standing official dollar-peso US$1=1 parity would be abandoned.[46] The government has been reluctant to adopt such policies for two reasons. First, they necessarily imply a certain additional loss of political control, given the additional heavy costs of adjustment that Cubans would need to bear to correct this policy error. Second, they would require the development of a whole new financing structure, for which Cuba is not ready institutionally or economically, not just politically.

Oligopoly formation. A second cluster of problems is institutional, that is, how the government has reorganized state enterprises. The quasi-private state enterprise policy creates tight oligopolies to favor the already favored. This is evident in the international tourism sector where partial privatization reforms are most extensive. By the end of the 1990s, two quasi-private state enterprises, Cubanacán and Gran Caribe, monopolized 91 percent of the supply of five-star hotels, jointly with their respective international partners. Another quasi-private state enterprise, Horizontes, controlled 66 percent of the supply of two-star hotels and 47 percent of the supply of four-star hotels, also jointly with its international partners.[47] The government used its discretion to carve out non-competitive niches for these firms even in the most dynamic sectors, weakening competition and creating opportunities for profit that are artificially generated by government policy for the benefit of one or two firms—oligopoly rents.

The government reorganized some of its more lucrative state enterprises and assigned them to favored insiders without a competitive bid or meritocratic process. The state owns these enterprises but, through bonuses and other means, managers set their own compensation in these quasi-private enterprises at levels far above those prevailing in the "plain" public sector. This Cuban-style partial privatization poses a high risk that privileged managers on their own will privatize these state assets at some future point.

The government has also tolerated lawless behavior on the part of many enterprises. Cuba's domestic financial imbalances at the enterprise level are most readily evident through what some Cuban authors call "the chain of non-payment,"[48] that is, Enterprise X finances itself by failing to pay what it owes to Enterprise Y, which in turn fails to pay Enterprise Z, and so on. Such illegal behavior on a massive scale creates enterprise liquidity but threatens the country's financial system. In 2000, enterprise non-payments amounted to about one-fifth of GDP.[49] Contract enforcement would provide better discipline for enterprises and reduce the likelihood of further abuse.

Levels of corruption in Cuba had been low before 1990. Since 1990, instances of corruption are reported in the Cuban press with regularity. In 1998 alone, the Cuban Communist Party conducted 1,159 investigations of corruption involving its members, most of whom in these instances were high officials. Among the officials most commonly accused of corruption and found guilty are associated with the quasi-private state enterprises in international tourism and other dollar-generating sectors.[50] The combination of new markets, strong state intervention in shaping those markets, and extremely wide executive discretion is the tripod on which corrupt practices can be built in any society.

The formation of oligopolies is sometimes justified as an attempt to retain the main economic assets in the hands of nationals as change accelerates.[51] It surely serves to protect the power and income of the national elite. This is the nationalism of scoundrels appropriating public property for private gain—the antithesis of the values of revolutionary socialism. If this process persists, Cuba will find a path to crony capitalism.

Suboptimal foreign direct investment regime. A third set of problems has arisen regarding the regime for foreign direct investments. As already noted, Article 15 of the 1992 Constitution permits foreign direct investment in the most backhanded way. Cuba has received remarkably modest and oscillating flows of foreign investment for various reasons. Its economy is small and weak. U.S. policy no doubts deters some potential investors, but Cuba's Constitution is hardly a good example of reliably rooted property rights. Law 77 (1995) cannot guarantee more rights than the Constitution itself. The Constitution must be changed, not in this instance to alter the political regime but to make it possible for the socialist regime to generate better economic results. Property rights cannot be just an exception to a uniform policy of state ownership, subject to the discretion of the executive committee of the Council of Ministers, and still expect substantial foreign investment, which has been the motor for Cuba's economic recovery.

The government could also use its Law 77 to authorize foreign investments in local firms wholly owned by the international enterprise, instead of insisting as a practical matter on joint ventures. The government would gain information and expertise in coping with foreign firms of different sizes, styles and capacity to invest. The paltry ability to bring in foreign investment is caused more by the restrictive fashion in which the government interprets the law than by the law itself. The desire to retain political control seems to be one obstacle to a change the current use of Law 77.

Cuba's approach to foreign direct investment also fosters non-competitive oligopolies. The executive committee of the Council of Ministers tends to grant concessions per product line or geographic site, thus making it unnecessary for foreign firms to compete against each other. The previously cited example of oligopoly outcomes in international tourism also applies to Cuban quasi-private state enterprises and their international partners. These non-competitive outcomes deprive Cuba of the opportunity to receive better terms from foreign firms and to benefit from likely efficiencies from greater competition. The government foregoes such benefits for the sake of retaining executive discretion in the allocation of sectoral and territorial resources. A better policy—more efficient and less vulnerable to corruption—would significantly liberalize the foreign direct investment regime and curtail the discretionary powers of the concession-granting agencies.

The complaints reported by Canadian firms investing in Cuba illustrate some problems created by the Cuban government's management of the investment regime:

- Inability to set prices for products at a rate that would encourage sales, which typically would mean lowering prices to encourage demand
- Inability to hire skilled labor freely, being confined, instead, to the labor pool of the Ministry that was the parent for the joint venture
- Ministries transferred workers trained by the joint ventures—against the firm's wishes—to other parts of the Ministry, after the investor had paid for the training
- Excessive restrictions on the ability to offer incentive payments to workers
- Refusal to renew visas for foreign managers before Cubans were ready to take over management jobs
- Unexpected new taxes and fees, set often by government

entities that had had no role in the initial joint venture
negotiations

- Imposition of the US\$1 = 1 peso exchange rate on internal
  transactions, when the joint venture incurred all of its costs in
  dollars[52]

Moreover, the "chain of non-payment" described above also affects
joint ventures operating in Cuba. Some foreign firms suffer from this
institutional climate, so lax in contract enforcement and timely payment of bills. The chain of non-payment is especially harsh on foreign
firms that cannot themselves collect the dollar earnings of their enterprises offshore, that is, they sell through Cuban partners in the Cuban
market. At the international level, many Cuban state enterprises and
other government agencies do not honor their obligations to international suppliers, some of which are the same firms that invest in Cuba
since lawfully authorized forms of investment include "investment
through supplies."

Cuba stopped servicing its international hard-currency debt in
1986. Since the 1990s, it has made commendable efforts to clear up
arrears in its multilateral debts and it has brought down some of its
debt with certain governments. The total hard-currency debt peaked
at US\$11.1 billion in 1999, dropping to US\$10.9 billion in 2001.[53] But
Cuba replicated at the international level what its enterprises do within
the country, namely, not to pay suppliers as a means to obtain international financing. The reason for this is simple: Cuba could not obtain
convertible-currency funds in any other way. This is not a sustainable
long-term strategy but it has sustained the Cuban government already
for a long term.

Non-payments to international suppliers grew by 73 percent from
1997 to 2001, thereby financing Cuba's economic recovery. In 2001,
non-payment of international suppliers amounted to 19 percent of
all of Cuba's international hard-currency debt. And the value of the
non-payments that year well exceeded the value of all of Cuba's goods
exports. Many of these international suppliers are the same firms that
already invest in Cuba or that might invest in Cuba if it had a more
secure property rights regime.

The partial-reform equilibrium that marked Cuba's political economy at the start of the twentieth century is driven by strong political
incentives. The multiple exchange regime gives the illusion of control
even as severe distortions work their way through the Cuban econ-

omy, contributing to the sugar industry's bankruptcy. The formation of strong oligopolies rewards elite cadres, prevents substantial denationalization of the ownership of the means of production, and retains control while elements of privatization trickle out. The cost is a severely anti-competitive regime, with the prospect of increasing levels of corruption. The foreign investment regime maximizes executive discretion to allocate resources at the cost of foregoing many potential gains from foreign direct investment. These three sets of policies are obstacles to Cuba's efficient and sustained long-term economic growth prospects. All inflict harm on its economy. All deserve reform. Because strong vested interests have been created through these processes, only President Castro's strong leadership can reform this "reform" in Cuba's current political system.

Adopting New Socialism-Compatible Economic Reforms

In addition to correcting the adverse results of some of its economic reforms of the 1990s, the government should also deepen the economic reform program. For this section as for the previous one, I impose on myself the restriction that these new, deeper reforms should be compatible with the socialist system enshrined in Cuba's Constitution and defended by the ruling party.[54] This section discusses four topics. The first three are liberalization measures (illegal markets, deregulating agricultural markets, small Cuban private business firms), and the fourth (pensions) bears on long-term fiscal health. Each recommendation extends procedures already employed or readily available within Cuba's current socialist framework.

Illegal markets. One of the sources impelling Cuba's economic reforms in the early 1990s was the illegal market. With the economic collapse, Cubans fended for themselves, ignoring economic regulations. Government and Communist Party officials and ordinary citizens alike engaged in massive lawlessness. Starting in the late 1980s, Cuban officials somewhat tolerated illegal markets because they appeared to be means to cope with adversity and complemented the legal economy. A 1989 survey of "gray" (semi-legal) and "black" (illegal) markets showed that Cubans searched mainly for services in these markets. From 1989 to 1993, however, they increasingly searched for food and household essentials, bidding prices up by a factor of 25 to 30—an inflation rate that official prices sought to repress.[55] Individual desperation deepened.

The government and the party could not imprison millions of Cubans. They had repressed illegal economic activities before the late

1980s and did so more selectively after 1990.[56] The preferred strategy after 1990 was to find a new equilibrium. State security had better things to do than to chase peasants trying to sell their products. Agricultural private markets, legalization of holding and using dollars and self-employment were responses, in part, to the state's accommodation to the behavior of its people and its effort to re-establish the rule of law to the extent possible.[57] The size of the illegal market abated though it did not disappear. Aspects of this state response have been common, of course, to other communist or once-communist countries, even North Korea.[58]

Agricultural markets. Following the same principles, the Cuban government can liberalize other aspects of economic behavior to further shrink the size of the illegal market. Fully liberalizing agricultural markets is one example. Such measures would likely increase output substantially, make the most important component of illegal markets disappear, and relieve the Interior Ministry from having to arrest peasants and ordinary citizens for simple food retail transactions.

Previous sections have shown that the sugar cane UBPCs suffered from various ills but one of them surely was being paid in relatively unchanging and low prices for their agricultural production while remaining under continuing excessive state control. Sugar cane UBPCs were *de facto* prevented from diversifying into other crops while being paid low prices in pesos. State agricultural marketing boards exercised oligopsony power to set prices and output levels. That is one reason why the sugar cane UBPCs were not profitable in the immediate aftermath of their creation. Lo and behold, many UBPCs became profitable when the government liberalized some agricultural prices in late 1994, granting access to market prices to UBPCs engaged in non-sugar production as well private farming cooperatives and individual farmers.[59] These rural enterprises performed well for the remainder of the decade.

Production of fruits and vegetables increased substantially between 1994 and 1998 because of market prices and agricultural policy deregulation. By 1998, many product lines of agriculture had recovered their 1989 levels. And yet, the heavy hand of the state agricultural marketing boards persisted, paying at prices appreciably below those prevailing in the free agricultural markets—prices at which producers were compelled to sell by law. Even late into the 1990s, the Ministry of Agriculture continued to behave toward peasant producers as if they were state employees, issuing excessive regulations and interfering.[60]

Yet, as China's example shows, the deregulation of agricultural markets can generate substantial improvements in economic performance, feed the cities, provide for exports and contribute significantly to economic growth. Remaining regulations would uphold market-conforming rules and enforce health codes. Full agricultural liberalization would most likely greatly increase food output, end illegal markets in food and lead to a more efficient allocation of resources.

Small businesses. Cuba's approach to property rights in directly productive activities is unusual by world standards. It permits and promotes state firms and foreign firms but prohibits privately owned national firms. Since the 1960s, the government has allowed individual farmers to contract for some labor through state agencies. It promoted private agricultural cooperatives. In the 1990s, the liberalization of self-employment, as noted, permits paying relatives but not hiring non-relatives. The creation of UBPCs might have been an interim step toward wider entrepreneurial autonomy. In the early to mid-1990s, Communist Party and government officials as well as academics discussed the utility of authorizing small and medium sized private Cuban firms.[61] The economic recovery begun in 1994 seemed to some decision makers to make such a further opening unnecessary, however.

And yet, the case for authorizing small- and medium-sized Cuban enterprises in the private sector remains strong. In the early 1990s, underemployment in the state sector approximated a fifth of that labor force, that is, some 800,000 workers.[62] Cuba's self-employed have been creative and productive in many endeavors, notwithstanding government barriers and a weak economy.[63] However, in this sphere, too, a partial equilibrium has created problems: Cuba lacks a private wholesale market so private entrepreneurs often rely on illegal markets to obtain their supplies. Some of this illegal entrepreneurship comes at the expense of state enterprises. The severe constraint on the potential growth of small business firms also fosters an illegal labor market. Cuban scholars find that, for each lawfully registered self-employed worker, 3.5 workers have not registered; many of the latter are not relatives. In 1995, that meant that over one million Cubans were self-employed, dropping to about 600,000 in 1997.[64] Authorizing small business firms would reduce the incentive to engage in such illegal behavior.

Carranza, Monreal, and Gutiérrez have made a good case for the role of small and medium sized enterprises within the political framework of a socialist Cuba.[65] They recommend imposing capital and employment constraints on the size of Cuban enterprises that could be owned and operated privately. They also recommend relying on provincial and municipal governments to regulate small and medium sized Cuban firms, lifting the weight of micro-regulation from the national government.[66] Carranza, Monreal, and Gutiérrez note the advantages of scale that such modest-sized firms would have in many lines of production and services. These firms would have no claim on government subsidies. Although each firm would employ few workers, the growth in the number of such firms could reduce overt and hidden unemployment and improve efficiency. They would pay taxes. They are suited to certain dynamic activities such as software technology development or service operations in which the Cuban economy is severely deficient.[67] Such small business firms could make a significant economic contribution. Authorizing them would imply some further loss of political control but one that the current socialist system can well manage.

Pensions. Financing old-age pensions is a daunting problem for Cuba. Cuba has been below the population replacement rate since 1978. By 2015, about one-fifth of the population will be 60 or older; that proportion will reach one-third in 2035 and remain at that level for decades to come. One out of every six Cubans is likely to be over 75 in 2050. This is, of course, a consequence of long-term improvements in education, health, nutrition, and in the greater capacity of adults to control their reproductive lives. Even without emigration, the population is scheduled to start shrinking in 2025; with emigration, its shrinkage could begin by 2015. This means that Cuba's system for pension financing will reach crisis proportions soon.[68]

Cuba authorizes women to retire at 55 and men at 60. It provides a defined-benefit system. In 1998, already 1.4 million people received pensions.[69] In practice, some adjustment has been taking place because pensions are paid in pesos. Their purchasing value falls as the economy dollarizes. However, this approach to pension policy adjustment is profoundly inegalitarian and arbitrary. Far preferable, at a minimum, would be to raise rapidly the age for retirement and pension eligibility, eliminate the gender differential, increase the rate of contributions from all workers in the state and private sectors, and shift gradually toward a defined-contribution system. No Cuban political regime can escape making such reforms.[70]

Conclusions

Cuba's economic reforms of the first half of the 1990s succeeded. The government responded pragmatically and effectively to the economic crisis. The reforms stopped the economic crisis, set the basis for economic recovery, stabilized both fiscal accounts and the political system, and retained albeit frayed a social safety net. The political regime persevered and changed little, remaining highly centralized and dependent on a key leader. Cuba continued to invest in health and education and it moved appreciably toward energy self-sufficiency. These results gained political support at the time of greatest peril for the regime in the first half of the 1990s. Substantial support remains for state socialism and gradual approaches to economic reforms along with official skepticism of market-oriented reforms.

Yet Cuba suffered an economic debacle from which it has yet to recover. It may not reach the 1985 GDP per capita levels until this century's second decade. Its economy is plagued with industrial dinosaurs; it remains an ineffective exporter of agricultural products. Its balance of payments is unsustainable because it is financed through non-payment of international financial obligations. Its fiscal situation is out of balance because inflation is repressed and partly hidden through illegal markets and dualistic markets. There is no sustainable equilibrium in its domestic or international accounts.

Several of Cuba's economic reforms were only partial. Partial reform equilibrium is a long-term recipe for disaster; it delays microeconomic reforms indefinitely. Such equilibria in the reform or privatization of state enterprises open the window for high levels of corruption as well as for state capture by quasi-private interests and their foreign partners for private gain. Cuba is vulnerable to these ills because its procedures governing quasi-private enterprises risk the unlawful privatization of public assets and create oligopolies that already choke off inter-enterprise competition. The government has been reluctant to sell off state enterprises to foreigners. Its nationalist political preference, explicit or implicit, for insider privatization could lead easily to crony capitalism.

Socialist Cuba could exit this partial-reform equilibrium. It should correct policy mistakes. It should unify its exchange rates to eliminate severe distortions to its economy, set a stronger institutional basis for property rights and adopt further deregulation in sectors where foreign firms and quasi-private enterprises already operate, and introduce elements of competition to break up counterproductive newly created official oligopolies. In addition, it could easily liberalize its agricultural markets within its current socialist system, thereby increasing output and curtailing illegal markets, to the glee of the Finance and Interior Ministries. These measures would also improve the fiscal balance. It could register significant efficiency, productive, and learning gains from liberalizing markets for small nationally owned private businesses. And it should take steps now to address the fiscal time bomb embedded in its pension policies.

In 1990, Cuba launched an experiment in political economy. It adopted some market means in order to rescue its socialist political and social system. And yet, it adopted fewer such changes than the most successful socialist governments—China and Vietnam—have. Nor has Cuba learned sufficiently the lessons from the new political regimes of Eastern Europe and Central Asia that have much to teach it. Cuba is proud of its internationalism. Now is the time to learn from comparative experiences to generate prosperity and improve its people's prospects for human development.

Author's Note

This paper was first written for a project sponsored by the Inter-American Dialogue. It has been modified for this book and is printed here by permission. I am grateful to the Inter-American Dialogue and Harvard University's David Rockefeller Center for Latin American Studies and Weatherhead Center for International Affairs for their general support of my work. I am also grateful to Shahid Javed Burki, Daniel Erikson, Jeffry Frieden, Omar Everleny Pérez Villanueva, and Michael Small for comments on earlier versions. All mistakes are mine alone.

Notes

1   *Granma Weekly Review*, 1 July 1990, 1.

2   Ibid., 27 May 1990, 2–3.

3   The price deflator most likely underestimates "true" inflation. It fails to take fully into account the illegal or "black" markets, takes no account of time waiting as a measure of inflation as felt by people, and probably underestimates the effect of dual dollar/peso markets on living standards.

4   For further discussion, see Jorge I. Domínguez, *To Make A World Safe for Revolution: Cuba's Foreign Policy* (Cambridge, Mass.: Harvard University Press, 1989), chapter 4.

5   Comisión Económica para América Latina y el Caribe, *La economía cubana: Reformas estructurales y desempeño en los noventa* (Mexico: Fondo de Cultura Económica, 2000), Table A.2. Hereafter, CEPAL. See also *Granma*, 21 December 2002, for the Economy Minister's report to the National Assembly, and http://www.cubagob.cubaweb.cu/des_eco/mep/cuba2000.htm

6 Oficina Nacional de Estadísticas, *Anuario estadístico de Cuba, 2002* (Havana: 2003), Tables II-14 and XIV-3. Hereafter *AEC 2002*. Infant mortality in Washington, D.C., was 10.6 in 2001, http://www.census.gov/statab/ranks/rank17.xls

7 Task Force on Education, Equity, and Economic Competitiveness in Latin America and the Caribbean, *Lagging Behind: A Report Card on Education in Latin America* (Washington, D.C.: Partnership for Educational Revitalization in the Americas (PREAL), 2001), 33.

8 Centro de Investigaciones de la Economía Mundial, *Investigación sobre desarrollo humano y equidad en Cuba 1999* (Havana: Caguayo S.A., 2000), 59, 82, 100.

9 Viviana Togores and Anicia García, "Consumo, mercados y dualidad monetaria en Cuba," Table 4. Centro de Estudios de la Economía Cubana, Universidad de La Habana.

10 Ángela Ferriol Muruaga, "Política social cubana: Situación y transformaciones," *Temas*, 11 (1998), 91.

11 Calculated from *AEC 2002*, Table II-3.

12 Ángela Ferriol Muruaga, "La seguridad alimentaria en Cuba," in *Cuba: Crisis, ajuste, y situación social 1990–1996*, ed. Ángela Ferriol Muruaga et al. (Havana: Editorial de Ciencias Sociales, 1998), 94.

13 Silvia M. Domenech, ed., *Cuba: Economía en período especial* (Havana: Editorial Política, 1996), 15.

14 Computed from *AEC 2002*, Table XII-11.

15 Calculations from Oficina Nacional de Estadísticas, *Anuario estadístico de Cuba, 1996* (Havana: 1998), 99. Hereafter *AEC 1996*.

16 Cuba's policies resemble Bulgaria's, which at the start of the 1990s continued to subsidize enterprises to sustain the Bulgarian Socialist Party in power. In Bulgaria as in Cuba, the economy had not collapsed prior to the end of the Soviet Union and the well-educated population was tolerant, perhaps supportive, of the communist regime. Cuba's policies also resemble Uzbekistan's, which continued to invest in health care and education and relied extensively on subsidies, also to sustain in power a political regime that changed little.

17 Darío Machado, "¿Cuál es nuestro clima socio-político?," *El militante comunista*, 9 (September 1990), 6, 7.

18 Calculated from *AEC 1996*, 98.

19 Calculated from *AEC 1996*, 98, 99.

20 Noel Chaviano Saldaña, "El tipo de cambio en la economía estatal cubana," in *Economía y reforma económica en Cuba*, ed. Dietmar Dirmoser and Jaime Estay (Caracas: Editorial Nueva Sociedad, 1997), 309.

21 Computed from *AEC 2002*, Table IV-4.

22 For an early assessment of these reforms, see Carmelo Mesa-Lago, *Are Economic Reforms Propelling Cuba to the Market?* (Coral Gables, Fla.: North-South Center, University of Miami, 1994), chapter 3.

23 Armando Nova González, "El cooperativismo en la agricultura cañera de 1993 a 2000," *Economía y desarrollo*, 129 (June-December 2001), 49.

24 Ibid., 54.

25 See, for example, Fidel Castro's remarks at the conclusion of the 1986 Third Congress of the Communist Party of Cuba, *Informe central: Tercer Congreso del Partido Comunista de Cuba* (Havana: Editora Política, 1986).

26 Computed from Oficina Nacional de Estadística, *Anuario estadístico de Cuba, 2000* (Havana: 2001), 103. Hereafter, *AEC 2000*.

27 Carmen D. Deere et al., *Güines, Santo Domingo, Majibacoa: Sobre sus historias agrarias* (Havana: Editorial de Ciencias Sociales, 1998), 369–370.

28 *AEC 2002*, Table V-1. Cuban statistics on unemployment fail to account for widespread under-employment. See Centro de Investigaciones de la Economía Mundial, *Investigación sobre desarrollo humano y equidad en Cuba, 1999*, 67–69. In 2002, the official open unemployment rate was 3.3 percent. *Granma*, 20 December 2002.

29 Oficina Nacional de Estadísticas, *Anuario estadístico de Cuba, 2001*, (Havana: 2002), Table IV-4, hereafter *AEC 2001*. For discussions regarding entrepreneurship in Cuba and the barriers to its development, see Philip Peters and Joseph Scarpaci, *Cuba's New Entrepreneurs: Five Years of Small-Scale Capitalism* (Arlington, VA: Alexis de Tocqueville Institution, 1998); Benjamin Smith, "The Self-Employed in Cuba: A Street-Level View," *Cuba in Transition*, vol. 9 (Silver Spring, MD: Association for the Study of the Cuban Economy, 1999); and Ted Henken, "Condemned to Informality: Cuba's Experiments with Self-Employment during the Special Period (The Case of the Bed and Breakfasts)," *Cuban Studies*, 33 (2002): 29.

30 *AEC 2000*, 128, 137; *AEC 2001*, Tables VI-1, VI-8; CEPAL, Table A.30; CEPAL, *Cuba: Evolución económica durante 2002 y perspectivas para 2003*, LC/Mex/L.566 (United Nations), Table 17.

31 *AEC 2000*, 128, 241, 248, 256; *AEC 2002*, Tables XI-13, XII-1, and XII-11.

32 *AEC 2002*, Tables VI-8 and VII-1.

33 Omar Everleny Pérez Villanueva, "Foreign Direct Investment in Cuba: Recent Experience and Prospects," in *Development Prospects in Cuba*, ed. Pedro Monreal (London: Institute of Latin American Studies, 2002), 52.

34 Humberto Blanco Rosales, "El factor gerencial y el perfeccionamiento de la empresa estatal cubana," *Economía y desarrollo*, 126 (January-June 2000): 11–39.

35 George Carriazo Moreno, "Cuba: Cambios económicos," *Economía y desarrollo*, 120 (June 1996), 23.

36 Omar Everleny Pérez and Alejandro Beruff, "Desempeño de la economía cubana: Primer trimestre de 1996," *Economía y desarrollo*, 120 (June 1996), 36.

37 Vilma Hidalgo de los Santos, Pavel Vidal Alejandro, and Lourdes Tabares Neyra, "Equilibrios monetarios y política económica," *Economía y desarrollo*, 127 (July-December 2000), 79.

38 Carriazo Moreno, "Cuba: Cambios económicos," 27.

39 *Granma*, 20 December 2002. For an analysis of the reasons leading up to this productive catastrophe, see Jaime Sperberg Fuentealba, "El sector azucarero cubano entre reformas y estancamiento," *Cuban Studies*, 33 (2002): 30–47.

40 Nova González, "El cooperativismo en la agricultura cañera en Cuba de 1993 a 2000," 51. See also Lázaro Peña, "The Sugar Cane Complex: Problems of Competitiveness and Uncertainty in a Crucial Sector," in *Development Prospects in Cuba: An Agenda in the Making*, ed. Pedro Monreal (London: Institute of Latin American Studies, 2002), 107–108, 113.

41 *AEC 2002*, Table X-5.

42 Alfredo González Gutiérrez, "Economía y sociedad: Los retos del modelo económico," in *Cuba construyendo futuro: Reestructuración económica y transformaciones sociales* (Madrid: Fundación de Investigaciones Marxistas, 2000), 202–203.

43 Ferriol Muruaga, "Política social cubana," 89–90.

44 Hiram Marquetti Nodarse, "La economía del dólar: Balance y perspectivas," *Temas*, 11 (1998): 51–62.

45 Karl Marx, "Critique of the Gotha Programme," in *Marx and Engels: Basic Writings on Politics and Philosophy*, ed. Lewis S. Feuer (Garden City: Anchor Books, 1959), 115–120, quotation from 119

46 For a thoughtful general assessment of Cuba's exchange rate regime, see Archibald R. M. Ritter, "La unificación de los sistemas monetarios duales y los sistemas de tasa de cambio en Cuba," in *Cuba: Reestructuración económica y globalización* (Bogotá: Centro Editorial Javeriano, 2003).

47 Alejandro Durán Cárdenas, "Turismo y economía cubana: Un análisis al final del milenio," *Economía y desarrollo*, 127 (July-December 2000), 41–42.

48 International economists sometimes call this process the "triangular debt," common in the public sector in the developing world.

49 Hidalgo de los Santos, Vidal Alejandro, and Tabares Neyra, "Equilibrios monetarios y política económica," 75–105.

50 Jorge Pérez-López, "Corruption and the Cuban Transition," *Cuba in Transition*, 9 (Silver Spring, MD: Association for the Study of the Cuban Economy, 1999): 453–477.

51 Such enterprise protectionism resembles similar experiences in Russia, Eastern Europe, and Central Asia. It could have the corrupting effects evident Russia and Bulgaria. In Slovakia, a similar process was defended on similar nationalist grounds.

52 I am grateful to Michael Small, Canada's former ambassador to Cuba, for these examples.

53 Banco Central de Cuba, *Cuban Economy in the Special Period, 1990–2000*, 14; *AEC 2002*, Table V1.2.

54 To be transparent, I favor a peaceful transition in Cuba to a democratic political regime, not just the enactment of economic reforms compatible with the current political system. In this work, however, my political preferences are not pertinent.

55 Alfredo González Gutiérrez, "La economía sumergida en Cuba," in *Economía y reforma económica en Cuba*, ed. Dietmar Dirmoser and Jaime Estay (Caracas: Editorial Nueva Sociedad, 1997), 241–243.

56 For discussion, see Jorge Pérez-López, *Cuba's Second Economy: From Behind the Scenes to Center Stage* (New Brunswick, NJ: Transaction, 1995), 97–109, 145–150.

57 I have visited Cuba every calendar year but one since 1991. These sentences summarize many interviews and personal observations.

58 On the start of economic reforms in North Korea, *The Economist* 13 March 2004, 41–41.

59 Niurka Pérez Rojas and Dayma Echevarría León, "Participación y producción agraria en Cuba: las UBPC," *Temas*, 11 (July-September 1997): 69–75.

60 Minor Sinclair and Martha Thompson, *Cuba Going Against the Grain: Agricultural Crisis and Transformation* (Boston: OXFAM America, 2001), 20, 22, 31, 33, 40. See also George Carriazo Moreno, "Cambios estructurales en la agricultura cubana: la cooperativización," in *Economía y reforma en Cuba*, ed. Dietmar Dirmoser and Jaime Estay (Caracas: Nueva Sociedad, 1997), 195–199.

61 I had such conversations with high party and government officials.

62 Ángela Ferriol, "El empleo. Próximo desafío," in *Economía y reforma económica en Cuba*, ed. Dietmar Dirmoser and Jaime Estay (Caracas: Editorial Nueva Sociedad, 1997), 361–362.

63 See Ana Julia Jatar-Hausmann's excellent account in *The Cuban Way: Cap-*

italism, Communism, and Confrontation (West Hartford, Conn.: Kumarian Press), chapter 7.

64 Lilia Núñez Moreno, "Más allá del cuentapropismo en Cuba," *Temas*, 18 (1998), 45–46.

65 This project was incubated and developed at the Centro de Estudios sobre América (CEA). One year after the publication of this book, and possibly because of its impact, the Communist Party Central Committee intervened the CEA, removed its leaders, and compelled its leading scholars to leave the CEA and disperse.

66 Their recommendation approximates the township and village enterprises that have developed successfully in the People's Republic of China.

67 Julio Carranza Valdés, Luis Gutiérrez Urdaneta, and Pedro Monreal González, *Cuba: La reestructuración de la economía, una propuesta para el debate* (Havana: Editorial de Ciencias Sociales, 1995), 89, 94–95, 154.

68 Alberta Durán Gondar and Ernesto Chávez Negrín, "Una sociedad que envejece: Retos y perspectivas," *Temas*, 14 (April–June 1998), 60; Ricardo Donate-Armada, "The Aging of the Cuban Population," *Cuba in Transition*, 11 (Silver Spring, MD: Association for the Study of the Cuban Economy, 2001): 481–488.

69 CEPAL, 269.

70 For an excellent assessment of Cuba's pensions system, see Carmelo Mesa-Lago, "La globalización y la seguridad social en Cuba: Diagnóstico y necesidad de reformas," in *Cuba: Reestructuración económica y globalización*, ed. Mauricio de Miranda Parrondo (Bogotá: Centro Editorial Javeriano, 2003).

3

The Cuban Economy Today and Its Future Challenges

by Omar Everleny Pérez Villanueva

The transformation and economic restructuring of Cuba that began in the 1990s has been especially complex. Various economic policy measures implemented in the crisis years have now been consolidated; the changes sparked by these profound reforms have not been exhausted. Cuba, above all else, has attempted to maintain social stability and political control in the context of these transformations, despite the fact that the level of equality has been altered as a result of economic restructuring. The Cuban economy did experience an economic upturn in the mid-1990s, but its buoyancy was not sustained over the decade. The emphasis on the tourist industry and telecommunications has transformed it into a service economy. In other words, a new pattern of growth has been formed.

To assess the current state of the economy and present policy considerations for future decision making, this chapter briefly presents the evolution of the Cuban economy through its principal macroeconomic and sectoral indicators. While this chapter mainly analyzes the internal aspects of the Cuban economy, this cannot be done without recognizing that the country is affected by external factors, such as the economic blockade[1] that limits the undertaking of a series of concrete policy measures.

Macroeconomic Indicators

In 1994, the Cuban economy began to experience an upswing, following a precipitous decline in GDP of more than 35 percent between 1989 and 1993. The implementation of a series of economic policy measures aimed at reactivating economic growth included, among others, the reforming of state enterprises, the opening of the economy externally and decentralizing functions. Although these measures decelerated in some years, overall growth was positive. More recently, however, indicators of efficiency have performed poorly. Some subtle positive movements did begin, however, in 1999, specifically in improved labor productivity, which in turn has translated into increments in the average minimum wage, and also a decrease in energy consumption as a share of GDP.

Figure 3.1 GDP Growth in Constant 1981 Prices, 1989–2001
(percentage)

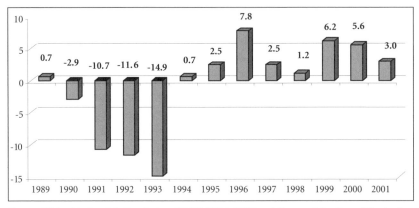

Source: Oficina Nacional de Estadísticas (ONE) (1996, 2000) and Report of the Central Bank of Cuba (2001)

Figure 3.2 GDP Growth in Constant 1997 Prices, 1997–2003
(percentage)

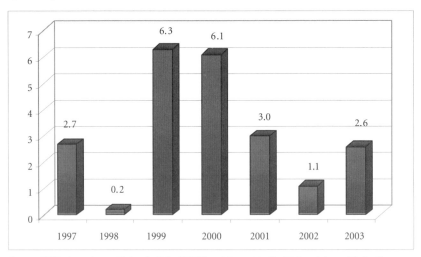

Source: ONE, *Anuario estadístico de Cuba* (2002) and Report to the National Assembly by the Ministry of Finances and Prices (2002)

In 2002, the price index used to measure the gross domestic product (GDP) was changed to 1997 constant prices. Both Figure 3.1, which presents GDP figures in constant 1981 prices, and Figure 3.2, which uses the new index based on 1997 prices, show that there was a deceleration in the rate of economic growth after 2000. This trend indicates that the time required for the economy to surpass 1989 levels will be extended.

Despite the economic model's achievements, an analysis of per capita GDP in constant 1981 prices (Figure 3.3) indicates that this variable remains deteriorated. That is, the trend for GDP per capita growth should be moving towards surpassing these values in the least possible time, which for economists means increasing output. However, financial resources in foreign exchange were needed to fuel this growth. The scarcity of these resources constitutes an important restrictive factor for the Cuban economy.

Figure 3.3 GDP Per Capita, 1990–2001
(in constant 1981 pesos)

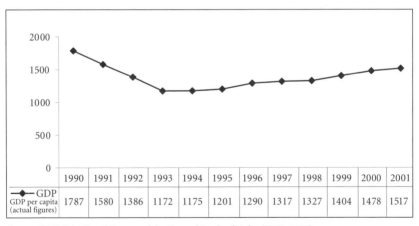

	1990	1991	1992	1993	1994	1995	1996	1997	1998	1999	2000	2001
GDP per capita (actual figures)	1787	1580	1386	1172	1175	1201	1290	1317	1327	1404	1478	1517

Source: ONE (2000) and Report of the Central Bank of Cuba (2000, 2001)

The relative share of agriculture, construction and transportation relative to GDP has tended to decrease over time, while that of mining, electricity, gas, water, finances, trade, restaurants and hotels has increased. By 2003, as Figure 3.4 indicates, services contributed 66 percent to GDP, signifying the transformation of Cuba into a service economy. In the future, investments should be increased to correspond to an industrial strategy that is needed to adapt to the increasing share of services as part of the economy. Otherwise, the trade deficit will continue to increase with the continued burgeoning of imports.

Figure 3.4 Composition of GDP by Economic Sector, 2003

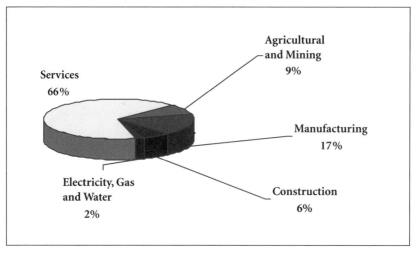

Source: ONE (2004). *Panorama Económico y Social, Cuba 2003*

Evolution of Investment

Based on an analysis of aggregate supply in GDP in 2001 and 2002, the production of goods and services increased relative to intermediate consumption, which implies a smaller share of material spending on production. Thus, in terms of supply, the economy was able to generate a better utilization of available resources. On the demand side, gross capital formation decreased in 2001 relative to 2000. However, it should be noted that this indicator has deteriorated with respect to 1990 levels, although it has partially recovered, as illustrated by Figure 3.5.

Figure 3.5 Gross Capital Formation, 1990–2001
(in constant 1981 millions of pesos)

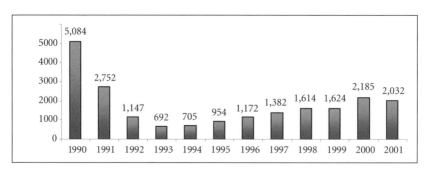

Source: ONE (1999) and Report of the Banco Central de Cuba (2001)

Although industrial capacities have been somewhat better utilized, as of 2003 the economy is still far from the levels of production achieved prior to the crisis, especially in industries specializing in consumer goods. In other words, a portion of industrial firms have achieved production levels above those achieved prior to the early years of the "Special Period," which is what the reform and adjustment process following the collapse of trade with the Soviet Union in 1989 is called in Cuba, in areas such as nickel, mechanical production, automotive and electricity sectors. However, the remaining portion of industrial production geared towards consumer goods such as food, clothing, footwear, etc. is still below necessary levels. In other words, demand for consumer goods is greater than their supply.

The transition to the effective upturn of the economy requires achieving rates of investment similar to 1975–1989, which on average were equivalent to 25 percent of the gross national product. In this regard it is appropriate to recall that the acquisition of these levels of accumulation were possible because of the combined effect of existing restrictions on personal consumption and beneficial financing terms granted by socialist countries. However, aspiring to achieve these growth rates in investment, at least in the short term, is difficult to imagine. First, the consumption of the population is depressed and requires an obligated restoration. Second, no objective possibilities exist for Cuba to once again enjoy the international conditions it had in 1989 (González 1998). Given these constraints, Cuba's ability for reaching consonant rates of investment depends on its ability to generate additional levels of domestic savings. In the absence of alternative sources of finance, the most feasible means of reaching this goal is by using existing resources with greater efficiency. However, even with greater efficiency, ensuring sustained levels of investments is problematic as the scarcity in foreign exchange reserves further limits Cuba's capacity to finance the purchasing of costly imports, such as machinery.

Greater economic growth occurred in part because of the volume of investments, initially on the rise in this period, although receding in 2001, and continuing to be low relative to the levels needed to compensate for the de-capitalization of capital assets and level of physical infrastructure. Furthermore, capital spending in equipment necessary for the modernization and improvement of production remains low (Figure 3.6).

Figure 3.6 Investments in Construction and Equipment, 1989–2002
(millions of pesos)

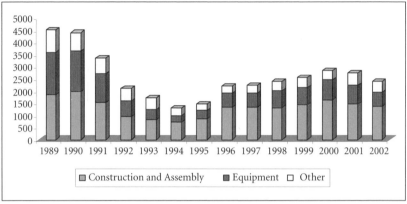

Source: ONE (1996 and 2002)

Evolution of Consumption

In the period between 1989 and 1993 total consumption, which until that time had been growing, began to decrease due to the reduction of social, government and private consumption. Several factors contributed to this decrease in consumption. The supply of goods and services contracted and remained very depressed because of the reduction of resources in the most important market—the rationed[2] market—and by the disappearance of the parallel markets[3] as a legal alternative. The boom of the black or underground market with its constantly rising prices also limited consumption. The consumer price index also increased in this period from 1.4 to 6.6, leading to a reduction of the real wage and limiting consumption possibilities. Furthermore, paper currency in Cuban pesos accumulated in the hands of the population without a material counterpart. In a short time, monetary liquidity reached the equivalent level of wage expenditures for fourteen months. This high monetary concentration, a trend that continues, was also reflected in the increase in bank deposits. As a result, the consumption of goods and services not distributed through the rationed market became polarized.

Consumption tended to grow after 1993 in response to different government policies (Figure 3.7). The improvement in the consumption dynamic has been possible because of a series of factors such as increase in production, increase in household income and other eco-

Figure 3.7 Evolution of Consumption, 1989–2000
(in constant 1981 millions of pesos)

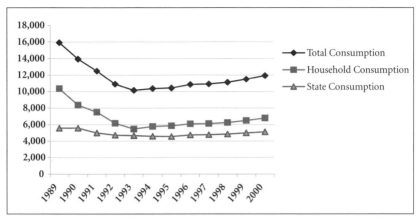

Source: ONE (1996 and 2000)

nomic transformations related to property, public finances and the market. Because these factors have an unequal effect on differing levels of income, a brief analysis of this relative impact is warranted and analyzed in the sections that follow.

Income

Income is an important variable since demand and consequent consumption of the population in different markets depends directly on its availability. The evolution of nominal income shows a historical trend toward growth. This marked improvement in the performance of income has been achieved through a set of factors that will be elaborated in the following paragraphs.

The nominal average monthly wage—characterized by either stability or growth—has maintained its performance over time (Figure 3.8). In 2002 average nominal monthly wage earnings reached 262 pesos, which, compared with the existing level in 1989, signified a large increase. Even so, this tendency has not managed to overcome the deterioration caused by the increase in the consumer price index (CPI). This increase in prices has caused duress for the majority of the population relying on wages as their most important source of income.

The distribution of income in the Cuban case is differentiated. The importance of the remunerations from state employment and payments for social security and welfare in Cuba is corroborated by the

Figure 3.8 Evolution of Nominal and Real Monthly Average Wage, 1989–2002 (pesos)

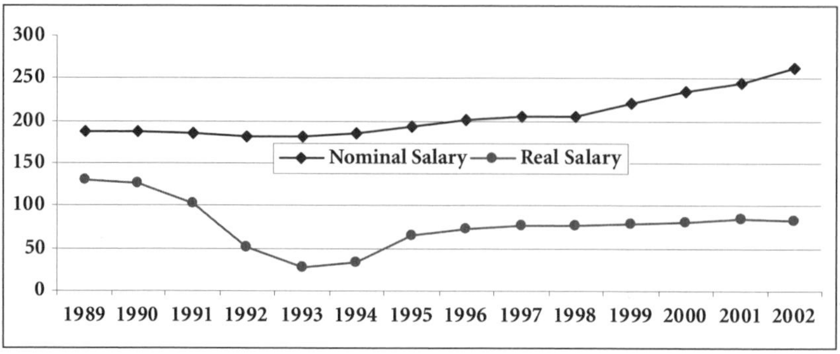

Source: Togores (2002) and Author's estimates

fact that the public sector generates 75 percent of employment. Furthermore, the majority of the dependent population also relies on this income source, especially youths and school-age adolescents, because of their increasingly limited income and consumption possibilities.

A not-insignificant number of workers employed by the state and cooperative sector receive stimulus compensation, which improved consumption for a small portion of the population. In 2002,

- 1,150,266 public workers received increases in wages;
- 1,342,000 workers were in compensation systems based on performance; and,
- 1,432,185 workers were in compensation systems with stimulus payments in foreign exchange.

The amount of remittances received from abroad has tended to consistently increase. Finding an accurate way to determine this increase is challenging. For example, if consumption in stores for the recovery of foreign exchange (TRD) is used as a reference, these sales increase continually. Together, these sources of income have increased the number of people who have access to foreign exchange. In 1997, 49.5 percent of the population was estimated to have access to foreign currency. By 2000, this figure reached 62 percent, although the amount was geographically disproportionate. Furthermore, the Cuban peso has substantially appreciated in the domestic foreign exchange market. Its value had declined from 95 pesos to the dollar in 1994 to between 20 and 22 pesos per dollar between 1997 and 2001. However, by the end of 2001, a new devaluation of the currency occurred increasing the exchange rate to 26 pesos per dollar.

The consolidation of a set of recent economic transformations has contributed to the reduction in the prices of products supplied in different markets. While supplies are still not adequate, the accelerated decrease in the consumer price index (CPI) has led to the recovery of real wages after 1993. But even so, due to the insufficiency of income to cover expenditures, a certain portion of the population has basic needs—especially dietary ones—that continue to be unmet.

Public Finances

Financial measures, and others focused on the organizational character of the central administration of the Cuban state, have permitted the fiscal deficit to be reduced by a significant degree between 1994 and 2002. The fiscal deficit has not exceeded 3 percent of GDP since 1996. In other words, the successful implementation of the financial stabilization program begun in 1994 can be observed by the positive results in public finances. The fiscal deficit as a share of GDP presented in Figure 3.9 illustrates this assertion, as the indicator reached 2.5 percent in 2001. Currently, however, this level of performance is being challenged and higher rates of income will need to be generated in order for greater expenditures to be continued in those spheres that are most necessary.

Figure 3.9 Fiscal Deficit as a Share of GDP, 1989–2003
(% of GDP)

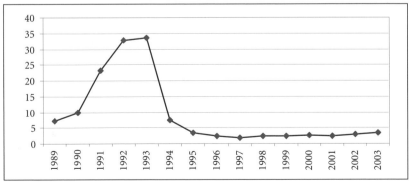

Source: Based on reports to the National Assembly by the Ministry of Finances and Prices, various years

The national budget has a very favorable situation. Inter-firm finances between state enterprises should be delved into further as these firms set their level of expenditures according to allocation in the state budget, but do not necessarily honor payments to other state enterprises. In other words, the settlements of payments among state enterprises currently experience high limits of insolvency. Part of the fiscal deficit reduction may indeed be quasi-fiscal debt in the banking sector (in particular, the loans provided to cooperatives which do not turn out to be profitable, or the accumulation of accounts receivable debt among public companies [CEPAL 1997]). Greater autonomy in management has permitted most of these state entities to finance themselves independently of state subsidies and therefore curb their burden on the national budget. Even so, the soundness of the fiscal adjustment and the permanence of achievements attained thus far will continue to depend on the scope and continuity of the structural and institutional reforms.

Structure and Evolution of Public Sector Budget Expenditures

In spite of the economic crisis already described, the national budget's tendency to increase current expenditures has been characteristic of the 1990s. A significant part of these expenditure increases were destined to sectors considered to have greater social impact. Figure 3.10 below shows these increases by sector as a share of the national budget.

Cuban economic policy has been characterized by a marked emphasis on social policy. Since 2001, an even greater emphasis has been placed on maintaining free and quality services in education and health, guaranteeing social security, protecting the elderly, the disabled and those most affected by current inequalities. In addition, the state has maintained spending aimed at alleviating a problem of increased sensitivity to the population—the growing deterioration of the housing stock, an inherited problem that worsened after 1960.

In response to a growth in population and a need to improve quality, state expenditures on education have increased over time. Numerous schools were constructed following the demographic explosion of the 1960s, but the amount of money spent on education fell beginning in 1990. This drop can be attributed to two causes. First, the baby boomers exited the educational circuit. Second, the crisis required reductions in material expenditures, as well as a decline in salaries for personnel who moved toward better-paid jobs outside of education. Increased num-

Figure 3.10 Select Public Expenditures of the National Budget, 1990–2004
(millions of pesos)

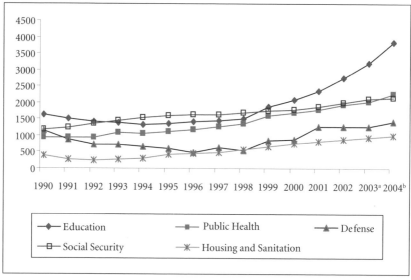

a. Expenditures in 2003 are estimates.
b. Expenditures in 2004 are projections.
Source: Based on reports to the National Assembly by the Ministry of Finances and Prices, various years

bers of students per professor and the deterioration of installations and modalities for teaching threatened the quality of education (García and Togores 2002). In response to these pressures, efforts were made to improve the quality of education. Wage increases were provided to teachers, a broad plan of investments in education was introduced and new prioritized educational programs were created. Together these efforts were designed to clearly improve educational indicators.

Defense spending has notably been reduced as a share of the national budget because of factors such as the reorganization of the armed forces, the increase in military enterprise self-financing, and the development of its own state enterprises. The restructuring of the armed forces included personnel reductions, changes in military tactics to respond to contemporary threat perceptions, as well as the adoption of "best business practices" (*perfecionamiento empresarial*) for military-run enterprises. Military-run enterprises were among the first to be re-structured; that process led also to the creation of large industrial groups focused on productive industrial, agricultural, service and retail-oriented activities. As a result, military-run enterprises are in better condition to face the challenge posed by the collapse of the Socialist Bloc. In addition, this portion of the budget also includes internal security expenditures for policing. Since police salaries were increased after 1998, this share began to slightly increase in subsequent years.

In the case of public health, the rate of expenditures has increased as a result of attempts to continue to improve the level of health, as well as to diminish the effects from losses in the quality of health care. In the 1990s integrated medical emergency services were created, and alternative sources of financing sought to help cover expenditures required for medical services. Thus, health tourism was introduced, as well as the marketing of medical equipment and biopharmaceutical products derived from R&D spending in the sector. The delivery of foreign technical services by physicians and nurses also helped finance the health system. Efforts have also been directed at rehabilitating deteriorated facilities such as polyclinics, hospitals and pharmacies. The combined efforts of this strategy have allowed Cuba to reach levels of health indicators comparable to those found in developed countries as an integral part of its development strategy. It is notable that in the midst of a severe economic crisis, the shortages and limitations did not lead to deterioration in the fundamental indicators that characterize the state of health of the population.

State Spending on Productive Activity

The share of the national budget attributable to transfers to state enterprise has been reduced significantly (Figure 3.11). By and large, subsidies to cover state enterprise losses have decreased as a result of effective policies focused on creating a sizable number of profitable Cuban state companies. An exception to this trend is that subsidies to state enterprises for price and product differences have not been reduced at targeted levels in some years due to increases in fuel and food prices in the international market. The state's subsidies to state enterprises that produce goods for the rationed market, including products such as milk, meat and eggs, have not been reduced as significantly in order to keep prices low both for consumers and for intermediary firms that purchase these products for the rationed market or for social services.

Evolution of Liquidity

Monetary liquidity has exhibited few signs of progression towards

Figure 3.11 Transfers to State Enterprises, 1990–2004
(millions of pesos)

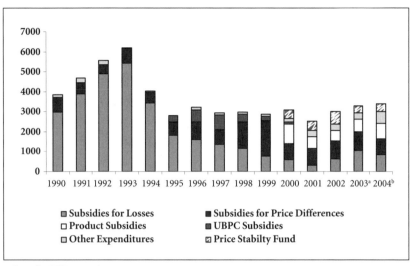

a. Data for 2003 are estimates.
b. Data for 2004 are projections.
Source: Ministry of Finances and Prices, various years

Figure 3.12 Cumulative Liquidity, 1980–2003
(millions of pesos)

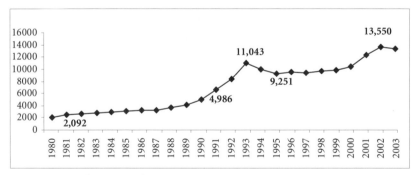

Source: Ministry of Finances and Prices, various years

decreasing, contrary to the expectations of government authorities
after 1995. Instead, a reversion of the trend has taken place, as liquidity has increased (Figure 3.12). For example, cumulative liquidity in
2002 amounted to more than 13,550 million pesos. This has conspired
against efforts to reduce prices, a measure exceedingly necessary for the
population.

Although the share of monetary liquidity in the hands of the population has declined, it increased in 2001 and 2002 (Figure 3.13).

Figure 3.13 Monetary Liquidity as a Share of GDP, 1993–2002
(percentage)

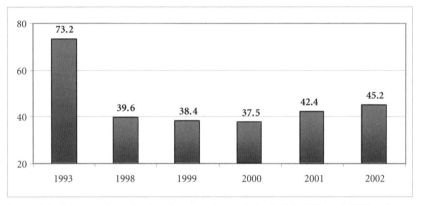

Source: Calculations by the author based on *Anuario estadístico de Cuba* (1996 and 2001) and reports to the National Assembly of the Ministry of Finances and Prices

Rather than the total quantity of money in circulation (both in cash and in ordinary savings), the fundamental problem with respect to excess liquidity is its concentration. This characteristic continues to negatively affect other movements, especially the relation between prices and income, and consequently between the standard of living and equity. It is important to recognize that the weight of foreign currency circulation in the domestic economy creates a quite complex process of internal financial balances. Added to this phenomenon, the number of bank accounts in foreign exchange has increased continually.

Limitations in the volume and the structure of available supply have impeded the reduction in monetary liquidity anticipated by government authorities. This situation demonstrates that the initial measures for internal financial balancing, in other words the marginal benefit of these measures, have been exhausted. As a result, there is a search for new mechanisms of monetary absorption. For example, goods and services should be directed to the rural sector in a way that encourages it to increase food production. Additional measures should also be directed at those who have high levels of pesos in banking accounts by providing them with goods at a greater value added. At the same time, it should not be forgotten that the monetary surplus can be absorbed through increased consumption, rather than higher levels of savings.

It should be reiterated that the circulation of foreign exchange in the domestic economy presents challenges for achieving internal financial balance. However, the creation of a consumption sector operating in foreign exchange has been one effective instrument in transforming the domestic economy, stemming from the 1993 de-penalization of the use of foreign exchange in Cuba. This domestic market in foreign exchange has become one of the most important engines driving the dynamism of the national consumer goods industry, which currently supplies between 50 percent and 60 percent of domestic consumption.

Agriculture and Natural Resources

The existence of three types of property (state, cooperative and private, which includes farm owners and tenants), four forms of ownership (state, cooperative, farmers and tenants), and properties held in usufruct (UBPC, *Unidades Básicas de Producción Cooperativa*[4]), farmers and tenants) introduces further complexity into Cuban agriculture. Analysts must differentiate mechanisms, methodologies and economic instruments, paying attention to the particular features of each property sector. In addition, 43 percent of Cuba's total territory is not used for cultivation (Figure 3.14). It is important to emphasize that the agrarian structure for traditional crops, especially those for export, has not been modified. These include sugar cane, citrus fruits and other crops.

Figure 3.14 Agricultural Structure and Its Utilization, 1999
(percentage)

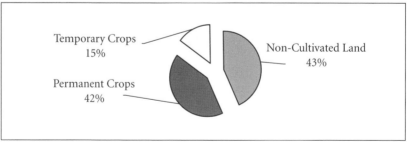

Temporary Crops
15%

Non-Cultivated Land
43%

Permanent Crops
42%

Source: Ministry of Agriculture (1999)

State production levels are recovering, but the non-state sector is exhibiting the greatest proportion of the generalized upswing in Cuban agriculture. In recent years, those crops with the highest yields have been vegetables[5], tobacco, beans and certain fruit trees. It is necessary to consider that these crops have maintained very low productive levels historically, which makes their growth notable (Figure 3.15).

Figure 3.15 Crop Output, 2001–2002
(millions of quintals)

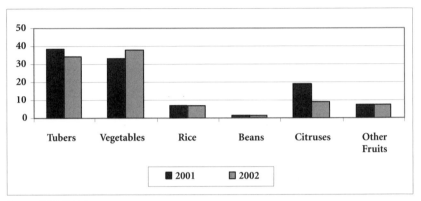

Source: ONE (2003)

The results of increased crop production, particularly in the non-state sector, reflect in the buoyancy of the sales of the agricultural market (Figure 3.16).

Figure 3.16 Sales in Agricultural Markets, 1995–2003
(millions of pesos)

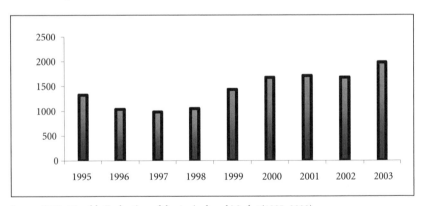

Source: ONE, Monthly Evaluation of the Agricultural Market(1995–2003)

The drastic reduction in availabile resources to cover the basic necessities of the sugar industry, the lack of producer incentives, particularly in agriculture, and the lack of priority given to the sector in the nineties had unfavorable repercussions for sugar crop production, yields and processing. These patterns led to significantly fewer exports and, consequently, fewer earnings and fewer credits that could be financed through sugar exports for the national economy (Figure 3.17 below).

While Cuba averaged 7.7 million tons in the 1980s, the average volume of sugar harvested between 1991 and 1998 was 4.3 million tons (Rosales del Toro 1999). As a result, the Ministry of Sugar initiated the restructuring of agriculture and the adoption of "best business practices" (*perfecionamiento empresarial*). In agriculture, UBPC's were created. Efforts were directed at the restoration of stocks in relation to the varieties and soil and climatic conditions of each region in early 1998. Sugar cane harvesting has been halted in order to increase the average age of plantations. Governmental authorities have set new targets for more intensive sugar harvests among their priorities.

Figure 3.17 Production of Physical Raw Sugar, 1985–2003
(thousands of tons)

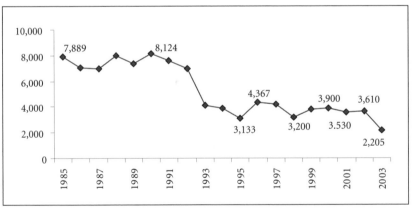

Source: Calculations by the author based on *Anuario estadístico de Cuba* (1996, 2000 and 2002) and Report to the National Assembly of the Ministry of Finances and Prices (2002), as well as experts' estimates

After 1995, external financing to increase sugar cane production was linked to pre-financing of sugar output per province or territory. The fresh flow of resources permitted the purchase of fertilizers, pesticides, repair parts, as well as other basic inputs, particularly for agricultural production. In the 1996–1997 harvest, Cuba reaped US$ 330 million in revenues. However, these external credits eventually stopped because Cuba has yet to solve the basic problems in sugar cane harvesting, prepare more efficiently for climate change, provide incentives for producers, or better organize the use of such external financing.

Other factors that contributed to the lack of improvements in sugar cane production included insufficient food for producers and their families from the rationed or subsidized food system as well as problems related to unmet housing needs. Technical factors also contributed to the decline in harvesting. First, there was a reduction in the cultivable lands dedicated to sugar cane harvesting. Second, given the poor quality of soils (requiring significant investments to improve soils prior to planting), there were significant difficulties associated with the planting of cane. And finally, the seeds utilized were inappropriate. Under these constraints, producers in UBPCs could not become autonomous from the state. Moreover, oftentimes the goals set for the UBPCs were unreachable and beyond the resources available to them, which depended on costly and resource-draining inputs and functioning with inadequate agricultural machinery and other inputs.

The aforementioned situation led authorities to decide to close down half of the sugar mills on the island, and convert some 14 mills into honey producers in 2002. Sugar and its derivatives will most likely continue as one of the country's economic pillars, both because of their potential contribution to the country's balance of payments and their multiplier effect on the domestic economy. Consequently, restructuring and new organizational measures are expected to bear fruit in the coming years.

The mere shutdown of the sugar mills along with decommissioning the agricultural, automotive, and railroad machinery devoted to this sector does not, however, solve the fundamental problems in agro- industry, even if it reduces fixed costs and subsequently overall production costs. The sector remains financially insolvent under the current financing scheme to which it is subject. Agro-industry has lost half its productive capacity. It is physically run down. Clearly fresh financing is required to ensure the sector's reactivation, seeking to return to acceptable levels of sugar cane production that would be consistent with the industrial capacity necessary to produce sugar and its derivatives. Secondly, reforms should focus on a much-needed agricultural transformation (production of various crops and forestry and animal products) in search of diversification, modernization and industrial flexibility. Without the required financing, agroindustry is unlikely to attain the goals foreseen in the restructuring process. Another risk is that the share of idle land would increase. The reality is that the process of restructuring requires capital to cover current expenditures and necessary investments. As part of this revised strategy, the participation of foreign capital could represent an important source of financing, which could contribute to the successful realization of the reforms already begun and targeted at restructuring agriculture (Nova González 2004).

The restructuring process must also confront the complex situation of finding jobs for the 100,000 sugar cane workers laid off in 2002, who have since undergone retraining. There is no doubt that the Agro-industry undoubtedly requires restructuring but this process must not just close a number of inefficient enterprises but also concentrate production and capacity to foster modernization, flexibilization and diversification of the agricultural and industrial sectors. That would allow Cuba to become competitive in international markets according to various scenarios.

One sector particularly affected by the economic crisis is the livestock sector. It has, as a result radically changed its operation, shifting away from dependence on imported food and reducing the proportion of feed derived from sugar harvests. Notably, UBPCs specializing in livestock have had significant performance results. Clearly, changes in land use have led to the need for replacing the present centralist and bureaucratic management methods and systems with new economic-financial instruments. In this particular sector, the state should limit itself to policy design, the creation and establishment of adequate instruments for their operation, guarantees of scientific and technical services and environmental protection. Decisions about management and production of livestock should be surrendered to microeconomic agents. (See the section on food consumption in the chapter by Togores and García.)

Based on an evaluation of agrarian transformations and agriculture's role of in economic restructuring, we conclude that thus far changes have been limited to the development of cooperatives and the delivery of parcels under usufruct to families for personal consumption and for specialized production of tobacco and coffee. These results can be evaluated as positive, despite their being generally slow advances due to the duality of the simultaneous operation of two models. The traditional model—supported by antiquated methods and already obsolete administrative practices—exists alongside a second one based on decentralized models of self-financing with new economic actors.

Although related issues with respect to natural resources and indus-

trial development during these years will be discussed in Pérez Villanueva's chapter on foreign direct investment, the substantial success of
the Ministry of Basic Industries in increasing oil, natural gas, and nickel
production should be noted here (Table 3.1 and Figure 3.18). Technology, modern managerial methods and new organizational measures
were obtained from foreign firms partnering in the development of
these sectors in both oil and nickel production.

Table 3.1 Oil and Gas Output, 1989–2003

	1989	1999	2000	2001	2002	2003
Petroleum (thousands metric tons)	500.0	2136.5	2695.3	2773.4	3553.4	3691.0
Natural Gas (millions cubic meters)	0	460.0	574.5	594.6	584.7	653.0

Source: ONE, *Anuario estadístico de Cuba (2002)*

Figure 3.18 Nickel Output, 1993–2003
(thousand metric tons)

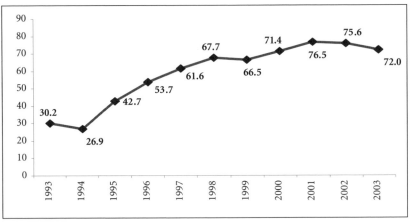

Source: Calculations by the author based on *Anuario estadístico de Cuba* (1996 and 2002) and
Report to the National Assembly of the Ministry of Finances and Prices (2002)

Services

The Cuban economy has been a process of transition toward a service
economy, given the contribution of services as a share of GDP—particularly in the areas of tourism and communications—both of which
have started to exhibit increased contributions to GDP.

Tourism

Tourism has introduced new operational modalities in the 1990s, driven by various forms of joint ventures with foreign investors. The Gran Caribe, Horizontes and Isla Azul chains, as well as the CUBANACAN and Gaviota corporations (hotel groups, restaurants and other specialized services), have been formed with foreign investment. The Cuban tourist sector is buoyant. The average number of visitors grew at annual rates of 14 percent between 1990 and 2003 (Figure 3.19). Gross revenue is more than 30 percent annually; the construction of hotel rooms at a rate of 13 percent annually made this sector very appealing for foreign investment.

Figure 3.19 Gross Revenue from Tourism and Number of Visitors, 1990–2003

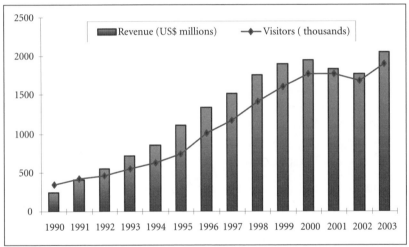

Source: Source: Calculations by the author based on *Anuario estadístico de Cuba* (1996, 2000 and 2002) and Annual Report to the National Assembly (2003), as well as statistics from the Ministry of Tourism

Policies to attract foreign investment in the sector have sought to open new markets by attracting tourists and acquiring new technologies, management expertise and fresh capital flows. Joint enterprises, comprised of Cuban state-owned firms in partnership with prestigious foreign entities, have been constituted, mostly in the hotel sector, based on a 50–50 split between Cuban and foreign capital. These same partners in Havana and Varadero Beach, both regions of greater maturity and international demand, have directed priority for initial investments to new tourist regions. The terms of agreements have been set at 25 years and extendable to 50 years, should both parties decide this is advisable.

Domestic investment has been decisive in the development of the sector. Of the available hotel rooms, 89 percent were state-owned and the remaining 11 percent were under joint venture management with 50 percent state participation. In 1990, Cuba received 327,000 tourists with 12,900 available rooms for international tourism, most of which required rehabilitation (ONE 1998). Management expertise in tourist centers was limited due to the previous lack of priority given to the sector, which led to the promotion of a long-term development program. A key element in that program was the transfer of managerial capacities through hotel management contracts and the creation of semipublic enterprises in hotels and non-hotel facilities.

By 2001:

- Twenty-four semipublic enterprises with 1.089 billion dollars in capital were established.
- These included twenty hotel firms with 15,600 rooms, of which 3,889 were in operation, and the rest either in the project or construction phase.
- Fifteen foreign offices from six countries with 50 hotels with 17,865 rooms under foreign administration had been established.
- Eighty-nine percent of the hotels under operation were in the 4 and 5 star categories.

Tourism as such has been heavily reliant on imports and hence Cuba has been increasing the production of some goods, many of them financed by foreign capital. In addition, plans and studies were being undertaken to strengthen extra-hotel infrastructure. Because Cuba is already part of the Caribbean tourist circuit and in order to become a more attractive site, its investment program should be accelerated in the coming years to increase the interest of international hotel proprietor chains. This infrastructure should be directed to the construction of theme parks, golf courses and docks for cruise ships.

Cuba is changing its productive structure in order to address this strategy; the results show that the domestic economy has been increasing its share of the supplies to the sector. In 2003, national industry contributed 69 percent of the inputs required by tourist installations. As a way of increasing tourist arrivals and guaranteeing stable flows, the administration of a group of hotels was contracted to specialized international companies, who in turn developed promotional campaigns to advertise globally through their contacts and indispensable marketing partnerships. Throughout this period these contracted firms, who contribute their brands and quality standards, have been a source for management and worker training and, at times, they too have financed the modernization of facilities.

Through the renting of rooms in private homes and the opening of small, family-run restaurants (*paladares*), tourism has also permitted the recuperation of the private sector, especially in areas that are already better developed for tourism. Tourism has also fueled the growth of the informal sector, which supplies these businesses with inputs, including among others, the sale of Cuban handicrafts. In short, tourism is being converted into the locomotive of Cuba. This means that FDI for tourism's branches should be completed in order to ensure the comprehensive development of the sector, with the vision that the rest of the Caribbean is a complement and not a source for competition.

Telecommunications

The development of Cuban telecommunications has advanced as a result of the more than 714 million dollars invested since 1995. The largest of Cuba's joint ventures, the telecommunications company ETECSA, was created as a result of an agreement between the Cuban government and foreign investors, primarily Italy's STET, leading to investments to modernize all aspects of telecommunications infrastructure. This has resulted in the exponential increase in telephone density per 100 inhabitants. Figures 3.20 and 3.21 illustrate the steady increase in installed telephone lines and digital plants.

Figure 3.20 Development of Fixed Telephony, 1990–2002
(thousands of installed telephones)

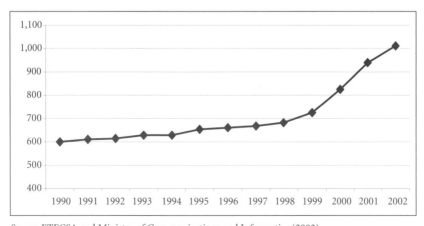

Source: ETECSA and Ministry of Communications and Informatics (2002)

Figure 3.21 Digitalization of Telephone Systems, 1995–2003
(% of Digitalized telephone plants)

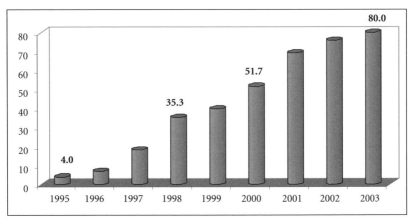

Source: ETECSA statistics and Ministry of Communications and Informatics (2002)

External Sector

Foreign Trade

Resulting from the economy's gradual adaptation to a new international environment, Cuba's foreign trade has experienced very complex and significant transformations relative to where it stood in 1990. Progress has been achieved in institutional, organizational and functional aspects. On the other hand, transformations of a structural nature have experienced very little progress, especially those related to the adverse balance of payments situation of the country's finances, the enhancement of export competitiveness and the modification of existing restrictions on the export portfolio of the island (Marquetti 1997).

Large trade deficits characterize Cuban foreign trade performance in recent decades, though starting in 1991 the real effects were different. Since then, the trade deficit has been driven by the lack of credits to finance trade, the lack of export expansion, whose underlying causes were the reduction of traditional exports and the fall of their prices, and the high level of imports.

Commercial trade declined successively between 1990 and 1993, due to the fall of both exports and imports (Figure 3.22). In 1994 total trade showed a minor increase—3.3 percent—compared to 1993. A 15.8 percent growth in exports, caused by higher international prices for the country's main exports, accounted for this slight improvement. Additionally, imports decreased by 6.3 percent with imported volumes

Figure 3.22 Exports and Imports, 1989–2003
(US$ million)

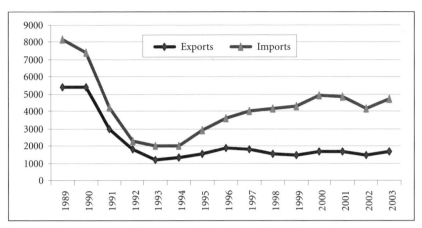

Source: ONE, various years and Report to the National Assembly (2002)

slightly greater than two billion dollars in the same year. In 1995, trade increased by an average of 30.1 percent, of which exports increased by 12.1 percent and imports by 42.9 percent. In the case of exports, these increases were due to the growth in nickel sales and the relative improvement in trade for traditional products, such as seafood, tobacco and some light manufacturing. Cement and other construction materials, as well as steel, exports, also increased. Nevertheless, declining sugar production and to a lesser extent a drop in pharmaceutical sales in foreign markets starting in 1995 prevented export performance from reaching expected levels. With respect to export earnings, a gap between the actual and potential revenue exists relative to levels achieved during the late 1980s, when exports ranged between 1.9 and 3.0 billion dollars (Álvarez 1994).

Two periods can be distinguished in terms of the evolution of commercial trade. The first, from 1990 to 1993, was characterized by the substantial reduction in the trade deficit. The second period, beginning in 1994, witnessed a decline in both the value and quantity of trade. The effects of the process of geographical reorientation of Cuban foreign trade with the end of the Soviet bloc and the rapid readjustment that external relations of the island suffered in those years accentuated these trends. The economy was slow to recuperate from this transition; sugar and other export prices declined; imported goods such as fuel and food became more expensive; the country's foreign reserves dropped to minimum levels. The trade deficit constitutes one of the problems to which policy makers must pay attention, since excessive growth of the deficit will place increased pressure on the current account balance. Figure 3.23 illustrates the evolution of trade in the last five years by hemisphere. Whereas Europe in entirety has become Cuba's principal commercial partner, the share for the American hemisphere has begun to increase.

Figure 3.23 Cuba's Cumulative Trade (Imports and Exports) by Hemisphere, 1998–2002 (US$ millions)

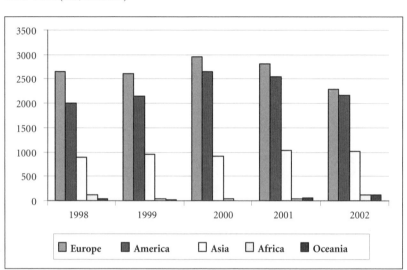

Source: Anuario estadístico de Cuba, 2002. Report of the Central Bank of Cuba (2001) and Report of the National Assembly (2002)

Distribution of Exports

Changes in international conditions did not result in a substantial variation of the commercial composition of Cuban exports. Minimum modifications occurring during this period correspond directly with the reduction of the sugar industry's contribution to the generation of income, whose productive irregularities led to losses greater than the two billion dollars between 1992 and 1996 (Figure 3.24). Initially, sugar exports suffered due to the fall in prices in the 1990s. Nevertheless, afterwards, the sugar industry continued to experience subsequent decreases in production. Moreover, the reductions in sugar production not only reduced export earnings, but also represented the loss of a source of financing, which the country received according to the share of these exports in the form of credit guarantees. No other branch of the economy has managed to compensate for the collateral function played by the sugar industry.

Figure 3.24 Distribution of Exports by Product Groups, 1989–2002
(% of total exports)

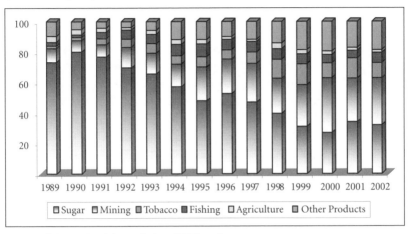

Source: Oficina Nacional de Estadísticas (ONE), various years

After the production and export of nickel experienced consecutive falls between 1990 and 1994, an impressive reversal occurred in both indicators starting in 1995. Due to substantial production increases and favorable international prices, the nickel industry has surpassed production levels prior to the crisis. These results have been further influenced by organizational and productive transformations introduced after 1991. In particular, the agreements reached with Canada's Sherrit Inc. in 1994 resulted in the creation of a joint venture company that facilitated the island's access to the international cobalt market.

Tobacco exports were affected severely between 1990 and 1993 by different factors, including the reduction in the amount of cultivated land historically designated to tobacco cultivation, difficulties of an organizational nature with respect to commercial management, and the inability to use certain name brands that had been utilized to market the Cuban *habano* in Western Europe during several decades due to unresolved trademark disputes on these brands. The Cuban company Cubatabaco signed important agreements in 1993 with the state companies of SEITA in France and Tabacalera S.A. in Spain. These agreements included guarantees for the supply of fertilizers and other inputs for tobacco production, the re-utilization of given name brands for the sale of the *habano*, as well as the corresponding marketing and payment terms expected in return.

At the same time, other decisions were adopted related to the organization of production, enhancement of international marketing for the *habano* and stimulus of workers in that sector. Starting in 1996, Figure 3.25 shows that these approved agreements served as the foundation for the gradual productive recovery of tobacco exports. By 1998, because of the reactivation of this sector, production levels and export earnings surpassed 1989 levels. Currently, the *Habanos* company is part of the ALTADIS Corporation, which is capable of distributing twice the amount of the company's current available production through its worldwide distribution network.

During the 1990s, the performance of fishing exports was affected by climatic problems, delays in planned investments, reduction of gross

Figure 3.25 Production and Sales of Tobacco, 1990–2002
(millions)

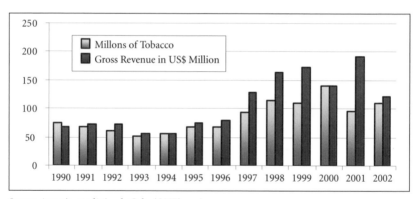

Source: Anuario estadístico de Cuba (ONE), various years

catch rates, as well as fuel shortages and technological problems of boats destined for lobster fishing. As a result, export earnings fell from 153 million dollars in 1989 to 84 million in 1993. In 1994, the government applied a set of organizational and stimulus measures that facilitated a modest increase in exports in this sector. However, the trend consolidated in 1995 when shellfish and other maritime exports exceeded the previous year's exports by 25.5 percent. Fisheries achieved a similar performance in 1996.

An analysis of export patterns between 1990 and 2002 shows that traditional sectors—sugar industry, mining, crops and light manufacturing—were driving Cuba's specialization and international integration processes. In the short and medium term, it is unlikely that nontraditional export[6] categories will produce earnings that surpass traditional export earnings. Furthermore, it should be noted that traditional export sectors still have unfulfilled potential: the value chain must be altered to favor those products with greater value-added contribution. The need for varying the value chain of traditional exports also arises because this group of products is characterized by erratic price patterns, whose performance in the last five years has been characterized by a marked downward trend and whose negative effects on the island's economy have been significant.

Cuba's economic performance shows that the sizeable reduction in foreign trade experienced in recent years will be difficult to recover in the short and medium term. Nevertheless, the utilization of the maximum potential of the traditional exporting sector, combined with other existing reserves in other economic branches, can be decisive in the revival of the Cuban economy and its long-run self-sustainability.

Structure of Imports

Overall, imports declined after 1989, although these reductions were concentrated in the quantity of imported fuel, raw materials and capital assets. With respect to the latter, purchases virtually disappeared between 1992 and 1994. Figure 3.26 shows that by 2002, purchases had still not increased to adequate levels, though imports of capital goods

Figure 3.26 Structure of Cuban Imports, 1989-2002
(millions of Cuban pesos)

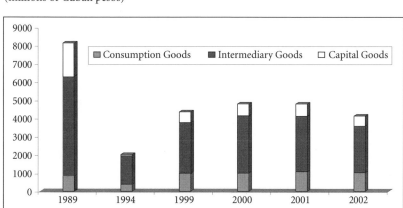

Source: Oficina National de Estadísticas (ONE) 1989, p. 261 and 2002, p. 141

increased. Factors of a structural nature combined with political economy priorities have caused food, medicines and fuels to together make up more than 60 percent of total imports. In the short term, it will not be possible to alter this distribution. Furthermore, the acquisition of these goods has required the utilization of approximately 80 percent of the country's foreign exchange income, a situation that will be untenable in any economic forecast for the coming years.

Lowering the high share of total intermediate good imports can only be achieved through the implementation of previously mentioned policy reforms in coordination with a greater degree of economic integration and effective modification of the productive and technological model. In general, the situation faced with respect to the level and composition of imports requires a higher level of integration between industry and agriculture. These changes will gradually introduce variations in energy consumption patterns and allow greater control and efficiency in the utilization of these resources, as well as maximizing economic potential. Cuba historically has had a structural dependency on the growth of the economy reliant on its importing sector. In view of the fact that more than half of Cuban imports were for food and fuel needs, the variation of the current structure of imports will be highly complicated and must be sensitive to providing guarantees that the population's basic needs are met in light of the fact that these needs were already at minimum levels.

External Finance

The negative impact of trade deficits affects the balance of payments of the country. Currently, Cuba faces a very difficult balance of payments position, with its monetary reserves practically null; this position hinders the daily operation of various national entities. Since 1995, the deficit in the balance of goods and services has varied, increasing and decreasing at times. Yet, despite the increase in the exports of services such as tourism, air transport and international communications, three of the most dynamic sectors in the domestic economy in recent years (see Figure 3.27), this deficit has increased since 1999.

The current account deficit stands quite high and increases every year despite compensations to this deficit by net current transfers that have grown from 470.2 million dollars in 1994 to 812 million in 2001. This account includes remittances and donations, with the delivery of money from Cubans living abroad to family members on the island corresponding to the largest share of these flows. As Carranza (1998) notes, to stake for a greater expansion and impact of this factor (remittances) requires further reflection, since in order to surpass current levels it would be necessary to delve further into economic reform and to make it possible that these capitals could be used for a family's small and medium investments, in addition to seeking new ways in order to increase the capture and mobilization of these savings. However, a decision of this nature cannot be made only with a view to promoting net current transfers, since policy reforms would be touching on a very sensitive part of the economic model. A decision—positive or negative—on this issue should be part of a comprehensive consideration concerning the economic changes and the restructuring character which should be promoted.

The other capital account that includes assets and short-term liabilities (in addition to errors and omissions) shifted from a negative balance of 555 million pesos in 1994 to a positive sum of 227 million in 2001. These movements were explained by adjustments in errors and omissions, and the varied impact that short-term credits have had, according to their amount and moment of payment, on the recovery of GDP.

Figure 3.27 Contribution of Specific Exports to Earnings, 2001
(percentage)

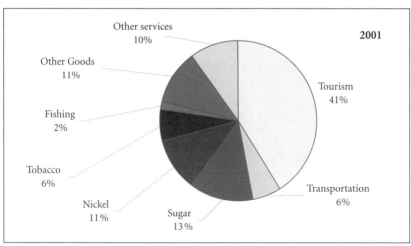

Source: Anuario estadístico de Cuba (ONE), various years.

Foreign Debt

By the end of 2001, Cuba's foreign debt stood at 10.8 billion dollars (Figure 3.28). The decrease in its value since 1998 was mainly the result of the depreciation of the principal currencies in which the foreign debt is denominated. External finances constitute a topic of utmost importance and also a source of pressure. However, these pressures do not represent a new burden; rather, these patterns revert to the beginning of the 1980s when international economic trends and the pressures of the blockade resulted in a drastic reduction of credits in freely convertible currency.

Figure 3.28 Total External Debt of Cuba, 1993–2001
(US$ millions)

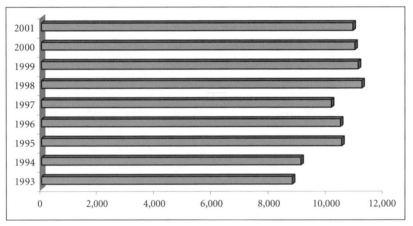

Source: Report of the Central Bank of Cuba, various years

In 1982 the Cuban Government asked its creditors to renegotiate its external debt, which stood at US$2.91 billion dollars. As a result of this negotiation, a reasonable agreement was reached. However, it did not free the country from financial strains. On the contrary, the situation continued to worsen as a result of negative trends in the world sugar market. In 1984 and 1985 new payment schedules were reached. But, in 1986, additional factors worsened Cuba's economic situation, thus diminishing the possibilities of meeting debt service requirements according to the negotiated conditions. As a result, the Cuban government requested a new debt renegotiation with its creditors. Although the governments of creditor countries signed the new agreement, commercial banks refused to grant the new financing that had been accorded under the latest accord. Under these conditions, Cuba found it impossible to continue to make the corresponding payments on each step and these have remained suspended since the second semester of 1986.

As a result, the Cuban economy has virtually lost its access to medium and long-term international credits in freely convertible currency. The movement of the value of the dollar in international markets is a factor that acts indistinctly on the level of Cuba's external debt, as the majority of this debt has been contracted in other foreign currencies as a corollary of the economic blockade. When the U.S. dollar depreciates or the value of other observed currencies appreciates, the debt of the country rises, as occurred in 1998. Japan, Argentina, Spain, France and the United Kingdom hold 66.1 percent of the total amount of the debt. Cuba's debt with the ex-socialist countries of Europe (the most important of which is with the former Soviet Union) is not included (Figure 3.28). This debt has followed a very complicated course of negotiations, largely the result of the fact that the actors, institutions, currency and an important part of the countries with which that debt was contracted no longer exist, as well as the fact that the conditions under which these economic agreements were signed have been radically modified. This is because much of the foreign debt with socialist countries contracted by Cuba occurred as part of agreements within the now defunct Council for Mutual Economic Assistance (COMECON). That debt was denominated in convertible rubles, a currency which disappeared without an agreed upon exchange rate with the U.S. dollar. Moreover, much of the debt was incurred for projects that were never concluded, thus rendering the debt unproductive. Examples include the Juraguá thermonuclear plant as well as nickel factories and petroleum refineries.

The debt to GDP ratio (in current prices) has recovered in recent years, but remains very high (Table 3.2).

Table 3.2 Debt as a Share of GDP, 1990–2001
(percentage)

1990	1991	1992	1993	1994	1995	1996	1997	1998	1999	2000	2001
34.0	—	52.1	58.2	47.3	48.5	46.5	44.2	48.2	43.9	39.66	37.4

Source: Carranza Valdés, Julio (1998) calculations based on ONE, *Anuario estadístico de Cuba* 1997, 1998 and 2001 and Report of the Central Bank of Cuba (2001)

Similarly, the share of debt relative to the value of exports of goods, the most adequate indicator to measure the debt's impact of the debt on Cuban resources of the country, denotes these strains (Table 3.3). Although neither the magnitude of debt payments per year, nor its ratio as a share of the value of exports of goods and services, has been reported officially since 1997, it can be inferred that service on the debt has been reduced.

Table 3.3 Debt as a Share of Exports, 1989–2001
(percentage)

1989	1993	1994	1995	1996	1997	1998	1999	2000	2001
114.6	759.5	678.4	704.2	565.9	556.5	776.0	764.9	648.4	655.6

Source: Calculations based on ONE, *Anuario estadístico de Cuba*, 1990–1996 and Reports of the Central Bank of Cuba, various years

Cuba's current external finance panorama has moved positively with concrete progress on external debt negotiations with the agreements reached with Japan, Italy, France and Spain. The agreement with Japan was an unusual one, uncharacteristic of standard commercial debts. The agreement between Cuba and Japan resulted from pressures due to the exceedingly high debt, more than 770 million dollars, which affected 182 Japanese firms (some of whose financing prospects depended on the solution of this problem), as well as Japan's economic recession and the advantages of the economic opening with Cuba for small firms, as was the case of the majority previously indicated (Marquetti 1998). In addition, renegotiation agreements have been reached with the United Kingdom and Belgium's Official Agencies of Credit Insurance for Exporting.

The analysis of external finances is fundamental to the study of the current situation of the Cuban economy and its prospects. Its review leads to comprehensive considerations of the process of economic change underway and the advances Cuba has made towards resisting hostile external forces. Though the Cuban government has made significant advances, efforts aimed at improving Cuba's external balances should be strengthened. Expanding the limited trade involved in Cuba's food purchases from the United States since 2001 could decrease the high costs of transportation incurred when importing food from more distant markets and, if there were to be reciprocity, U.S. purchases of

Cuban goods would provide resources for reinvestment in further purchases from the United States, thus benefiting both countries.

Final Considerations

The indicators utilized, as well as several considerations set forth in this analysis, show us that the Cuban economy is still in a stage of resuscitation in which certain constraints—primarily the economic blockade, the misshapen economic structure, the depreciation of capital assets and the levels of internal efficiency—remain significant problems. The growth of the economy starting in 1994 has still not been able to recover the loss in gross national production suffered during the years of acute contraction (1990–1993). The overall utilization of installed industrial capacity was estimated in 2001 to be at lower levels than those of 1989. Investment, the evidence suggests, is depleted and has not played a significant role in the economy's recuperation—a worrisome trend given that this factor makes growth most sustainable and likely to persist in the long run. To grow is strategic, since only that which is produced can be distributed. In view of the exhaustion of the measures previously adopted to increase production, new mechanisms are necessary. As Triana (2003) explains, the sources of growth fueled by tourism, FDI and foreign exchange markets are not depleted, but they have become fatigued and require new conditions to ignite their operation.

The Cuban economy continues to be characterized by low levels of integration among its principal sectors. Adding to these trends, the country is dependent on technologies requiring high energy consumption and a high degree of imports of intermediate goods, both of which are necessary for the operation of installed capacities. However, there is a paradox that is key with respect to the economy's performance—that without having surpassed the phase of the economic crisis in its entirety, the conditions to maintain a dynamic of irreversible growth in some branches have been created. These were found in the productive chains that have surged around tourism and the increased importance of the segment of the national market that operates in foreign exchange.

The socioeconomic reforms implemented have had an effect of resuscitation and growth of the economy, but have also had a negative impact on social equity. The Cuban government still has not managed to achieve an optimal solution in terms of income for the majority of Cuban families. Of greater concern, segments of the population are still not able to cover their expenditures with the amount of formal income they receive, which in turn forces them to resort to alternative strategies or to deny themselves access to a certain set of goods and/or services. The set of applied economic policy measures requires an adaptation of social policy, based on the formation of an optimal balance between distribution mechanisms through rations and markets.

The so-called "best business practices" (*perfecionamiento empresarial*) have demonstrated that spaces still exist to increase labor efficiency and productivity, although macroeconomic restrictions hindering these objectives may endure. These restrictions must be reduced. Progress has been made with regard to prices, financial restructuring and in reduction of the exchange rate for the dollar, but consumption and income continue to be strapped, presenting serious challenges for the government. A rethinking of policy and strategy for agriculture is necessary. That strategy should be consistent with existing development conditions and present new forms that promote labor potential. Any strategy should be focused on gradually eliminating the sector's high dependency, promoting sources of cooperative production, establishing necessary autonomy, elevating the share of territory in decision-making processes and readjusting pricing policy for producers. The process of economic reforms must be examined further, seeking solutions to compensation for workers in those sectors in which wages have not increased, thus elevating productivity to accelerate the modest advances in the processes of restructuring and industrial transformation, which includes "best business practices" (*perfecionamiento empresarial*).

Employment is an important component of the social development model. Despite its transformation by factors related to the economic crisis and structural changes in the Cuban economy's regulation and operation, specific areas must be targeted. For example, in recent years the granting of licenses to self-employed persons, especially in certain trades, has been paralyzed, with the doubly negative consequence of reducing the supply and quality of a group of provided services. Even worse, this framework has created sectors with quasi-monopolistic control, therefore facilitating the concentration of wealth in the hands of a few. An alternative to self-employment can be the promotion of a cooperative sector in services and in sectors complementary to the state-run industrial sector, which will contribute to improving overall efficiency, increase demand and employment, increase workers' incomes and serve as a source of competition to the individual private sector (Triana 2003).

Nevertheless, at the beginning of the new millennium, Cuba is in a better situation than in 1993, the year of the most critical point of the crisis. The purchasing power of a segment of the population has definitely improved. The progress of social indicators has been maintained and confirms the state's prioritized concern about the improvement of the living standards of the population.

Cuba is thoroughly analyzing roads of growth and economic development. In order to make congruent those efforts of growth with those advances in knowledge and education created and being strengthened by the government, the pathway of long-term sustained growth should be associated with strengthening what we call the" knowledge sector." Accordingly, the future strategic design should be directed to the search for growth alternatives that are sustained and grow through the balancing of political, social and economic factors. Beyond the objective factors that explain the complexity of the economic crisis, a debate concerning the alternatives that can reduce its impact is indispensable, although any proposal or opinion is, of course, polemical. However, it is necessary to journey through this debate logically, within the frameworks of the socioeconomic system that has been implemented in the last 40 years.

References

Álvarez C. Elena. 1994 "El ajuste importador en la economía cubana: apuntes para una evaluación." *Boletín de Información de Economía Cubana*, No.14. Havana: CIEM

Anuario Estadístico de Cuba, various years. ONE: Havana.

Report of the Central Bank of Cuba, 1997, 1999, 2000, 2001. Central Bank of Cuba: Havana.

Carranza, Julio. 1998. Las finanzas externas y los límites del crecimiento (Cuba 1996–1997). Havana: CEEC.

Centro de Estudios de Economía Cubana. Universidad de la Habana. 1997. Proceedings from the Workshop "La economía cubana en 1996: Resultados, Problemas y Perspectivas." Havana: CEEC.

CEPAL. 1997. "La economía cubana. Reformas estructurales y desempeño en los noventa." México: Fondo de Cultura Económica.

Fernández, María Antonia. "Las zonas francas y la economía nacional. Cuba en este proceso." *Boletín informativo de la economía cubana*, Número 31. Havana: CIEM.

Ferriol, Ángela. 1997. "Política social cubana: Situación y transformaciones. *Revista Temas:* Número 11.

García, Anicia. 1998. "El mercado agropecuario." *Cuba: Investigación económica.* INIE: Havana.

García Álvarez, Anicia and Viviana Togores González. 2002. "El acceso al consumo en Cuba y su repercusión en la vida cotidiana." Havana: CEEC.

García, Mercedes. 1997. *El financiamiento externo actual.* CIEI: Havana.

García, Mercedes. 1996. "Los mercados financieros internacionales: Tendencias actuales y participación de los países en desarrollo." Havana: Centro de Investigaciones de la Economía Internacional.

González Alfredo. 1996. "Situación actual y perspectivas de la economía cubana." Conferencia Magistral Annual Event of Instituto Nacional de Investigaciones Económicas (INIE).

González Gutiérrez, Alfredo. 1998. "Economía y sociedad: retos del modelo económico." *Temas*, No.11. Havana.

González, Alfredo. 1993. "Economía emergente: Logros, dificultades y perspectivas." Havana: INIE.

Lage, Carlos.1997. Clausura de la II Reunión Nacional del Ministerio de Economía y Planificación. *Granma*. Havana.

Lage Carlos. 1995. Speech delivered at the Economic Forum in Davos, Switzerland. Granma. Enero 28, 1995. Havana.

Marquetti, Hiram. 1998. "Proceso de renegociación de la deuda." *Negocios en Cuba.* Havana: Prensa Latina.

Marquetti, Hiram. 1997. "Reordenamiento funcional e institucional del comercio exterior de Cuba: Evolución y perspectivas," Documento del Centro de Estudios de la Economía Cubana (CEEC). Havana.

Ministerio de Finanzas y Precios. 1998. "Resultados de las medidas de saneamiento financiero aprobadas por la Asamblea Nacional del Poder Popular." Havana.

Monreal, Pedro and Julio Carranza. 1997. "Problemas del desarrollo en Cuba: Realidades y conceptos *Revista Temas*, Número 11. Havana.

Nova González, Armando. "Redimensionamiento y diversificación de la agroindustria azucarera cubana." CD-Rom, Special Publication Commemorating the Center for the Study of the Cuban Economy's 15th Anniversary, May 2004. CEEC: Havana.

Oficina Nacional de Estadísticas (ONE). 2004. "Panorama económico y social, Cuba 2003." ONE: Havana.

Pérez Villanueva, Omar Everleny. 1996. "Las reformas económicas en Cuba en los 90's." Published by the Universidad de Santiago de Compostela, España at the Conference on "Galicia—América Latina."

Pérez Villanueva, Omar Everleny. 1998. "Cuba's Economic Reforms: An Overview" in *Special Studies No 30: Perspectives on Cuban Economic Reforms* (edited Jorge F. Pérez-López y Matías Travieso-Diaz). Center for Latin American Studies Press, Arizona State University.

Pérez Villanueva, Omar Everleny. 1998. "La inversión extranjera directa en los países subdesarrollados: El caso cubano." Doctoral thesis. University of Havana, Havana.

Rodríguez, Santiago. 1998. Las transformaciones en la agricultura cubana. Havana: CEEC.

Rosales del Toro, Ulises. 1999 "La agroindustria azucarera en Cuba: Transformaciones y perspectivas." 5th Roundtable with the Goverment of Cuba, February 22nd–24th. Havana: Hotel Meliá Cohiba.

Salas, Carola and García, Mercedes. 1997 "Las finanzas externas de Cuba. Situación actual y perspectivas." Havana: Centro de Investigaciones de la Economía Internacional.

Togores González, Viviana. 1999. "Efectos de la crisis y el ajuste económico de los 90's en el desarrollo social cubano." Havana: CEEC.

Triana Cordoví, Juan. 2002. "El desempeño económico en el 2002." Eighth Annual Seminar on the Cuban Economy at the CEEC. CD ROM. Havana: CEEC.

Author's Note:

This is a revised version of a chapter that originally appeared in Spanish in Mauricio de Miranda (ed), Cuba: *Reestructuración económica y globalización* in 2003.

Notes:

1 This is the standard word used in Cuba to characterize the set of U.S. policies toward Cuba.

2 This market was created in 1962 with the objective of permitting equitable access to essential consumer goods for all social strata.

3 Parallel markets were state-run with prices fixed above those in the rationed market, where goods could be purchased without limits on the quantity. Among the goods that could be purchased were food, clothing, hygiene and cleaning products.

4   UBPC (*Unidades Básicas de Producción Cooperativa*) or Basic Cooperative Production Units were created in 1993 as part of the economic reforms from old state farms. In these cooperative units, workers now derive a share from the profits of their farm.

5   Vegetable production based on organic farming has presented an important dynamic in recent years. Of the 791,900 tons of vegetables produced in 1998 in the country, 440,900 belonged to organic farms, which is more than 60 percent of total production.

6   Although, there has been a gradual increase in sales of laminated steel, cables, cement and in other construction products, these have not structurally altered the composition of Cuban exports.

PART

II

The International Economic Context

4

Globalization and the Dilemmas of Cuba's Economic Trajectories

by Pedro Monreal

Without a doubt, Cuba at the end of the 20th century is an exceptional country. The reasons are various and the nation's peculiarities have been widely reported. Among the multiple representations of contemporary Cuba an image stands out of a country that, in my judgment, represents a powerful metaphor concerning the dilemmas that the island faces in the context of the global economy: the vision of the island as an unusual enclave of old cars that function miraculously, rarely in impeccable condition. The image of an old Chevrolet with a tropical landscape in the background has converted itself into part of the tourist iconography of a country that has found a powerful means for its "modernization" through the "leisure industry." However, the abundance of very old cars can also evoke a different vision of the future. After all, their operation requires technical capability and productive ingenuity that make many countries envious, including some which are attributed a high expertise with regard to "reengineering" and who have managed to become prodigious manufacturing exporters. Accordingly, an old auto could also be, from this other perspective, part of the future, although a very different future from a tourist-related one.

What lesson could this metaphor suggest for Cuba? Should autos be confined to the backdrop for tourism or could they indicate technical aptitudes that reveal the starting point for an exporting reindustrialization of the country? In more precise terms, should one bet, in the context of a global economy, on a development strategy intensively utilizing natural resources with reindustrialization oriented basically toward domestic markets? Or, on the contrary, should one bet on an economy concentrated on export reindustrialization, based on the intensive utilization of a skilled workforce, with high potential for learning? Which option would be the most promising in terms of the country's development?

This is, in essence, the dilemma that this brief chapter attempts to explore, although not to exhaust. The problem certainly has not been overlooked by other analysts in the debate on the Cuban economy of the post-Soviet era. Though several subjects have been debated, the long-range possible trajectories of the Cuban economy have received growing attention on the part of policy makers and academicians from the island, in particular during the so-called "recovery phase" that, in the second half of the 1990s, followed the profound crisis of the first years of the decade.

The proliferation of academic texts, official declarations, and studies by government experts, with views on "restructuring," "industrial policy," "flexible specialization," "industrial upgrading," "sectoral positioning," "strategic areas of specialization," and "export diversification," constitutes a clear example of the interest in the subject.[1] However, the issue of the alternatives to the different development trajectories still has not received the attention it deserves.[2] The predominant treatment has been focused, fundamentally, on a sectoral approach, almost always associated with an "adaptive" view of the development model. The texts published in Cuba that have addressed these problems in greater detail have done it especially from a sectoral viewpoint; that is, as alternatives within the industry sector, or as the exploration of alternatives to the "exporting sector."[3] In general, the alternatives focus on the possible development trajectories as a part of the Cuban economy's adaptation to the international one, but assume as a premise that any current "correction" in the path of development should be subordinated to a more general model of development whose essential determinations are anchored in past conceptions. In other words, the adaptation would be unavoidable and convenient, but relatively secondary and limited. It would involve upholding—through the minimum essential adjustments—a development model based, to a great extent, on conceptions previous to the very changes that made adaptation necessary.[4]

I share an important group of assumptions with the supporters of these conceptions, among them, the idea that development should necessarily include social justice, environmental conservation, respect for culture, and a humanistic ethic. I share also a socialist perspective of society and of social transformations, the importance of preserving and consolidating the achievements of the Cuban revolution; and the desirability of a "gradualist" approach to the necessary changes. However, I distance myself from any perspective that confines the possible trajectories of development of the country within the constraints of "sectoral studies" or that considers them only as an accessory element (adaptive) of the development model.

The problem is whether the Cuban economy should be put on a trajectory in which international integration is based on the intensive use of natural resources and a reindustrialization designed to substitute imports, or whether, on the contrary, it should be led on a path of exporting reindustrialization, sustained by the intensive utilization of a skilled workforce and not limited to a sectoral approach, although the latter is very important. Neither should the "adaptation" of a previous model to the new conditions be the fundamental issue.

From my perspective, the dilemma of the possible routes to develop the country represents the central axis of the discussion concerning the configuration of a development strategy for Cuba. The sectoral dimension of the possible trajectories should be treated as a basic component of that configuration, to the extent that what is sectoral is not secondary, nor neutral, to the goals of development, but this sectoral dimension must be understood in the context of a more comprehensive policy framework. Even more important, according to my criteria, is that the dilemma of the possible trajectories does not refer so much to the possibility of introducing "adaptations" to a previously existing model, but rather to the need for a "new" and distinct model of development.

However, the gradualism of the transformations, which the majority of the analysts on the island recognize as unavoidable, should not be assumed as a glorification of continuity of the existing development model. It should also be seen as an instrument for favoring discontinuities, when necessary. Precisely, this is a point that should be clarified in any analysis of possible development trajectories. The lack of rigorous definitions with respect to the matter—the need or lack thereof of a new model—can yield more uncertainties than clarifications in regards to thinking about Cuba's development strategies under current conditions.

One of the most important problems that, in general, should be noted in the predominant approaches in Cuba concerns an ambivalent stance toward the subject. The tendency exists to assume the possibility of a stable coexistence between essentially different alternatives. The notion, to my judgment correct, that the development of the country

should encompass multiple components—utilization of natural resources and a skilled workforce, as well as the substitution of imports
and exports, among others—is not equivalent to assuming that a core
set of strategic alternatives should not be adopted as they will forcibly
exclude others.

A strategy based on the export of technology-intensive manufacturing does not exclude, by necessity, the existence of processes of import
substitution, nor does it exclude exports derived from natural resources;
but it does indeed reject them as definitive axes of development policy.
In a strategy of development there should exist flexibility, but not a lack
of definition with regard to its core. However, it would not be enough
to restore the centrality of what, in appearance, constitutes a sectoral
issue, nor is it sufficient to specify a need for a new model of development rather than an adaptation of the existing model. Simply pointing
to the drawbacks of an ambivalent position will not solve the problem
of an adequate design.

The reflection on a development strategy for contemporary Cuba
requires, at least, the consideration of three additional and important
points. In this regard, the prevailing thinking in the country is lacking
in precision.[5] The first point involves the nature of the connection between Cuba and the world economy or, in other words, how we should
live globalization from the perspective of a country such as Cuba. The
second is the fundamental dimension that should be considered upon
thinking about development; that is, what it means for Cuba to be
developed. Finally, Cuba must undertake a categorical identification
of the principal assets upon which the country depends in order to
achieve development.

One of the most important findings in the evaluation of the international economy is the surprising stability of the unequal relative distribution of income among developed and underdeveloped nations.
The rise of some countries of this latter category in previous decades
has been the exception; so much so, that they have been referred to as
"economic miracles." Development is a process with an accompanying
anomaly that, although despite its indisputable appearance, is seldom
found clearly formulated in Cuba: the development of the island would
amount to creating an "economic miracle." The discussion concerning
the viability of such tremendous effort should occupy center stage of
any analysis of the Cuban economy and the reflections concerning the
strategy of the nation's development.

For a country such as Cuba, globalization should be faced, accordingly, from a perspective of exceptionality. The economic performance required to reach development must be so singular, that there are very few spaces for errors and omissions. The factor of time gains utmost importance, and thus high rates in the growth of the gross domestic product (GDP) and of productivity are required in order to shorten the rates of transformation, since the global economy heavily penalizes the slowness of change. Consequently, solutions that are discontinuous with respect to the previous status should prevail. In an era of globalization, it is difficult for economic performance that is not exceptional to lead to development.

To develop oneself in the midst of this context should not be limited, however, to undergoing this process solely based on a perspective of exceptionalism. It also requires the resignation to any notion of self-centered development and a redefinition of the strategy's unit of analysis. The first requirement does not indicate, in any way, the abandonment of national interests, nor of the active role that the nation-state should have in the process. Instead, what is important to understand is that, in the current period, those interests are promoted more effectively if the nation-state recognizes existing limits for actions that assume that some policies can be undertaken by embarking on patterns of development with relative independence or disdain for the dynamics of the global economy. The assumptions that could have justified self-centered notions in another historical period are no longer viable. The state can still act in favor of development, but under very different assumptions.

It also becomes evident that the traditional assumption that the nation is the most adequate unit of analysis for the design of development strategies should be re-examined. The most dynamic activities of the international economy are organized as parts of global production chains, and it is at this level—and not within a given national sphere— where there can exist the greatest opportunities to develop a country such as Cuba.

In thinking of development, it would be worth clarifying that it is a complex, multidimensional process and that, similarly, unilateral attempts to emphasize single dimensions can impoverish the analysis. Nevertheless, without underestimating the importance of those most frequently specified—for example, social justice or its sustainability—I wish to emphasize the dimension of development focused on the process of positioning a substantial part of the country's workforce in rising trajectories of technological and organizational learning. That perspective has not been pointed out sufficiently in the analyses on Cuba and, yet, it is vital for the design of a correct strategy. In the first place, this perspective makes it possible to identify a substantial connection between the country's potential of progress and the dynamics of the global economy, in a globalized world that penalizes those societies incapable of constantly elevating their educational, scientific and technical standards, as well as the capacity to implement these in innovative forms. Second, this focus is vital for the design of a correct strategy because it emphasizes the role of the workforce, particularly skilled human resources.

A workforce with a relatively high skill level and with a high capacity for learning is the principal asset on which the country can count to develop itself. The greatest potential for development of Cuba is based, without a doubt, on its people. From my standpoint—one that emphasizes an export-oriented reindustrialization development of the country—the industrial workforce and that employed in related productive services are particularly important. The key to ensuring the country's ability to guide itself successfully through the stages of technological learning depends on a complex interaction between many categories of workers: from the primary school teachers to the most distinguished scientists of the nation, from physicians and other health workers to the unpretentious sanitation service workers, from engineers and technical personnel to the factory workers and the farmers in the furrow. Advancing along the technological learning curve requires a strong commitment to educational excellence, to workers' health, to continuous systems of training, and to labor retraining and, especially, to the creation of the incentives and other conditions that support innovation as a continuous process. Development, in a globalized context, amounts in essence to a struggle over the distribution of shares of the material foundations of modern-day production. This is a complex process that far surpasses the simple "adaptive" incorporation of the country into the international economy. In this process, two aspects become indispensable: the quality of available human resources and the capability of the state to implement policies that promote development.

Finally, I would like to make a brief note concerning the concept of "export substitution," which occupies a central place in my arguments. In no way do I attribute the innovation of the concept to myself. In any case, I have tried to introduce it for the first time—to the best of my ability—into the study of the Cuban case.[6] The concept should not be confused with that of "export diversification," at least in the way in which it is habitually used in Cuba. I believe, as many do, that Cuba's road toward development is forcibly through the growth of exports, but not growth by any means. It must not only involve increasing traditional exports, but also their "diversification" through their extension into additional exportable categories, including manufacturing and services.

An effective diversification of exports should not be understood as indiscriminate aggregation of new exportable categories, quite the reverse, it should be understood as the selective expansion—absolute and relative—of exports based on technological factors and on the intensive utilization of a relatively skilled workforce. That is, these exports should be associated with the concentrated application of knowledge in the form of technical and organizational methods applied to production processes, as well as knowledge embedded in efficient equipment. These types of activities would mostly involve the so-called "high tech" industries such as pharmaceuticals or software development, as well as the "upgrading" of processes and products in traditional sectors such as the transforming of raw sugar into special types of alcohol. The key point should be the extent to which these new technologically intensive exports succeed in growing as a proportion of total exports until becoming the majority. In other words, some exports should be substituted for others in the country's exporting structure.

Returning to the metaphor of old cars, the archaic flotilla of autos that circulate in Cuba could be a good starting point to undertake the adventure of development. Development is the type of "miracle" that if largely extended with an exporting bias, could lead to another "miracle." The elderly Chevrolets continue to be, after all, quite safe vehicles, particularly in order to go up steep hills.

The Fissures of the "Adaptation" of the 1990s

The last decade of the 20th century has been a scenario of an inconclusive transformation of Cuba's economic structure. The model of development adopted during the first thirty years of the Cuban revolution (1959–1988), which was fundamentally focused on a national agro-industrial complex with guaranteed financing, technology, and markets from the socialist camp, has gradually been transferred—at least partially—into a new structure in the 1990s. This new configuration is outwardly-oriented toward foreign markets—as in the cases of tourism and mining—and towards other spheres whose growth has been fueled by the expansion of a domestic market in foreign exchange. The latter has been promoted, in considerable measure, by tourism and by net current transfers, especially family remittances, and other sources of "hard" currency income associated with "spillovers" derived from tourism and workforce incentives in "hard" currency for a segment of the country's population.

For an open economy such as Cuba's, the transformation of its economic structure towards development occurs within a framework of restrictions. First, the economic structure should guarantee a role for the insertion of the country in the international economy. The opportunities for autarkic whims are practically nonexistent and their consequences would be disastrous. For Cuba, there are no viable options outside of those "outward-oriented strategies," an always-problematic though not impossible alternative, while the country is submitted to the U.S. economic blockade.[7] The second restriction is that, for the practical purposes of the design of development strategies, "the country" cannot be regarded as the most adequate unit of analysis. The advances gained by technological and organizational learning are currently derived more from one's progress in the context of global chains of production than from one's self-centered promotion of "national industries."

The third restriction refers to the need for restructuring the economy as a part of a broader process of social change that transcends the partial reform of the economy's traditional, centrally planned apparatus. The probabilities for a successful reorientation of the economic structure are not very high in the absence of relatively significant transformations of fundamental economic institutions and property rights.[8] Another very important restriction is that the identification, selection and promotion of the sectors and activities that will have to constitute the new economic structure should be understood as part of a complex process that will be determined, to a great extent, by social and political considerations. No transformation of the economic structure will be sustainable nor desirable, in the long run, if it is done at the expense of the well-being and the expectations of the majority of the population.

The fact is that from the beginning of the 1990s a change occurred—in a number of significant specific aspects—in the pattern of development followed by Cuba from the mid-1970s. The more visible causes of change, although not the only ones, were located basically in external factors. In this respect, what happened in Cuba is registered in quite well-defined historical patterns. Across countries and across time, changes in external conditions have been a central factor in the transformation of development strategies.[9]

The central axis of Cuba's development strategy had been defined in 1975 as "the industrialization of the country."[10] By the 1990s, although this process had not fully managed to fulfill the delineated tasks, it had succeeded in achieving a relatively higher share of industrial output within total supply, diversified industrial production, and expanded its support infrastructure. It had also extended and deepened the business network, created a capacity for administration and for management, and fostered the expansion of a relatively skilled industrial workforce. By the late 1980s whole industrial sectors had been vastly expanded and new manufacturing branches had been established, fundamentally with the goal of import substitution. New productive capacities were created in a rather wide spectrum of industries such as metal processing, industrial machinery, assembly of transportation equipment, naval construction, food processing, pharmaceutical, medical equipment, fertilizers, agro-machinery, construction supply materials, electronics and textile plants. Deficiencies and limitations of the process have been widely pointed out by many authors. What I wish to indicate here is that the existing situation at the beginning of the 1990s was not the culmination of this development strategy, but rather a starting point of the search for possible and existing alternatives.

The changes introduced into the pattern of development of Cuba during the 1990s have significantly marked the composition of the balance of payments[11] and other areas of the economy—for example, the incentives structure and social mobility. But, despite all the changes, the old agro-industrial structure still predominates in terms of total supply and employment today, although a good part is not viable under current conditions, nor compatible—in its current form—with the needs for the future development of Cuba. By the beginning of the 21st century, it is evident that the transformation has been inconclusive. This is not only because of the unfinished character of the reforms, but because of the unclear direction of the economy's new structure. The development of tourism does not indicate, necessarily, that the country is redeeming itself by unavoidably moving toward becoming a "service sector economy," nor should the expansion registered to date in a group of activities be regarded as the solution to the formidable challenge to substantially modify the current demand structure of the country's economy. The implications of the transformations of the 1990s for the future development of the country can be valued more clearly if they are evaluated even superficially by two of its central dimensions: international reinsertion, on the one hand, and the patterns and the strategy of development, on the other.

The King Has Died, Long Live the King!

Evaluated retrospectively, and with the advantage of hindsight, the Cuban economy undertook international reinsertion based on three pillars in the 1990s: the intensive utilization of natural resources, the access to external rents (family remittances), and the limited revenue derived from foreign loans and investment. This pattern of development is different from the previous (1976–1989) period with regard to the mode of insertion into capitalist world markets, now in competitive terms, versus the previous access—guaranteed and in compensated terms—to the markets of the Council for Mutual Economic Assistance (COMECON), of "real socialism." For this reason, the specific ties connecting the country to the international economy have changed, with tourism partially replacing sugar and foreign investment and family remittances unsuccessfully attempting to replace the compensating transfers coming from COMECON. However, the development pattern of the 1990s maintains an impressive continuity with the previous one, to the extent that it has continued to be, in essence, a process of industrialization by means of import substitution.

Since the second half of the 1970s until the end of the 1980s, the explicit emphasis of the development strategy was industrialization—specifically directed to replace imports.[12] The increase in exportable resources as a result of that industrialization was also a declared objective. However, as the facts demonstrated, this objective was very secondary compared to import substitution. The latter constituted the key part, but not the only one, of the pattern of development in effect during that period. Another pattern was the export development of primary products or products with a minimum degree of processing such as sugar, minerals and citrus fruits. However, this component was subordinated to the first one inasmuch as it was regarded as a source of resources to finance industrial investment and as a starting point for new industrial products—for example, sugar cane derivatives or steel outputs based on mineral reserves. In addition to substitutive industrialization and the promotion of primary product exports or exports with a low degree of processing, there existed a third component of that development pattern: the promotion of industrial exports that performed a very secondary role and yielded limited results. During the 1976–1980 five-year plan, 115 new exportable items were added, but these corresponded to a practically insignificant number in the total value of the exports of the country.[13]

As a result, the pattern of development entered in crisis at the beginning of the 1990s is, essentially, an industrialization model by means of import substitution.[14] And, it is precisely this central feature that becomes unsustainable, given the impossibility of continuing to count on the external mechanisms of compensation that permitted their expansion and even their operation. The second feature—the export of primary products—was not capable of serving as a source of accumulation for financing industrialization in the absence of the preferential prices previously paid by socialist countries. In fact, exports of primary products also entered in crisis upon not being able to ensure their expanded propagation as a consequence of the commercial and financial dislocations resulting from the bankruptcy of European "real socialism." The third component comprised of industrial exports was marginal to the essential operation of the pattern of development.

In retrospect, what is noteworthy at the beginning of the 1990s is that the new pattern—that was arising from the collapse of the previous one—essentially resulted in the continuity of the earlier model. In the 1990s industrialization by means of import substitution was not renounced as the central component of a vision in the long-run development of the country. What indeed was modified was the means of connection to the international environment through the type of industrialization anticipated for the future.

In the midst of the crisis and the severe balance of payments restrictions in the 1990s, industrialization by means of import substitution could not be carried out through *new* industrial investment. Instead, the strategy that was adopted attempted to preserve, as much as possible, the previously created industrial structure, while introducing the necessary adaptations and partially modernizing it, awaiting a return of more propitious conditions that would make it possible to reinitiate new investments for those targeted industries. The greater priority that some exporting sectors received in the 1990s with regard to investment—for example, tourism, nickel, and pharmaceuticals—was not conceived as a substantial modification of import substitution industrialization, but instead as the creation of improved conditions for the strategy's continuation. This resulted in relatively important adjustments in the following two other components of Cuba's pattern of development.

First, exports should be increased. This was understood to be possible through two means: first, trying to augment new exports based on the intensive utilization of natural resources; and second, trying to give a "leap forward" to a few industrial exports, especially in high technology such as pharmaceutical products based on biotechnology and medical equipment. Second, along with the export of primary commodities or those with low level of processing—i.e. related to an intensive utilization of natural resources, the impetuous development of tourism added a relatively new component in the Cuban economy with annual growth rates close to 20 percent. Although tourism often is presented as the "industry without chimneys" or the basis of a supposed "new service economy" for the country, tourism is also, to a great extent, based on the intensive use of natural resources.[15]

This does not mean, in any way, that it is a sector that should not be developed, in fact, quite the contrary. Cuba has unquestionable competitive advantages in this area and in addition, as will be discussed further on, tourism currently constitutes the only sector of the Cuban economy with the ability to act as the "leading sector" for development. However, its take-off in the 1990s has represented an additional expansion of natural resource-based exports, rather than the emergence of a new ingredient for the country's development pattern that could be augmented with other assets, such as skilled labor, science or technology. It is necessary to consider as well that in the long run an economic structure that enables a country to travel upwards through trajectories of technological learning is of great importance. In this process, the sectoral composition of the economy is not a "neutral" factor. Furthermore, the bet on industrial exports essentially relied on pharmaceutical production derived from biotechnology and, to a lesser extent, medical equipment. In this regard, industrial exports were not promoted in an extensive spectrum of activities, but in a very selective way. Nevertheless, the existing expectations at the beginning of the 1990s in this area have been reduced considerably in recent years.

The industrial structure created before the crisis was functioning in the early 1990s with very low levels of utilization and, in fact, it remained subject to a process of de-capitalization, especially acute in some branches.[16] It had not been created in order to compete internationally (thus it could not, in general, count on foreign markets as a possible distribution outlet) and, in addition, it was highly dependent on imports. Given severe balance of payments restrictions it was unable to produce for domestic markets as well.[17] However, part of that resulting structure was favored by the expansion of a practice that has grown in importance and has been called "exports within the borders." These consist of Cuban domestic markets that function in foreign currency (basically the U.S. dollar), whose demand originates from two fundamental sources: a growing number of national, foreign, and mixed companies that basically operate in "hard currency," (i.e. tourist activities), and the demand generated by a part of the population that possesses dollars, to a great extent thanks to family remittances and to other sources of income associated, as previously explained, in some cases with the "spillovers" derived from tourism and in others with the establishment of mechanisms of foreign currency- denominated bonuses delivered to a segment of the workforce.

The fact that they are referred to as "exports within the borders" reveals the importance of the availability of foreign exchange for the internal operation of the Cuban economy. The lack of "hard currency," rather than the paucity of other productive assets, is generally the strangulation point of productive processes. By creating domestic markets operating in "hard currency," a growing number of enterprises now have direct access to such a critical resource, thus "exports within the borders" have made it possible to place some industries originally designed to replace imports on a parity with export-oriented industries in terms of direct access to foreign exchange. However, the term should not be understood as a part of the process of export promotion because it actually facilitates import substitution in the new context by revitalizing industries which produce for domestic markets. Hypothetically, domestic markets in foreign exchange could act as a "springboard" for the generation of real exports, but that possibility has yet to be materialized in the recent experience of Cuban industry.

Based on domestic market demand for foreign exchange, new productive links have been created and pre-existing channels have been reconfigured. "Exports within the borders" have favored the formation of business networks, in some cases of a very dense character, that have permitted the reactivation of a part—still insufficient—of the import substitution industry.[18]

At least two lessons are derived from the experience of "exports within the borders" during the 1990s. First, relatively inefficient industries have managed to be reactivated and even be partially modernized, especially because their sales take place in markets in which the levels of efficiency are less than would be required by global markets.[19] Under these conditions, the development of strong incentives for export should not be expected to emerge. Hence, the potential for this mechanism to act as a "springboard" for exports will be met with major difficulties. Secondly, "exports within the borders" have acted as an important mechanism of social and political stability in the 1990s, as they have allowed for higher levels of employment—as a result of a smaller relative efficiency—than those which would be possible under an alternative predominant pattern based on "real" exports.

Having argued that the adjustment experienced by Cuba's development pattern in the 1990s was concentrated on its international integration and not the modification of its essential structure—that is, in the degree of the quality of its industrialization process by means of import substitution—it is advisable to summarize some of the most outstanding characteristics of that process:

1. The insertion of Cuba in the world economy during the 1990s consisted, basically, of the expansion of exports based on the intensive utilization of natural resources, particularly through the promotion of tourism services, an area whose potential had been unexploited at the beginning of the decade.

2. The performance of different activities within this export group has been very heterogeneous. While tourism revenue grew spectacularly, the sugar exports were reduced in a no less spectacular fashion. The losses associated with the contraction of the sugar sector substantially lessened the positive effects of the growing contribution of foreign exchange earnings from tourism.

3. In terms of international integration, tourism dethroned sugar, but its rise has not modified the fact that the country continues to be, as it has for centuries, basically an exporter of natural resources. What is innovative about tourism is that it has incorporated services as part of the list of exports derived

from these resources. The share of Cuban exports of activities based on other types of assets is minimal—for example, transformative industries, skilled labor or the utilization of science and engineering. The expectations that surrounded the medical-pharmaceutical complex in the first years of the 1990s did not materialize at expected levels by the end of the decade.

4. The type of international integration arrived at in the 1990s demonstrates that there is an astonishingly low level of utilization of the country's principal economic assets: a relatively skilled workforce and, especially, with high potential for learning.

5. Under limited possibilities for financing balance of payments deficits, the reduction of the country's total exporting capacity led to an "import substitution" pattern that was economically recessive; that is, imports lost their relative weight as a share of gross national product due to an adjustment through "compression" of imports.[20] This situation was particularly critical during the first half of the decade, and although improved in later years, it is still far from being resolved. In other words: the level of the country's exports in the 1990s was not capable of ensuring the operation of an industrial structure created to replace imports.

6. The partial reorientation of this structure toward what some authors have described as a "closed cycle scheme" has permitted a somewhat limited type of reindustrialization through "exports within the borders."[21] The demand for foreign exchange associated, to a great extent, with mechanisms of international integration—tourism, foreign investment, access to credit, and family remittances—has functioned as a source for reactivating industrial supply by generating investment that has modernized and restructured national industry segments, directing them toward domestic markets.

7. Tourism has played an important role in the country's process of limited reindustrialization. Not only has this sector provided foreign exchange and jobs, but it is the only segment of the Cuban economy that has met three simultaneous conditions, making it the current "leading sector" for development: 1) the existence of potential and still insufficiently-met de-

mand; 2) a relatively large scale of activity and intersectoral ties—permitting the dissemination of its growth to the rest of the economy; and 3) an "exogenous" growth rate, that is, relatively independent of the general average growth rate of the domestic economy.[22] As a "leading sector" in the economy, its contribution has been much more significant than solely its generation of export earnings; in fact, this alternate role is what is most important in the long run. Tourism offers potential links—particularly with respect to industry and other services of greater technological complexity including air transport, telecommunications, information technology and engineering projects—that would facilitate advances in the structure of the economy and the workforce towards international trajectories of technological learning. In that way, tourism—a service of little technological complexity in some of its predominant activities (for example, lodging and gastronomy), and based on the intensive use of natural resources—could act as a gateway for the development of industrial activities and of more technologically advanced services, both with much greater income earning potential.

8. Foreign investment was concentrated during the 1990s in activities related to natural resources—tourism, mining, oil, agriculture, the development of infrastructure (for example, telecommunications), and certain industrial outputs that function as "exports within the borders" such as light manufacturing and food industries.[23] The direct impact of foreign investment with respect to the utilization of established industrial plants and skilled workforce has been insignificant. The problem is not only based on relatively stringent domestic regulations with regard to foreign investment, but more importantly the existence of more general economic and political conditions—the existence of the U.S. economic blockade against Cuba, the persistence of imbalances in the balance of payments, the lack of business flexibility, the limited possibilities for the functioning of effective workforce incentives, and the absence of sufficient mechanisms for economic innovation, among others—that limit the country's attractiveness to foreign investment, particularly in the manufacturing sector.[24]

The "Combined Reindustrialization" of the 1990s and the Limits of a Development Strategy

At times, development strategies have been identified as such from the beginning; this was the case of Cuba in the mid-1970s. But on other occasions what sometimes is classified as strategy is, strictly speaking, the result of a gradual process and this is significantly dissimilar from the other. That seems to have been the case of Cuba in the 1990s. Development strategies "do not necessarily represent the existence of comprehensive economic plans or of major blueprints for industrial transformation"; on the contrary, oftentimes, they result from practical and fragmented decisions that attempt to respond to immediate crises and to short-term problems, rather than to strategic considerations.[25] Several specialists hold that the majority of policy actions referred to as "development strategies" actually have been "discovered" as such only with the passage of time; that is, its retrospective study has made it possible to attribute certain coherence to economic programs that, in their time, only were designed to respond to the situation at hand.[26]

In conceptual terms, there exists an important difference between *development strategy* and *pattern of development,* to the effect that the first always refers to an ideal representation at the policy level, while the second consists of a given sequence of events and economic and social outcomes. The distinction is relevant to the extent that most of the controversy concerning strategies revolves around what governments can actually do, so that the study of the past (the patterns of development) reveals their capabilities or lack thereof. That knowledge, consequently, can be utilized as an initial condition for the design of new strategies.[27]

Having defined these points, the following summary does not refer, strictly speaking, to a review of Cuba's development strategy in the 1990s, as if one had existed; nor does it concern an examination of the archetypes that could have existed in the mind of policy makers, but it does allude to the pattern of development observed during that period. The analysis of the observable characteristics in the decade's pattern serve as a starting point in order to advance some provisional considerations with regard to the development strategy during that period:

1. The pattern of development observed in Cuba during the 1990s—sufficiently well defined by the end of the decade—does not correspond with an explicit new strategy of development that had been formulated at the beginning of the decade.[28]

2. From the beginning of the 1990s at the level of the state apparatus an economic strategy was observed in Cuba in the sense of the existence of a series of principles, assumptions and prognoses that had as a purpose "the essential objectives of confronting and surpassing the effects of the crisis, distributing as equitably as possible its impact on the society, while there were created conditions for the reinstitution of Cuba into the world economy,"[29] but that resistance strategy—without a doubt very important—should not be confused with a *new* development strategy; i.e. with an essentially different ideal archetype contrary to the existing one concerning the manner in which to develop the country.

3. What is at times described as a development strategy in Cuba possesses coherence only retrospectively. What at the end of the 1990s could be regarded as such a strategy had resulted from the measures gradually adopted in the early 1990s as a part of a strategy to resist the dire consequences for the Cuban economy of the collapse of the Soviet Union and the persistence of the U.S. blockade.

4. More than a new strategy of development, the adjustments introduced due to the crisis resulted in *a different phase* than that predominating since the middle of the 1970s. If the phase that extended during the period 1975–1990 could be characterized as "industrialization by means of import substitution under conditions of high external subsidies" (in order to abbreviate: subsidized import substitution), the 1990s opened a new stage of what, in essence, was the same strategy, which can be called "reindustrialization by means of import substitution with superimposed export orientation" (in order to abbreviate: *combined* reindustrialization).

5. In the new phase, the assumption that industrialization by means of import substitution should be the principal component of the development strategy was maintained. What was recently modified was the perception that, under the new conditions, the following were indispensable: a) the reconfiguration the industrial structure to take advantage of the emergence of new domestic markets in foreign exchange; b) the promotion of a few, new specific exports with the ability to rapidly become sources of accumulation and articulating links for

productive chains that permit partial reindustrialization; and c) the inclusion of foreign investment as a route to access financing, technology and markets. What is new has been, then, a relatively greater emphasis on the creation of new exports in the short term. However, beyond this general invocation on the need for a "will to export," a change in the paradigm of import substitution based industrialization has yet to be identified.

6. Despite its important limitations, the new phase of combined reindustrialization has the virtues of almost every policy designed and implemented under pressure, basically its practical character and high degree of flexibility. For that reason, although it does not manage to displace the idea of the substitutive industrialization from the center of the strategy—which constitutes an emphasis not much adjusted to the current circumstances—a relatively large emphasis on a certain reorientation of the economy towards exports is given, that, without a doubt could be the basis from which to advance a different industrialization paradigm. The new phase of the development strategy has a problem of emphasis, but a great potential given its "flexible" character.

7. The two most important limitations of the new phase of the development strategy are the following:

- The level of new sources of foreign exchange and the potential for productive links that the sectoral leader (tourism) is capable of generating is considerably less than that required for reconfiguring and reactivating the existing industrial basis, which had been created in order to replace imports. A considerable part of latent supply corresponds to an industrial model that is not viable under current conditions. Given the assumption that the economic program should try to optimize existing productive plants and the industrial workforce, a general reindustrialization oriented towards import substitution objectives is not plausible for Cuba. The extension of import substitution to a development strategy will lead to a dead end.

- The export orientation of the 1990s is sustained by natural resource-supported activities, but these do not have the potential for significant expansion with the very important exception of tourism. In some cases such as mineral and oil reserves, the natural resources that sustain them have insurmountable material limits, while in others, the market imposes current limitations, whether in the restricted supply that should be the basis for an exclusive product, such as *habanos* or in relatively stagnant demand as is the case of sugar. It is certain that a part of the agricultural sector could be reoriented towards export, but even doing so, would represent a limited export option. Furthermore, the experience of "large stake bets" on a few industrial activities, not only seems to have a not too convincing record, but also does not maximize the widely available productive plants and industrial workforce. The notions that export orientation should be aimed at sectors with clear "comparative advantages" (natural resources) and toward a few industrial activities are not a plausible assumption for Cuba's development strategy. The almost exclusive emphasis on an exporting program based on natural "comparative advantages" or in a "great leap" of some branch of industry could also lead to a dead-end street.

At the dawn of the new century, as was the case at the beginning of the 1990s, an opportunity to rethink the country's development strategy is once again available. My view is that import substitution should be replaced—although in no case excluded—as the center or nucleus of the strategy by one that emphasizes exporting.

Rethinking the Debate on the Development of Cuba

The development of Cuba requires, among other factors, the reindustrialization of its economy. However, this should not be conceived as a process of reconstructing the industrial framework directed toward the reactivation and diversification of supply which is basically oriented towards the domestic market. Under new international economic conditions, the creation of the internal foundation necessary for the systematic development of the country's productive forces should be the result of a reindustrialization process whereby a share of the industrial base is oriented towards contemporary global production.

Cuba should aspire to convert itself, in the short and medium terms, into a new site for the manufacturing of global products in a series of branches, based on modalities of insertion that—prospectively—make it possible for national industry to advance "upwards" toward trajectories of technological and organizational learning. This should not involve postulating the need for a "new" strategy of "outward-oriented industrialization," allegedly opposed to an "old" one based on import substitution. This can be explained in at least three ways. In the first place, existing historical evidence indicates that, with sufficient certainty, the majority of the world's industrialization processes have relied on a combination of both approaches for relatively long periods of time, although at a given time the emphasis was placed on one or the other. In the long run, the two approaches have been complementary and non-exclusive.[30] In the case of Cuba, export substitution could represent the nucleus of a new strategy: it could benefit from factors that, as the skilled workforce, were promoted throughout the long period during which import substitution occupied the center of the country's development strategy.

The second reason is that export-oriented industry in many localities, countries, and regions are successfully being structured as *clusters* (agglomerations) of products and services focused on foreign market manufacturing, but the sector's resulting density has also favored expansion to domestic markets. In other words, a *cluster* permits the development of an internal supply network that serves as a basis for productive activities directed toward external markets. From that perspective, the traditional contours among outputs for "domestic" and "external" markets are quite blurred.[31] Thirdly, because my reasoning refers particularly to the case of Cuba, a country in which, given its current industrial structure based on import substitution, any step to reorient a part of the industrial supply toward exports should not be understood as excessive neglect of the part of the industry that produces for domestic markets.

What Cuba needs is a reindustrialization with export substitution, that is, the adoption of a pattern of development in which "technologically intensive" exports replace those products and services based on the intensive utilization of natural resources, as the dominant part of the country's total exports. The foregoing would represent a radical modification in the pattern of development observed thus far, as it would displace industrialization by means of import substitution as the central component. It would imply a change of emphasis—with qualitative implications—regarding the development strategy phase followed in the 1990s, since the export orientation of reindustrialization would cease being an overlapping component and become the central aspect, the essential component. Another fundamental difference that exists between reindustrialization for export substitution and the previous orientation would be that not only would the industrial share occupy a growing part of total exports, but a relatively broad spectrum of activities also would be produced.

The proposal of a reindustrialization strategy with export substitution surely would be contested on several fronts. On the one hand, there exists a theoretical objection that this would threaten the exploitation of Cuba's comparative advantages in providing products and services based on the intensive utilization of natural resources; on the other, there exist objections on a practical level, including various arguments, among them, that this strategy has not been carried out successfully in many countries that have attempted the same route, as well as the existence, in the case of Cuba, of powerful structural factors that impede the rapid growth of industrial exports.

With regard to the first objection, two brief observations would perhaps suffice. First, national development is very complex and too important to be determined by the attachment to a theory that, like that of comparative advantages, cannot adequately explain some of the most outstanding aspects of the process of restructuring the global industry.[32] Second, the availability of several technical conditions in contemporary Cuba facilitates the adoption of a more technologically intensive path of development, even after taking into account the negative consequences of the crisis of the 1990s. Cuba has a relatively skilled industrial workforce with demonstrated high potential for learning. Although in many sectors of the Cuban economy, technical and organizational skills do not meet world class standards, the combination of a high level of general education with basic, but widespread, technical skills, and a tradition of technical inventiveness has established a general profile of very fast assimilation of new techniques by the Cuban labor force, as recognized by foreign investors. In addition, the existence of a relatively diversified industrial base (metal processing, industrial machinery, assembly of transportation equipment, naval construction, food processing, pharmaceutical, medical equipment, fertilizers, agromachinery, materials for construction, electronics, and textile plants), and business networks are in economic terms, more important assets for Cuba than the natural resources of the country.

With regard to the practical objections on a practical level, although the implementation of a successful industrialization strategy with export substitution has not been very extensive, there indeed exist sufficient cases that support its viability. My argument consists, precisely, in emphasizing that in Cuba there are exceptional conditions—and it is reasonable to think that others can be created—that render a pattern of industrialization development through the export substitution viable. Cuba, unlike the majority of underdeveloped countries, can take advantage of a series of opportunities that exist in the global economy.

In addition, a strategy of reindustrialization through export substitution stems from the assumption that existing structural limits should not be accepted, but instead attempts should be made, precisely, to surpass them. The domestic economic reforms that this would require have elsewhere been referred to as "fundamental"[33] but, in addition, it would be necessary to utilize the opportunities offered by foreign investment and global production networks in aiding the country's journey across technological and organizational learning trajectories.

The debate on the development of Cuba should give more attention to factors such as:

- The consideration of uncertainty as one advantage that the global economy offers the country
- The challenges that are posed by a globalized world where slow change is severely penalized
- The realistic expectations that Cuba will be able to insert itself in global networks of production
- The country's power of negotiation with respect to transnational capital that articulates these global networks.
- The modalities of insertion that would be more propitious to "advance" along these production chains
- The internal institutional transformations that would make it possible for the country to take advantage of foreign investment and global production networks as factors for development
- The clarification of the different dimensions and methods of measuring "progress" in the context of these global networks

In summary, the economic transformations that occurred during the 1990s cannot be regarded as the solution to the formidable challenge of substantially modifying the current supply structure of the economy in order to be able to access development. The reconstruction of the Cuban economy is—despite the changes that have occurred in this decade—an incipient process with a high degree of ambiguity. It concerns, succinctly, a challenge yet to be resolved.

For an open economy such as Cuba's, a transformation of its economic structure focused toward development is a process that occurs within a framework of unavoidable restrictions, particularly the inherited structure and the existence of the U.S. economic blockade. Nevertheless, development is possible. Under current conditions, the most adequate strategy for Cuba consists—in my opinion—of undertaking a process of reindustrialization with export substitution that makes it possible to advance the country along rising trajectories of technological and organizational learning. In terms of the future, the alternative vision of Cuba as a "techno-island" (industry) or as an "intelligent island" (innovation) should stand out against the current predominant vision of an "island-paradise" (tourism). Human capital, knowledge and technical skills should take precedence over natural resources as the foundations of national development in this era of globalization.

Notes

1   Among the most proficient academic texts of the second half of the 1990s that address the subject the following ones could be cited: Adriano García, Hugo Pons, José Somoza and Víctor Cruz, "Bases para la elaboración de una política industrial," *Cuba: Investigación económica*, A. 5, N. 2, Havana, April–June, 1999; Hugo Pons, "Cuba: industrialización y desarrollo," *Cuba: Investigación económica*, A. 4, N. 1, Havana, January–March,1998; Hiram Marquetti, *La industria cubana en los años 90: Reestructuración y adaptación al nuevo contexto internacional*, (tesis doctoral), mimeo, Centro de Estudios de la Economía Cubana, Universidad de La Habana, julio de 1999; Elena Álvarez, "Cuba: Un modelo de desarrollo con justicia social," *Cuba: Investigación económica*, A. 4, N. 2, April–June, 1998; Oscar Echevarría, "Cuba: la antesala de la crisis," *Cuba: Investigación económica*, A. 4, N. 2, Havana, April–June, 1998; Adriano García, "La reestructuración industrial en Cuba," *Cuba: Investigación económica*, A. 2, N. 2, Havana, April–June 1996; Mario Fernández Font, "La reestructuración tecnológica de la economía cubana en los próximos años," *Economía cubana. Boletín informativo n. 23*, CIEM, Havana, September–October, 1995; and Gerardo Trueba, "Reflexiones sobre la reestructuración industrial en las condiciones de la actualidad cubana: las pequeñas y medianas empresas," *Economía cubana. Boletín informativo n. 23*, CIEM, September–October, 1995. Government official positions on the subject have appeared in various documents during the second half of the 1990s. The most complete official

vision is probably the "Economic Resolution of the V Congress of the Communist Party of Cuba" (*Granma*, Special Supplement, Havana, November 7, 1997). There have also been frequent declarations of important Cuban policy makers, in particular those of Carlos Lage, Secretary of the Executive Committee of the Council of Ministers, and José Luis Rodríguez, Vice President of the Council of Ministers and Minister of Economy and Planning. Among its many declarations, the following ones could be cited: Carlos Lage, *Intervención en el V Pleno del Comité Central*, Ministerio de Economía y Planificación, Havana, March 23, 1996; José Luis Rodríguez, "Cuba 1990–1995: Reflexiones sobre una política económica acertada," *Cuba socialista*, N. 1, tercera época, Havana, 1996; *Perspectivas económicas de Cuba en 1996* (World Economic Forum, Davos, 1996), Ministerio de Economía y Planificación, Havana. Although there are no detailed texts published and broadly circulated authored by government agency experts, authors such as Hugo Pons, Adriano García, and Hiram Marquetti cite a considerable body of studies of experts of different ministries in their academic works that, without a doubt, reveal the intense investigation underway by analysts in the state's central administrative bodies.

2   The article of Hugo Pons is the only one that expresses clearly the existence of a dilemma between productive specialization alternatives that could imply differing levels of economic and social costs for the country (inter-industry specialization versus intra-industry specialization). Even though the author's perspective is basically of a "sectoral" sort, the identification of the dilemma has clear implications for the overall development strategy (not only for industry), although the author, unfortunately, did not develop this point. Recognizing the unquestionable significance of this work, Dr. Pons' position with regard to the viability of the concurrence of the two specialization alternatives identified in his article, however, does not seem to me sufficiently argued.

3   Among the published academic texts that correspond with an "industrial sector" perspective should be noted the doctoral dissertation of Hiram Marquetti and research conducted by Adriano García, Hugo Pons, José Somoza, and Víctor Cruz. Among those works that deal with the "export sector" perspective, the work of Elena Álvarez should be acknowledged.

4   This viewpoint is found in relatively more accentuated form in the official documents and in the declarations of government officials, although it also appears in the majority of the aforementioned academic texts.

5   I refer to the cited texts previously.

6   I have utilized the concept following the notion introduced into development studies by René Villarreal in his chapter "The Latin American Strategy of Import Substitution: Failure or Paradigm for the Region," in Gary Gereffi and Donald L. Wyman, comps., *Manufacturing Miracles: Paths of Industrialization in Latin America and East Asia*, Princeton University

Press, New Jersey, 1990, p. 310. In the case of the most recent discussion on Cuba, those who have come closer to the concept, without completely adopting it, have been Adriano García, Hugo Pons, José Somoza and Víctor Cruz.

7   This is the standard word used in Cuba to characterize the set of U.S. policies toward Cuba.

8   See Julio Carranza, Luis Gutiérrez and Pedro Monreal, *Cuba: la reestructuración de la economía. Una propuesta para el debate*, Nueva Sociedad. Caracas, 1997.

9   Christopher Ellison and Gary Gereffi, "Explaining Strategies and Patterns of Industrial Development," in *Manufacturing Miracles: Paths of Industrialization in Latin America and East Asia* (Gary Gereffi and Donald L. Wyman, eds).

10 The Programmatic Platform approved in the First Congress of the Communist Party of Cuba, which met in December 1975, expressed that "the central task of development plans for the promotion of the domestic economy for the next 5-year period 1976–1980 will be the industrialization of the country" (*Plataforma Programática del Partido Comunista de Cuba. Tesis y Resolución*, Departamento de Orientación Revolucionaria del Comité Central del Partido Comunista de Cuba, Havana 1976).

11 In the 1990s gross revenue from tourism displaced the dominant role of sugar as the principal source of foreign exchange of the country, which had prevailed for over two hundred years.

12 "The principal task of industrialization consists of creating the necessary domestic foundations for the systematic development of productive forces, to supply equipment and materials to industry, to agriculture and to livestock; to elevate exportable resources; replace imports, and to produce varied items available for widespread consumption by the population." (*Plataforma Programática del Partido Comunista de Cuba. Tesis y Resolución*, p. 77).

13 Humberto Pérez, "La plataforma programática y el desarrollo económico de Cuba" *Cuba Socialista*, N. 3, Havana, 1982, p. 39.

14 Cuban official statistics recorded vast participation of the industrial sector in domestic production (Global Social Product), which reached 46% in 1988. The majority of the 22 branches classified as a part of the industrial sector were oriented toward production for the domestic market. See: *Anuario estadístico de Cuba 1988*, Comité Estatal de Estadísticas, Havana 1989.

15 The notable expansion of tourism in Cuba during the 1990s has been accompanied by speculation with regard to the supposed advantages that the country gains in moving towards a service sector economy. However, as

far as I know, these arguments have not managed to establish a convincing conceptual rationale, nor have they been able to explain adequately what should be done with the existing industrial structure, or how the country's deindustrialization could lead toward development.

16 The period of Cuba's economic decline in the 1990s took place from 1990 to 1993, when GDP fell by approximately 35%. In 1994, growth was practically zero, but at least represented the end of the recession. Since 1995, a recuperation of the economy in relative terms has occurred.

17 There exists an excellent analysis of Cuban industry in the 1990s, which studies its problems and readjustments as a consequence of the crisis in detail. See Hiram Marquetti.

18 Ibid.

19 It is certain that, ordinarily, the companies that generate "exports within the borders" have been restructured and today are less inefficient than before; but even so, they are usually less efficient than they could be if they had to operate under conditions of international competitiveness.

20 CEPAL, *La economía cubana. Reformas estructurales y desempeño en los 90*, Fondo de Cultura Económica, Mexico D.F., 1997, pp. 147– 59.

21 The concept of "closed cycle" or "comprehensive cycle" firm is part of a business typology utilized by some authors in order to explain the transformations of the Cuban economic model in the 1990s. It refers, specifically, to one of the regulatory mechanisms that enable firms generating foreign exchange to utilize directly a part of these resources for the financing of their own production. For this group of firms, a significant change in state-run centralized planning has occurred to the extent to which the initiative has been given to the producer. See Alfredo González, "La transformación del modelo económico y los retos futuros," paper presented in the Taller Anual de Investigaciones del Instituto Nacional de Investigaciones Económicas (INIE), Havana, 1999; and by the same author, "Economía y sociedad: los retos del modelo económico," *Cuba: Investigación económica*, a. 3, n. 3–4, INIE, July–December 1997. Havana.

22 Robert E. Looney, "Manufacturing Contribution to Pakistan´s Economic Expansion: Commodity or Service-Led Growth," *Development Policy Review*, v. 12, 1994.

23 Omar Everleny Pérez, *El papel de la inversión extranjera directa en los países subdesarrollados. El caso de Cuba* (tesis de doctorado), Centro de Estudios de la Economía Cubana, Universidad de La Habana, 1998. Havana.

24 Claes Brundenius and Pedro Monreal, "The Future of the Cuban Economic Model: The Longer View," in Claes Brundenius and J. Weeks, eds., *Globalization and Third World Socialism: Cuba and Vietnam*, Macmillan Press, London, 2000.

25 Gary Gereffi, "Paths of Industrialization: An Overview," in Gary Gereffi and Donald L. Wyman, p. 55.

26 Ronald Dore, "Reflections on Culture and Social Change," in Gary Gereffi and Donald L. Wyman, p. 354.

27 Ibid.

28 For example, "exports within the borders" were never publicly identified as a significant adaptation mechanism, at the beginning of the decade.

29 José Luis Rodríguez, "Cuba 1990–1995 . . . ," p. 20.

30 See Gary Gereffi and John L. Wyman.

31 San Diego Association of Governments (SANDAG), "San Diego Regional Employment Clusters. Engines of the Modern Economy," *SANDAG Info*, San Diego, California, 1998; and "The Complications of Clustering," *The Economist*, London, 2 de enero de 1999, pp. 53–4.

32 In many cases, the emergence of exporting industries in a number of countries is not explained by their comparative advantages in these areas, but by the existence of a complex set of "negotiated access" agreements. Through them, transnational companies are "induced" by governments of those countries to transfer technological and productive capacity in exchange for access to their markets that, in many cases, are very dynamic. That factor—not comparative advantages—is what makes it possible to understand why Boeing incorporated China into the chain of production for one of its most sophisticated passenger airplanes (B-777). See William Greider, *One World, Ready or Not. The Manic Logic of Global Capitalism*, Simon & Schuster, New York, 1997.

33 See: Julio Carranza, Luis Gutiérrez and Pedro Monreal.

5

Challenges of Cuba's Insertion in Caribbean–U.S. Trade

by Jorge Mario Sánchez Egozcue

What are the structural elements that will determine Cuba's foreign trade trends in the next two to six years? The regional perspective must be considered, and this chapter seeks to analyze factors favoring the trend toward convergence with neighboring countries in the medium term. It alternatively considers the scenario of Cuba's continued status as an isolated case, albeit with the benefits and drawbacks implied by the status quo. In addition to this regional contextualization, the chapter examines the impact of a possible relaxation of current restrictions and the reestablishing of trade with the United States. Although this scenario is a more uncertain one, it is no less important in thinking about medium term possibilities; we focus here on economic considerations, without speculating on the political process of achieving such a commercial re-approximation with the United States. We seek to explore the significance of this hypothetical re-opening for Cuba and the Caribbean, analyzing whether the best alternative for Cuba would be trade liberalization through bilateral trade agreements, such as Chile's Free Trade Agreement with the United States or, on the other hand, regional insertion into a Caribbean agreement following Mexico's free trade agreements with the EU and North America.

This chapter evaluates the strategic options for Cuban trade. To orient trade policy most advantageously for Cuba, comparative weaknesses and strengths at regional (Cuba-Caribbean) and bilateral (Cuba-U.S.) levels must be identified. Previous studies have raised similar questions but from substantially different assumptions, for example, schemes based almost exclusively on foreign assistance for an eventual reconstruction of the country as a consequence of a political transition, or a priori guaranteed access to the United States market without practical considerations. In this study, a simpler and more pragmatic approach

is adopted. The transformations derived from the collapse of the Socialist Bloc are assumed to be irreversible, making it critical to consider
the options of integration within international and regional trends of
trade and investment.

In the case of the Caribbean community of nations, increased policy
harmonization of reciprocal trade is already taking place. The question
is not whether Cuba should or should not participate in these accords,
rather how far trade policy should be advanced in that direction. Likewise a definitive shift has also taken place as a result of the awakening of
interests by U.S. business executives in pursuing trade and investment
options with Cuba and the relaxation of bilateral trade restrictions
as a result of U.S. approval for Cuban purchases of U.S. agricultural
commodities since 2001. While trade with Cuba's closest North American neighbor was regarded with a high degree of uncertainty in the
1980s, it has become one of the factors of greatest potential influence
on Cuba's economic future, together with tourism and remittances. To
answer these questions, the relevance of how significant bilateral trade
with the United States will become for Cuba in the medium term is
examined in this chapter using a sufficiently conservative estimate in
order to measure its "minimum" probable impact.

An attentive reader will note surely that the approach of deploy-
ing an analysis based on world trends was avoided, and relatively little
space is dedicated to historical factors and institutional inertia. In the
case of global patterns, both Cuba and the Caribbean as a whole are
small actors with respect to large-scale international forces. Therefore, this study focuses on potential impacts given the respective scale
of these economies in international trade markets. This chapter also
presents its findings based on the assumption that the improvement in
U.S.–Cuba trade relations is a given, the result of specified policies and
particular consensus.

Regional Trends: Opening and Access to Markets

Trade Openness and Economic Growth: Theories and Empirical Results

With increased internationalization of trade relations, studies focused
on the linkages between openness to trade and economic growth[1] have
developed considerably in recent decades. The predominant view is
that greater openness is correlated with greater economic growth, independently of allotment conditions, including country size, resource

endowment, natural trade barriers, political environment, and cultural and historical background. The literature widely concurs that trade flows are ultimately not more than an imperfect "proxy" for trade orientation, and that tariffs and exchange rates in and of themselves do not capture the spectrum of real restrictions and factors that distort prices and the relationships between trade regime and economic growth.

Openness can stimulate a positive effect in terms of growth, many studies contend, particularly the so-called "new theories" on growth developed by Romer (1986) Lucas (1988), and, at a more empirical level, Martin (1992). Another approach builds on the idea that countries with greater openness have more flexibility to take advantage of the technological advances generated in other nations, thus benefiting growth rates; researchers favoring this interpretation include Romer (1992), Grossman and Helpman (1991), Barro and Sala-i-Martin (1995) and Obstfeld and Rogoff (1996). Along these lines, other models have shown that distortions to trade induced by tariffs and exchange rate controls act to reduce growth in small countries with limited resources, where imports are essential for production, basically by reducing per capita GDP by the share derived from distortions in exchange rates and tariffs (Lee 1993).

Some authors, however, have opposed this view or questioned the impact of these variables on economic growth. Helleiner (1986) argues that a minimum level of development is required before the benefits of international trade can completely be realized. Grossman and Helpman (1991) develop a theoretical model showing that there is a negative relation between the degree of trade liberalization and growth. Krugman (1994) and Rodrik (1995) found that the effect of the degree of economic openness on growth turns out to be insignificant, or at least not as large as other studies postulate. In addition, the indices[2] utilized to measure the degree of openness have been strongly criticized with regard to their capacity to capture the entire range of causal factors that frequently do not distinguish between trade factors and those of macroeconomic policy (Rodrik 1995). One study on the variety of measures of openness in order to verify the soundness of the interrelationship between economic growth and trade restrictions found that all the statistically significant indices showed a positive relation between more open trade regimes and economic growth (Harrison 1993). Other studies have addressed the subject, for example, using the growth of exports and the ratio of trade dependency as proxy variables for openness, such as Balassa (1982). The principal limitation of such indices is that they are not necessarily associated with trade policy.[3] Some methods are better accepted since they are derived from more "observable" variables.[4] Perhaps the most encompassing approach is that used by Edwards (1997) in which nine indicators for openness are analyzed for a sample of 93 countries. Edwards reports that his findings concur with authors who previously had found evidence of a positive relationship between economic growth and openness to trade.[5]

Having examined this theoretical framework pointing to the merits of trade liberalization on economic growth, this chapter departs from the premise that Cuba's access to trade with the Caribbean and other regions potentially promises to yield long-term benefits for the country's overall growth strategy. However, at the same time, as noted in the aforementioned literature, trade levels and strategies must be analyzed to understand how overall cross-country trends translate into the outcomes for particular countries such as Cuba.

Cuba and the Caribbean: Commonalities and Divergences[6]

The economies of the Caribbean Basin all share a similar profile with regard to size, income level, as well as their most important economic sectors and commercial structures. However, a more detailed comparison shows important asymmetries. Some Caribbean countries are extremely dependent on oil revenue as their primary source of income, others on financial services, and still others on tourism, or the export earnings from raw materials and food. Within the set, Cuba has certain advantages. For example, its size is relatively large compared to the regional average.[7] The size of its merchant and aviation fleet provides advantageous capability for use in intraregional trade. In addition, its workforce is relatively well-qualified, and its domestic market is relatively large compared to the rest of the Caribbean.

Nevertheless, certain unique characteristics prevent Cuba from being analyzed homogeneously with other countries in the region. The development of its financial and tourism industries, restricted access to foreign borrowing, domestic financial systems, as well as structural economic differences, are the most relevant characteristics which attest to its heterogeneity with respect to the rest of the region. For example, of the nine procedures that form the Caribbean Single Market Economy (CSME) project[8], the most difficult short-term factors for Cuba's accession are requirements related to fiscal convergence, exchange rate stability and international reserves. These differences are particularly significant in the case of Cuba because of its strong disparities with respect to macroeconomic policy and market orientation in comparison to its neighbors. Nevertheless Cuba's likely membership in the Association of Caribbean States (ACS) should act as the natural bridge toward deeper integration in the Caribbean's free trade area, thus altering these existing disparities. In addition, there is consensus that Cuba's full insertion into the agreement could positively improve trade and investment flows for the region.

In terms of trade, the level of access Caribbean countries, other than Cuba, have to the U.S. market is particularly relevant. U.S. initiatives or special agreements provide guarantees and preferential treatment for the region that would normally be unavailable in the international market. These factors, to a greater or lesser extent, condition the probability that a pattern of short-term "convergence" will take place in terms of trade and regional investment with Cuba. Likewise, these factors are determinants for evaluating the relative impact stemming from the possible trade scenarios under which Cuba's trade with the United States improves in the medium term.

Before undertaking a more detailed analysis of Cuba's trade strategies, it is first necessary to characterize the principal special features of other Caribbean economies, comparing them to Cuba in terms of size, income levels, economic sectors, growth patterns and trade structures.

Size

In terms of the region,[9] Haiti, the Dominican Republic, and Cuba are the larger countries, each with 7 to 11 million inhabitants. However, classified by population in world terms, these same countries rank towards the bottom third of smallest countries. Nine of the region's 15 economies have fewer than 300,000 inhabitants. Accordingly, these economies are characterized by their small size, below the world average and lower than the average for developing countries. At the regional level, Cuba stands out as one of the larger countries given its population and geographical surface area, which in principle permits it to have advantages on the flows of trade, investment and services.

Size not only is important from the perspective of the regional integration, but also influences the establishment of trade agreements with other regions or partners. However, Cuba has not participated in almost any of the trends in regional trade for the last 30 years. Lacking access to the U.S. market, it also remained excluded from all the modalities of collective agreements (such as the Brady Plan, and the Caribbean Basin Initiative and the more recent law, United States-Caribbean Basin Trade Partnership Act). It also has not participated in the 1986 CARIBCAN agreement with Canada that permits duty free access to 7.5 percent of the Caribbean's exports, nor in the current negotiations to expand its coverage.[10] However, since the mid-1990s Cuba's approximation to the region, including recent steps such as joint agreements for economic collaboration in tourism, transportation and trade,[11] has been gradually increasing through the Caribbean Community and Common Market (CARICOM).

Income Level

The majority of Caribbean countries are middle income, according to World Bank classification (see appendix). Nine have above-average per capita income levels relative to all middle income countries. Haiti is the only country in the low-income category (less than US$755 per capita on an annual basis), while the only country classified as high income is Bahamas. As the global trend in the flows of financing has been found to be clearly adverse for low-income countries, whereas middle income countries have been favored by greater flows, this factor represents a relative advantage for the Caribbean.

Cuba ranks in the lowest third within the low middle-income category, which would locate it among the nations with the lowest access to international flows. However, in practice this factor is not really the one that determines the degree of Cuba's access to investment flows. More critical factors include the high value of the country's risk,[12] the moratorium of payments since 1986 on the private foreign debt with the Paris Club, the low level of reserves[13] (domestic saving), its exclusion from the International Monetary Fund (IMF) and the World Bank, and provisions contained in U.S. laws, particularly the blockade and the Helms-Burton Bill, which veto or penalize almost any international financial transaction with Cuba.

Key Economic Sectors

The extraction of primary products has a relatively large significance in the Caribbean's economic activity, a characteristic shared with poor countries throughout the world. The provision of services also is a common feature of poor countries, with tourism common in almost all poor countries, and financial services and transportation in a few. In Cuba, exports of primary products represented 90 percent of total exports[14] between 1994 and 1998, while tourism has expanded significantly, displacing sugar as the principal foreign currency income source since the mid-1990s. Likewise, there is a great similarity with the products and services exported by the region. Except for oil that is dominant in only some countries, all have the same export base: crops and their derivatives (sugar, fruits, tobacco, beverages, etc.), minerals, seafood, and tourism-dominated services. It is also worth noting that the percentage share of export-oriented manufactured goods has accelerated in recent years, basically due to new provisions of market access to the United States and Europe.

Economic Structure

The richer the Caribbean country, the greater is the proportion of the service sector in the gross national product. In the four richest countries, services are roughly two-thirds of the gross national product. In the rest of Caribbean countries, the proportion is higher than the average for developing countries. That is, services have a determining influence on the level of economic activity. Their pattern of expansion points to the consolidation of a model based on the intensive use of labor and natural resources, rather than the expansion of the sector based on the utilization of knowledge, technologies and enhanced management techniques, as well as standards and procedures for quality control.

Growth

The Caribbean's real growth performance was 0.9 percent per year in 2003, significantly below the 2.6 percent average for Latin America (excluding the Caribbean). Since 2001, a change in growth trends has occurred due to the following factors:

a) Slowdown of world economic growth, especially of the U.S. economy, which reduced the growth rate of international export demand that had been increasing steadily for more than 10 years

b) A decline in world prices for primary commodities and manufactured goods that are based on primary goods

c) Characteristic difficulties for Caribbean economies that had to make numerous adjustments to maintain moderate inflation rates

Due to the impact of the fall in sugar prices and the instability of oil prices, as additional contributing factors, the Caribbean's export volumes were reduced in 2001. Imports of goods, however, surpassed the average for Latin America, increasing trade deficit pressures. In addition, the drop in tourism earnings related to the events of September 11 in the United States made it difficult for most countries in the region to finance their trade deficit.

As a result of the crisis that followed the shock in foreign trade with the Socialist Bloc, the Cuban economy contracted by 6.15 percent on average between 1989 and 1994 This trend reversed between 1994 and 1999 when annual growth rates averaged 3.45 percent, a relatively high percentage for the Caribbean and for Latin America during the same period. However, Cuba's growth rate fell to two percent per year from 2000 to 2002.

Trade Structures

In the economic and commercial integration process underway in the Caribbean, two basic patterns of incorporation can be identified. The first one is based on the formation of vertical flows for the production and export of manufactured goods destined primarily to the United States, basically comprised of textiles and components for the manufacture of several types of electric appliances and equipment. Although this trend is relatively higher in Central America and Mexico, there is a proportion of this trade that is distributed among countries in the Caribbean.

The second type of integration is one based on the merging of services, and involves several sectors and branches. Compared with the rest of Latin America, commercial services occupy a much greater proportion of total exports in the Caribbean, representing approximately one fourth of the income generated for all countries, regardless of profit levels. The share from manufactured earnings represents a much lesser share of GDP, although there has been a growing level of activity with respect to assembly for re-exporting in recent years. With respect to the change in the composition of exports, recent trends point toward a reduction of traditional crops and primary goods. For example, oil and coffee fell from 60 percent of overall exports to only 15 percent in 15 years. This displacement has been over-compensated by the increase in the share of exports derived from manufactured goods, assembly production, services (tourism and financial) and nontraditional agricultural goods (Table 5.1).

Table 5.1 CARICOM Distribution of Exports by Technology-Intensiveness, 1999–2001

(percentage)

Primary Products	Manufacturing based on natural resources	Manufacturing based on poor technology products	Manufacturing based on intermediate technology products	Manufacturing based on high-technology products
30.8	37.9	8.1	14.1	1.1

Source: Comisión Económica para América Latina y el Caribe, 2003. *Panorama de la inserción internacional de América Latina y el Caribe, 2001–2002*, Chapter IV, based on COMTRADE (United Nations Commodity Trade Database)

Intra and Inter-Regional Trade Patterns

Trade patterns—both within and with other regions—determine a set of restrictions inherent to the Caribbean with respect to a trade strategy promoting insertion in world markets. The region's principal trade partner is the Western Hemisphere and in particular North America (the United States and Canada acquire three-fifths of the exports and supply almost half of imports of the Caribbean), followed by the European Union (a fifth of exports and supplier of a sixth of imports) (Figure 5.1). Excluding intraregional trade, less than 3 percent of the Caribbean's trade is channeled toward Latin America. The enormous concentration of Caribbean trade toward North America has fallen as a consequence of the loss of competitiveness that resulted from the entry of Mexico into the North American Free Trade Agreement (NAFTA).

Figure 5.1 Caribbean Basin and Cuba: Trade with Other Regions, 1999
(percentage)

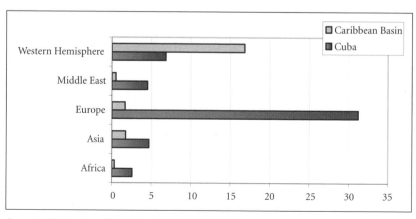

Source: IMF, *Direction of Trade Statistics Yearbook* (2000)

The preferential access now enjoyed by Mexican exports has displaced several relatively more competitive regional exporters, significantly affecting the region's revenue share.

With respect to intraregional trade, integrationist arrangements have helped increase trade to 21.4 percent of total trade in the Caribbean. However, this figure remains low. Historically, Cuba's trade with the Caribbean has been almost irrelevant (lower than two percent), and in addition, even after the increase that was caused in recent years by the trade re-orientation that followed the collapse of the COMECON, the relative weight of the Caribbean in the Cuban balance of trade continues to be very low,[15] averaging less than 4 percent between 1990 and 1999.

Limiting Factors for the Caribbean's Trade Strategy

The small size of domestic markets and their limited export base creates a lack of domestically generated resources to carry out significant restructuring processes in the short term. Export concentration in a small number of goods and services—chiefly primary products, *maquila* assembly, tourism and services— accentuates the region's vulnerability to changes in world markets. For example, *maquila* assembly exports depend entirely on unilateral preferential treatment granted by the United States, an agreement that can be modified at any moment for political reasons without consideration of local interests, which are less significant in comparison to U.S. domestic interests.

In turn, the social costs derived from modifying trade policies (tariffs, exchange rates, etc.) have an immediate impact that is amplified by the very structure of the economies. The profits that trade reform could return to the region's principal trade partners do not provide significant incentives to cause them to respond significantly in terms of trade volumes. This characteristic implies a paradox: the road to modifying the pattern of economic development in alignment with the course of the most dynamic global trends implies growing liberalization of the trade regime and progressive transformation of the current distribution of exports from primary products toward manufactured goods and services. However, the very structure of Caribbean economies, with their strong concentration on the export of a few goods and concentrated market destinations, creates a very rigid framework for maneuver that severely restricts the possibilities for carrying out trade reform.

This creates "trade-offs." On the one hand, there is pressure for rapid policy changes to restore export growth, thus avoiding both marginalization from new trade blocs and exclusion from preferential regime agreements. Even initial exclusion means that the opportunity to enter and be a part these accords will decrease. On the other hand, to accelerate beyond what is recommended in these processes has a strong likelihood of resulting in failure, given the high vulnerability and limited available resources for adaptation.

Moderate levels of economic growth highly dependent on European and North American markets also constrain the region. Although intra-Caribbean trade has increased, it remains relatively small, given the similarity in exports.[16] This helps to consolidate a strong asymmetry of a historical and insolvable character: trade with the Caribbean has very little relative weight in the U.S. trade balance, while the U.S. role in the region's external sector is decisive and tending to increase. Simultaneously, the European market is contracting, reducing or eliminating preferential treatments toward the region.

The current trend of the growing displacement of traditional primary exports towards services and manufactured goods such as assembly and textiles emerges from the characteristic need to accommodate investment and trade flows from the U.S. market in light of increases in European and Asian competition in Latin America (Gunn, 1997). The trend is a response, rather than a representation of an increase in regional productivity, in negotiating capacity or increased flexibility of tariff regimes. Manufacturing constitutes one of the most dynamic sectors in the general process of the region's restitution of exports. Within the manufacturing sector, textiles for some time have been one of the categories with better U.S. market access. However, in relative terms, this sector does not represent a key sector with respect to the U.S. trade balance. In this realm, the most recent initiative, the U.S. Act of Trade and Development for the Caribbean (TDA2000), also known as the U.S.–Caribbean Basin Trade Partnership Act of 2000 (CBTPA), constitutes an illustrative example in this regard.

Role of Trade in Development Strategy

There is an important difference that defines the role the external sector plays within a general development strategy. A development strategy constituted in an environment in which foreign trade is the principal focus is not the same as one in which the external sector is one of many elements and does not represent a priority determining the rest of the interrelationships within the economy. Cuba and other Caribbean countries all share the characteristic that the external sector is not one within several factors, but the vital axis for economic activity. To a greater or lesser extent, Caribbean Basin countries are all small economies with respect to international markets, incredibly open–given the limited diversity of domestic outputs—as a strategy to meet a significant proportion of their needs. To this end, they simply cannot reach rates of sustainable economic growth without externally financed support and provisions for market access.

Free Trade, Market Power and the Best Option for the Caribbean: Unilateral Liberalization or Collective Agreement?

The relatively small size of the of the Caribbean economies' combined market with regard to that of its principal partner, the United States weakens their capacity to implement a strategic trade policy agenda. In formal terms, under "classical" assumptions, conventional theory tends to identify as a "better option" the movement from tariff-protected markets toward free trade. Many studies, embracing different perspectives, frequently recommend this option.[17] Even when data indicates that trade liberalization is not necessarily the best option, it is argued that the results are not conclusive or at least insufficiently strong so as to rule out the trade liberalization strategy. Accordingly, the removal of trade barriers is at least a matter of "improving the benefits for at least one country without worsening outcomes for the rest (Pareto efficiency)" in which national interests and the relative power of economies do not influence the most efficient assignment carried out from and for the market.

Nevertheless, despite substantial tariff reductions in almost all countries in recent years, tariffs of one or another type still predominate in today's world. Significantly, incentives still exist in particular for large countries—with their technological endowments and human and natural resources—to maintain tariffs, challenging the precept that free trade brings Pareto-efficient distribution through which all benefit. The explanation for this situation partly has to do with the capacity of a country to influence prices, the effect of country "size," and how this is expressed in practice with respect to tariff policy.

Small countries (price takers) do not have any influence on world market prices. Sufficiently large countries, on the other hand, find themselves in a similar situation to that of a monopoly, being able to select the volume of export production to the degree that it influences world market prices and thus maintain production levels in order to maximize profits. Trade theory has proven that under traditional assumptions, there exists an optimal tariff that can improve the trade conditions of a large country, though this has parallel effects that distort production and consumption, "because the profits from an improvement in the terms of trade through tariffs exceed the losses due to distortions" (Chichilnisky 1995 and Krugman and Obstfeld 1998). This advantage of one country over others naturally raises the counterpoint that in response, others may also seek a "strategic" maximization of tariffs resulting in a scenario of interactions concluding with a "balance of optimal tariffs." This already differs in practice from the balance achieved by the free market whereby some countries are better than others in view of their capacity to influence prices based on their greater economic size (Kennan and Riezman 1988; 1990). This is nothing else but the "rational" response to maximize via the economic incentives of "market power" instead of Pareto-type optimization.

The same argument can be extended to interactions between regional commercial blocs. The creation of free trade areas renders greater market share for agreement members who can utilize their collective strength to impose or maintain higher tariffs than those that apply within member countries to nonmember countries. Accordingly, although economic theory posits the desirability of moving economies in the direction of trade liberalization, in practice the most advisable strategy for smaller countries is not to liberalize "on their own" without first "harmonizing" themselves purposely toward regional options for free trade zones.

Despite various efforts aimed at consensus building, the real outcomes for Caribbean countries have progressed in the opposite direction. The composition of current tariffs demonstrates that these have been shaped on the basis of a process of historical accumulation of policies taken at different times for dissimilar reasons. Each country has adopted tariffs and quantitative restrictions to specifically respond to particular circumstances or in order to "protect" or respond to the interests of specific domestic groups. The disparity of these measures indicates that an attempt has not been undertaken to identify "social" returns based on comparative advantages or of potential comparative advantages.[18]

The utilization of discretionary and non-tariff restrictions have increased social costs, thus putting more pressure on the appreciation of the exchange rate. In turn, the stronger exchange rate further hinders movements aimed at liberalizing trade and reducing the power of domestic agents who benefit from restrictions that generate artificial profits. In the end, regardless of whether domestic pressures to maintain a certain level of tariff protection or limit market access are justified, it is a fact that the low relative weight of Caribbean economies gives them little to almost no capacity to influence decision-making processes concerning trade both at the international level and in its principal market, the United States.

Access to the U.S. Market

The trade relations of the Caribbean with the United States have two fundamental axes: the Caribbean Basin Initiative and the United States-Caribbean Basin Trade Partnership Act as a part of the Trade and Development Act of 2000 (TDA2000). U.S. policies and trade practices toward Latin America have become more complex with regard to the instruments and the means for guaranteeing both greater effective access for Latin American exports and a more diversified protection for U.S. producers who could be affected by these same measures. The following trends with respect to U.S. trade policy should be noted:

- Promotion of agricultural U.S. exports through financing for exporters in terms of research and development, openness of markets, development of trademarks and credit guarantees for imports
- Imposition of antidumping and countervailing duties (particularly in case of key outputs for the region, such as food, minerals and chemical products)
- Preferential access granted on the basis of bilateral or multilateral agreements
- Application of quotas (especially sugar, which turns out to be particularly restricted due to the interests of U.S. corn producers)
- Escalation of tariffs, which increase as the proportion of the manufactured content of these goods rises (at the same time that this also confers on them a greater value-added

For example, credit guarantees for exports are covered under the new Law of Agricultural Security and Rural Investment administered through the U.S. Department of Agriculture that grants credits of six months to three years (GSM-102), and from three to ten years (GSM-103). Moreover, the Commodity Credit Corporation (CCC) for agricultural products can cover up to 98 percent of the principal and part of the interests of the credits granted by U.S. financial institutions to select foreign banks, that in turn issue bills of credit for importers of U.S. products.

Financing

Trade expansion is greatly determined by access to financing. In case of the United States, a network of government-affiliated institutions traditionally has played a role in supporting and promoting trade, particularly in the case of Caribbean countries. These institutions include:

- FCIA, Foreign Credit Insurance Association: insurance for U.S. exporters against commercial and political risks

- Eximbank, the Export-Import Bank of the United States: export financing through direct loans, intermediate loans for third parties (banks or companies), insurance and guarantees for purchases of goods produced in the U.S. bound for export

- CCC, Commodity Credit Corporation: financial services for goods of an agricultural origin

- OPIC, Overseas Private Investment Corporation: a self-financing federal corporation aimed to assists U.S. investors in developing countries and emerging economies through project financing, investment insurance and investor services

- USAID, U.S. Agency for International Development: assistance programs and development projects through economic support funds, special assistance initiatives and development assistance for small development projects (apart from economic policy and structural adjustment programs)

- SBA, Small Business Administration: protection and support for U.S. business with information and special services for small exporters, such as its Export Legal Assistance Network and its International Trade Loan Program that guarantees up to 85 percent of loans up to US$1 million for business that meet its size requirements

- TDA, U.S. Trade and Development Agency: funding for various forms of technical assistance, feasibility studies, training, orientation visits and business workshops that support the development of a modern infrastructure and a fair and open trading environment

The latter framework is particularly relevant for this study since TDA has served as the point agency for the most recent political commercial initiative for the Caribbean—United States-Caribbean Basin Trade Partnership Act in 2000.[19] The TDA represents a shift in the strategy promoting closer economic ties with the Caribbean. In practice, the negotiation model based on "fast track," which Congress rejected on several occasions, has been replaced with the "NAFTA Parity Bill," a regimen oriented toward specific commercial initiatives that assumes a selective and step-wise treatment across time. On the one hand, this increases the tendency toward the conditionality of U.S. assistance toward these countries. On the other hand, it facilitates the Congressional approval process. The enactment of the TDA was the first time in ten years that the U.S. Congress has approved a trade policy not under a "fast-track" scheme and the first trade legislation approved in six years.

Tariffs

The tariff systems in Latin America and the United States differ in systems and methods. Latin America uses an ad valorem system of the FOB value at the point of export, while the structure in the United States and the European Union is much more heterogeneous, including:

- Specific tariffs (by unit of weight, volume, number of parts, and seasons)
- Tariff quotas (quantitative restrictions)
- Special regimes

Policies and business practices are another facet of the problem. In several instances, these have proven to have an impact greater than tariffs, which on average tend to be short-term with a tendency to decrease over time. In 2001, CARICOM countries had tariff-free access to the U.S. market for 72.7 percent of the total goods, if the applied ad valorem duties are taken as a reference (Table 5.2). However, a more detailed examination reveals that tariffs are levied well above the average for those products providing true sources of income such as food and manufactured goods, including textile, footwear, leather, tobacco, chemicals and sugar. In other words, there is a high dispersion in the U.S. tariff structure; the standard deviation is greater than the average at more than two and one-half times (Table 5.3). For example, there are specific and composed tariffs (for chemical products, textiles and sugar) and in the case of tobacco the value paid (ad valorem) is 350 percent.

Table 5.2 Ad Valorem Duties: Charged by the U.S. on CARICOM Imports
(US$ million)

Total Value (US$ million)	Taxable Value (US$ million)	Perceived Duties %	Duty-Free %	Taxable Ad Valorem Equivalent %	Tariff Rate as % of Total Import value
3,899	1,065	15	72.7	1.4	0.4

Source: Comisión Económica para América Latina y el Caribe, 2003. *Panorama de la inserción internacional de América Latina y el Caribe, 2001-2002*, Chapter IV, Table IV.1

Table 5.3 U.S. Tariff Structure, 1996–2000
(percentage)

Indicators	1996	1998[b]	1999[b]	2000
Simple average tariff[a]	6.40	5.90	5.70	5.40
Agricultural products (WTO definition)[b]	10.00	10.30	10.70	10.40
Non-agricultural products (WTO definition)	5.70	5.00	4.70	4.50
Items with tariffs above 15% (as a percentage of the total)	8.90	7.70	7.40	7.00
Standard deviation	13.40	12.90	13.30	13.10
Coefficient variation	2.10	2.19	2.34	2.38

a. Contingent tariffs are excluded.
b. Includes Chapters 1–24, except fisheries and fish products, and the SA 2905.43, 2905.4, 3809.10 and 3823.60 sections, as well as other categories covered in SA 33.01, 35.01–35.05, 41.01–41.03, 43.01, 50.01-50.03, 51.01–51.03, 52.01–52.03, 53.01 and 53.02.

Source: Comisión Económica para América Latina y el Caribe, 2003. *Panorama de la inserción internacional de América Latina y el Caribe, 2001-2002*, Chapter IV, Table IV.2

Fiscal Aspects, Role of the Tariffs in Terms of Income

The high relative share of fiscal revenues derived from tariffs is essential for Caribbean economies. This factor creates an important limitation both from the standpoint of macroeconomic policy and the commercial side. Despite the trend toward decreasing tariff revenues, these continue to be a source of income without a short-term substitute for some countries (Table 5.4). Though Cuba has gradually been reducing its average tariffs, the share of tariff revenue as a share of GDP has been increasing, though at a moderate rate (Tables 5.5 and 5.6).

Table 5.4 CARICOM and Cuba: Tariffs as a Share of Fiscal Revenues, 1996

Country	Percentage
Anguilla	77.00
Antigua and Barbuda	66.10
Dutch Antilles	39.16
Bahamas	59.98
Barbados	8.60
Belize	52.39
Dominica	56.50
Granada	16.77
Cayman Islands	42.16
Jamaica	14.00
Montserrat	52.50
Dominican Republic	44.80
Saint Lucia	58.70
St. Vincent and Grenadines	40.80
St. Kitts y Nevis	55.20
Suriname	41.70
Trinidad and Tobago	10.40
Cuba*	*1.85*

Sources: Except for Cuba, data is from CEPAL (1999) *Panorama de la inserción internacional de América Latina y el Caribe* 1997–1998, Table VI.1, page 128. *Data for Cuba is from ONE, *Anuario estadístico de Cuba* 1999, page 96

Table 5.5 Tariff Revenue, 1995–1998
(millions of pesos)

Year	GDP in Current Prices	Income from Tariff	Tariff Income as a % of GDP
1995	21,737	269	1.24
1996	22,815	423	1.85
1997	22,952	351	1.53
1998	23,901	386	1.61
1999	25,504	410	1.61

Sources: Calculations based on ONE, *Anuario estadístico de Cuba* 1999, page 96

Table 5.6 Cuba: Annual Average Tariff, 1989–1999
(percentage)

Year	Average Tariff
1989	0.700
1990	0.515
1991	0.340
1992	0.238
1993	0.238
1994	0.238
1995	0.238
1996	0.238
1997	0.107
1998	0.107
1999	0.107

Source: Author's estimates based on interviews with experts

Competitiveness and the Regional Framework

Traditional Comparative Advantages and Economies of Scale

In recent years, Latin American exports have evolved generally toward growing dynamism in several exports due to the benefits of agreements of integration or free bilateral and multilateral trade. However, a significant part of that evolution is the result of the Mexican-side of the North American Free Trade Agreement (NAFTA) and the strengthening of trade within MERCOSUR and the Central American Common Market. In that overall export evolution process, the Caribbean has scarcely participated. In fact, recent studies show that there has been a concentration toward few exports whose growth rates have only increased as a consequence of the progressive application of the TDA2000, and not as a result of insertion of more dynamic international production chains. The composition of Caribbean exports shows that despite changes in recent years towards exports with greater technological content, most are still primary commodities and manufactures based on natural resources, with low degree of "technological intensity" compared to the average for Latin America (Table 5.7).

Table 5.7 Export Structure by Technology-Intensiveness, 1999–2001[a]
(percentage of total exports)

Regions	Primary Products	Natural Resource Based Primary Products	Manufactured Goods with Low Levels of Technology	Manufactured Goods with Intermediate Levels of Technology	Manufactured Goods with High Levels of Technology
Latin America and the Caribbean	27.3	17.5	12.2	26.1	16.9
CARICOM[b]	38.8	37.9	8.1	14.1	1.1

a. Some of the totals exclude some groups—351, 883, 892, 896, 911, 931, 941, 961 and 971— as these pertained to special categories.
b. The average between 1999–2001 roughly corresponds to the information for 1998–2000.

Source: Comisión Económica para América Latina y el Caribe (CEPAL), 2003. *Panorama de la inserción internacional de América Latina y el Caribe, 2001–2002.* Table III.1, pg.4. based on COMTRADE (UN Commodity Trade Database)

In this panorama, Cuba constitutes a separate case. Despite the strong geographical reorientation of foreign trade which followed the Socialist Bloc's collapse, the structural composition of its trade portfolio remains dominated by primary products with a very low level of participation of other exports with greater technology or human capital content (Table 5.8). Contradictorily, the displacement toward tourism as a primary source of income has only transferred the structural problem from sugar to services. Tourist services reflect essentially the same type of trade insertion. They too do not take advantage of already accumulated labor resources accrued from years of investment in education and professional training. This trait, together with an appropriate infrastructure, "potentially" could permit the retrofitting of industries towards the production of manufactured goods and electric appliances bound for export. However, this assumes that Cuba could obtain similar access to the U.S. market as the rest of the region, with relatively minimal costs.

Competitiveness of Cuba within the CARICOM Framework

Several products and services are likely to be exported successfully by U.S. companies in joint ventures as exemplified by the Central American market, once Cuba is able to participate in an equal playing field.

Table 5.8 Cuba's Exports: Dynamics and Composition
(US$ million)

Product Group	1998 Value	1994–98 % Growth	% of 1998 Exports
Primary Products	1181	0	90
Manufactured Goods Intensive in:			
Natural resources	61	26	5
Labor	5	4	0
Technology	31	−26	2
Human Capital	20	5	2

Source: WTO International Trade Commission—ITC (2001). Calculations based on statistics of COMTRADE. For further detail see, http://www.intracen.org/countries/htm99/cub.htm

This change could be associated with an important increase in the use of technologies and quality improvements. Such is the case of services in computer technologies, communications, materials, and services for the construction industries, tourism, air and maritime transport, products and techniques for agricultural application, to cite a few examples. It will be necessary to delve further into the evaluation of these alternatives with more precision, but as first approximation, the options of insertion in the regional market based on the trade-offs in competitiveness should be identified in order to effectively orient future studies. The selection of "indicator areas" presented below does not constitute in itself a "definitive" criterion for valuation, at the most a minimum comparative reference, prepared with aspects that are most frequently taken into account for agreements of this type and summarized in Table 5.9. [20]

- *Availability and the cost of capital.* In this case, Cuba is severely restricted, with a high country risk, without membership in the principal international finance institutions, with a low level of foreign currency reserves, with a high level of external debt depending on negotiations and pressures from the North American blockade. In this aspect, Cuba should be qualified below the country average in the region with respect to access to credit.

- *Government regulation.* Despite having reformed the system of state monopoly on foreign trade, a strong level of trade regula-

Table 5.9 Cuba's Comparative Advantages in Comparison with CARICOM

Source	Valuation
Availability and the cost of capital	*Insufficient*
Government regulation	*Above average*
Skilled labor	*Above average*
Macroeconomic and fiscal policy	*Moderate*
Marketing	*Insufficient*
Design and quality of exportable goods	*Below average*
Productivity	*Below average*
Quality of administration and control	*Insufficient*
Natural resource endowments	*Above average*
Tax structure (tariffs and non-tariff barriers)	*Below average*
Technology (industrial factories)	*Moderate*
Transportation infrastructure	*Above average*
Salaries	*Below average*

Source: Author's estimates based on interviews with experts. The level is classified with reference to CARICOM standards. The scale has been created with the following values: above average, moderate (equal to the regional average), below average and insufficient.

tion still exists in Cuba compared with that of its neighbors. This represents an advantage with regard to the mobilization of limited resources, but a disadvantage in terms of prioritized projects. However, it constitutes a disadvantage for those companies not ranked among its priorities, as well as for medium and small businesses.

- *Skilled labor.* The general and professional levels of education in Cuba guarantee great flexibility with respect to technology assimilation and advancement of productive procedures.

- *Macroeconomic and Fiscal Policy.* Institutional and regulatory reform has been undertaken with caution and gradualism in the Cuban economy. Although numerous and yet unresolved structural problems persist, the government has been consistent with the adjustment strategies undertaken. In general, international observers generally accept the evaluation that it is not worth anticipating drastic changes in the medium term.[21]

- *Marketing.* If a few products whose identity, brand names, or exclusive character does not make them representative (tobacco, rum, nickel and some intellectual property rights) are excluded, marketing activity in Cuba is not comparable with the average levels in the CARICOM. This is also influenced by the fact that an important part of the region's marketing services are imports or benefits of first-rate international agencies based in highly developed economies such as the United States and United Kingdom.

- *Design and quality of exportable goods.* In the past three years, Cuban industries have advanced in important ways, particularly in regard to the so-called "exports within the borders" or outputs destined for the domestic market in foreign exchange. However, on average, these are still below the levels of presentation and regional quality, although great varieties of outputs in tourism (and a few services) have demonstrated notable improvement in quality.

- *Productivity.* Cuba's productivity rate has slowly recovered, but is still insufficient to sustain a sufficiently strong rate to compensate for other adverse factors and bring about economic recovery. Taking into account only outputs linked to exports, the average indicator is above average, but the value of this assessment is questionable because the calculations of labor costs are made on the basis of an overvalued exchange rate.

- *Quality of administration and control.* Greater efforts to achieve reliable accounting systems in the companies by central Cuban economic management agencies remains. Even in those sectors linked and ranked among the highest in terms of foreign exchange income, this indicator is considered below average, largely a result of the absence of a control system that includes bankruptcy and a market for domestic financial claims—an indispensable prerequisite that is still in the midst of an unfinished merging process.

- *Natural resource endowments.* In this regard, Cuba has a very favorable situation. In addition, it has advantages of scale, since it far surpasses resources in broad proportions in terms of volumes compared with other CARICOM countries (for example, tourism, sugar, nickel mining, fishing, citrus fruits).

- *Technology (Industrial Factories).* This element was classified as moderate. Although high levels of technological obsolescence remain in some branches, an important level of reserves exists in terms of productive capacity that can be exploited in very little time with minimal investments for its reactivation. As a result of investments made in previous decades that maintained a configuration characterized by "low efficiency and an abundance of resources to be invested,"[22] many industries use technologies that consume a great quantity of energy, contaminate the environment and are generally inefficient in terms of current requirements. However, the situation is complex to diagnose. Alongside these obsolete plants, another generation of new investments has been incorporating state-of-the-art technologies that are highly competitive, precisely in the sectors linked with electric generation, oil and gas extraction, services, and exports, in short, those with greater weight in this analysis.

- *Tax structure (tariffs and non-tariff barriers)*. Although Cuban tariffs by the standard of origin are lower than those in the Caribbean, existing structural barriers, such as the lack of access to the domestic market and bureaucratic controls, are a constant subject in discussions among foreign business executives and representatives.[23] Consultation mechanisms that seek to create more expeditious approval procedures for the approval of product lists, facilitation of transactions and other transactions are being promoted. However, in practice, there are additional procedures that make the insertion in the world market complex. This factor was classified as below average for the time being because it is not compatible with Caribbean levels.

- *Transportation infrastructure*. Cuba has above-average infrastructure in terms of its communication, roads, ports, and airport networks, although the sector requires significant investment in order to modernize its services to satisfactory operational levels. Relative to the scale in the CARICOM, the country has a fairly significant aviation fleet, as well as maritime container services that operate separately or in association with contractors.

- *Salaries*. The compensation systems in export-linked industries do not resemble the remaining procedures in this area. Although wage stimulation mechanisms have permitted notable increases in productivity in some outputs, this problem is often cited for the effect it has in generating incentives toward the double payment of the workforce in resident companies in Cuba. This indicator is classified as below average.

Cuba: Revealed Comparative Advantages

From a standard perspective, the evaluation of revealed comparative advantages of export-oriented production for Cuba offers some interesting elements. In trade simulations, as well as in terms of real performance, Cuba's external sector is oriented toward a structure that consists of a high relative proportion of goods including fresh food (in real terms), textiles, minerals and processed food (in the simulations, see Figure 5.2). In the real case, this is due to the high share of sugar as a proportion of total exports of goods (around 90 percent). This is confirmed in the two simulations[24] by Preeg and Levine (1993) and Montenegro and Soto (1996) but at a reduced rate due to the presence of differing levels of exports of textiles, processed foods and mining products in the proxy countries.

As Figure 5.2 indicates, the profile that is obtained in real terms, as well as in simulations, underscores a trend towards a specialization in

Figure 5.2 Revealed Comparative Advantages for Cuba in Actual and in Two "Proxy" Versions

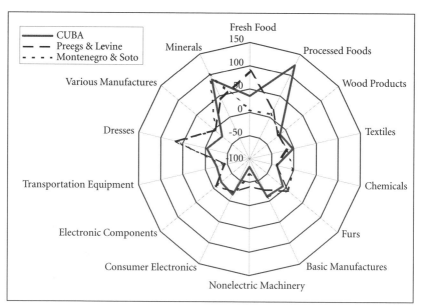

Source: Prepared by the author with data from the WTO-ITC and proxies obtained from Preeg and Levine (1993) and Montenegro and Soto (1996)

primary good exports and a low share of manufacturing or goods with a high share of human capital, such as electronic products (consumer goods, components) manufactured textiles (dresses) and non-electrical equipment, which are precisely the sectors with the greatest growth overall in world trade. Consequently, despite Cuba's existing potential with respect to existing human capital and infrastructure endowments, its trade structure continues to be regressively oriented toward the primary sector, whose overall share is declining in world trade as manufactured trade continues to expand.

Trade with the United States: A Gravity Model Simulation and its Results

A common and widely accepted technique for estimating potential trade volumes between countries or trade blocs is the gravity model,[25] whose name alludes to the principles embodied by the law of physics with the same name. It is based on the premise that trade flows between countries are determined by two opposing forces—the overall level of economic activity and income levels that are comprised by the export and import demand potential and the obstacles to trade including transport costs due to distance, trade policies and cultural differences. The combination of both forces has proven to be a reliable predictor in empirical estimates of trade (Havrylyshin and Pritchett (1991), Frankel and Wei (1993), Bayoumi and Eichengreen (1995) and are widely used by the World Trade Organization.[26] The theoretical foundations for the gravity model were developed by Bergstrand (1989) and Helpman & Krugman (1985). In essence, the method consists of identifying a pattern of trade for a specific geographic area or group of countries based on real flows of trade. Based on estimates obtained from standardized parameters, expected values of commerce are estimated for the countries under study. The contrast between real commercial values and those obtained by simulations allows one to identify if the country is above or below its expected value.

Gravity models are only a limited way of expressing determinants of trade and prices. These models use variables that depend on comparing data in a systematic form. However, their utilization, which began in investigations on bilateral trade began in the 1960s, has steadily increased, particularly in the past decade. The surge in new trends of integration and global trade expansion, has spurred the use of gravity models, proving their usefulness in analyzing the effects of incorporation into or exclusion from trade agreements.[27]

Gravity models use regression equations to obtain a "natural" or anticipated trade pattern by modeling the flow of a defined independent variable—free trade, exports or imports—between country "r" (reporter) and country "p" (partner) as a function of key factors such as the size of the economy, understood as the level of economic activity and/or income. A larger economy can be assumed to have greater demand for imports and a larger supply of exports, depending on its degree of trade liberalization and population density. In a similar manner, per capita income is used as a factor to identify economies with higher income levels, a factor that creates a stronger demand for consumer products, and hence the probablility of more imports.

Another key factor in gravity models is the geographic distance[28] between countries in a broad sense of the word, including communications and services. These distances determine the costs of transportation. Complementary variables such as trade agreement participation, cultural and language affinities, shared borders, and specific trade policies provide a high—or quite acceptable—level of consistency as an explanation for variability in the data.[29]

In the case of potential trade between Cuba and the United States, the trade simulations performed to date have utilized three approaches:

- Identification of the trade volumes expected by sectors and in aggregate terms based on restricted foreign currency resources and a conventional trade model (USITC 2001)

- Adjustment for the level of distortion in Cuban trade with respect to trade between other countries in the Caribbean and the United States (Montenegro & Soto 1996)

- Factoring of the impact of possible participation in differing trade integration schemes with Latin America and its possible impact on bilateral trade between Cuba and the United States (Selva 1997)

This section presents the results of a gravity simulation model. The purpose of these estimates is twofold:

1) To verify whether there were significant changes with respect to previous estimates, given that significant trade re-orientations have taken place in the short term during the latter part of the 1990s and the notable increase in market volatility with Cuba's trade partners

2) To establish how income level in aggregate and per capita terms impact trade flow stimulations

The results presented in Table 5.10 were obtained from the application of a conventional gravity model for a first sample of 65 countries as "reporter" and 100 countries as "partner" from which was derived an "aggregate" model, where economies that were not considered appropriate were not included. Both large countries and economies heavily dependent on oil exports were excluded as these distort the reference values. A second version of the model was run limiting the "reporter" countries to the 13 members of the CARICOM and this is called "Caribbean Basin" following the approach taken by Montenegro and Soto (1996). The data utilized for 1997 was taken from IMF's Direction of Trade Statistics. Three variants from the simulations are presented in Table 5.10. The first variant includes all the variables. The second attempts to quantify the impact of the Heckscher-Olin effect, that is, to measure to what extent the level of income (economic activity) of each country could affect potential trade. The third variant excludes per capita income in order to control for the probable distortion that stems from the increase of the presence of high flows of income reported by Caribbean countries whose economies have an important share of financial service operations.

What is interesting in this exercise is that in the final version, the sign of the coefficient for per capita income (GDPPC) has a smaller variability in magnitude between the global version and the version estimated for the Caribbean Basin. Concerning the coefficient for the NAFTA variable, there is an increase in the value associated with this coefficient when the estimate was run for countries in the Caribbean in the third variant. This is due to the fact that the relative effect of the increase in trade in the case of Mexico (being a part of NAFTA) is much greater if it is compared with the Caribbean than that which is estimated from the group of 65 countries in the "general" sample. The initial results of Montenegro and Soto (1996) were confirmed, although on this occasion greater precision is given to the role of regional factors in the configuration of trade flows. Finally, a value of U.S.–Cuba trade in the first year equivalent to some US$2,602 000 million was estimated, which locates the projection well within the range already obtained by previous studies (Montenegro and Soto 1996, Selva 1997 and USITC 2001), with different methodologies, but quite convergent assumptions (Figure 5.3).

Table 5.10 Trade: Estimates from Gravity Model Simulations
a) Global (65x100 countries) b) Caribbean Basin (13x100 countries)

1997 (Method: TOBIT Canonic)	Model I				Model II: Heckscher-Olin Effect				Model III: Final Version			
	(a) Global		(b) Caribbean Basin		(a) Global		(b) Caribbean Basin		(a) Global		(b) Caribbean Basin	
	Coefficient	Z-statistic	Coefficient	Z-statistic	Coefficient	Z-statistic	Coefficient	Z-statistic	Coefficient	Z-statistic	Coefficient	Z-statistic
Intercept	4.187409	11.63209	5.654618	4.553174	5.030874	15.32729	5.038719	4.824124	4.235649	11.82535	4.772360	3.878782
GDP	0.719968	50.85403	0.415529	10.44909	0.758913	61.18631	0.395658	11.87072	0.720832	50.93661	0.413681	10.30745
GDPPC	0.114657	5.582700	-0.057694	-0.915246	0.043963	2.749837	0.189535	4.035797	0.097450	6.045999	0.089807	1.816542
Dif.GDPPC	-0.026126	-1.289274	0.224328	3.713893								
Distance	-0.918100	-24.53333	-0.704393	-6.429134	-0.914159	-24.32121	-0.689288	-6.359562	-0.919222	-24.58001	-0.655242	-5.969830
Border	0.827969	5.818587	0.586240	1.237126	0.834103	5.835182	0.598155	1.261853	0.847418	5.986018	0.531995	1.112846
Language	0.561968	7.583898	0.086761	0.432404	0.603140	8.142398	0.074593	0.372314	0.573194	7.781440	-0.037030	-0.185422
Island	0.097365	1.749645	0.767849	5.457189	0.116533	2.088507	0.759981	5.407420	0.097438	1.750701	0.766969	5.400065
NAFTA	-0.093176	-0.089285	1.676650	1.188194	-0.149693	-0.142800	1.712559	1.213256	-0.112334	-0.107631	1.875047	1.317526
CARICOM	0.249875	0.863996	0.140437	0.315279	0.391852	1.354258	0.128499	0.288393	0.264478	0.914831	0.192386	0.428135
APEC	1.573202	11.56779	0.767400	1.450426	1.624995	11.92268	0.778339	1.470432	1.587487	11.70884	0.631386	1.185212
ANDEAN	0.446351	1.196250	0.447886	0.655847	0.515745	1.376753	0.459531	0.672541	0.465657	1.248713	0.375855	0.545528
CACM	1.062420	3.108029	0.081501	0.154640	1.148548	3.348190	0.109358	0.207694	1.062378	3.107344	0.267134	0.504449
Adjusted R²	0.650223		0.317039		0.646067		0.317010		0.649100		0.303306	

Figure 5.3 Cuba and the Caribbean Basin, Trade with the U.S., 1999
(percent)

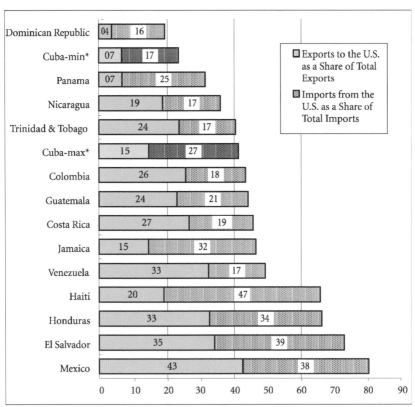

* Cuba-min represents a minimum estimate of exports to the United States. *Cuba-max* represents a maximum estimate of exports to the United States.

Source: Results obtained by the author based on gravity models described above with separate estimates for exports and imports based on data from IMF, *Direction of Trade Statistics Yearbook* (2000). In the case of Cuba, two estimates were computed.

This methodology has its limitations since it excludes other factors that might indeed be significant. For example, it does not take into account drastic changes in conditions regarding access to financing for trade and/or the external debt, as well as unforeseen modifications in investment flows and in access to current markets, whether for political reasons or necessities generated by Cuba's domestic situation. Another important element in the limitation of this methodology is the uncertainty about the way in which Cuba will come to terms with bilateral trade. Up until now, both parties have conducted themselves in a pragmatic fashion through trade operations authorized by special licenses, with totally atypical agreement terms—including transportation, cash payments, insurance and other conditions—in the context of general trade practices. Paradoxically, this circumstance makes the Cuban market the only risk-free market today in terms of payments. The fact that Cuban purchases are made today throughout the United States contributes to creating a perception of demand that probably would not exist in normalized trade conditions.

Conclusions

For the Caribbean as a whole, the strategic limitations of integration and commercial policy are due to the following factors:

- As the size of economies is small, "market power" is weak and there is a reduced level of influence in terms of volumes and prices in world trade (price and quota takers).

- Intraregional trade is insignificant, as is the level of macro-economic convergence (international reserves, exchange and fiscal stability) due to internal asymmetries.

- The industrial structure is minimally diversified and is highly dependent on foreign trade and preferential market access mechanisms.

- Exports are concentrated in "less dynamic" products with regard to the international flows (primary products—mining and food, as well as manufactures with limited technological applications—textiles and dresses) resulting from "adaptive" processes and not "proactive policies" of incorporation into international investment and trade chains.

- The structural pattern of integration into international trade is based on mixed schemes: a) "vertical" flows of manufactures, and b) services (tourism, financial, transportation), with goods intensive in the use of labor and natural resources. There is limited incorporation of technology and knowledge, in particular in the area of information technologies and communications that constitute a decisive factor in the merger of institutional frameworks, commercial practices and more effective policies.

- There is high dependency of fiscal revenues derived from tariffs.

- Although significant share of exports do not pay tariffs in the

U.S. market (72 percent in 2001), there is a strong vulnerability with respect to principal exports (food, textiles, minerals, tobacco) at restrictive treatment from the United States by means of specific tariffs, special regimes, policies of progressive, scaled-up tariffs and quotas.

This set of elements results in a scenario of "continuity" in the medium term (two to four years). It is expected that principal efforts will be oriented toward a combination of attempts aimed at preserving the preferential trade arrangements that have been secured to date in primary products—mining and food—together with a parallel effort to diversify and expand the growth of services (tourism) and manufactures of low technological complexity (textiles, assembly of electric appliances).

Despite similarities in productive structure, exports and macroeconomic limitations, Cuba's trajectory shows more differentiation than convergence with the other Caribbean countries. Cuba's lack of access to the U.S. market marks the most important difference, explaining the current totally different geographic trade pattern. Based on the estimates using a gravity model, trade with the United States in either of the two versions of the model presented, (one derived from a general scheme, the second on a Caribbean scale), the expected maximum and minimum volumes do not represent an important short-term increase in Cuba's current trade. This result implies that the "diversion" of trade instead of the "creation" effect will predominate in the near term. This estimation indicates that Cuba would be below the Caribbean median or near the minimum level by current regional standards with respect to U.S. trade.

In a scenario of steady increase in trade between Cuba and the United States, the estimated potential rise of Cuban exports and imports does not substantially reduce Cuba's current trade deficit due to a relatively high share of domestic absorption and the continuing need for short-term credits with high interest rates. This calculation of potential trade assumes that Cuba will not receive special financing flows different from the regional average. It also assumes that Cuba will not be a party to the preferential access enjoyed by its principal potential competitors in the Caribbean, since this access has resulted from bilateral or multilateral treaties of long standing. For Cuba, unlike the rest of the region, under the established assumptions increased trade with the United States should not be expected to result in changes in its:

1) Foreign trade portfolio

2) Rate of dependency of current Cuban economic growth on access to external financing

3) Dominant role of domestic absorption in sustaining most dynamic Cuban industries

Thus, the current core differences with regard to geographical environment should persist in the next few years.

References

Anderson, James E. and Peter Neary. 1994. "Measuring the Restrictiveness of Trade Policy." *World Bank Economic Review*, 8:1, 151–169.

Anderson, K., J. Francois, J., T. Hertel, B. Hoekman, and W. Martin. 2000. "Potential Gains from Trade Reform in the New Millennium," paper presented at the Third Annual Conference on Global Economic Analysis, Monash University, Mt. Eliza, Australia.

Balassa, Bela and Associates. 1971. *The Structure of Protection in Developing Countries*. Baltimore: published for the International Bank for Reconstruction and Development and the Inter-American Development Bank by the Johns Hopkins Press.

Balassa, Bela. 1982. "Development Strategies in Semi-Industrial Countries." Baltimore: published for the World Bank by Johns Hopkins University Press.

Barro, Robert J., and Sala-i-Marti, Xavier. 1995. *Economic Growth*. New York: McGraw Hill.

Bayoumi, Tamin and Barry Eichengreen. 1995. "Is Regionalism Simply a Diversion? Evidence from the Evolution of the EC and EFTA." NBER Working Paper 5283.

Bergstrand, J. 1985. "The Gravity Model in International Trade: Some Microeconomic Foundations and Empirical Evidence." *Review of Economics and Statistics*, 67: 474–481.

Chichilnisky, Graciela. 1995. "Strategies for the Liberalization of the Trade in the Americas," in *The Liberalization of the Trade in the Western Hemisphere*. Washington D.C.: IDB and CEPAL.

Clark, Ximena and Tavares, José. 2000. "A Quantitative Approach Using the Gravity Equation." Development Discussion Paper No. 748. Central America Project Series, Harvard Institute for International Development.

Davis, Donald R. and David E. Weinstein. 1997. "Economic Geography and Regional Production Structure: An Empirical Investigation." NBER Working Paper 6093.

Davis, Donald R. and David E. Weinstein. 1997. "Does Economic Geography Matter for International Specialization." NBER 5706.

Dollar, David. 1992. "Outward-Oriented Developing Economies Really do Grow More Rapidly: Evidence from 95 LDCs, 1976–1985." *Economic Development and Cultural Change*, 40: 523–544.

Edwards, Sebastian. 1993. "Openness, Trade Liberalization and Growth in Developing Countries." *Journal of Economic Literature*, 31(3), p. 1358–93.

Edwards, Sebastian. 1997. "Openness, Productivity and Growth: What Do We Really Know." NBER Working Paper 5978.

Comisión Económica para América Latina y el Caribe CEPAL. 2003. "Panorama de la inserción internacional de América Latina y el Caribe, 2001–2002." Accessed at http://www.cepal.cl/cgi-bin/getProd.asp?xml=/publicaciones/xml/3/11663/P11663.xml&xsl=/comercio/tpl/p9f.xsl#

———. 1997. *Panorama de la inserción internacional de América Latina y el Caribe 1997.*

Economist Intelligence Unit, EIU. 1997 (2000) "Cuba: Country Risk Service." 2nd quarter 1997, and 4th quarter 2000.

Evenett, Simon J. and Wolfgang Keller. 1998. "On Theories Explaining the Success of the Gravity Equation." NBER Working Paper 6529.

Finger, Michael J., Isidro Soloaga and Francis Ng. 1998. "Trade Policies in the Caribbean Countries: A Look at the Positive Agenda." Paper presented for the meeting of the Caribbean Working Group for Cooperation on Economic Development. Washington, D.C.: World Bank.

François, Joseph, Håkan Nordström and Clinton Shiells. 1996. "Transition Dynamics and Trade Policy Reform in Developing Countries." Staff Working Paper RD-96-005. Geneva: World Trade Organization.

Frankel, Jeffrey, Ernest Stein and Shang-Jin Wei. 1993. "Continental Trading Blocks: Are They Natural or Super-Natural?" NBER Working Paper 4588.

García, Tania and Nancy Quiñones. 1996. "Research concerning the opportunities for integration of Cuba in the Caribbean Basin." University of Havana, *Bulletin of Research*. Center of the International Economy.

Grossman, Gene and Elhanan Helpman. 1991. *Innovation and Growth in the Global Economy.* Cambridge, Mass.: MIT Press.

Gunn, Gillian. 1997. "Divergent International Perspectives on the Caribbean: The Interaction between the Ongoing Caribbean, U.S. and European Adaptations to the New Global Economy." Georgetown University, Caribbean Project, Manuscript.

Harrison, Anne. 1993. "Openness and Growth: A Time Series, Cross-Country

Analysis for Developing Countries." Manuscript. Washington D.C.: World Bank.

Havrylyshyn, Oleh and Lant Pritchett.1991. "Eastern European Trade Patterns after the Transition." Working Paper Series No.748. Washington D.C.: World Bank.

Helleiner, Gerald K. 1986. "Outward Orientation, Import Instability and African Economic Growth: An Empirical Investigation" in *Theory and Reality in Development: Essays in Honour of Paul Streeten* (Sanjaya Lall and Frances Steward, Eds). London: MacMillan.

Heritage Foundation. 2002. *Index of Economic Freedom.* http://www.heritage.org/index.

Helpman, Elhanan and Paul Krugman. 1985. *Market Structure and Foreign Trade.* Cambridge, Mass.: MIT Press.

International Monetary Fund. 1997. *International Financial Statistics.* Washington D.C.: IMF.

International Monetary Fund and World Bank. 2001. "Market Access for Developing Countries' Exports" (Prepared by the Staffs of the IMF and the World Bank).

International Trade Commission and World Trade Organization. 2002. "Trade Information, Country Specific Trade Analysis—Cuba: National Export Performance." ITC-WTO http://www.intracen.org/countries/htm99/cub.htm

Kennan, J. and R. Riezman. 1988."Do Big Countries Win Tariff Wars?" *International Economic Review*, 29(1):81–85.

Kennan, J. and R. Riezman. 1990. "Optimal tariff Equilibria with Custom Union." *Canadian Journal of Economics*, XXIII(1), 70–83.

Krugman, Paul R. 1995. *Development, Geography and Economic Theory.* Cambridge, MA: MIT Press.

————. 1993. "Empirical Evidence on the New Trade Theories: The Current State of Play," in *New Trade Theories: Look at the Empirical Evidence.* London: Center for Economic Policy Research.

———— 1991. *Geography and Trade.* Cambridge, Mass.: MIT Press.

————. 1990. Introduction to *Rethinking International Trade.* Cambridge: MIT.

Leamer, Edward. 1988. "Measures of Openness" in *Trade Policy and Empirical Analysis.* Edited by Robert Baldwin. Chicago: University of Chicago Press.

Lee, Jong-Wha. 1993. "International Trade, Distortions, and Long-Run Economic Growth," *IMF Staff Papers* 40–2: 299–328.

Levine, Ross & Renelt, David. 1992. "A Sensitiveity Analysis of Cross-Country Growth Regressions." *American Economic Review*, 82–4: 942–963.

Lucas, Robert E. 1988. "On the Mechanism of Economic Development." *Journal of Monetary Economics*, 22–1.

Marquetti Nodarse, Hiram. 1999. "The process of industrial resuscitation, principal outcomes, and problems" in "Financial Statement of the Cuban Economy at the end of the 1990s," Proceedings of the annual seminar, Center of Studies of the Cuban Economy.

Martin, K. 1992."Openness and Economic Performance in Sub-Saharan Africa: Evidence from Time-Series Cross-Country Analysis." WPS 1025. Washington D.C.: World Bank.

McIntosh, Andrew. 2001. "Chrétien Vows to Look Out for Smaller Economies, Canada to Consider Separate Regional Free Trade Deal." *National Post*, January 20, ftaa-l-request@lists.tao.ca

Michalopoulos, Constantine. 1999. "Trade Policy and Market Access Issues for Developing Countries: Implications for the Millennium Round." Policy Research Working Group Paper 2214. Washington, D.C.: World Bank.

Montenegro Claudio and Raimundo Soto. 1996. "How Distorted is Cuba's Trade? Evidence and Predictions from a Gravity Model." *Journal of International Trade and Economic Development*, 5:1 p.45–68.

New York Times. 5 July 2000. "Trade Deal between Caribbean, Cuba."

Obstfeld, Maurice and Kenneth Rogoff. 1996. *Foundations of International Macroeconomics*. Cambridge, Mass.: MIT Press.

Organization for Economic Cooperation and Development. 1997. *Market Access for the Least-Developed Countries: Where Are the Obstacles?* Paris: OECD.

Preeg, Ernest and Jonathan Levine. 1993. "Cuba and the New Caribbean Economic Order." Center for Strategic and International Studies (CSIS) Significant Issues Series, Vol. XV, No.2. Washington, D.C.: CSIS.

Rodrik, Dani. 1995. "Trade Policy and Industrial Policy Reform" in *Handbook of Development Economics* (edited by Hollis Chenery and T.N. Srinivasan) Vol. 3B. Amsterdam, North Holland, NY: Elsevier Science Pub. Co.

Romer, Paul. 1992. "Two Strategies for Economic Development: Using Ideas and Producing Ideas." World Bank Annual Conference on Economic Development. Washington D.C.: World Bank.

Sánchez Egozcue, Jorge Mario. 1999. "Cuba–Canada Economic Relations in the 1990s: A Review from the Caribbean." Paper presented at the annual meeting of the Canadian Association for Latin American and Caribbean Studies (CALACS): "Latin America and the Caribbean into the Coming Millennium: Equity, Democracy and Sustainability" in Ottawa, Canada.

————. 1997. "Cuba, Inflation and Stabilization." Paper presented at the annual meeting of the Latin American Studies Association Congress (LASA).

Selva, Gustavo. 1997. "Principales tendencias en el comercio cubano: Evaluaciones y predicciones desde un modelo de gravedad." Instituto Nacional de Investigaciones Económicas (INIE).

U.S. Department of Agriculture, Economic Research Service. 2000. "Impacts of Possible Lifting of U.S. Trade Sanctions with Cuba," November 6. www.ers.usda.gov

U.S. International Trade Commission (USITC),. 2001. "The Economic Impact of U.S. Sanctions with Respect to Cuba." Investigation No.332–413, Publication 3398. www.usitc.gov

Wolf, Holger. 1993. "Trade Orientation: Measurement and Consequences." *Estudios de Economía.*

World Bank. 1997. *World Development Report: The State in a World in Transformation.* Washington D.C.: World Bank.

World Trade Organization (WTO) and International Trade Commission (ITC). 2001. Profile of Cuba at: http://www.intracen.org/countries/htm99/cub.htm

————. 2004. Market Analysis Section (TradeSim). See http://www.intracen.org/menus/countries/toolpd99/nep.

World Trade Organization (WTO). 2001. "Examen de las políticas comerciales-Estados Unidos." WT/PR/S/88. Geneva: WTO.

Appendix 5.1   Classification of Economies in the Americas by Income Level, 2001

Income Classification		
Low		Haiti
Middle	Low	Belize Bolivia Colombia Costa Rica *Cuba* Dominican Republic Ecuador El Salvador Guatemala Guyana Honduras Jamaica Paraguay Peru St. Vincent and Grenadines Suriname
	High	Antigua and Barbuda Argentina Barbados Brazil Chile Dominica Granada Mexico Panama Puerto Rico St. Kitts and Nevis St. Lucia Trinidad and Tobago Uruguay Venezuela
High	*OECD*	Canada United States
	Non-OECD	Aruba Bahamas Bermuda Cayman Islands Dutch Antilles Virgin Islands

Source: World Bank, *World Development Report* 2002

Notes

1   The arguments presented on this subject are taken for the most part from Edwards (1997), Francois, Nordström & Shiells (1996), Michalopoulos (1999), Anderson & Neary (2000), IMF & World Bank (2001). An exhaustive review of the literature in this regard is referred to in Edwards (1993) Rodrik (1995), IMF (2001).

2   The nature that trade policy itself, which is carried out by several instruments including tariffs, quotas, licenses, exchange rate controls, etc., as Edwards (1997) explains, "suggests that attempts to construct a single indicator of trade orientation may be futile, and will tend to generate disagreements and controversies."

3   A country can substantially alter its trade and continue to be highly dependent on it.

4   Some of the most interesting are: Corden (1966), Anderson and Neary (1994), Pritchett and Sethi (1994), Levine and Renelt (1992), Leamer (1988), Wolf (1993), and particularly Easterly (1993), who analyzing a sample of 57 countries using a similar index of price distortion to that of Dollar, confirms the existence of a negative relationship between price deviations and growth. The theoretical model utilized showed how distortions of relative prices caused by commercial policy had notable effects on growth as a result of distorting investment decisions.

5   The fundamental results were in the direction of confirming the positive relation openness-growth, which is interpreted as a demonstration of the consistency of the relationship. Human capital and per capita income are more relevant variables than the degree of openness in six of the nine regressions where the index of openness had a lower value. It is understood that every index of openness "captures" a different aspect of commercial policy and thus, a "composite" index was employed to verify these results. In general terms the previous results were confirmed.

6   The evaluations in this section are based on statistics from the World Bank's *World Development Report 1997*, the IMF's *International Financial Statistics 1997* the study by Finger, NG and Soloaga (1998) and CEPAL (2003) report.

7   This refers to the insular Caribbean, which excludes Mexico.

8   In 1968 several Caribbean countries launched their own integration system, the Caribbean Free Trade Area (CARIFTA). In 1973 CARIFTA was replaced by the Caribbean Community and Common Market (CARICOM) which never came close to a common market, in part because the individual islands relied heavily on tariff revenue and in part because intraregional trade was extremely limited. "CARICOM pursued and intensified its efforts to consolidate Caribbean integration but progress has nonetheless been slow, particularly in terms of the common external tariff and the start–up of the

Caribbean Single Market and Economy (CSME), which had been scheduled for 2002. Macroeconomic convergence, which is important for these countries' progress and integration, will be hard to achieve in the current economic context." Economic Commission for Latin America and the Caribbean (2003), pp.2728.

9　Observe that Mexico is excluded purposely because, although it is part of the member countries of the Caribbean Basin, its membership in NAFTA renders it a special case.

10　"Chrétien Vows to Look Out for Smaller Economies, Canada to Consider Separate Regional Free Trade Deal." Andrew McIntosh, *National Post,* ftaa-l-request@lists.tao.ca, January 20, 2001,

11　*New York Times.* 5 July 2000. "Trade Deal between Caribbean, Cuba."

12　See EIU Country Reports (The Economist Intelligence Unit Dec.2000: D, on a scale from A to E) http://www.eiu.org and The Heritage Foundation, Index of Economic Freedom (2001): 4.75 on a scale from 0 to 5) http://www.heritage.org/index.

13　According to The Economist Intelligence Unit, the level of foreign currency reserves in the Central Bank between 1996 and 1999 has been 1.0 (months of coverage of imports), and in 2000 and 2001 was estimated to be 1.2 months in coverage (EIU, Cuba, Country Risk Service, December 2000, p. 9).

14　International Trade Commission (ITC) World Trade Organization, (2002) Trade Information, Country Specific Trade Analysis—Cuba: National Export Performance: http://www.intracen.org/countries/htm99/cub.htm.

15　Calculations by the author show that Cuba's imports from the Caribbean were 0.3 percent on average, with an average standard deviation of 0.8 percent, and exports were 0.1 percent on average with a standard deviation of 0.3 percent in the period between 1990 and 1999.

16　"In 1996 the value was US$843 billion, 16.2 percent of which were CARICOM exports. (CEPAL, *Panorama de la Inserción Internacional de América Latina,* 1997).

17　Further details are described in the section on trade openness and economic growth.

18　On the role of the protectionist measures in the formation of trade policy in underdeveloped countries see Balassa (1971).

19　The United States-Caribbean Basin Trade Partnership Act H.R.434, 2000. Trade and Development Act of 2000. (TDA), Title II—Trade Benefits for Caribbean Basin, Subtitle A—Trade Policy for Caribbean Basin Countries, SEC. 201. United States–Caribbean Basin Trade Partnership Act. (CBTPA).

20 Taken from Jorge Mario Sánchez E. (1999) "Cuba–Canada Economic Relations in the 1990s: A Review from the Caribbean," presented at the Annual Meeting of the Canadian Association for Latin American and Caribbean Studies (CALACS): "Latin America and the Caribbean into the Coming Millennium: Equity, Democracy and Sustainability" in Ottawa.

21 "The Cuban authorities still have at their disposal, through the fiscal management and the price controls, sufficient tools to maintain macroeconomic stability," The Economist Intelligence Unit, Cuba, Country Report, 3rd quarter 1999, p8. A similar evaluation was issued by the same source in its report of November 2002.

22 Marquetti (1999: 24).

23 Controls in terms of regulations on market access, as well as restrictions on the employment of the labor force, leasing of housing, office and pricing systems, create an environment that forces foreign businessmen to "adapt" to a situation that is atypical in terms of regional practices.

24 Each simulation is based on a country "proxy" made up of: a) Preeg and Levine (1993), Jamaica, the Dominican Republic and Costa Rica; and, b) Montenegro and Soto (1996), Jamaica, Dominican Republic and Trinidad and Tobago.

25 This is also known as Tobit model or "canonical censored regression model."

26 WTO Research Division, Market Analysis, (TradeSim), at: http://www. intracen.org/menus/countries/toolpd99/nep.

27 Evenett S. & Keller W. "On Explaining the Success of the Gravity Equations," http://www.nber.org/paper/w6529

28 Given the fact that countries with large geographical areas have different ways of perceiving closeness in relation to other geographical areas, there is more than one method to determine distance, for example, distance between capitals, between the countries' economic hubs, the average of regional markets and other procedures. For a detailed discussion of this issue, the following authors discuss the method of the "great-circle-route" of the most important city up until New York, in Fitzpatrick & Modlin, (1986), also: International Trade Data, Useful Gravity Model Data "great-circle," Haveman, John (2000) http://www.eiit.org/Trade.Resources/Data/ Gravity/dist.txt, also in Wei (1995) and Linneman (1966).

29 International Trade Center, UNCTAD/WTO, TradeSim, The ITC Simulation Model of Bilateral Trade Potentials: Background Paper, p. 5.

6

The Role of Foreign Direct Investment in Economic Development: The Cuban Experience

by Omar Everleny Pérez Villanueva

An economic reform process of adjustment, crisis management and external opening unfolded in Cuba at the beginning of the 1990s in response to the severe economic crisis. Initially, the island nation needed to secure immediate outside resources to compensate for the collapse of the country's trade ties with the former Socialist Bloc. Before long, this opening would be decisive in reactivating the Cuban economy and reinserting its participation in world markets. The most important aspects of this economic opening in the external sphere were: the promotion and opening of the economy to foreign capital investments, the restructuring of foreign trade and the rapid development of international tourism.

Because sufficient levels of resources to fuel growth and development in the foreseeable future could not be generated from domestic savings, foreign financing became an urgent and first order priority for the Cuban economy. The difficulties in increasing foreign financing, however, have been sizable. While normally this source has been considered an important complement to domestic savings in increasing investment and helping to promote sustained levels of economic growth, such had not been Cuba's experience. Generally, foreign credits or loans help mobilize material and technical resources that promote new production, thereby making it possible to generate domestic savings, acquire technologies and elevate the quantity of exports necessary for the repayment of financing credits. However, Cuba has had to confront well-known restrictions in securing capital, as well as to face the challenge of its own limited export diversification.

Most loans that Cuba has received since 1991 have been short-term export credits with high interest rates. Contracts with creditors have been established under conditions that can also be classified as rigid. Credits under favorable terms have been fixed and limited. Foreign assistance through donations and technical assistance have evolved with minor growth margins. Hence, the Cuban state has begun to study and analyze how to utilize foreign investment without bargaining away either the country's resources or its sovereignty. Satisfactory results have been achieved though a complicated exercise in decision making under tight constraints. The entirety of all these source of financing have permitted the country to obtain certain resources to attenuate the difficulties experienced as a result of the crisis and to continue with economic reform. However, these resources are insufficient, expensive and have limited growth possibilities until problems—including the external debt and its servicing— are solved.

The purpose of this chapter is to show how foreign direct investment (FDI) became a reliable means for Cuba to acquire financial resources and accordingly the technology capable of competitively improving its outputs and services in the 1990s. Before turning to the case of Cuba, the importance of foreign direct investment in developing countries in recent decades is worth reviewing. FDI has played a decisive role in the financing of development in many countries, particularly in East Asia with encouraging results and in some Latin American countries. However, this does not mean that FDI generates development in all cases. Nevertheless, FDI has generated resources utilized by governments for the development of specific activities or regions. It can also play an important role in the development of receiving economies, since it can provide a vehicle for the acquisition of technologies, theoretical and business knowledge and other important foreign-origin elements including integration into international marketing, distribution, and production networks and the improvement in the international competitiveness of firms and national economies, in addition to contributing capital flows.

No matter what, neither the entrance of FDI nor the benefits derived from these flows are automatic. In other words, governments must direct attention towards examining where FDI should be channeled in order to fuel the development of their economies by establishing policies that guide the optimal form of investments and promoting the utilization of these resources on behalf of society as a whole. Driven by the need to have stable sources of external financing, many economies have promoted and liberalized their foreign investment regimes, especially in developing countries in recent decades.

A number of ex-socialist countries have based their economic reform programs on high levels of foreign financing with very positive results. Most East Asian countries that have emerged as industrial powers have demonstrated that economic development results from a state's close links with businesses. Their experiences show that the combination of a coherent and respected bureaucratic apparatus with appropriate technical knowledge, and suitable communication links between that state and the owners of domestic and foreign capital are key factors in promulgating an economy's industrial development. The coordination and linkages between businesspeople and public sector officials are among the most central factors that have allowed these countries to become winners in terms of gains of their economic development indicators over the last 20 years. At the same time, developing countries are finding that they cannot obtain access to high technology without giving a greater share of control to the foreign owners of these innovations and simultaneously increasing investments in their own technological development. In other words, developing countries have found the need for more openness and liberalization of regulations related to foreign investment flows because of these global trends.

Foreign Companies, Exports and Development

Those responsible for economic policy seeking to promote development focus efforts on improving "export competitiveness." Although this includes efforts to increase market share, it requires much more. Efforts at improving competitiveness require diversification of the country's export composition, maintaining higher rates of growth and enriching the technological content and skilled personnel in exporting activities, as well as expanding the productive base of those national companies capable of competing in international markets. Through these efforts, competitiveness becomes self-sustainable and is accompanied by an increase in income.[1]

The need to increase exports is understandable as it allows for the acquisition of foreign exchange that can then be used to import products, services and technologies that countries need to increase productivity and raise living standards. Improved export competitiveness also has many benefits. It helps countries to diversify their exports and thus reduce their dependency on the export earnings from a few commodities. It contributes to elevate the levels of skilled knowledge and technology in production processes—an essential component in increasing local value-added to products and maintaining growth in the well-being of workers. Exporting also makes it possible for countries to obtain greater economies of scale and of diversification, since it opens more varied and larger size markets. In turn, exporting strengthens the capacities that help to sustain competitiveness. Indeed, it forces companies to confront superior standards. Furthermore, it provides firms with opportunities to have easier access to information, which encourages national companies to make increased efforts to acquire new capacities and expertise. Ideally, the increase in market share should be accompanied by all these other advantages so that the impact on development is maximized.

Foreign companies can help increase competitiveness in developing countries, although unlocking this potential is a complex task. Intense competition exists among emerging economies for managing to succeed in getting transnational firms to locate their export-oriented production in each country's particular economy. Moreover, even countries that obtain this objective face difficulties in maintaining competitiveness as wages rise and market conditions change. It is essential to have the support of coherent policies if one wants the export production activities of transnational companies to be inserted firmly into the national development strategy. As this chapter will attempt to show, this is one of the policy objectives of foreign investment in Cuba, although greater integration of a comprehensive nature is still needed.

Export competitiveness is an important goal that is full of difficulties, but should be seen as a means for reaching an end—development.[2] Transnational companies are the source of a considerable proportion of exports in many developing countries, and their spheres of operation extend to all economic sectors. In the primary sector, in addition to minerals and oil, they have contributed to natural resource export development particularly in the food and horticulture industries. In the manufacturing sector, transnational companies tend to be leaders in production and marketing of export products, especially the most dynamic ones, which must be connected to international marketing and distribution networks.

Transnational companies can take on various forms in their international systems of production. These forms range from systems based on FDI that stimulate production in which subsidiary trade between respective divisions of transnational companies dominates those based on networks of independent suppliers with non-ownership ties responding to buyer demand (such as occurs in international sub-contracting and contract-based manufacturing). The growing commercialization of services opens new export possibilities. To date, the best-known example is that of the Indian software industry. Those possibilities also extend to services such as regional headquarters, purchase centers, shared service centers and R&D activities.[3]

In many technologically complex activities, a sizeable proportion of transnational firms' own trade is within their own international systems of production. Trade of parts and components, especially those manufactured in dynamic industries, has gained increased importance— a sign of the growing trend towards the specialization of trade derived from international systems of production. The most dynamic products in world trade are primarily manufacturing products such as those of the electronic, auto, and clothing industries, rather than those based on the exploitation of natural resources. Transnational companies have had an important role in the growth of these products' exports, although through varied mechanisms.

Current transformations in business strategies and in production systems present developing countries with new possibilities for entering into technologically intensive production activities and for orienting production towards exports, which could otherwise not be initiated, and for integrating their economies into international systems of production. The foregoing does not mean that transnational companies are a fundamental element in the development of an economy. Rather, governments should maximize the advantages that may be derived from these companies as efficiently as possible, while recognizing their limitations and adverse effects so as to minimize these through policy-making decisions.

Improving export competitiveness is beneficial for countries. In terms of market share, only 20 economies total more than three-fourths of the value of total world trade. Developed countries, especially Germany, the United States and Japan, are large global competitors. However as Figure 6.1 shows, developing economies, especially countries such as China, Mexico, Taiwan, the Republic of South Korea, Singapore and Thailand, and transition economies, such as Hungary, Poland and the Czech Republic, have registered the greatest increases in market share during 1985 to 2000. In fact, due to the increase in market share in recent years, seven of these developing economies now belong to the top 20 exporters of the world, whose FDI market share gains are denoted in Figure 6.1 below. In other words, spectacular changes are occurring in the composition of world trade, with several developing countries and transition economies as the chief beneficiaries.

Figure 6.1 The 20 Winner Economies Based on Export Market Share Gains, 1985–2000 (percentage)

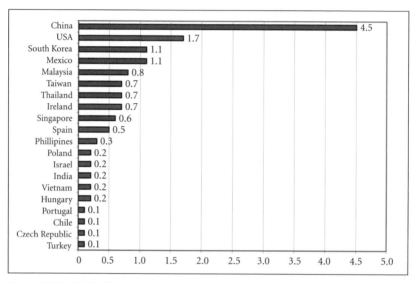

Source: UNCTAD. *World Investment Report, 2002: Transnational Corporations and Export Competitiveness,* Figure VI.I

The growth of exports in many of these winning economies directly relates to the expansion of national production systems, especially in the electronic and auto industries. For example, foreign subsidiaries already realize approximately half or more of the manufacturing exports of a few of these countries (see Table 6.1). It is possible that the buoyancy of exports experienced by these "winners" will extend to other developing and transition economies as international production gathers impetus and expands geographically. However, the bulk of exporting activity to date resulting from the presence of transnational companies has been concentrated in a group of countries, mainly in East Asia and in the border regions of North America and of the European Union. China, Costa Rica, Ireland, South Korea and Mexico—countries selected by UNCTAD for analysis—also experienced a change in export structure: from non-dynamic products to dynamic products and from relatively low technologically intensive activities to intermediate and high technologically intensive activities, in addition to the anticipated strong increase in market share.

Table 6.1 Shares of Foreign Affiliates in the Exports of Selected Host Economies, All Industries and Manufacturing
(percentage)

	Year	All Industries	Manufacturing
Developing Economies			
Argentina	1995	14	
	2000	29	
Brazil	1995	18	
	2000	21	
Chile	1995	16	
	2000	28	
China	1991	17	16
	2001	50	44
Costa Rica	2000	50	
Malaysia	1985	26	18
	1995	45	49
Mexico	1995	15	
	2000	31	
Singapore	1994		35
	1999		38
Central and Eastern Europe			
Estonia	1995		26
	2000	60	35
Hungary	1995	58	52
	1999	80	86
Poland	1998	48	35
	2000	56	52
Czech Republic	1993		15
	1998		47

Source: Table elaborated by the author based on Table VI.3 of UNCTAD's *World Investment Report 2002*

Most governments prioritize export promotion and maintenance for greater development or higher levels of resources to channel towards improving their economies. Just as companies are obliged to create more competitive production systems, countries must design strategies in which industries increasingly contribute greater value-added to national output. There are many ways in which transnational companies can enhance a country's export competitiveness. In order to attract FDI towards export activities and investment that benefits development, countries must seek the most effective means so that their location can favorably influence the types of exports they wish to promote. Even countries that traditionally receive a considerable amount of FDI oriented toward export activities must continue to improve their systems to cope with wage increases and maintain their competitiveness as exporters.[4]

Incentives have been an important component of the development strategies of many countries, especially of those that have succeeded in attracting FDI to their export activities. Some of those countries have adopted an increasingly selective criterion when seeking to attract particular types of investments. Developing countries considering offering incentives in order to promote export-oriented FDI should balance the costs against the benefits. When introduced effectively, incentives generally have been used to complement other measures designed to improve aspects such as expertise, technology and infrastructure. Attempting to compensate for important shortages by offering incentives is perhaps not always a prudent strategy since there is greater risk that public funds will be spent on projects that do not offer the externalities necessary for justifying such incentives to investors.[5]

If one does not improve business conditions by creating those that are most propitious for investment and production and which integrate FDI into the local economy, one increases the risk that investors will leave once the incentives have been depleted. FDI recipient countries have instruments necessary for making investments more effective in terms of development at their disposal. Governments can design policies geared toward creating political and macroeconomic stability, as well as focus on developing science and technology policies, labor laws, and commercial policies, among others.[6]

The overall trend is towards the liberalization of regulations on foreign direct investment. However, merely opening an economy is not sufficient for attracting sustained levels of FDI and ensuring that these flows contribute development advantages. Transnational companies base their investment decisions on economic criteria such as market size, production costs and efficiency, infrastructure quality and access to skilled personnel. The domestic development of skilled personnel and of entrepreneurship takes on special importance in order to attract quality FDI and to ensure the necessary absorptive capacity to fully take advantage of knowledge transfers. The degree to which one manages to create an environment in which businesses are more inclined to undertake investments, introduce improvements and establish linkages, the less likely it will be that investors will abandon the country once incentives are exhausted.[7]

Foreign Direct Investment in Latin America and the Caribbean

Cuba is inserted within a very dynamic region with respect to foreign investment. Hence it is necessary to briefly analyze its regional context with respect to Latin America and the Caribbean. In net value (inflows minus outflows), FDI was the only positive element of the private capital directed at developing countries and transition economies during 2000 and 2001. In spite of the effects of weakened demand in the world's leading economies, the long-term prospects of FDI are unswerving and transnational companies will continue in their expansion.[8] Latin America and Caribbean have received a systematic inflow of financial resources through FDI (excluding 2002). Although these flows still remain directed predominately at developed countries, Figure 6.2 shows that overall the share of investments directed at Latin America and the Caribbean has been steadily increasing for over a decade.

Figure 6.2 FDI Inflows to Latin America and the Caribbean, 1988–2002
(US$ billion)

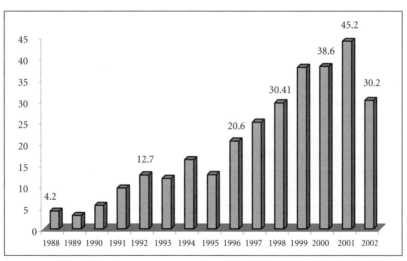

Source: World Investment Report, UNCTAD. United Nations, New York and Geneva, various years.

According to UNCTAD's 2001 World Investment Report, "the current volume of FDI in Latin America and the Caribbean has reached values that were unthinkable *just a decade ago.*" Investment prospects, as well as sectoral breakdowns, differ according to country and the sub-region in question. After Mexico, the Dominican Republic received the highest proportion of foreign investment (32 percent of the total of foreign investment in Latin America and the Caribbean), followed by Trinidad and Tobago (17 percent), Guatemala, Costa Rica, and Jamaica, each sharing 12 percent respectively. While FDI has traditionally targeted tourism in Caribbean countries, the Dominican Republic and several Central American countries—Costa Rica, Guatemala, Honduras and El Salvador—have received resources targeted towards their manufacturing sector. This orientation of foreign investment[9] responds to:

- Incentives granted by local governments for export processing zones, in the context of the Caribbean Basin Initiative
- Incentives granted by the United States government based on shared production, which provides preferential market access to U.S. suppliers
- The search for greater efficiency and lower costs on the part of transnational companies

Together these factors have encouraged a strong expansion of FDI in manufacturing, mainly linked to low-skilled assembly industries. For example, investments in textile industries for exporting to the United States market have expanded in the cases of Honduras, El Salvador and the Dominican Republic. Recently, however, FDI also has been attracted toward sectors requiring more complex skills, as the electronics and information technology industries. Central American countries, for example, have received increased interest from transnational companies seeking to install call and cost centers.

Several countries in the region have implemented strategies targeted towards the development of these new sectors, not only on the part of their governments, but also by transnational companies themselves. This includes U.S. transnational companies that had previously reduced their investments. Between 1997 and 2002, Costa Rica managed to concentrate the highest proportion of FDI in its industrial sector, particularly in its electronic sector. Noteworthy investments in this area were concentrated on the manufacturing of electronic, magnetic and telecommunications components, microprocessors, as well as the production of medical devices, including the manufacturing of surgical equipment, computer programs medical preparations, monitoring equipment, surgical instruments and laser medical equipment.

Due to the international recession and excess production, several electronic and telecommunications companies suffered strong contractions in profits and market values, forcing them to restructure and close factories in 2001. However, this process did not affect Costa Rica. Indeed, the investments to this country have not diminished and are projected to increase in these sectors in the coming years.[10]

Although Latin American and Caribbean economies are undergoing privatization and attracting foreign investment toward infrastructure, the magnitude of flows for this sector was limited in 2001. Investment flows continue to be concentrated in services, including communications, tourism and financial services. While there are moderate increases in manufacturing, the share accruing to this sector is decreasing as a percentage of total FDI flows.

Distinct Features of Foreign Direct Investment in Cuba

In terms of attracting foreign direct investment, Cuba has followed trends similar to those of Latin America and the Caribbean, experiencing substantial surges in funds especially in investments targeted towards services such as tourism and telecommunications, as well as for mineral exploration and exploitation, namely nickel and oil. Hence, it is important to undertake a detailed analysis of the evolution of foreign investment in Cuba and the special features in areas where its presence is most significant.

In the late 1980s, the process of opening the Cuban economy to foreign investment was initially oriented towards solving specific problems, including the need to diversify the quality and quantity of exports, acquiring raw materials, to secure fresh capital flows, to integrate the economy into new markets, to acquire advanced technologies and introduce modern business management practices. Collaboration between the Cuban state and foreign investors has demonstrated that the adoption of confidence building measures can diminish risk and uncertainty. Foreign investment also has played an important role in terms of nourishing the scarcity of capital and technology and improving the channeling of investments toward economic projects that contribute to both societal well-being and greater profits.

Without failing to acknowledge the restrictions that foreign investors attempt to impose on the economic policy design concerning resource allocations, the preferences of the investors are not always predetermined. In addition, these preferences have been redefined during negotiations with the state.[11] In other words, foreign investors will always attempt to maximize profits, but the strategy they adopt will depend on the political and institutional context that they encounter in the host country.

Despite the negative impact of the imposition of foreign laws impeding the flow of resources of FDI toward Cuba on its country risk evaluation, the number of joint ventures has grown over the last thirteen years. Viewed in this light, foreign direct investment flows gain importance far above their quantitative value or a simple comparison with the flows of investment toward other countries in the region. As Figure 6.3 shows, the number of joint ventures rose from 20 in 1990 to 403 by 2002, but decreased to 342 in 2003.

Figure 6.3 Number of Joint Ventures with FDI in Cuba, 1990–2003

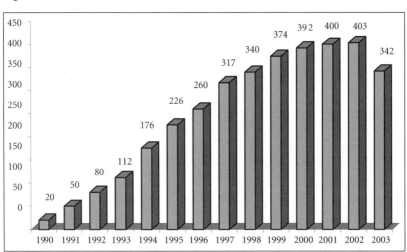

Source: Report of the Ministry of Foreign Investment and Economic Collaboration (MINVEC), various years

The results of foreign direct investment in 2003 were disappointing. The number of dissolved joint ventures was the highest since Cuba began to promote FDI in the late 1980s, while the number of authorizations of new projects was the lowest since 1990. In addition, the volume of foreign capital inflows showed only a modest recovery from the sharp decline experienced two years earlier. However, a few new agreements with foreign partners were signed, some existing investors expanded their operations in the Cuban market, and the presence of joint ventures operating abroad became increasingly important. In 2003, 68 joint ventures operating in Cuba were dissolved. Tourism was the most affected sector with 21 dissolutions, followed by 12 in basic industry and 7 in light industry.

Many joint ventures, for the most part formed in the first half of the 1990s, simply dissolved because of the expiration of the regular contract between the Cuban state and the overseas investor. These joint ventures generally involve small and medium-sized firms whose profits have been disappointing, in part because of the lack of adequate financing. The changing priorities of the Cuban authorities toward foreign investment may have also played a role in this turn of events, however. Other joint ventures dissolved because of the anticipated withdrawal of the foreign partner. The existing restrictions on the operation of enterprises, excessive bureaucratic practices and failure to achieve pre-established targets are among the most common causes.

In the last few years, Havana authorities have subjected each existing joint venture to close scrutiny to verify whether satisfactory economic results and the state's original objectives for establishing the enterprise have been achieved, above and beyond the initial scrutiny of the proposal. At the end of 2002, more than half of the 403 active joint ventures operating in Cuba failed to generate profits for different reasons. For the most part, these joint ventures were in the process of dissolution, waiting for additional documentation to begin operations, or performing an undefined social function.

The amount of foreign direct investment in Cuba has decreased significantly. After a peak of US$448 million in 2000, the level of inflows fell to only US$389 million in 2001 and only about US$100 million arrived in 2002. The world economic crisis, the U.S. blockade and the deteriorating relationship with the European Union account for such a trend, although the decline in FDI also mirrors a general tendency throughout Latin America and the Caribbean.

Further calculations based on the levels of gross fixed capital formation at current prices between 1993 and 2002, totaling US$27.5 billion, and balance of payments statistics reporting that FDI exceeded US$2.1 billion dollars over the same period, the contribution of FDI to gross capital formation can be estimated to be 8.2 percent. Although far from the needs of the Cuban economy, the contribution of FDI to gross capital formation in Cuba is comparable with world averages. As Figure 6.4 below indicates, the annual variance remains significant. According to UNCTAD's 2002 *World Investment Report,* FDI was small in absolute terms in the 49 least developed countries. However, it continued to contribute to local asset formation, especially given the high proportion of FDI relative to gross domestic capital formation in several of these countries. Overall, it represented an average of 7 percent of total investment during 1998 and 2000 in these 49 countries.

Figure 6.4 FDI as a Share of Gross Capital Formation in Cuba, 1993–2002
(percentage)

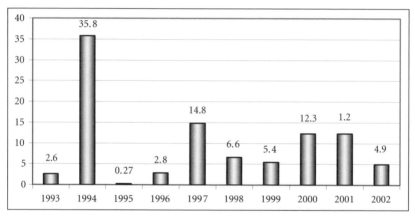

Source: Elaborated by the author based on reports from the Central Bank of Cuba, various years

Foreign investments have impacted some economic sectors very positively in terms of quantitative and qualitative effects, in particular, tourism, nickel, fuels, communications, food industry, steel and services. More than a decade of the novel presence of foreign capital in Cuba has elapsed; as a result, these investments have undergone a process of maturation with positive results. For example, joint ventures have increased their total sales of goods and services. As Figure 6.5 demonstrates, these reached US$2,068 million in 2002, while exports amounted to US$963 million. During the same year, direct capital flows into the country totaled US$287 million. In addition, foreign direct investment has both tangible and non-tangible benefits. In other words, joint ventures create positive spillovers, which are difficult to quantify. An example of these includes the development of local managerial capabilities.

Compared with the country's total exports of goods, exports by joint ventures have had a high and growing participation (Figure 6.6). The share of exports from joint ventures averaged more than 40 percent of total Cuban exports in recent years. This trend follows previously analyzed global patterns, though proportions differ. Similarly, the share of exports

Figure 6.5 Gross Sales of Goods and Services in Cuba by Joint Ventures, 1995–2002 (US$ million)

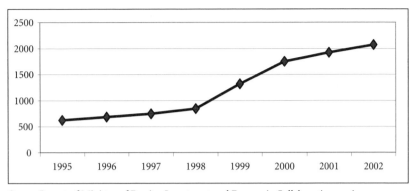

Source: Report of Ministry of Foreign Investment and Economic Collaboration, various years

Figure 6.6 Exports by Joint Ventures, 1993–2002 (percentage of total exports of goods and services)

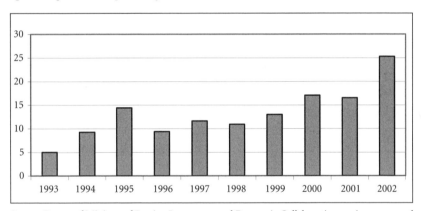

Source:. Report of Ministry of Foreign Investment and Economic Collaboration, various years and Comisión Económica para América Latina y el Caribe, 2003

by joint ventures relative to the total value of goods and services is presented in Figure 6.6. These results show that the share has averaged above 15 percent since 2000.

The greatest percentage of foreign enterprises rests in the industrial sector, especially in basic industries. Mining and oil are the dominant sectors, with tourism and to a lesser extent other spheres following. In general, ventures are most limited in those areas of greater value-added or with higher technological requirements. Given that human capital is the asset of greatest value, foreign direct investment agreements are moving in the opposite direction from patterns found in other developing countries, where the proportion of FDI directed at sectors that are intense in human capital has increased in recent decades.

In the last two years, Cuba has established joint venture enterprises abroad in high-technology areas. In a Chinese-Cuban joint venture enterprise, Cuba began constructing a plant in China for the production of monoclonal antibodies for combating neck and brain cancer.[12] Another joint venture enterprise was established in Malaysia between Malaysia-owned Bioven Holdings Sdn Bhd and Heber Biotec S.A., the trading company for Cuba's Center for Biotechnology and Genetic Engineering (CIGB). The company, 70 percent Cuban property, has enabled Cuba's participation in an important project focused on the Malaysian Bio Valley. In the first phase of the project, the new company will concentrate on marketing Herbert Bioven products in the Malaysian and South East Asian markets. In the second phase, the project is conceived to focus on technology transfers through joint research. Cuba's Center of Genetic Engineering and Biotechnology is participating in three of the five products that Bioven intends to present for consideration to Malaysian authorities.[13] The strategy to attempt to enter new markets with products of recognized international endorsement should make it possible for Cuba to further penetrate high-technology markets, which has become a highly trans-nationalized market. Perhaps these incipient initiatives represent the beginning of greater ventures.

FDI in Select Economic Sectors

Analysis of foreign domestic investment in some sectors, especially in high performing sectors such as tourism, mining, beverage and liquor industries, and communications, clearly shows that progress has been made in the industrial productivity of Cuban companies, and how the international circuit of trade flows has included many Cuban companies (Figure 6.7).

Since the 1990s, the presence of various forms of joint ventures with foreign capital led to industry restructuring and introduced new operational modalities. Chains such as Gran Caribe, Horizontes and Islas Azul were formed, in addition to corporations like Cubanacan and Gaviota. Together, these comprise of a number of related activities including hotels of varying quality, as well as restaurants and other specialized services. The dynamism of the Cuban tourist sector contributed to making the sector extremely attractive for FDI. Visitor growth rates av-

Figure 6.7 Number of Joint Ventures by Sector, 2003

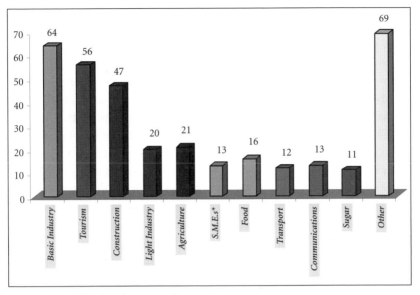

* S.M.E.s are small and medium enterprises.
Source: Report of the Ministry for Foreign Investment, various years

eraged 14 percent annually between 1990 and 2000; gross revenue was more than 30 percent annually, with room construction rates growing at 13 percent annually.

In the tourism sector, foreign investment policies have sought to open additional markets, attract new tourist flows, obtain innovative technologies, improve management practices and attract fresh capital flows. In response, joint venture enterprises—mainly in hotels—have been constituted with entities of recognized international prestige, with participation distributed evenly between Cuban and foreign capital. Initially, investments as a matter of priority were first channeled to undeveloped regions before the same firms could invest in Havana and Varadero, which are more developed regions that benefit from high international tourism demand. The operational period of these contracts was established for 25 years and is extendable to 50 years when deemed advisable. The theoretical framework of oligopolistic rivalry with its preventive character helps to explain why many companies have shown an interest in the Cuban market as these players foresee the future when more powerful companies in the U.S. or the North American tourist market will seek access into Cuba.

In 1990, Cuba received 327,000 tourists with 12,900 available rooms, most requiring rehabilitation. Foreign firms administered 1,300 of these rooms. Tourist centers found a limited pool of local managerial abilities, since the industry had not been prioritized in prior decades. As a result, these forces led to the preparation of a long-run tourist development program in Cuba. One of the program's key elements was the transfer of managerial abilities through hotel management contracts and the creation of joint ventures in hotel and non-hotel installations.

The globalization of the world tourist industry has taken place through horizontal and vertical mergers by hotel chains, airlines and tour operators. As a result, transnational companies significantly influence the direction of mass tourist flows. In order to increase tourist arrivals and guarantee stable flows, the Cuban government has followed a policy to contract hotel administration to a group of specialized international hotel companies, which in turn develop promotional and global-scale advertising campaigns, taking advantage of the necessary contacts and indispensable partnerships for their marketing.[14] During these years the contracted firms—which contribute their "brand names" and quality standards—have been a source for the training of managers and the domestic workforce, as well as a source of financing for the modernization of installations. After a decade, the supply of rooms for tourism reached some 37,200 rooms in 2001; foreign companies administered 47 percent of these. Joint venture enterprises have an average of 4,300 rooms in operation. Figure 6.8 illustrates the growing and positive trend of the increase in hotel rooms in Cuba and the important role that different foreign companies play in the development of these installations.

Within the development of new hotel installations, the number of hotels constructed by different joint venture enterprises is a growing trend (Figure 6.9). Based on the advanced progress of projects under study, evaluated and already in the construction phase, it is estimated that joint venture enterprises will have built more than 10,000 rooms by the year 2006. This represents between 20 to 25 percent of the total number of rooms that will be in operation by that year.

The development of tourism in Cuba has required a significant amount of imports as inputs. Hence, Cuba has been increasing domestic production of some products, many of them necessarily financed by foreign investment. In addition, plans are being developed to study the strengthening of extra-hotel services, such as theme parks, golf courses and marinas. Cuba has become part of the tourist circuit of the Carib-

Figure 6.8 Hotel Rooms under National and Foreign Administration in Cuba, 1990–2001 (thousands of rooms)

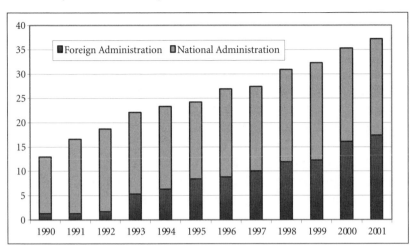

Source: Elaborated by the author based on ONE (various years) and Ministry of Tourism (MINTUR) statistics (2001)

Figure 6.9 New Hotel Rooms Constructed by Joint Ventures in Cuba, 1991–2001

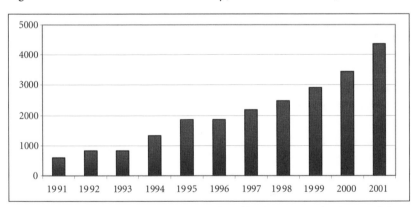

Source: Elaborated by the author based on the number of hotels inaugurated each year and the number of rooms as reported by the press

bean. Its investment program should be accelerated in the coming years for this very reason. Cuba is changing its productive structure in order to serve future tourist demand, and the domestic economy has been steadily increasing the share of domestically-produced supplies for the tourist industry. In 2001, domestic industries produced 68 percent of the inputs needed in tourist installations. In short, tourism has been converted into Cuba's locomotive. As a result, foreign direct investment should be directed at creating a comprehensive supply of Cuba's tourist industry, with the vision that the Caribbean is a complement in this path to development and not a competitor.

Nickel

Cuba's mining industry centers on the exploitation of its polymetallic sediments. The country has the greatest number of reserves in nickel, followed by cobalt. A historical level of nickel production was achieved with the extraction of 74,400 tons in 2001 with almost half of these resources obtained by the joint venture enterprise of Moa Nickel. The solid metals of copper, gold, silver, chromium, magnesium, lead, zinc and nickel are all either in the evaluation, exploration or exploitation stages in Cuba. The Cuban company Geominera S.A. has signed bilateral contracts with foreign companies on the basis of risk contracts. Furthermore, contracts have included agreements on selling these minerals, except in the case of nickel, where the volume of reserves has had an independent structure. Currently, the three types of mining contracts are 1)contracts of exploration at risk by foreign companies; 2) exploration contracts, with the risks shared between the Cuban and foreign counterparts; and 3) joint ventures enterprises participating in mining exploration.

The Cuban metallic mineral processing plant, Moa, obtains a sulfide from nickel and cobalt (Ni+Co), an intermediate product with reduced value in international markets. Prior to 1990, Cuba's production was refined in the Soviet Union. When the Russian government interrupted nickel exports in 1991, Cuba's company nickel and cobalt plant was left without markets. Coincidentally, sulfide deposits of nickel and copper that had supplied the metallurgical refinery in Canada were exhausted during the same year. In 1992 the Cuban sulfide of Ni+Co began to be exported to the Canadian refinery.

In 1994 three joint venture enterprises were created. Moa Nickel S.A., a venture between the Cuban Nickel Union and the Canadian firm Sherritt International, which operates the mining and processing of nickel in the "Pedro Soto Alba" plant in Moa, Cuba. A second enterprise, the Cobalt Refinery Co. Inc. was created to serve the Port Saskatchewan in Alberta, Canada installations for nickel refining. The final enterprise, the International Cobalt Company Inc. located in the Bahamas was created for marketing operations. As a result, the Canadian company (Sherritt) became the owner of half of Cuba's plant and its deposits. The Cuban company

(Cuban Nickel Union) became the owner of half of Canada's refinery and the third joint venture enterprise (International Cobalt Company Inc.) markets the nickel and cobalt products in global markets.

If Cuba had decided to construct a new sulfide refinery in 1992, nickel and cobalt mining would have been paralyzed during construction. Similarly, without minerals to process, the refinery in Canada would have had to close its operations. These experiences demonstrate that foreign direct investment does not necessarily represent a zero sum game. Indeed, in this case both parties netted gains from the transaction.

Sheritt has introduced technological improvements, making it possible to lower production costs and increase production volumes to original capacity levels. The company has had the following clear objectives as its goals: 1) elevating international competition in terms of quality and costs; 2) increasing the recovery of the nickel and cobalt contained in the mineral at international levels; and 3) reasonable cost reduction through improvements in plant energy efficiency. In addition, this plant's results were combined with the modernization of two other existing plants, as well as the renovation of mining equipment, trucks and conveyor belts. By 2001, these investments resulted in the following achievements:

- Ten percent of world cobalt was produced by Cuba.
- Cuba became the sixth largest nickel producer worldwide.
- Market share was recovered with exports to more than 30 countries.
- New production records were established.

The joint Cuban-Canadian enterprise Moa Nickel S.A. has managed to increase continually its share of total nickel exports. Since 1995, these have represented more than 40 percent of the total export of Cuban mining exports (Figure 6.10).

Oil and Gas

The introduction of cutting-edge modern technologies through foreign investment partnering with foreign investment has produced very significant results in the oil and gas sector. Dozens of important companies in Canada, France, United Kingdom, Sweden, Brazil and Spain have signed at-risk contracts to explore and drill oilfields. The new

Figure 6.10 Sherritt's Share of Total Cuban Mining Production, 1995–2003 (percentage)

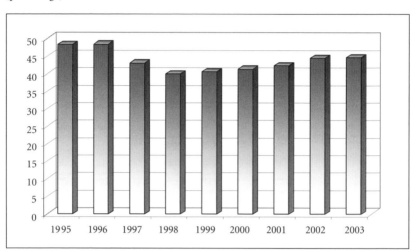

Source: ONE, *Anuario estadístico de Cuba,* various years, and Sherritt International Corporation Annual Report, various years

technologies have permitted the increase in crude oil and related gas production, as well as more efficient utilization. Technologies introduced include:

- Horizontal perforation and multi-pipe, which has reduced perforation by 4 or 5 times and increases production levels to 5 or 6 times higher than standard levels.
- Improvements in pumping system using ROTAFLEX, which has increased productivity by 2 or 3 times.
- Utilization of the gas associated with electricity generation and in domestic consumption, eliminating contamination and recovering sulfur.
- Construction of ducts for the transportation of petrol and gas, which reduced transport costs and increased safety.
- Construction of raw treatment plants that reduced the share of water and salts required and eliminated hydro-sulphuric acids, resulting in time and energy savings (Ministerio de la Industria Básica 2000).

As a result of these technologies, for example, production of petroleum equivalent oil increased six fold between 1991 and 2001 (Figure 6.11). By 2001, the utilization of oil and gas in electric power output,

Figure 6.11 Crude Oil Production, 1988–2003
(thousands of metric tons)

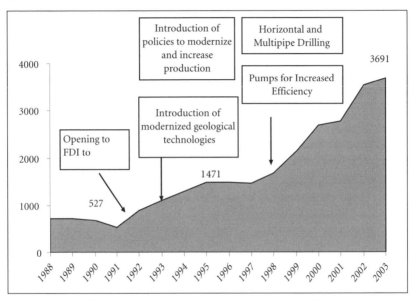

Source: Ministry of the Basic Industry, "Report on business opportunities," Havana, October 2001 and ONE, *Anuario estadístico de Cuba*, 2001 and 2002

cement, nickel and household fuel (gas) resulted in production levels that had an import substitution effect greater than US$450 million.

The joint venture enterprise ENERGAS, the result of a merger between a Cuban company and the Canadian-based Sherritt International Corporation, has joint investments of more than US$150 million. These have financed the construction of a 210 Mw electricity plant. This project also produced a significant environmental benefit since the natural gas derived from petroleum extraction that previously contaminated the northern coast of Havana and Matanzas is now being utilized (Figure 6.12). As a result, 20,000 tons of sulfur and 12,000 tons of LPG, formerly released into the atmosphere, are now being recovered and harnessed to produce electricity. In 2002, the plant's completed expansion with an additional 150 Mw of capacity followed the installation of two gas and combined cycle turbines with an investment of approximately US$120 million. Following significant investments and the signing of important agreements, Sherritt International's oil and gas operations in Cuba have increased extraordinarily in recent years. More than 30 percent of the oil that is extracted in Cuba comes from Sherritt (Figure 6.13).

Figure 6.12 Increase in the Use of Companion Gas to Eliminate Contamination, 1994–2003 (millions of cubic meters)

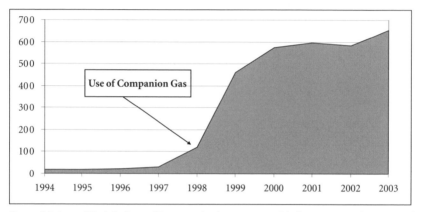

Source: Ministry of Basic Industry, "Report on business opportunities," Havana, October 2001 and ONE, *Anuario estadístico de Cuba*, 2001 and 2002

Figure 6.13 Sherritt's Sales as a Share of Total Petroleum Production, 1997–2003 (percentage)

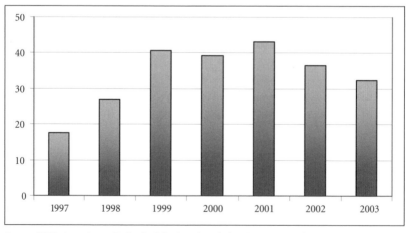

Source: ONE, *Anuario estadístico de Cuba* (2002) and Sherritt Inc. Annual Report (various years)

Telecommunications

One of the most important FDI agreements in Cuba was the 1994 creation of the joint venture firm ETECSA. A venture between the Cuban state telephone communications firm and Mexico's CITEL, the company is valued at more than US$1.6 billion. The agreement granted ETECSA a concession for 55 years, stipulating a US$740 million investment in the project's first seven years. This agreement was exceptional as it encompassed Cuba's entire telephony infrastructure, resulting in the creation of organizational structures with a very centralized character, contrasting with the territorial or decentralized structure that had prevailed in the 1970s and 1980s. Although CITEL originally owned 49 percent of ETECSA's shares, it sold 25 percent of its shares to STET International of Italy in April 1995. When STET purchased an additional portfolio of shares that were in the hands of CITEL in 1997, it became the majority stakeholder (CONAS 1996–1997). In 1997 Sherritt of Canada acquired part of CUBACEL, Cuba's cellular communications operator.

Overall, foreign direct investment in the telecommunication sector has produced positive results, especially considering that the joint venture enterprise ETECSA put an end to Cuba's profound deterioration of communications services by constructing modern digital plants and installing microwaves in different parts of the country, as well as introducing state-of-the-art technologies such as fiber optics in local networks. Plant modernization and other investments have been impressive, but what is most important is that the improvement of service has been palpable to users, who have been offered new communications services for the first time in 30 years.

One of the additional advantages of partnering with an internationally renowned European company has been that service quality indicators have greatly improved. For example, the services available today are well above those available to consumers under obsolete infrastructure. That is, ETECSA's investment of more than US$500 million dollars has permitted unprecedented achievements in this sphere (Figure 6.14). Forecasts predict that the telephone density per every 100 inhabitants will rise to 20 telephones per 100 inhabitants for Havana and 9 telephones per 100 inhabitants as the nationwide average (Figure 6.15).

Figure 6.14 Investments in Fixed Telephony, 1994–2003
(US$ million)

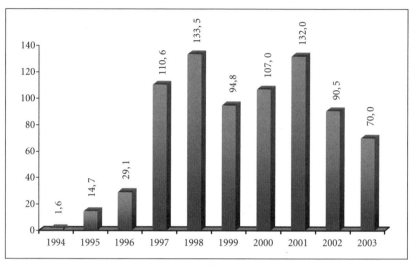

Source: Report of the Ministry of Information and Telecommunications (2000, 2001 and 2002)

Figure 6.15 Telephone Density, 1996–2004
(telephones per 100 inhabitants)

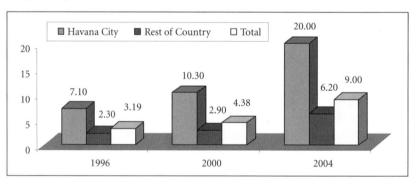

Source: Report of the Ministry of Information and Telecommunications (2000, 2001 and 2002)

Food and Beverage Industry

In 2001, the Food Industry Ministry (Ministerio de la Industria Alimenticia–MINAL) developed two private corporations with state financing to work with the 16 companies with foreign investment operating in Cuba. In 1995, the ministry introduced financing schemes to allow the industry's companies access to foreign exchange resources financed both by their own income earned from their participation in domestic foreign exchange markets and from export activities (González 1998). Competition from better quality foreign products increased the competitiveness of nationally-produced products and broadened the range the goods available in given markets. Seventeen financing arrangements in foreign exchange were available for each top business management executive committee (Organización Superior de Dirección Empresarial) in 2001.

In 1993, the Corporación Cuba Ron S.A. was constituted with the signing of a 30-year agreement with the French company Pernod Ricard for the marketing of "Havana Club" rum. Revitalizing exports of this traditional category, this corporation is a Cuban private entity made up of four factories and two trading companies, one of which is a joint venture, Havana Club International S.A. This joint operation is a well-balanced partnership in which a quality product is being combined with a well-established international distribution network. Sales have increased from 250,000 cases in 1994 to 1,250,000 cases in 1999. In a period of no more than 10 years, the goal is to reach production and distribution of 5 million cases. Havana Club sold US$43.9 million in 2003.

In 1996, the Corporación Alimentaria S.A. (Coralsa), a Cuban private entity, was created to fuel the development of foreign investment opportunities organically by pursuing market expansion, technology investments and development financing of the rest of MINAL's industries except for alcoholic beverage production. In addition, this cor-

Figure 6.16 Joint Venture Sales to the Ministry for Food Industry, 1994–2000
(US$ million)

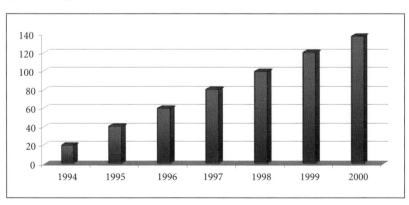

Source: Cámara de Comercio de Cuba, 2000 Foreign Trade No. 3 and Ministry of Food Industry (MINAL)

poration was charged with strengthening the capture of income from undertakings with joint ventures. Overall, the sixteen joint venture enterprises belonging to the Food Industry Ministry account for 6 percent of total food production. Though small, these represent a valuable contribution in terms of shares in domestic and export markets.

In addition to increased sales by joint venture enterprises, technological improvements have been made as well. The associated quality improvements have also translated into better packaging and product presentation. The brewing company, Cervecera Bucanero S.A., is a joint venture enterprise between the Coralsa Corporation and the Canadian firm Cerbuco. This corporation owns the beer plant for manufacturing Bucanero Antigua Mayabe, the brands of Cristal, Bucanero and Mayabe in the beer category and Maltina and Mayabe in the malt category. It has increased continually its production and export by more than 15 percent annually, thanks to the foreign company's introduction of new technologies to reduce costs, improved packaging and presentation.

The company Industrias Cárnicas Hispano-Cubanas (Bravo S.A.), a joint venture enterprise between Coralsa and the Provalca Company of Valencia, Spain, operates in the meatpacking industry. This firm takes advantage of the experiences and the "know how" of the Spanish meatpacking industry adapted to Cuban conditions. The company is considered a leader in its profitability in the food industry sector and it is expanding into the Caribbean and Central American markets. Moreover, an outstanding factor is the quality of state-of-the-art technology introduced that has permitted the growth of production by 30 percent in 1999 and 25 percent in 2000.

In the case of the Los Portales S.A. Company, ownership is shared between the Cuban company Coralsa and the Swiss group NESTLE. This company produces and markets some of the most important mineral waters and beverages, as well as owning several mineral water bottling factories. In addition, Los Portales S.A. has introduced the use of the PET container for bottling refreshments and new bottling lines for canned goods. With growing annual sales reaching 12.6 million cans in 1998 and more than 16.7 million in 1999, sales exceeded US$20 million by 2001. The advance in the quality of the obtained products has also enabled the company to enter the Caribbean and MERCOSUR markets.

Investments by foreign partners total more than US$100 million, which added to the contribution of Cuban partners, represent total investments of more than US$150 million (González 1998). In the food and alcoholic beverages industries, foreign investment has permitted the achievement of goals such as:

- Remodeling of beer production capacities
- Creation of a new line of bottled beers at a cost of US$16 million
- Creation of a new wheat milling plant with capacity to process 80 MT per year
- Construction of a dry yeast factory in Santa Cruz
- Remodeling and construction of sausage factories
- Restitution of ice cream production and the introduction of new milk lines in long-lasting containers
- New lines of Tetra Brick for packaging evaporated milk
- New soybean processing plant in Santiago, Cuba

Enterprises stimulated by sales in foreign exchange have rethought their linkages with the Cuban agricultural sector. They have entered into agreements on the delivery of good quality raw materials in exchange for advanced distribution of inputs and financing for farm producers, with advantageous prices for both sectors. In the future, agro-industrial relations should be developed in greater depth, as well as integrated into more dynamic, direct and less bureaucratic forms of trade, especially because of the new forms of production that have emerged in the agricultural sector.

Free Trade Zones

The establishment of free trade industrial zones to create efficient infrastructure and eliminate bureaucratic transactions in a given place has been an instrument commonly utilized to promote FDI in export activities. In fact, the majority of "winning countries" in Figure 6.1 established this type of activity in strategic sectors (or other arrangements that share some of its characteristics, such as export processing zones). In addition, several of these countries produce most of their manufactured goods exports which are not based the exploitation of natural resources in free trade zones. However, the operation of free trade industrial zones depends a great deal on the adoption of other policies; particularly those aimed at improving training for human resources and creating the necessary infrastructure that attracts and improves export-oriented foreign direct investment. Those zones have given excellent results in countries such as China, Costa Rica, Philippines, the Dominican Republic and Singapore.

Free trade industrial zones have registered changes in both their composition and utilization in recent years. Export quantity requirements have been reduced in many countries, thus permitting a considerable increase in the volume of sales to domestic markets. National companies are now more significantly represented in these zones. Governments are now promoting linkages between foreign branches and national companies, as well as the education of local workers and the development of adequate levels of technical and technological infrastructure.[15] Whereas manufacturing activities were characterized by low technological intensity, high levels of labor intensiveness with accompanying response to incentives, the assembly of electronic products and electronic design, as well as testing services and research and development, have become much more frequent.

Free trade industrial zones have continued to have an important role in the general strategy of the countries seeking to promote FDI in their export activities. Countries interested in strengthening exports have continued to exempt company exports from indirect taxes (as sales taxes), border taxes (for example, consular rights) and import duties. Regimes that permit the reimbursement and exemption of import duties are also permitted. Although regimes that permit the recompense of duties may include specific criteria pertaining to capital assets utilized to produce exported goods, it is possible that many smaller member countries of the WTO barely produce these capital assets, which means that they could consider the possibility of reducing or eliminating import duties on these goods. Furthermore, it is noteworthy that most structural advantages, such as effective infrastructure operation and the simplification of administrative formalities, are not affected. Partly for this reason, several countries, among them some developed countries, are beginning to convert their free trade industrial zones into industrial polygons or scientific parks that can serve as catalysts for the formation of agglomerations of companies (*clusters*).[16] The success of the free trade industrial zone should not be measured only by its capacity to attract FDI or to increase exports and foreign exchange income. To correctly assess the zone, the extent to which they help reach broader economic and social objectives should be evaluated.

Countries that adopt more integrated measures to attract FDI in export activities, such as protections for workers' rights and participation of the same groups in business decisions, are more successful in obtaining results. To achieve maximum benefit from government intervention, the promotion of FDI in export activities should be an integral part of an overall national development strategy. The success of a recipient country in attracting and improving export-oriented FDI and in promoting development resulting from this investment depends crucially on its ability to develop internal capabilities and its know-how in achieving deregulation.

In Cuba these free trade zones were created through the Decree-Law 165 in 1996, which established the benefits granted to these zones, which with a few exceptions were the same benefits given to FDI. In 1997, the first three free trade zones began operations in Cuba. Wajay was inaugurated on May 5, 1997 with a total of 51.9 acres (21 hectares). The free trade zone of Havana (Berroa) was inaugurated two days later with 602.8 acres (244 hectares). Mariel was inaugurated in November of the same year with 1365.1 acres (553 hectares). Each zone was fitted with ample manufacturing and office space. Concessions were helped by CIMEX and Almacenes Universales corporations. Of the 365 operators in free trade zones in 2000 the free trade zone of greatest coverage was in Wajay with 141 operators, followed by Berroa with 125 operators and finally Mariel with 99 operators (Figure 6.17).

Figure 6.17 Number of Approved Operators in Free Trade Zones, 2000

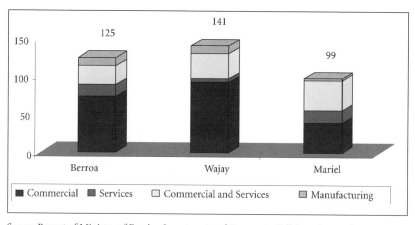

Source: Report of Ministry of Foreign Investment and Economic Collaboration, various years

The results from free trade zones operations, show a significant growth in exports from 1997 to 2001 (Figure 6.18). Despite the fact that most of the companies were productive and provided advantages in job generation and technology acquisition, the results obtained have for various reasons not reached the levels targeted in the original proposals.

Figure 6.18 Exports from Free Trade Zones, 1997–2002
(US$ million)

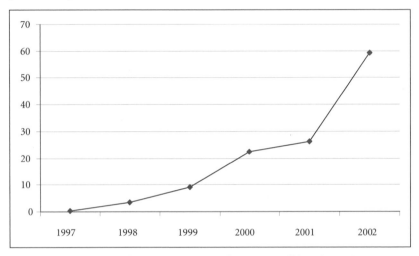

Source: Report of Ministry of Foreign Investment and Economic Collaboration, various years

International experiences that attest to the increasing returns resulting from the positive spillovers derived from the location of more complex industries in which positive technology transfers enable the efficient utilization of trained human resources, such as the pharmaceutical or biotechnology industry, chemistry, optic or electronic equipment and medical equipment, have not been given due importance in Cuba. A challenge for Cuba is to succeed in obtaining meaningful cooperation from foreign companies and the rest of national companies to focus on these higher growth areas.

The role of free trade zones in Cuba's developing trajectory should be reconsidered. Greater involvement of foreign operators should be permitted in order to incorporate their experience and demands into the building of a strategy for their insertion into local markets. This should include encouraging greater reduction of export goals of the free trade zones, following examples by winning economies. Foreign investment as a source of financing can still contribute a great deal. Its contribution will depend, to a large extent, on the way in which it is articulated in an organized manner with the rehabilitation strategy of the Cuban economy. Some foreign researchers who analyze the impact of foreign investment in the development of the Cuban economy also have recognized the impact of this on the improvement of the competitiveness of Cuban products (Spadoni 2002).

Conclusion

Collaboration between the Cuban state and foreign investors has demonstrated that risk and uncertainty can be diminished through the adoption of confidence building measures. Foreign investment has also played an important role in nourishing the scarcity of capital and technology and improving the channeling of investments toward economic projects that contribute both to society's well-being and higher profits. The overall balance of these types of joint venture enterprises has been positive for Cuba. Markets were secured for Cuban products, a task which otherwise would have been more complex. In addition, foreign direct investment has permitted Cuban firms to learn from the types of rigorous experiences that are required by insertion and competition in various world markets. Hence, it is advisable that these possibilities should be expanded in the immediate future.

Since the 1990s, the problems associated with securing foreign sources of financing for the Cuban economy has become a fundamental task, since it is no longer feasible to rely on sufficient levels of domestic savings to fuel growth and development. While foreign financing normally has been considered an important complement to domestic savings, as both increase investment and help promote sustained levels of economic growth, such has not been Cuba's recent experience. In the search for financing abroad to supplement this gap, the capability of acquiring high-level foreign technologies should be linked even more to this search for investments.

Recent experience shows the importance of the application of economic policies by recipient capital countries on the maintenance of a stable investment flow. But, it also demonstrates that in order to attract foreign capital in significant levels, healthy macroeconomic policies are not sufficient. In addition, the application of profound internal reforms in economic and financing policies is required. The growing level of speculation in international financing activity has helped to accentuate the exclusion of underdeveloped economies, while the level of risk and exposure in the transactions of capital, especially short-term, has been increased.

Taking these trends into account, Cuba should continue the process of opening to foreign direct investment, while enhancing the rules that are established to regulate these flows. It should promote FDI without surrendering sovereignty over the nation's resources. Foreign direct investment should be promoted in strategic sectors, such as sugar. In addition, FDI should also be encouraged in the most deficient services such as transportation. However, the strategy to attract FDI should focus on directing these flows toward the formation of joint ventures. Through these arrangements, the state can ensure its continued participation in decision making and the flow of benefits from such investments in the national interest.

The experiences of FDI in developing countries considered "winners" in terms of their current levels of international trade demonstrate that the support of coherent policies is essential to guaranteeing that transnational companies' export production activities are inserted firmly into the national development strategy. Polices toward foreign capital in Cuba strive to achieve this goal, but still need to become more comprehensive. On the other hand, FDI is not the panacea that is painted by international organizations. FDI inevitably maximizes transnational capital profits, and this capital represents geopolitical interests. Thus, the ability to balance virtues and defects by receptor governments is indispensable if the advantages of capital are to be obtained.

In sum, the experiences in the different sectors analyzed in this chapter make it possible to conclude that the process of foreign investment has been successful in Cuba. It has enabled the acquisition of technologies and managerial capabilities, and has been an important source of export growth as well. Industrial progress has been achieved in those sector with significant foreign investment. This should serve as a guide for advancing toward the development of other sectors, especially those with greater buoyancy in world trade. Cuba is inserting itself in the world economy that is being shaped in the new century, athough the rigid blockade imposed by the United States on the island remains in place.

References

Ariovich, Laura. 2000. "Análisis sobre el estado y los intereses económicos." *Revista Nueva Sociedad,* 170, November–December.

Banco Central de Cuba. Various years. *Informes económicos.* BCC: Havana.

Centro de Estudios de Economía Cubana. Universidad de la Habana. 1997. Proceedings from the Workshop "La economía cubana en 1996: Resultados, problemas y perspectivas." Havana: CEEC.

CEPAL. 1986. *La planificación y las políticas públicas en 1982–1984 y perspectivas para la segunda mitad del decenio,* Cuadernos del ILPES, no. 31. Santiago de Chile: CEPAL.

CEPAL. 1997. *La economía cubana. Reformas estructurales y desempeño en los noventa.* Mexico: Fondo de Cultura Económica.

Dahlman, Kart. 1988. "Inversión extranjera y transferencia de tecnología" in *Comercio exterior: Apertura comercial y proteccionismo; fomento industrial e inversión extranjera,* Colegio Nacional de Economistas, AC, Mexico.

Europa Press. 2002. October 4, 2002.

Fernández, María Antonia. 1997. "Las zonas francas y la economía nacional. Cuba en este proceso." *Boletín informativo de la economía cubana.* Havana: CIEM, no. 31.

Figueras, Miguel. 1998. "Reflexiones sobre los acuerdos regionales y eventuales acuerdos multilaterales de inversión."Speech delivered at the Reunión de Expertos sobre Acuerdos Regionales y Multilaterales Existentes y sus consecuencias para el desarrollo. Geneva: UNCTAD.

———. 2002. *El turismo internacional y la formación de clusters productivos en la economía cubana.* CEEC.

Foreign Trade. 2000. No. 3. Havana: Cámara de Comercio de la República de Cuba.

García, Mercedes.1997. *El financiamiento externo actual.* Havana: Centro de Investigaciones de la Economía Internacional.

García, Mercedes. 1996. "Los mercados financieros internacionales: Tendencias actuales y participación de los países en desarrollo." Havana: Centro de Investigaciones de la Economía Internacional.

González Cruz, Víctor and Guillermo Riech Benítez. 1998. "Diagnóstico sobre los bienes de consumo alimenticios manufacturados del MINAL." Havana.

Gunn, Gillian. 1991. "The Sociological Impact of Rising Foreign Investment," Georgetown University, Cuba Briefing Paper Series, Issue Number 1.

Granma, Havana, January 28, 2003.

Ferradaz, Ibrahim.1997. Remarks at "The Economist Intelligence Unit: Cuarta Mesa Redonda."

Lage, Carlos. 1997. Clausura de la II Reunión Nacional del Ministerio de Economía y Planificación. *Granma*. Havana.

———. 1995. Speech delivered at the Economic Forum in Davos, Swizterland. *Granma*. January 28, 1995. Havana.

Ministerio de la Industria Básica. 2000. "Informe sobre la evolución del Ministerio de la Industria Básica."

Ministerio de las Inversiones Extranjeras. 1996. "Guía para el inversionista en Cuba." Centro de Promoción de Inversiones de La Habana.

———. Various years. Balance Anual del Ministerio. Havana.

ONE. Various years. *Anuario estadístico de Cuba*, ONE: Havana.

Pérez Villanueva, Omar Everleny. 1995. "La inversión extranjera en Cuba" in *El sector mixto en la reforma económica cubana*. Havana: Editorial Félix Varela.

———. 1998. "Cuba's Economic Reforms: An Overview" in *Special Studies*, No. 30, *Perspectives on Cuban Economic Reforms*, edited Jorge F. Pérez-López y Matías Travieso-Diaz. Center for Latin American Studies Press, Arizona State University.

———. 1997. "La inversión extranjera en Cuba. Peculiaridades." Paper presented at XX International Congress LASA 97. Guadalajara, México.

Romero, Antonio. 1996. "Las transformaciones económicas en Cuba." CIEI.

Salas, Carola and García, Mercedes. 1997. "Las finanzas externas de Cuba. Situación actual y perspectivas." Centro de Investigaciones de la Economía Internacional.

Spadoni, Paolo. 2002. *Foreign Investment in Cuba: Recent Developments and Role in the Economy*. University of Florida.

The Star. October 2, 2002.

UNCTAD. 1987. "Reactivación del desarrollo, el crecimiento y el comercio internacional, evaluación y políticas posibles." Document TD/328/add. 2. Geneva: UNCTAD.

———. 1999. World Investment Report 1999: *Foreign Direct Investment and the Challenge of Development*. Geneva: UNCTAD.

———. 2001. World Investment Report 2001. Geneva: UNCTAD.

———. 2002a. "Informe sobre las inversiones en el mundo 2002" in *Las empresas transnacionales y la competitividad de las inversiones*. Geneva: UNCTAD.

———. 2002b. *La dimensión del desarrollo de la IED en el contexto nacional e internacional. Cuestiones de política que han de examinarse*. TD/B/COM.2/EM.12/2. Geneva: UNCTAD.

Vera, Ignacio and Molina, Elda. 1999. "¿Incide el NAFTA en los Niveles Actuales de Inversión Extranjera en Cuba?" Havana: CIEI.

Notes

1   UNCTAD. 2002a. *World Investment Report 2002: Transnational Corporations and Export Competitiveness.* New York and Geneva.

2   Ibid.

3   Ibid.

4   Ibid.

5   Ibid.

6   UNCTAD (2001).

7   UNCTAD. 2002b. "La dimensión de desarrollo de la IED en el contexto nacional e internacional. Cuestiones de política que han de examinarse," TD/B/COM.2/EM.12/2. September 23, 2002. New York and Geneva.

8   UNCTAD (2002a)

9   CEPAL. 2002. *La inversión extranjera en América Latina y el Caribe,* 2001. CEPAL: Santiago de Chile.

10 Ibid.

11 Ariovich, Laura. 2000. "Análisis sobre el estado y los intereses económicos." *Revista Nueva Sociedad,* no. 170, November-December, 2000.

12 *Europa Press.* October 4, 2002.

13 *The Star.* October 2, 2002.

14 Figueras (2002)

15 UNCTAD (2002a)

16 UNCTAD (1999)

Commentary:
Economic Reforms in China and Vietnam: Are There Lessons for Cuba?

by Dwight H. Perkins

No two countries are exactly alike and so one country cannot simply adopt the policies of another and expect to achieve the same results. That said, China and Vietnam are seen as two nations that adopted market reforms that achieved rapid economic growth without seriously challenging the rule of the Communist Party. Are there lessons for Cuba?

The first thing to note about the reforms in China and Vietnam is that, at the start, the leadership in both countries had only a very general idea about what they hoped to achieve. The principal goal was to increase the nation's wealth and power while preserving socialist values in some form. Deep dissatisfaction with the slow GDP growth rates of the two decades prior to the beginning of reform in 1978 led to a determination to raise that rate closer to the rates achieved by China's (and Vietnam's) East Asian neighbors. The approach was one of trying something to see if it moved the country toward that goal. If it did, the experiment was pursued further; if it did not, the experiment was abandoned and replaced by another approach.

This reform process in Asia has often been described as a strategy of gradual reform to contrast it with "shock therapy" practiced in parts of Eastern Europe. But in both China and Vietnam, certain quite radical reforms were introduced rapidly, the rural reforms for example, while other sectors such as the state-owned industries experienced slow and generally ineffective reform for more than a decade after the beginning of the reform process. It was not until the middle of the 1990s, a decade and a half after the reforms started, that China's leadership finally agreed that the goal was to create a full market economy integrated into the world economic system. Vietnam started the reform process much later (the critical change in political leadership occurred in 1986 followed by major economic reforms in 1989) but was able to move faster toward a market economy in part because it could learn from the successes and failures of the Chinese experiment next door.

Much of the success of the reform process in China and Vietnam can be attributed to the fact that the reform process started with "winners." In both countries a process was set underway that led within three to four years to the complete abandonment of collective agriculture replacing it with household-based agricultural production. A freeing up of rural markets for most agricultural crops accompanied this change, although the state retained a major role in the purchase and sale of grain. This was not a partial reform involving the expansion of private plots that had supplemented collective agriculture even during the height of the Commune or collective period—it was a near total transfer of production and marketing to the household. The resulting impact on farm output in both China and Vietnam was dramatic. Higher output plus higher farm purchase prices meant that rural incomes in China between 1978 and 1984 increased by more than 50 percent. Prior to these reforms, Vietnam was an importer of rice. A year later, with the reforms more or less completed in the south, Vietnam became a rice exporter again. The one thing not freed up in both China and Vietnam was the right to buy and sell land. The local governments continued to determine who farmed what land, occasionally redistributing it as some families moved to the cities and higher paying jobs.

The other change at the outset of the reform period was both countries' decision to encourage imports from hard currency, which in turn required the country to find sources of foreign exchange to pay for these imports. In Vietnam, this process was complicated by the continued existence of the U.S. embargo that was not lifted until the mid-1990s. In the case of China, the embargo had been lifted in the late 1960s and hence was not a factor. The Vietnamese experience is the one with the most relevance to Cuba. As late as 1988, most Vietnamese trade was with COMECON and Vietnamese. Imports, heavily subsidized by the Soviet Union, were double export earnings. With the abrupt end of Soviet aid and the continuing embargo, Vietnam could have experienced a sharp decline in GDP. In actual fact, the GDP growth rate rose, and Soviet aid was rapidly replaced with new exports, including the aforementioned 1989–1990 switch to rice exports and the beginning of production by the White Tiger oil field. Subsequent years, but still before the end of the U.S. embargo, saw the rapid expansion of coffee and other agricultural exports, followed by manufactures such as shoes.

In China, to promote exports, the government began to break up control of foreign trade previously monopolized by corporations associated with the Ministry of Foreign Trade. China also early on made sure that it had an exchange rate that was most likely undervalued and hence a stimulus to exports. China continued to devalue its currency to ensure that its exports remained competitive. China did experiment for a time with a multiple exchange rate system but soon abandoned it. Vietnam, in contrast, freed up its foreign exchange market and let the currency float. For a time the Central Bank may have intervened to try to prop up the value of the Vietnamese dong, but by the latter half of the 1990s the exchange rate was clearly at a level that made many Vietnamese exports internationally competitive.

In the early phases of the reform in China most manufactured exports came from state-owned enterprises. But China has never succeeded in overcoming some of the built in inefficiencies of many of its state-owned enterprises. Increasingly exports of manufactures have come first from township and village enterprises that behaved like private enterprises, although they were officially registered as collective enterprises, and then in the 1990s exports increasingly came from foreign direct investment enterprises—firms that involved both joint ventures with local enterprises and others that were wholly foreign owned. In the case of Vietnam, most of the manufactured exports have come from foreign direct investment enterprises. Vietnam's state-owned sector is still highly protected and follows an import substituting model.

The increasing role of foreign direct investment in both China and Vietnam was a gradual process. The decision to allow FDI was made early on in both countries, but the supporting institutions needed to attract investors were not in place. In the case of China many overseas Chinese invested anyway, counting on personal ties of various sorts to give them the security they needed for their investments. In the early years, China also experimented with various methods of extracting funds from foreign direct investment, such as requiring foreign investors to pay artificially high wages, but these measures were soon abandoned because they clearly interfered with the expansion of FDI. Over time first China and then Vietnam began to put in place laws that gave FDI a more secure and predictable framework in which to work. The lack of a secure FDI institutional framework in the 1980s meant that the large multinational investors were not really a major factor in Chinese FDI (except for oil) until the mid 1990s when multinational participation succeeded in raising total FDI to over US$40 billion per year. For China, of course, there was the enormous attraction of the anticipated huge domestic market. Vietnam did not have such a large potential domestic market, but Vietnam by 1997 was attracting US$2 billion each year in FDI, although that number declined in the aftermath of the Asian financial crisis and the bureaucratic obstacles that some in the Vietnamese government continued to put in the way of foreign investors. In China, FDI is now a major element in almost all industries except for those directly related to the production of armaments. In few if any cases, however, does FDI dominate a major industry. Even at US$50 billion per year, the level of 2002–2003, that amount represents slightly less than ten percent of total Chinese investment.

Some of the most difficult decisions both China and Vietnam have had to make are those connected with whether to fully join the international economic system and, if so, what to do with the many state-owned enterprises that probably could not survive global competition. China has gone the furthest in this regard with its decision to join the World Trade Organization on conditions that require China to open up all aspects of its economy to foreign competition. The Chinese leadership, in making this decision, quite deliberately decided to use competition to force state enterprises to reform or to go out of business. The immediate result was the laying off of some 30 million workers in these enterprises over a three-year period, a process that is still continuing. It seems likely that China will eventually privatize most of its state enterprises, although the word "privatization" has been studiously avoided by both China and Vietnam. Many of the smaller state and collective firms in China, however, have effectively been privatized already. The larger state firms are now mostly shareholding enterprises, but the majority of shares are still controlled by the state. Vietnam also has introduced shareholding enterprises, but this process is not as far along as in China.

Global competitiveness, of course, involves more than just the question of ownership. Both China and Vietnam have had to consciously decide how far they wanted to go in making the Internet available to its citizens, for example. China, after some initial reluctance, has basically decided to make the Internet widely accessible, although efforts continue to try to limit access to sites deemed politically or socially unacceptable. Vietnam has followed a similar path.

By the year 2004, it is possible to say that China and Vietnam have abandoned all aspects of Soviet-style central planning, and that system has been gone for over a decade. What remains is an economic system that increasingly looks like the mixed private-public market economies of China's and Vietnam's East Asian neighbors. The government still plays an active role in promoting particular industries, but direct ownership and control of industry by the state is less than a quarter of total output in the case of China—a larger share in the case of Vietnam. In Vietnam's case these changes have produced more than a decade of 7 percent GDP growth. In the case of China there has been a quarter century of per capita growth of around 8 percent. Put differently, per capita incomes in Vietnam in the reform period have more or less doubled on average while per capita incomes in China have increased at least five fold. These increases have been achieved mainly by relying on reforms that emphasized individual incentives and a price system (including the exchange rate) that fostered efficiency and international competitiveness. China in 1978 was a minor economic player on the world scene with exports of less than US$10 billion that year. In 2003 China's exports were US$438 billion, roughly the same size as the exports of Japan. Vietnam has gone from having exports of only US$1 billion in 1989 with most of those directed to COMECON to a total export of US$17 billion in 2002 mostly with market economies.

The Social Consequences of Reform

In terms of average income and consumption, there is no question that the Chinese and Vietnamese approach to reform has been a success. But has everyone benefited from these reforms or have large numbers been left out of the process? China at the outset of reforms, it should be noted, made a conscious decision to allow some individuals and particular regions of the country to get rich faster than the others. At the same time the goal of ensuring that eventually all would benefit was retained and resources were devoted to assisting the poorest regions, but there is a question as to how well this latter effort has succeeded. On the favorable side, there has been a sharp reduction in poverty throughout both countries especially in the case of China. There are still pockets of extreme poverty and the number of people involved are in the tens of millions in China, but that is down from the hundreds of millions who lived on less than US$1 per day three decades ago. On the less positive side, there is rising inequality both within the cities and within the countryside, but particularly between the cities and the countryside. After the initial success in agriculture, farm output has slowed down and prices paid to farmers have come down as those prices have come into line with world prices. The resulting widening gap between average rural and urban incomes has created an enormous pressure to migrate from the farms to the cities. China still maintains a household registration system that restricts services in the cities available to rural migrants, but this system will have to change as these migrants increase from the current level of around 100 million workers to several times that number over the coming two decades.

Abolition of the collective system in agriculture and its replacement by market forces and household production has also led to the collapse of the rural public health system and most rural health insurance in China. Higher incomes have in many ways improved access to health care even in the rural areas, but access is highly unequal and family health catastrophes are a major reason why some families fall back into poverty. There are efforts underway to change this situation, but they are still in the experimental stage.

Education, in principle, is now compulsory for the first eight years and there has been a rapid expansion in both the quality and quantity of secondary and university level education, but the quality of education in the cities far surpasses that in the rural areas and rural migrants often have to provide for their children's education with their own resources with little help from the government.

Lessons for Cuba?

What, if any, lessons are there for Cuba in this experience? Certainly there are many specific measures undertaken by China and Vietnam that Cuba can learn from—everything from exchange rate policies to the failure of most attempts to reform the state-owned enterprises, but the real lesson from the Chinese and Vietnamese experience lies elsewhere. In a sense, the main lesson is the one that Japan understood as early as the 1880s, while it was not until a hundred years later in the 1980s that China reached a similar conclusion. If you are going to build a modern competitive industrial and service sector economy, one cannot do it with half-way measures or gimmicks. China in the nineteenth century tried to maintain the old Confucian system of governance and values supplemented with modern armaments and it did not work. Mao tried to create a fundamentally different kind of society and that kind of society could not produce rising standards of living either. Even a cursory review of Cuba's attempts at reform makes it clear that Cuba is still trying to hold on to too many of the trappings of a Soviet-style command economy for the country to achieve sustained economic growth. Cuba also appears to have put a much higher premium on the use of economic levers to maintain political control and on maintaining equality even if it is at the expense of rising standards of living for all.

China in 1978 and Vietnam in 1986 did not decide to abandon socialism and neither has made such a decision today. But both have clearly decided that they had to do what was necessary to achieve sustained increases in income if they were to survive as strong and independent nations. To achieve that goal, they have had to abandon virtually all of the trappings of the Soviet approach to economic development. They have also tended, albeit inadvertently, to neglect other basic socialist values that stress the importance of guaranteeing education and a certain level of health care to all, but both China and Vietnam are now wrestling with how to overcome that neglect. They now have the resources to do much in these areas, but they don't yet have workable systems for providing a minimum welfare standard for all.

Finally, neither China nor Vietnam has fully faced the consequences of their economic successes for the continuation of one-party rule. Both have been willing to abandon many of the economic levers of political control and rely instead on rapid growth to provide the main rationale for the continuance of rule by the Communist Party. How much longer that will continue to be the case and how well it will work remains to be seen.

PART

III

Social Policy and Welfare

7

Social Effects of Economic Adjustment: Equality, Inequality and Trends toward Greater Complexity in Cuban Society

by Mayra Espina Prieto

As a result of the crisis and reforms in the 1990s, the Cuban social sciences are now examining issues of poverty, its measurement and the design of policies aimed at counteracting its effects. Previously, these disciplines had excluded research and debate over poverty, primarily because poverty was considered a problem that had been eradicated during the socialist transition. At the very least, poverty was seen as significantly lessened as a result of the revolution's universal, integrative social policies. In this context, the relevance of poverty as a social problem had diminished and was considered practically solved (Rodríguez and Carriazo 1987). At the same time, strong influences and linkages with the academic community in the former Eastern European socialist camp, in whose agendas the topic did not appear, led to an examination of advances in the process of "social homogenization," as well as a tacit understanding, never declared, of the irrelevance of poverty as a topic of study for Cuban social sciences, based on the assumption that socialism had established a logic of universal coverage and uninterrupted, irreversible access for the popular sectors of the population.

Poverty has become a central theme for Cuban social sciences, at the same time that the analysis of poverty in policy circles and the social sciences has increased worldwide in the last decade and a significant portion of the Cuban population faces more scarcity and a lack of fulfillment of basic needs. This chapter seeks to place the discussion of poverty in Cuba and the policies for its eradication in a broader framework. In analyzing the relationship between equality and inequality, this study argues that poverty must be understood as a part of social relations and as an expression of the social structures derived from distinct inequalities. An analysis of poverty must be based on structural conditions, those that persistently reproduce themselves, rather than on the traditional reductionist position that considers poverty to be a circumstantial disadvantage for a limited sector. Only a structural framework will allow for the design of realistic policies to alleviate and eradicate poverty.

This chapter begins with a critical reflection on the social political model adopted during Cuba's socialist transition and its treatment of equality as a central axis of distribution. It then undertakes a characterization of the state of inequality in Cuba in regards to income, territorial differences and possibilities for advancing social mobility. The chapter concludes with an analysis of whether equality-based social policy can be reformulated towards an improved understanding of differences and diversity, in which the objective of providing equality through egalitarian homogeneity shifts towards one that emphasizes distributive mechanisms based on the equality of diversity.

The Cuban Model of Social Policy for Tackling Poverty

Cuban society's experience over the past 45 years or so may be interpreted as a process of thorough, widespread social change that has passed through different stages, including crisis periods. This process can be characterized by its construction of a model of social change, incorporating a wide range of social policies. The model has quite original features, especially when compared with the usual methods of tackling poverty in developing or peripheral countries. The most substantial feature—and the one that is truly original about this Cuban model—is its radical focus on the social dimension, and its departure from a narrowly economic focus on development.

A set of particular features characterize the social policies inspired by Cuba's model of social change including:

- Elimination of private property in the fundamental means of production and of the conditions that give rise to relationships of exploitation

- Social ownership by the state as the foundation for the vanguard role of the popular sectors and prioritizing those sectors in the social agenda

- Centrality of equality and social justice in policy formulation

- Need for adequate articulation between the economic and the social dimensions of development
- Leading role of the state in the design and implementation of social policies and of planning as a mechanism for prioritizing them
- Single centralized social policy to guarantee the broadest possible levels of universal basic social services
- Conception of human beings in which their needs are assumed to be both material and spiritual, and where spiritual needs play an essential role in individual and social development
- Centrality of distribution as an instrument of social justice
- Combination of individual and social consumption, in which the latter weighs heavily on distributive justice
- Presence of mechanisms of popular participation in actions for change
- Elimination of inequality and gradual flattening of incomes
- Mass access to employment
- Rationality of consumption and of needs as a model of overall life in Cuban society, not simply as a means for doing away with poverty
- Mass access to cultural goods
- Promotion of processes of de-stratification and social homogenization
- Conception of dealing with poverty as the implementation of development policies
- Orientation toward satisfying basic rational needs, systematically extended by placing priority on the educational and spiritual-cultural realm
- Creation of "spaces of equality" as an instrument of equal distribution and social integration
- Gradual weakening of the role of personal and household incomes in consumption and satisfaction of needs by enhancing "spaces of equality"
- Maintenance of these principles and of the inalienable and non-transferable responsibility of the state to guide social pol-

icy, regardless of the availability of economic resources and of the amount of goods to be distributed

As these features indicate, equality and social justice are implicitly assumed to not simply depend on monetary income distribution at the individual and household levels (that is to say that income distribution is not the decisive factor for assuring equality and social justice). Instead, these principles establish what I could call "spaces of equality." I define this concept as a distribution mechanism characterized by universality; its mass character; being free of charge or highly accessible; its status as a legally established right; having a state and government character; centrality and public character of its design and of the guarantee of access to it; societal involvement; preponderance of social over individual solutions; homogeneity; increasing quality; and the option of social integration under equal conditions for all social sectors, regardless of income. Historically, the Cuban model has seen the state as the only (or at least the leading) protagonist in these distribution spaces. Alternatives for having access to the goods distributed in the space in question either do not exist, or they are very low profile and cannot compete with the state option.

Cuban social policy has revolved around gradually broadening these spaces, especially in six areas: satisfaction of basic nutritional needs, education, health, culture, sports and social security. I believe that it is precisely the presence of strong state property, as a guarantor of the interests of the popular sectors, and the emphasis on "spaces of equality" as distribution mechanisms that have enabled the Cuban state to implement an innovative approach to dealing with poverty. Rather than merely providing assistance, the state has pursued the logic of development to assure essential conditions for its reproduction and has created universal and systematically extended social integration.

Critical Views on Cuba's Social Policy Model

I do not intend to conclude that this model and the practices that it has inspired have been perfect and always successful. Indeed, social research has made it possible to construct an interesting critical view of Cuban social policy and of the model of socioeconomic change pursued by the socialist transition, thereby adding interesting dimensions to this analysis. One critical line stemming from considerations from the field of the sociology of inequalities could very succinctly be summarized in issues such as absolutized statism as almost the sole formula for social ownership, which burdens the state, limits its efficiency and fails to utilize the innovative and productive capacity of other social actors and types of property; excessive centralism in decision making; formalization of participation and uniform distribution which lessen sensitivity for grasping and incorporating into policy design individual, group, and local differences and particularities in satisfying needs; the low profile of local actors and governments in the design of social policies at that scale; bureaucratization and expansion of the underground economy (Espina 1999).

Another essential line of criticism focuses on the defects in the economic model implemented, and hence on its weakness for supporting an ambitious social policy. While there is no single approach shared by specialists in this area, my own viewpoint is close to the following appraisal. Monreal and Carranza note: "A pattern of economic growth based on excessive utilization of inputs was the main feature of the evolution of the Cuban economy during the fifteen years preceding the deep crisis of the early 1990s. (. . .) Economic growth in Cuba during the 1975–1989 period was a resource-driven growth, that was not very efficient and bore a high level of external compensation (2000)."

The severe limitations of this extensive-growth model, note the authors, include the dependence on external financing as an indispensable condition for its operation, that is, its inability to be self-sustaining. Other limitations include the inefficient use of productive resources; inability to transform the large sums accumulated into expanded exports; insufficient degree of intersectoral integration of the national economy; high-energy-consumption technology; and the high vulnerability of growth to external factors. In concluding this analysis, they state, "The national economy thus retained powerful structural barriers to self-sustained growth which compounded the relative scarcity of natural resources."

Similarly, Álvarez (1997) notes:

> Until 1989 the Cuban economy was characterized by a high concentration of property in the hands of the state, which employed almost all the economically active population, with a high level of employment, but in many lines of work productivity indicators remained unsatisfactory. Investment was given enough priority to assure development (accumulation rates of over 20 percent), but the yield from basic funds was like-

wise disappointing. Hence it can be concluded that the model applied could not assure the levels of economic efficiency required for a successful process of intensive growth."

Excessive centralized planning methods further compounded the model's deficiencies. Centralized planning resulted in reduced autonomy for enterprises or regions; extremely restricted spaces for the market; little variation in the composition of exports (dependence on foreign revenues from sugar, nickel, citrus fruits, fishing and other scarce primary products); insufficient assimilation of advanced technology in industrial development; and, a concentration of 85 percent of international trade with the COMECON member countries (ibid 1997).

Research in sociology and economics concur in their assessments of the place of distribution and consumption in the Cuban model. While uniform egalitarianism in distribution can be effective for universalizing and extending to the masses the satisfaction of a broad range of needs, it is not sensitive to diversity and has the effect of artificially producing homogeneity in human beings and social groups, by equating their needs and the satisfaction of those needs. The upshot is that contrary to intention, this distribution scheme produces dissatisfaction, or partial satisfaction, and—likewise paradoxically—it ends up reproducing inequality, because it is very ill-suited to respond in an individualized way to the needs of sectors, who have a disadvantage from the start and are thus prevented from truly accessing distributed benefits under equality of conditions, and who accordingly would need "affirmative action" policies to eliminate the conditions that reproduce their disadvantages.

Likewise, undifferentiated consumption with little relationship to the results of labor and productive effort can no longer be a means for encouraging efficiency. Moreover, the undervaluing of individual consumption associated with individual and household incomes—and a certain demonization of it because of its differentiating character—has hobbled the expression of such individual consumption as a realm for the legitimate unfolding of individual abilities and needs, a mechanism for encouraging productive performance, and in general a social relationship stimulating production (Hernández, Espina and Togores 2002). Similarly, the tendencies to reduce popular participation to mere formality, combined with an excessive centralism in decision making, have hindered the concrete expression of some elements of the model.

A Model of Equality

Since a critical vision is basic for any effort at self-transformation of the Cuban experience, I wish to note that, in my judgment, the ideal of social policy for addressing poverty, as the guiding landmark for change and development in the Cuban transition to socialism, albeit with economic reform, is similar to what I have called a model of equality or ethical model. The term is suggested to us by the definition of social policy elaborated by the Brazilian Laura Tavares. She regards social policy a metapolicy that justifies the ordering of any other policy, the ordering of "tragic choices," rather than as one isolated policy, lost among others. From this point of view, social policy would be outside the economic calculus and would be situated instead in ethical accounting, in the area of conflict between values. It would constitute a metapolicy since it takes shape as a matrix of principles prioritizing tragic choices, principles of a changing and contradictory nature (Tavares 1999).

This definition points toward the complexity of decisions in the area of social policy and of their practical implementation, particularly because they cannot be designed with overall universal recipes taken out of context, and because they are always situated, at least in peripheral societies, before the imperative of establishing priorities between dramatic life-or-death options with very limited resources. The imperative splits into one of economic efficiency and another of an ethical nature; although the two aspects are not absolutely incompatible, they are unlikely to be combined without contradictions.

Neo-Liberal Social Policies

Analyzing social policies and policies for dealing with poverty in Latin America that have accompanied the neo-liberal types of reform, Bernardo Kliskberg (2002) identifies the ten assumptions (which he calls "fallacies" because they are wrong and turn reality upside down) on which they are based, from which I can infer a model of neoliberal social policies:

1) De-prioritization of poverty as a social problem, with the understanding that poor people have always existed everywhere

2) The solution of poverty as a matter of time ("being patient with history"), the time necessary to reach the economic goals

that will make it possible to have the resources for attaining social objectives

3) Economic growth as sufficient condition for solving poverty and attaining social development

4) Taking inequality for granted, as an inevitable, necessary phase of development that can be surpassed, with the idea that the concentration of resources on small groups produces investment capabilities that lead to economic growth

5) Downgrading social policy to a secondary level, something that is not a priority, since social spending is considered inefficient investment, while placing emphasis on economic policies such as increasing production capacity, attaining monetary and macroeconomic equilibrium and technological growth

6) De-legitimization of the state as an actor in development, inevitably linking it to corruption, ineffectiveness and bureaucratization, contrasted with the efficiency of the private sector and the market

7) Downgrading the role of civil society as an agent of progressive change on the basis of the superiority of the market in this realm and of the strength of economic incentives, maximized profits, and business management

8) Social participation controlled by the management of public affairs, to be handled by specialized technocratic leadership

9) Ethical evasion, in which technical and instrumental rationality replaces the centrality of values and evades discussion of the means

10) Absence of alternatives

Based on data on economic and social performance from Latin America and elsewhere, Kliskberg demonstrates what is wrong with these assumptions, severely criticizing their effect of devaluing social policy and its inability to solve the problem of poverty. He distinguishes five types of inequality: in income distribution, in access to productive assets and credit, in educational achievement and in access to information technology, empirically showing the inverse relationship between inequality and development and the insidious economic impacts of low-profile social policies which impede the formation of qualified social capital on a broadened scale. He thereby makes clear the need for social policy strategies based on the ethical dimension that recognizes how those strategies fuel the economy.

It is useful to consider these reflections at some length due to the fact that they help demonstrate the alternative character of the Cuban model, whose basic postulates are a response to the "ethics of urgency," which Kliskberg pits against "historic patience" toward poverty (Kliskberg 2002: 9). From my standpoint, the interconnected effect of the crisis on Cuba and the ensuing reforms following the collapse of the Soviet Union have interrupted the logic of systematically extending social equality. The crisis and its subsequent economic reforms have also produced social vulnerability and poverty, creating a situation in which society becomes more complex. As a result, there are demands for the state's leadership in this area to be redesigned. In this chapter, I will concentrate on some of the processes underway in Cuba illustrating the evolution toward greater complexity, in the forms of income re-stratification, the territorialization of inequality and the change in the pattern of social mobility.

Re-stratification of Income

Within the objective dimensions of inequality, sociological studies attempting to measure social differentiation have regarded so-called economic inequalities as the tangible and quantifiable element par excellence of stratification systems. Economic inequalities are the most obvious and the ones that are associated in some manner (as causes or effects) with the most varied structural constraints and expressions of heterogeneity and inequality present in a society at a given time and place. Economic inequalities are defined as differences in income distribution, in access to material and spiritual well-being and consumption (Heller 1987). They express the different degrees of resource availability and the endowment of abilities for satisfying the material needs of different social groups. In this trilogy of income, access to well-being and consumption, individual and household income constitutes the primary, although not the only indicator for measuring inequalities, poverty and social disadvantage. In this context, individual and household income is operationally understood as the amount of money that an individual or household receives in determined periods from different sources such as wages, pensions, profits, informal sources and illegal actions. These income measures are also an indicator of the ability to satisfy needs that must be achieved through markets and serve to measure social distances quantitatively.

The Reduction in Inequality in the Early Decades of the Revolution

Socioeconomic transformations of a socialist nature during the first three decades of the Cuban revolution were able to significantly reduce the asymmetries of the distribution of monetary income, lessen income inequality and minimize polarization by eliminating from the pyramid of social stratification the sharpest and most marked extremes such as an elite exploiting class, the unemployed, those in extreme poverty and outcasts. While the 10 percent of the population with highest incomes received 38 percent of total income, the lowest 20 percent received 2.1 percent in 1953. Only two decades into the revolution, in 1978, this relationship had changed substantially with the lowest 20 percent earning 11 percent of total income, and the 20 percent highest receiving 27 percent (Zimbalist and Brundenius 1989).

Indeed that central thrust of the structural and social changes proper to the transition to socialism was the expansion and predominance of the state sector in the national economy. Thus, this process of lessening income inequality came about as the state took over the economy and paid most individual and household incomes through wages to the workforce employed in state enterprises. The proportion of government workers in relation to the total occupied workforce, rose from 8.8 percent in 1953 to 86 percent in 1970, and reached 94 percent in 1988 (*Censo de Población y Vivienda, 1981* and *Anuario estadístico de Cuba*, 1998).

As the state became solely responsible for employment, a uniform centralized salary system was designed and implemented, thereby giving the state the greatest role in setting pay scales. Salaries were thereby separated from the practically abolished realm of labor market operations. Conditions for the greater equality in remuneration for work were thus created, while at the same time, it was proposed that equal pay be guaranteed for equal work.[1] As a result of these processes, household incomes became tied to wages and salaries.

The uniform, centralized salary system, together with the state's increased role in employment, meant that income lost its absolute and relative importance as a marker of inequality. The reason is that the "spaces of equality" were spread widely as equal distribution mechanisms, assuring ample access to material and spiritual consumption for the satisfaction of basic needs in terms of food, goods, health, education, sports and culture. Dependence on household and personal monetary incomes for consumption or well-being were thus reduced.

With the implementation of the 1983 General Salary Reform (*Reforma General de Salarios*), the parameters of the pay-qualification scale were set in a range of 13 groups, allowing a differentiation between maximum and minimum pay within a range of 4.5 to 1. According to 1988 Instituto de Estudios del Trabajo data, 93 percent of the workers that year fit within a range of only 2.3 to 1 (Nerey and Brismart 1999: 11). By 1986, the Gini index stood at 0.24 (Brundenius 1987). This very low level of income differentiation, especially for wage groups, combined with the great importance of social redistribution, created homogeneity in many dimensions of well-being, culminating in the mid-1980s. Wages were clearly significant as a factor of social-structure leveling, when their stratifying effect was reduced to a minimum. This effect was enhanced by an insurance and social assistance system that guaranteed the protection of universal coverage and a minimum guaranteed post- or extra-labor income, combined with social consumption funds. Adequate access to income for non-workers and dependents was thus insured.

But alongside the positive side of improved income equality, studies on this issue point to its negative aspects: the inability of salary to become a "mobilizing and corrective engine" of the social structure inherited from underdevelopment; the accentuation of imbalances between professions and sectors; constant labor shortage in priority economic activities that are not well paid (e.g., agriculture); the separation of salary increases and efficiency; extensive use of human resources; and the reduced ability of salary to offer incentives (Nerey and Brismart 1999).

The Rise of Inequality in the 1990s

The 1990s marked a rather radical change in the distribution system of individual and household incomes. The range between salaries was widened, with corresponding social distances. Different research projects conducted in the second half of the last half-decade identified a set of features and trends in this area which can be summarized as including:

- The impoverishment of vast sectors of the labor force and emergence of a worker elite

- The appearance of incomes and living standards unconnected to work
- The exclusion of significant population segments from consumption in certain markets, or at least reduction of their access to a very limited group of products distributed through these markets (Togores 1999)
- The rise in social re-stratification, "de-statization," and "de-salarization" of broad occupational segments, as well as concentration and polarization of incomes (Espina 1999)
- The emergence of a segment of the population that lives in poverty
- The superiority of average incomes of self-employed workers when compared with state wage-earners (Ferriol 1999)
- The diversification of workers incentive programs and practices
- The loss of the significance of salary in each household's financial capability, as the means to satisfy the needs of the population and as a factor for leveling social structure
- The widening of income levels for state workers
- The redistribution of the power to set wages and the loss of the absolute centrality of the state in redistributing income
- The quantitative and qualitative weakening of social services (Nerey and Brismart 1999)

This set of features, as studies indicate, points to a re-stratification process associated with the differentiation of individual and household monetary incomes. Unfortunately, regular ongoing Cuban statistics have still not reacted to these changes and do not allow for calculating real distances since they only distinguish five groups based on monthly per-capita monetary income: Group 1 (up to 50 pesos); Group 2 (between 51 and 100 pesos); Group 3 (between 101 and 150 pesos); Group 4 (between 151 and 200 pesos); and, Group 5 (201 pesos and more) (ONE 2001). Thus, we have to avail ourselves of other means if we wish to examine the real magnitude of social distances more closely or at least to infer their possible extremes with some accuracy. For example, for 1995, the INIE had estimated a ten-stratum income-group distribution (Table 7.1):

Table 7.1. Income Distribution, 1995

Income range (pesos)	Average monthly income	% of population
(0–50)	40	19.3
(51–100)	75	22.7
(101–200)	150	25.0
(210–300)	250	12.5
(301–500)	400	11.0
(501–800)	650	5.5
(801–1,200)	1,000	2.4
(1,201–1,500)	1,350	0.7
(1,501–2,000)	1,750	0.5
(Over 2,000)	6,000	0.4
Total		100

Source: Quintana, Didio. et al, 1995."Mercado agropecuario, apertura o limitación."*Cuba Investigación económica,* No. 4. INIE

There are reasons to believe that this distributional pattern has continued to change. Between 1995 and the present, personal and household incomes have not remained static. Salaries have risen in different sectors and activities in the national economy such as sugar agriculture, education, science and technology and security. In addition, the number of workers connected to foreign exchange payment systems has increased; the sector of self-employed or independent workers has diversified and the range of operation of the market has been extended—all of which influence income distribution. I draw on these estimates to show that by the mid-1990s a rather widespread stratification in the income structure of the Cuban population had already taken place. The Gini index is currently calculated to be about 0.38 (Ferriol 2002).

A set of recent research projects conducted in the city of Havana show us other aspects of income stratification and social distancing. These studies employed qualitative methodologies that rely on small samples and in-depth interviews and do not intend to statistically project their findings onto the nation as a whole. The study "Exploration of spatial-household inequalities in the city of Havana" (*La exploración de las desigualdades espacio-familias en la Ciudad de La Habana*) (Iñiguez et al. 2001) showed an income stratification ranging from a monthly per capita income of more than 928 to one of less than 214 pesos. The study classified income groups into four strata. Stratum I included those households with per capita income of more than 928 pesos. Stratum II was comprised of families with per capita income of between 535 and 884 pesos and stratum III had monthly per capita income of between 286 and 525 pesos. Those in the lowest group were stratum IV with monthly per capita income of less than 214 pesos. The study revealed that " the median incomes and monthly per capita household incomes in the stratum I group of families are practically 10 times as high as they are in stratum IV" (Iñiguez et al. 2001).

The CIPS Department of Household Studies (Departamento de Estudios de la Familia) (2001) uncovered a monthly household per capita income ranging from 69 to 1,200 pesos. The study "Social Components and Distances in the City" (*Componentes y distancias sociales en la Ciudad*) (Espina et al. 2002) identified a minimum per capita household income of 37 pesos and a maximum of 7,266, nearly 200 times higher. Setting aside this case, since it may not be common, the next highest per capita income is 1,025 pesos, 28 times as much as the lowest. Here higher income is associated with the combination of income sources obtained from remittances, state salary and other monetary incomes linked to private property.

It is striking that three different studies—using data gathered at three different times in the past three years and using qualitative typologies allowing for a choice of cases representing typical and fairly widespread Cuban socio-structural situations—all indicate that income spread is wider than can be discerned from the statistics. If we take the lower limit of incomes detected, 50 pesos (which the INIE statistics considered) and the highest one, 1,200 pesos (CIPS Department of Household Studies 2001) the higher income is 24 times higher than the lowest income. I stress that a calculation like this cannot be taken as a confirmed measurement of income inequality, but rather is used here as a hypothetical estimate sending a warning signal that official data may be quantitatively and qualitatively underestimating increasing economic inequality.

As we attempt to understand the evolution of the problem of poverty in the Cuban socialist experience, even without successive measurements of this phenomenon, analyses from the early 1980s point to a rise in economic performance indicators during the second half of the 1970s in the universality of social policies, and in the systematic rise of quality of "spaces of equality." Together, these developments provide a basis for the claim that poverty, and especially social exclusion had declined far enough that, from a basic needs approach, it could be concluded that poverty had been eradicated as a social problem in the country (Rodríguez and Carriazo 1987). Nevertheless, the exact scope of poverty reduction in the Cuban socialist transition remains an issue of debate.

In the 1990s, the pattern shifted markedly. The portion of the urban population "at risk," which was estimated at 6.3 percent in 1985, had widened considerably by 1995, when it reached 14.7 percent (Zabala 2002). That indicated an expansion of groups whose living conditions had become very poor and whose access to welfare have been seriously affected. If we add to this analysis the fact that the portion of urban poverty is currently calculated to be around 20 percent (Ferriol 2002), it is clear that income equality today contrasts with the pre-crisis and pre-reform periods because it now affects the area of basic needs.

Two additional factors have further complicated income distribution—access to incomes in foreign exchange and diversification of income sources. The phenomenon of access to income in foreign exchange is still poorly understood, though it is being studied. Part of the difficulty in measurement and quantification arises from the fact that the amounts and sources of household foreign exchange incomes often derive from informal channels and non-official employment. I will nevertheless try to discuss some aspects of this phenomenon. Ferriol (1999) indicates,

> In contemporary Cuban society the main source of inequality is determined by those having a source of income in foreign exchange. That reflects the appreciated exchange rate in effect along with the fact that meeting some essential household needs requires foreign exchange. This situation is closely connected to the institutional design set up for the consumption goods and services in the segmented market.

It should be kept in mind that the current official exchange rate is 26 pesos to the U.S. dollar. Various estimates confirm that average incomes of self-employed workers are much higher than those of state employees, particularly small restaurant owners and those who rent out their homes. (Ferriol 1999 and Espina et al. 2002).

The cited qualitative studies (CIPS Department of Household Studies 2001; Iñiguez et al. 2001, and Espina 2002) report a higher presence of non-state incomes in higher-income families, which is either greater than that from state income, or a substitute in cases in which no state income is received. Retirement and pension incomes are very low and by themselves are not sufficient to meet basic needs. Remittances, as well as employment in the joint venture and the emerging economic sectors, are important because of the incomes they provide. However, most effective higher-income earning strategies seem to include activities that are illegal or not approved by the current institutional framework, as well as linked with foreign capital. These studies provide suggestive evidence that the sources that provide above-average incomes, in order of importance, are remittances, employment in work with special advantages such as tourist-connected dining and sales in the black market. The most successful strategy is to combine several of these sources. Iñiguez (2001) found that 35 percent of the families studied were receiving remittances. However, this proportion rose to 63 percent in the high-income stratum, whereas it fell to 5 percent at the bottom. The study by Espina and colleagues confirms this finding and notes that, even though a small number of families receive remittances, this source of foreign exchange is associated with high per capita incomes, marking a significant difference between low and high income families.

Recognizing the impossibility of establishing the relative importance of these sources in definitive terms and the continuing debate about the primacy of remittances relative to other income sources, the available information does yield several important issues in spite of its limitations. The importance of work in general is declining and work in the state sector is not seen as providing high income or welfare. The role of salary as a source of income has weakened. In addition, income-earning strategies not associated with employment have increased in importance and the holding of private property has become connected to the availability of monetary income. Finally, illegal strategies constitute an ever-more efficient means of obtaining income.

I believe that the way in which information on income differences is currently gathered and processed makes it impossible to clarify the real distances between income groups, and thus to evaluate inequality according to this indicator. Income has become an essential marker of differentiation, to the point that it defines elites and the vulnerable. As the goal of the country's social security system includes enhancing more personalized and individualized methods and approaches to serving people, the design of policies and strategies, and general programs in this terrain (actions are not opposed to the previous purpose, but complementary) cannot fail to seek as detailed a knowledge as possible of the income profile and the most statistically explicit knowledge of stratification in the country.

Considering, on the one hand, the findings of the qualitative studies on social distances and, on the other, recent estimates of the cost of the consumption basket (between 170 and 190 pesos per month in per capita terms, according to estimates about the population's vulnerability investigated at Center for the Study of the Cuban Economy by Togores), it is possible to present a preliminary proposal of income groups that improves the sensitivity of statistics to the processes of economic differentiation taking place. It could encompass the following groups: *very low income brackets:* per capita monthly income lower than 180 pesos; *low income brackets:* 180 to 300 pesos; *low average income brackets:* Between 301 and 500; *high average income brackets:* between 501 and 1000; *high income brackets:* between 1001 and 3000; and, *very high income brackets:* more than 3000 pesos.

It is worth clarifying that the previous proposal is only illustrative, since there are no reliable and open data sets that would permit the author to test this stratification scheme empirically. Consequently, it is not possible to prove the proposed income structure. Rather, the analysis is presented to show the reader how the research findings translate into much higher income distances than those reflected by publicly available statistics. In light of the process of renewal and enhancement of social policy and of the confrontation of poverty in contemporary Cuba, this proposal also intends to emphasize that certain methodological requirements are unavoidable. A wider spectrum of strata by income must be incorporated into statistical measurements. In addition, greater statistical sensitivity is needed in order to capture the magnitude of existing economic inequalities and to avoid masking or underestimating this sphere of social differentiation.

Territorialization

I use the word "territory" to mean the set of economic, social, cultural, environmental, political and historical relationships and networks that make a geographical space a socioeconomic unit or subsystem. A territory is connected to a more extensive set, but with its own structuring and connectivity, granting it relative autonomy and specificities in its functioning in good part due to the peculiarities of environment and natural resources. Both advantages and limitations result from this subset of space in terms of the size and preparation of its human resources, its traditions and customs, and the degree of development of its economic structure.

The Cuban socialist transition had exhibited a clear tendency to include a territorial focus in the design of economic and social policies. The central principle of that focus was to balance out the social and economic level of Cuba's various regions in order to overcome the deep differences inherited from dependent capitalism, which had caused exclusion and differentiation among territories, with the eastern part of the country, and the rural and semi-urban sections being left behind. The goal was to provide all regions with possibilities for equal access to material and spiritual well-being.

I believe that these experiences faced limitations because the highly centralized economic model under which they operated offered little space for options of local self-transformation or for planning at the territorial level, merely reproducing national policies on a small scale. These views were articulated in a very interesting analysis prepared by the National Economic Planning Commission in 1988 (*Comisión Nacional del Sistema de Dirección de la Economía*), which denoted the primary flaws and needs for planning in Cuba. The report drew attention to the insufficient comprehensive territorial planning, the lack of coordination between economic branches and territorial divisions, the absence of any active aspect of territorial planning, the need to establish differentiation and the connections between property sectors on all levels of planning (Comisión Nacional del Sistema de Dirección de la Economía 1988).

These national circumstances are not disconnected from the international context. In the current phase of development, characterized by the globalized nature of economic relations, territory takes on new qualities under the impulse of globalization processes (Monereo

1997). A critical feature of globalization is that it shapes local development fundamentally, namely: *inter-territorial economic integration*, which goes beyond the borders of the nation-state and is coordinated by extranational agents. Basic to this form of integration is the transition from "Fordist" type economies of scale, based on final assembly, to a territorially scattered manufacture of component parts, known as "dispersed economy." The key to this dispersed economy is territorial *selectivity*, providing for selective integration, which takes into account dynamic competitive advantages and productive activities. As a result, areas are excluded from the process, and whole population segments are left completely or partially outside of the logic of globalized interrelationships. This excluding selectivity deepens previously existing inequalities and produces new ones.

Cuba has been marked by the global circumstances that have given territoriality a new meaning. The reinsertion of the Cuban economy into international markets, where the rules of neoliberal globalization reign, has meant an economic restructuring that emphasizes productive activities and spaces best able to respond effectively to market demands. Even when the effects of selectivity and accompanying territorial exclusion are cushioned by the state's redistributive action, dynamic local comparative advantages are playing a decisive role in the extent to which territories are included in strategies aimed at addressing the country's crisis and development. As a result, the steps taken to achieve readjustment have different concrete effects, depending on the target territory. Thus, Cuba also strongly reflects the heterogenization of local actors and societies, inter-territorial differentiation and multiplication of contacts between the local and the global. These, in turn, are changing the features of territorial social structures and their roles in the reproduction of social relations.

Territorialization in Cuba in the 1990s

Studies conducted in the second half of the 1990s enable us to infer the degree of territorial differentiation that has taken place in the country. Poverty research has found that 14.7 percent of Cubans can be classified as urban poor, and also demonstrated that the Cuban economy's contraction had most intense impact on the eastern area of the country, where the urban population at risk reached 22 percent (Ferriol 1998). Likewise, the 1996 measurement of the human development

index (HDI) in Cuba included the construction of an index to measure relative human development for each province (Martínez 1997).
This index encompasses five dimensions: longevity, education, income,
health, and basic services. The calculation of this provincial human
development index enables us to infer at least three major territorial
groups: provinces with a high HDI: Havana (city), Cienfuegos, Villa
Clara, Matanzas and Havana (province); provinces with medium HDI:
Sancti Spíritus, Ciego de Avila, Pinar del Río and Santiago de Cuba;
and, provinces with low HDI: Holguín, Guantánamo, Camagüey, Las
Tunas and Granma. According to an analysis of human settlements in
the lowest segment of human development, 36 Cuban municipalities,
all of which are located in provinces in the eastern part of the country,
were found to be in a highly "critical" or "severely depressed" development state (IPF 1998).

A study of spatial inequalities of well-being in Cuba showed that
"new processes" are manifested unequally in terms of territory with
most impact and to the best advantage in the city of Havana, Varadero,
northeast Holguín, northern Ciego de Avila, southern Matanzas, Pinar
del Río and the province of Havana (Iñiguez and Ravenet 1999). These
"new processes" range from the creation or encouragement of non-tra-
ditional forms of property and market mechanisms to the ranking of
sectors and economic activities and improvement of cooperative and
individual production and of household activity.

A team from the *Centro de Investigaciones Psicológicas y Sociológicas* (CIPS) found in its research project "Territorial expressions of the
re-stratification process" that Cuba's present economic map contains
provinces where a connection to revitalized economic forms (tourism,
joint venture enterprises, activities associated with foreign capital) has
been quickly established and others where that has scarcely happened
(Martín et al. 1999). The end result is a provincial territorial differentiation expressed in the following classification by groups in accordance
with the degree of their linkage with the emerging economy: *Group
1:* provinces that are very much integrated into revitalized economic
sectors (City of Havana, Matanzas, Holguín, Ciego de Ávila); *Group
2:* provinces with a medium level of integration (Pinar del Río, Camagüey, Santiago de Cuba, Sancti Spíritus, Isla de la Juventud, Cienfuegos, Villa Clara, Havana (province); and, *Group 3*: provinces that are
barely integrated (Las Tunas, Gramma, Guantánamo).

The study added a statistical correlation analysis, applied to data on the provincial social-class structures, including the structure of the economically active population by occupational categories and by property type—state, mixed, cooperative, and private. The analysis indicated that the reform has entailed the formation of four types of major territorial socio-structures:

1) *Mixed-state* (with strong presence of workers and leaders) in Matanzas, Santiago de Cuba, Isla de la Juventud

2) *Cooperatives (CPA and UBPC)* in La Habana, Ciego de Ávila, Cienfuegos

3) *Private (especially rural)* in Pinar del Río, Sancti Spíritus, Gramma, Villa Clara, Las Tunas, Camagüey, Guantánamo, Holguín

4) *State-foreign private, with a strong presence of intellectuals and office workers)* in the City of Havana

This typology indicates those structuring elements that are exercising the greatest differentiating power territorially. It also serves to highlight the distinctive forms that the economic readjustment is adopting in this space and offers indications on the socioeconomic actors playing an important role in various provinces. These findings indicate that territorial differentiation is one of the strongest processes accompanying Cuban reform. Likewise, heterogeneous design formulas and the involvement of local actors in the implementation of social policies are essential to building agendas and marshalling resources.

A New View of Territory in Cuba's Development Model

I agree with CEPAL when it states that the new circumstances of the development of local societies demand that policy and the social sciences firmly move away from the widespread conception of territory as a geographical support for national socioeconomic activities and as an object of physical planning. Instead, territory should be viewed as a factor of development, a concept centered on the heterogeneity of territory, which has the capacity for mobilization around various projects of self-transformation of the social actors emerging and being reproduced at that scale. The existence and possibility of access to strategic resources for local development and the shaping of socially organized territories to generate "positive synergies" among their different agents of production must also be recognized. Surely, the strategic and participatory involvement of territorial governments in planning social and economic development and their role in the creation of spaces where the different social actors can reach consensus must be utilized. The identification of territorially balanced and sustainable lines of development must also occur. Likewise, strategic business plans and institutional cooperation must be facilitated, especially in innovation, diffusion and adaptation of technologies, achievements of R & D activity, identification of local development initiatives in technology, training of specific human resources, and development financing (Albuquerque 1995).

This conception does not mean treating territory as an autonomous segment, disconnected from the nation as a whole, but proactively mobilizing local societies in order to identify their endogenous possibilities for development. It is also important to obtaining resources from external sources, which in turn can serve as the platform for connecting with the nation and other territories in a dynamic positive synergized network. Cuba's strength in the role of the state as an agent of development and guarantor of the security of society, conditions that practically do not exist elsewhere in the underdeveloped world, would permit the country to take on this conception, in which a centralized focus and universality are combined with a localized base and focus. In short, I am simply indicating that from the standpoint of the advantages and disadvantages linked to spatiality and the concurrent process of concentration of vulnerability and poverty that has taken place in Cuba, territoriality must be reclaimed. It should be used to embark upon a participatory and self-transforming approach to development, and it should become a primary locus for the design and implementation of social policy and for the retrieval of "spaces of equality."

New Patterns of Social Mobility

The notion of social and socio-class structure implicitly entails a certain *statics*, as a set of positions and interlinks reproduced with a certain stability in time and space. Likewise, it entails a type of *dynamics*, resulting from the nature of a complex system always moved by reproductive tendencies of self-preservation and change, some anticipated and others unforeseeable. One dimension of socio-structural dynamics is social mobility—the movement of individuals and social groups from one position to another in the social hierarchy, up or down. These shifts—excluding the role of chance and the involvement of intersubjectivity—appear as connected to the set of objective constraints present in a society and predefined as a repertory of possible movements in a given social-structure.

Mobility describes an important aspect of interclass relations and the interconnections between macro-social phenomena such as social-structure, economic, and political processes, as well as the connections to individual destinies. Mobility does indeed have a power to change personal trajectories. In this sense, it influences individual behaviors with its varying causes and tendencies, as well as the formation of group subjectivity.

Studies of socio-structural changes in Cuban society in the past four decades have documented the presence of three intense moments in this process (Espina 1999):

A. *Period of fundamental class changes, 1959–1975.* During this time, prior class relations were dismantled, private property as the fundamental means of production was eliminated and a new system of socio-structural components was constructed. The system was based on state centralization. Social de-stratification occurred as a result.

B. *Period of changes in the internal structure of fundamental socio-class components, 1976–1988.* The social-structure components typical of socialist transition (working class, intellectuals, and peasantry) were reproduced in a stable manner, they maintained their relative weight in the social structure and the more intense changes shifted within sectors as the socio-occupational division of labor gradually became more complex.

C. *Period of economic reform and social re-stratification, 1989 to the present.* One of the most significant effects of the economic crisis beginning in the late 1980s with its resulting adjustment strategy is that social distances and social inequality increased.

I will now take a closer look at the characteristics of social mobility in the different stages of the Cuban socialist transition and corresponding social-structural changes.

Period of Fundamental Class Changes

The data presented in Table 7.2 can be analyzed using a criterion of social-structural hierarchy ordered by the degree of socialization of ownership of the means of production. This ranking takes into account that socialist (in this case, state) property is the characteristic integrating mechanism in the new social system. Although the categories used in this table do not allow for the strict definition of their hierarchical order, I can use the dividing line of property type as an indicator of vertical upward mobility. Thus from 1953 to 1970, a significant structural dynamic took place with 84.3 percent of the population crossing class boundary lines. This was the most pronounced feature in the first phase of Cuba's socialist transition.

Table 7.2 Distribution of Employment by Economic Sector, 1953 and 1970 (percentage)

	1953	1970
State workers	8.8	87.5
Private employees	63.3	1.3
Self-employed	24.0	1.2
Other non-state workers	3.9	10.0
Total	100	100

Source: Censo de población y vivienda 1981. Table II, page 6

The most notable feature of the first decade of the Cuban revolution was the intense movement between classes, shifts that had not existed in Cuba before 1959. The massive movements from groups of private sector employees, small owners, semi-proletarians, and the unemployed toward the working class connected to the state sector of the economy are a prime example of this phenomenon. Similarly, the movement from the working class, the peasantry, and other social sectors toward various forms of intellectual work also illustrate this pattern.

During this period (1959–1975) the class location of a person became more likely to change to a position substantially different from that of his or her parents and grandparents. There were many cases of maximum upward mobility or complete inter-generational change of social class location, with differences between three generations and in the trajectory of each individual. The extension of the state sector, increase in levels of employment, diversification of professional alternatives and the massive increase of general, technical, and professional education operated as driving forces of this mobility.

In short, mobility in this period was characterized by a radical change in structural constraints. It was prompted by the replacement of one social class structure by another and the level of mobility was highly structural and generalized. With high fluidity, intensity and long-range inter-generational mobility, private sector employees shifted to state jobs; manual workers engaged in intellectual work, and unskilled, unqualified workers became skilled labor. These movements resulted in the configuration of a subjective pattern of high expectation of upward mobility, the pinnacle of which was considered to be highly qualified intellectual work.

Period of Changes in the Internal Structure of Fundamental Social Class Components

The pace of social mobility slowed down after the 1959–1969 period, where the socio-class components in the initial phase of the new socioeconomic system were shaped. In the next period (1976–1988), the need to reproduce these components in a stable manner and perfect their roles in the social system took precedence. Accordingly, the social mobility characteristic of the first stage of interclass social-structure transformation became less intense. Mobility became linked to the internal social and professional advancement within the fundamental social class components.

The analysis of this stage is based on data gathered in a broad, national investigation into Cuban socio-class structure, in which the period's intra-generational upward mobility was measured through a survey (Espina and Núñez 1988). In order to capture vertical mobility; this study used a socio-structural framework gradated by property form. State property represented the top of the structure, cooperative property an intermediate level, and small private property the lowest level. Criteria measuring job skills and qualifications, intellectual effort and degree of mechanization were also taken into account. Movements across property, levels of qualification, between intellectual and manual, mechanized and non-mechanized, and agricultural and industrial labor thus constituted vertical shifts. Upward movements were defined as those in the direction of state property, higher skill qualification, higher intellectual content of work and a greater extent of mechanization and technology.

The framework used was the following:

I. *State property:*

  (a) Workers whose efforts are primarily intellectual such as managers, specialists and technicians

(b) Office workers

(c) Working class employees whose efforts are primarily physical and manual labor, including the occupational category of service workers

II. Cooperative property: Agricultural production cooperatives

III. Private property:

(a) Individual small farmers

(b) Self-employed workers

The Cuban pay scale's criterion of "distribution of rewards" in effect in the state sector of the economy during the 1980s was utilized to define the level of household material and spiritual well-being. As a result, inequalities corresponded to these patterns. Accordingly, the working class displayed a negative mobility balance. Despite the tendency of the working class to maintain its members, the reduced proportion of departures was not compensated by entries from other social-structure positions. Thus, it appeared to be a "sender" to other groups with a poor ability to attract others. Its movements of entry and exit were primarily directed towards exchanges with the stratum of intellectual workers. The strongest mobility took place within the class itself, among adjacent groups, in shifts that entailed slight changes in skill qualifications, incomes or working conditions. This mobility took place in a way that makes it difficult to draw the line between vertical and horizontal movements. Within this class group, types of workers followed a behavior similar to that described in relation to other groups, with service workers becoming receivers more than senders.

Specialists—technicians whose work involves primarily intellectual efforts requiring high or upper medium qualification—whom I could broadly equate with intellectuals, were slightly more stable than the working class. This group was a receiver, one that attracted office workers and laborers. Movements in this latter group were indeed one of the most intensive shifts during the period. Very few peasants and self-employed workers were able to achieve the level of intellectual work, and this option seemed almost inaccessible to them during their lifetime, although perhaps not to their children.

Office workers, on the other hand, formed a mobile stratum. While generally excluding peasants and the self-employed, this stratum was open to the other branches connected to state property, and was basically a sending group. They tended to move upward, toward becoming specialists. The peasantry was the least mobile in this period; it retained 91 percent of its initial members, and very few moved toward it. Short-term shifts took place within it—from individual small farmers toward cooperatives. The routes outward went to the working class.

Self-employed workers were the most active in shifting from non-state to state property, but it was the sector that gained the most members as a result of social mobility, with 68 percent of its members coming from other social-structure positions. This trend clearly ran counter to the gradual elimination of private property and to the mobility "needed" or desired in accordance with the economic and political model in effect at that phase of the Cuban socialist transition. Although this stratum was relatively small in the 1980s Cuban socio-structural framework, highlighting the relative lack of mobility, it has the virtue of showing us a conflictive aspect of shifts in society from the standpoint of socialism as then widely understood.

In short, social mobility during 1976–1988 was characterized by the predominance of not very intense, short-term and limited mobility, taking place primarily within classes. Self-recruitment in intellectual spheres surfaced, while structural mobility and particularly greater changes in the levels of massive mobility declined. The pattern of individual upward mobility based on both skill classification and access to intellectual work was consolidated.

Economic Reform Period and Re-stratification

Empirical evidence about mobility during 1989 to the present-day conveys a quicker interaction between already existing groups and vigorous shifts toward socio-structural positions created or expanded by the reforms undertaken in the 1990s. Table 7.3 indicates that 20 percent of the population crossed class boundary lines between 1988 and 1998. As the data presented in the table is classified by broad categories of occupations, combining criteria based on property and the character and content of work, a relatively high degree of differentiation between each sector is presented. Based on these further defined categories, I can thereby infer that mobility has been far-reaching and of high intensity.

Table 7.3 Employment Structure by Occupation, 1988 and 1998
(percentage)

	1988	1998
Workers	48.4	38.7
Service Workers	12.7	16.5
Office Workers	6.5	3.3
Specialists	20.1	13.1
Managers	6.4	6.4
Workers in joint-ventures	0.0	3.2
Agricultural cooperatives	1.8	1.5
UBPC Farmers	0.0	5.7
Individual Farmers	3.0	8.2
Self-employed workers	1.1	2.7
Total	100	100

Source: ONE, *Anuario estadístico de Cuba* (1998)

The increase of structural mobility and the intensification of shifts compared to the previous period are corroborated by the data presented in Table 7.4, which indicates the dynamics and interchanges between strata by property sectors.

Table 7.4 Distribution of Employment by Economic Sector, 1977–1998
(percentage)

	1977	1988	1998
State	91.1	94.1	78.7
Joint venture	0.0	0.0	3.2
Cooperative	0.1	1.8	7.22
Private	8.8	4.1	10.8
Total	100	100	100

Source: ONE, *Anuario estadístico de Cuba* (1978 and 1998)

While the level of structural dynamic change between property boundaries was 5 percent for the period between 1977 and 1988, it rose to 15 percent between 1988 and 1998. With regard to mobility toward the informal sector, I believe that the statistics underestimate the sector's magnitude, because only registered informal work is recorded, but other equally important manifestations are not represented. ILO studies conducted indicate that as a rule, the real number of informal workers can be estimated by tripling the registered number of workers. Should such a procedure be adopted for the present case, the measure of structural mobility would certainly increase considerably.

Data from a 1999 survey by Espina et al. (1999) present further evidence of individual intra-generational vertical movement. According to this survey, office workers were the most mobile stratum during the 1990s, as during the previous period. After adding managers and self-employed workers, a map of the categories of most mobile groups—those whose mobility index is higher than overall mobility—is derived. However, it is worth noting that the behavior of these groups was more stable during the previous period.

By far, the least mobile were agricultural cooperative members, followed by state-sector technicians and workers. Managers, urban private-sector workers, farm cooperative members and joint venture workers are the groups acting as receivers, with positive balances between mobility of those entering and those exiting the group. The remainder, comprised of office workers, laborers and specialists, tend to be sending groups. In terms of paths of mobility, 38 percent of all exit movements from the initial group entailed shifts toward some non-state sector group, especially toward self-employment. Thirty percent of mobility went from the state sector toward the non-state sector.

Data available to date generally show that re-stratification is accompanied by a new pattern of social mobility. Increased shifting of positions, the opening of new routes of mobility, acceleration of shifts from state to non-state property and escalated intensification and increase in mobility characterizes this pattern. This new pattern also includes tendencies toward downward mobility for individuals and groups, associated with the pauperization found in a set of informal sector occupations. This downward mobility could especially be affecting women, who are significantly tied to informal work in dependent and subsidiary roles. In addition, many movements in the emerging sector are accompanied by de-professionalization. Income is becoming further concentrated, with a collective decline of entire socio-occupational groups due to the declining value of real wages and the emergence of poverty and unemployment. Mobility has increased, sometimes including upward mobility at least in terms of the possibility of higher income. However, a strong mobility deficit exists when measured in both objective and subjective terms. Moreover, selective upward mobility favors some social groups, namely some fragments of the working class, intellectuals, managers and the informal sector, which have been able to find a place individually or collectively in more lucrative positions.

Trends in Social Mobility

This analysis has enabled us to show very succinctly how different patterns of social mobility occurred during the three different stages of the Cuban socialist transition from 1959 to the present. These patterns have been shifting. Initially (1959–1975), movement was characterized by a highly fluid and intense situation of maximum mobility associated with a radical process in which one social structure was dismantled and replaced by another qualitatively different structure, composed of a new generation of components or a construction scarcely present in the preceding structure. In the following period (1976–1988), the processes of reproducing continuity prevailed, thereby lessening major mobility. These processes gave way to less intense shifts between positions close in the social-structure ranking, in which some social groups experienced processes of both efficient and inefficient self-recruiting. These shifts, which emerged and were consolidated during this period, centered on both professional mobility and higher job qualifications, which constituted the primary route for movements.

In the last period (1989 to present day), the pattern of mobility has been driven by the combination and simultaneous action of two processes: crisis and reform. This combination means that trends of selective social upward and downward mobility coexist. This pattern also includes the opening of new routes to mobility that had previously been closed or very narrow, such as movement from state to non-state property, without that being regarded as a downward movement. This new pattern is characterized by the presence of vertical shifts among groups, neither upward nor downward, through the economic devaluation or emergence of certain types of activity. Most noteworthy is that the new pattern corroborates both the growing heterogeneity and the complexity of the social-structure processes accompanying the reforms, as well as the range of contradictions contained in these processes as they create improvements and reductions in well-being, as well as shifts toward poverty. Thus, these transformations have important implications for social policy design.

Conclusions

The Cuban experience shows that poverty eradication can only be waged effectively if it is placed within a perspective that sets it apart from policies of simply giving charity or remedying problems. Its eradication must be placed in the relational dialectic between poverty, inequality and development, understanding poverty not as a social situation, but as fundamentally a social relation. However, there are weaknesses and limitations of implementing this model in practice. There is renewed need for understanding both the state and social policy dimension within socialism and the role of the state as central development agent.

From my perspective, the first challenge of this renewal is precisely that of the economic sustainability of Cuba's social development policy. Without embracing a narrowly economic viewpoint, or abandoning the ethical focus on social policy, formulas must be found for reintegrating the Cuban economy into international markets to stimulate domestic production and to provide social programs with sufficient funds. If this fails to occur, the programs will be facing a deficit and will themselves be in a critical condition. Under these conditions, the primary role of the state as the guarantor of well-being will be called into question. The second challenge, the one on which my research interests primarily focus, is that of attaining a new understanding of equality. Equality must be seen as an essential characteristic of social relations in society, particularly through distribution and access to satisfaction of material and spiritual needs, based on the understanding of diversity.

With regard to capitalism, Carlos Franco (1994) cites conclusions from his research in Latin America stating, "upon being exposed to and experiencing recurring inequality and poverty over generations, populations will end up accepting them as natural. Concurrently, how elites define the size of inequality that they regard as just, tolerable, or legitimate, affects how it is viewed objectively." In accordance with these reflections, the relations of exploitation and domination which serve as the pivot for the specific type of capitalist reproduction are "internalized" by the various social groups. Ultimately, they are signified as natural and irremediable, and "externalized" in concrete decisions about the design of development policies and strategies.

Obviously, in these conditions it is necessary to improve a new social policy of equality that should entail the following:

- As an indispensable methodological requirement, territory should be included as a factor in development. In order to accomplish this, the essential role played by local socioeconomic actors as agents of change, in the design of development programs or actions for change at the local level, must be recognized. This should entail empowering maximum local endogenous development and the creation of formulas of connection and transfer through the creation of networks of interterritorial synergistic relations to make possible a correction of the imbalances that cannot be resolved locally. Strategies centered on the sustainability of processes of change should also be designed with an understanding that the intensive use of wealth in terms of nature, culture, work skills, and history will assure its systematic regeneration. Traditions should also be respected and the innovation and installation of a lasting capacity for self-management and participatory self-organization of local societies should be encouraged (Albuquerque 1995).

- The possible repertory of forms of property ownership in small production and local services (community, urban cooperative, mixed property forms: state-cooperative, state-community, and state-individual, professional) should be diversified in a framework of integration, complementation, and competence in which all forms contribute directly or indirectly to spaces of markets and "spaces of equality"). Such a broadening will help concentrate state property on essential activities, and put aside activities that bloat it and lessen private appropriation of its benefits.

- The quality of "spaces of equality" should be recovered, especially those installations which, because of their spatial location, are availed primarily by groups who are less well off, which could attenuate the effect of income differentiation in widening inequality.

- The relationship between central planning and markets should be improved to make it possible to account for emerging differences and to better serve the needs of various social groups.

- The scope of the market that responds to the demands of higher income groups, thereby making it possible to finance similar or other demands in lower-income groups, should be widened.

In sum, the aim of this framework is to improve and enhance the role of the state, not through centralization and overall approaches that ignore other agents of change, but by strengthening its leadership, synergistically connecting it with other agents of social development and the positive expression of social diversity.

References

Alburquerque, Francisco. 1995. *Espacio, territorio y desarrollo económico local.* ILPES LC/IP/R. 160. Santiago de Chile: CEPAL.

Álvarez, Oneida. 1997. "La economía cubana."Papers, No. 52. Barcelona: Universidad de Barcelona.

Brundenius, Claes. 1987. *Revolutionary Cuba. The Challenge of Economic Growth with Equity.* Boulder, Colo. : Westview Press.

Centro de Investigaciones Psicológicas y Sociologicas (CIPS), Departamento de Estudios sobre Familia (Department of Household Studies). 2001. "Familia y cambios socioeconómicos a las puertas del nuevo milenio." Fondos del CIPS, Havana.

CIPS-ISPS. 1990. *Objetivos sociales y condiciones del desarrollo económico. Estudio comparativo RDA-Cuba.* Havana: Ed. Academia.

Comisión Nacional del Sistema de Dirección de la Economía. 1988. "Decisiones adoptadas sobre algunos elementos del sistema de dirección de la economía." *Cuba, economía planificada.* Año 3, No. 3, Havana: JUCEPLAN.

Comite Estatal de Estadísticas. 1981. *Censo de poblacion y viviendas*, 1981. Havana: CEE.

Espina, Mayra. 1999. "Transición y dinámica socioestructural en Cuba." Talk presented at the XX LASA conference Guadalajara, Mexico: Latin American Studies Association.

Espina, Mayra and Liliana Núñez. 1988. "Acerca del concepto de movilidad social y su utilización en la sociología marxista." *Estudio de la sociedad cubana contemporánea.* Anuario Havana: Ed. Academia.

Espina, Mayra, et al. 1999. *Reestratificación y movilidad social. Informe de investigación.* Havana: Fondos del CIPS.

Espina, Mayra, et al. 2002 *Componentes sociestructutrales y distancias sociales en la ciudad.* Informe de Investigación. Havana: Fondos del CIPS.

Ferriol, Ángela. 1998 "Pobreza en condiciones de reforma económica. El reto a la equidad en Cuba." *Cuba. Investigación económica.* Año 4, No. 1. Havana: INIE.

Ferriol, Ángela, et al. 1999. "Política social en el ajuste y su adecuación a las nuevas condiciones." *Cuba. Investigación económica.* Havana: INIE.

Ferriol, Ángela. 2000. "Ingresos y desigualdad en la sociedad cubana actual." Talk presented at the Seminario sobre la Estructura Socioclasista Cubana. Havana: C.C. del Partido Comunista de Cuba.

Ferriol, Ángela. 2002. "Explorando nuevas estrategias para reducir la pobreza en el actual contexto internacional. Experiencias de Cuba." Talk presented at the Seminario Internacional Estrategias de Reducción de la Pobreza. Havana: CLACSO/CROP.

González, Alfredo. 1998. "Economía y sociedad: Los retos del modelo económico." *TEMAS*. No. 11. Havana.

Heller, Celia S. 1987 (2nd Edition). "Economic inequality." *Structural Social Inequality. A Reader in Comparative Social Stratification*. The Macmillan Company, New York.

Hernández, Angel, Mayra Espina and Viviana Togores. 2002. "El consumo en el socialismo." Mesa redonda. Fondos de la Revista Temas, Havana.

Íñiguez, Luisa and Mariana Ravenet. 1999. "Desigualdades espaciales del bienestar en Cuba. Aproximaciones a los efectos de los nuevos procesos en las realidades sociales." Informe de Investigación. Centro de Estudios de Salud y Bienestar Humano. Universidad de la Habana.

Íñiguez, Luisa, et al. 2001. "La exploración de las desigualdades espacio-familias en la Ciudad de La Habana." Informe de investigación. CESBH. Universidad de La Habana.

Instituto de Planificación Física (IPF). 1998. "Diagnóstico de los asentamientos de la franja de base en los municipios críticos." Informe técnico.

Kliksberg, Bernardo. 2002. *Diez falacias sobre los problemas sociales en América Latina*. Ponencia presentada al Seminario Internacional Gobernabilidad y Desarrollo en América Latina y el Caribe. Montevideo: MOST-UNESCO.

Martín, Juan Luis, et al. 1999. "Expresiones territoriales del proceso de reestratificación." Informe de investigación. CIPS.

Martínez, Osvaldo. 1997. "Cuba y la globalización de la economía mundial." Talk at the Seminario Globalización de la Economía Mundial." Havana.

Martínez, Osvaldo. (Director). 1997. *Investigación sobre el desarrollo humano en Cuba*, 1996. Havana: Ed. Caguayo.

Monereo, Manuel. 1997. "Mundialización de las relaciones sociales." Talk presented at the event "El Socialismo en el Siglo XXI." Havana.

Monreal, Pedro and Julio Carranza. 2000. "Los retos del desarrollo en Cuba: Realidades, mitos y conceptos," *Cuba construyendo futuro*, Monereo, Manuel. Miguel Riera and Juan Valdés Paz. (coord.). Madrid: El Viejo Topo, Fundación de Investigaciones Marxistas.

Nerey, Boris and Nivia Brismart. 1999. "Estructura social y estructura salarial en Cuba: Encuentros y desencuentros." Trabajo de curso de la maestría en Sociología. Universidad de La Habana.

Núñez, Marta. 2000. "Enfoque de género: proposiciones metodológicas." *Temas*, No. 14. Havana.

Oficina Nacional de Estadísticas. 1999. *Anuario estadístico de Cuba 1998*. Havana: ONE.

Oficina Nacional de Estadísticas. 2001. *Anuario estadístico de Cuba 2000*. Havana: ONE.

Quintana, Didio, et al. 1995. "Mercado agropecuario, apertura o limitación." *Cuba. Investigación económica*, No. 4. INIE: Havana.

Rodríguez, José Luis and George Carriazo. 1987. *La eliminación de la pobreza en Cuba*. Havana: Editorial Ciencias. Sociales.

Tavares, Laura. 1999. *Ajuste neoliberal e desajuste social na América Latina*. UFRJ, Rio de Janeiro.

Tavares, Laura. 2002. "La reproducción ampliada de la pobreza en América Latina: El debate de las causas y de las alternativas de solución." Talk presented at the Seminario Internacional Estrategias de Reducción de la Pobreza. Havana: CLACSO-CROP.

Togores, Viviana. 1999. "Cuba: Efectos sociales de la crisis y el ajuste económico de los 90s." Fondos del CIEC. Havana.

Zabala, María del Carmen. 2002. "Situación de la pobreza en el Caribe: Actualidad y perspectivas de Cuba en el contexto caribeño." Talk presented at the Seminario Internacional Estrategias para la Eliminación de la Pobreza. Havana: CLACSO-CROP.

Zimbalist, Andrew and Claes Brundenius. 1989. "Creciendo con equidad: El desarrollo cubano en una perspectiva comparada." *Cuadernos de Nuestra América*. CEA. VOL VI: No. 13. Havana.

Notes

1 For further elaboration on this point, see Nerey and Brismart 1999.

8

Consumption, Markets, and Monetary Duality in Cuba

by Viviana Togores and Anicia García

Studies about consumption, necessarily complex, are especially so in Cuba's case because of the vast changes that have taken place during the last four decades. In theory, as Karl Marx showed in his *Contribution to the Critique of Political Economy* (1975: 223–244), consumption to satisfy the needs of individuals is the final purpose of production. Several elements must be included in the analysis of consumption, particularly with regard to Cuba. The portion of gross national product acquired by the private sector is a key part of consumption, including the purchase of food, movie tickets, payments to the plumber, and washing machine purchases. A set of government expenditures should also be included in estimates of consumption, however; in Cuba, such government outlays represent a significant share of consumption that does not reach the population through purchase and sale.

What have been the trends of consumption in Cuba? How have these changed in the last decade? How has the recently-introduced simultaneous monetary circulation of both pesos and U.S. dollars impacted consumption? To answer these questions, we first review the status quo prior to 1989 and then describe the changes adopted throughout the 1990s.

Aspects of Consumption

With the arrival of the Cuban revolution with its new government policy measures on behalf of the majority of the population, the existing workforce gained access to more stable, better-remunerated[1] and better quality jobs. That, in turn, resulted in more equitable national redistribution of income, thereby causing a substantial change in consumption.[2] On one hand, demand increased; on the other, the state became the principal supply source for the consumer market.[3]

As a rule, increased consumer demand is limited by price movements in which equilibrium is established without regard to the fact that those who cannot pay are excluded. However, in the case to be considered, the classical laws of the market are obviated. In Cuba, regulations about procurement of goods ensure that consumption takes place in a universal and egalitarian manner. In given periods, however, alternative modes that indeed function under the laws of "supply and demand" have operated along with quota-based distribution systems.

Figure 8.1 Patterns of Consumption, 1975–2000
(millions of pesos)

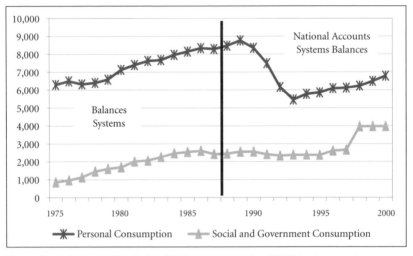

Source: Comité Estatal de Estadísticas (CEE) (various years) and ONE (various years)

Consumption rose in the three decades previous to the 1989 crisis (Figure 8.1). For example, social and government consumption grew by 207 percent between 1975 and 1989. This was primarily a result of the priority given to social development to eradicate problems inherited from the previous economic model. Personal consumption, however, was limited. Despite the increase in the number of people with access to overall consumption, personal consumption was limited by restrictions on supply imposed by rationing of almost all consumer goods and the absence of other market spaces outside of the network of gastronomic services or the black market. This situation improved in the 1980s, with the increase in supply resulting from the expansion of the state-run parallel market[4] of goods and services and the appearance of the farmers' markets for agricultural products.

From 1990 to 1993, consumption fell 31 percent from 1989 levels, with a 7 percent decline in social and government spending and a 39 percent drop in private spending. The reversal in direction resulted from the crisis experienced by the Cuban economy, in which gross domestic product (GDP) fell approximately 35 percent[5] between 1989 and 1993. This crisis, originated with a contraction of the supply of goods and services, a drop in the amount and variety of products for distribution in the primary market—the regulated one[6]—and the disappearance of parallel markets as substitutes for the former. The only alternative supply source became underground or black markets, where prices were considerably higher and rising because of the indexing of purchase prices to the U.S. dollar.

The implementation of a package of macroeconomic adjustment policies reversed the trend in declining overall consumption, starting in 1993. By 2000, total consumption had risen by 37 percent. Contributing to that increase was a 24 percent growth in household consumption and a 68 percent rise in social and government consumption.[7] Since 2000, investments in social consumption, such as public welfare, culture, health and education, have been gathering momentum due to the implementation of various social programs aimed at improving the quality of health and education services, which had deteriorated during the crisis, and at solving a set of new problems that have emerged since then.

What Are the Factors Determining the Change in Consumption Patterns?

By 1994, a process of consolidation began related to economic transformations in the areas of property, domestic finances and the market, which pre-condition higher production and income growth.

Household Income

Household income is an extremely important element of this analysis because its availability depends directly on demand, and hence consumption also does, in different markets. After the revolution came to power, Cubans' income underwent significant changes, especially because of increased employment and a higher number of salaried workers. Between 1960 and 1970, almost one million people joined the workforce, thereby increasing the country's labor force by 58 percent. Hence, the amount of money issued in the form of wages rose. Whereas

Box 8.1 Economic and Social Transformations in Cuba in the 1990s

- Decriminalization of the holding of foreign currency
- Opening to foreign investment
- Geographical reorientation and decentralization of foreign trade
- Extension of self-employment
- Expansion of cooperatives in farming with the creation of UBPCs in agriculture ("Third agrarian reform")
- Re-sizing and re-structuring of state enterprises
- Institutional and regulatory reorganization of central state administrative agencies
- Economic and financial reform
- New salary scales for the labor force (Resolution No. 6/94 of the MTSS.)
- Opening of farmer's markets
- Opening of markets for small-scale industrial and craft goods
- Decentralization of decision-making and greater autonomy at the territorial level for policy implementation
- New social programs launched

Source: Prepared by authors

wages represented an average of 71.6 percent of total household income in the 1960s, they grew to represent 77 percent by the 1970s. In the 1980s, wages rose to approximately 75 percent. However, they declined significantly in the 1990s, coming to represent only 56 percent of total income.

In short, income growth was based on job expansion up until 1989. However, the material counterpart was never enough to match income levels, primarily because of insufficient domestic consumer goods production, insufficient financial resources available to finance the demand deficit from imported goods and the general scarcity of services. Wages made up the primary source of household income, along with payments for social security and social welfare. These three income sources represented an average of 87 percent of total earnings during the entire pre-1989 period. Nominal income rose historically until 1989, when a 4 percent annual decline began, lasting until 1994. It should be noted that the government stance of criminalizing the possession of dollars also contributed to minimizing income inequalities, and therefore consumption access as well. The only differences in inequality permitted were those that resulted from differences in work. Other factors that could contribute to differentiated access, such as remittances from abroad, were limited as a matter of policy, at least in the legal, official economy, so as to ensure equity.[8] During this period, bank withdrawals from savings accounts played a fundamental role in the structure of income as a complement to the financial resources needed by families to maintain certain minimal living conditions.

Figure 8.2 Household Income, Expenditures and Liquidity, 1990–2001 (millions of pesos)

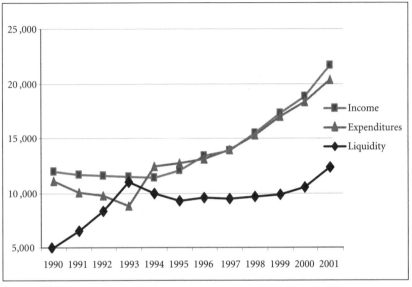

Source: ONE

During the first four years following 1989, household expenditures contracted, as seen in the increase in accumulated monetary liquidity due to the scarcity or disappearance of existing markets (Figure 8.2). In this situation, the only options for consumption were the rationed and the underground markets. The latter ultimately absorbed these balances and developed very rapidly. During this period, the estimated volume of black market sales reached the point of equaling and sometimes surpassing sales and distribution to the population by the state. After 1995, the transactions in the underground market declined because of the incorporation of these players into formal markets, which in turn increased supply and decreased prices of a significant portion of activities in the unofficial economy. Both these steps had a direct impact on lowering prices and improving possibilities of access to consumption. Even so, a significant volume of transactions for a particular group of articles, such as dairy products, beef and eggs, still continue to be sold in the informal market at prices lower than those in the only alternate option, the markets operating in U.S. dollars.

In sum, the period from 1989 to 2001 was marked by significant changes in the relative shares of the sources of income and the relative purchasing power of Cuban households (Figure 8.3). Wages lost their significance, although taken together with social security they are still the most important component of total income and represent an average of 67.4 percent of total earnings by 1997. Moreover, wages affect vast sectors of the labor force and the population, since the state sector provides 76.6 percent of employment, and these workers are responsible for most of the dependent population, especially school-age children and adolescents. State workers have been one the most affected group in terms of the decline in income and hence access to consumption.

Figure 8.3 Income Sources of the Population, 1989–1997

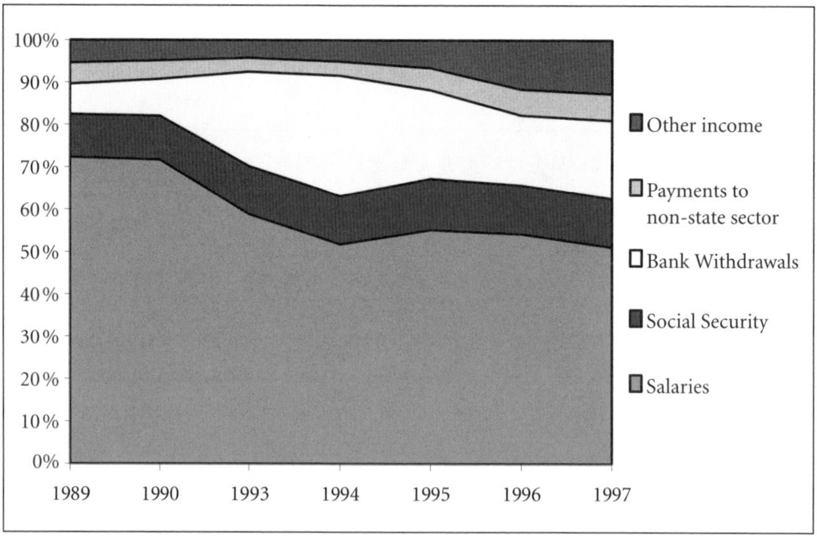

Source: ONE (various years)

The average monthly nominal salary has undergone significant variation since the onset of the crisis in the early 1990s (Figure 8.4). It declined between 1991 and 1994, but then began to increase moderately. By 2000, the nominal salary was 234 pesos, a 24 percent increase over the entire crisis period dating from 1989. Even so, the tendency of nominal wages to rise has not been able to offset the deterioration resulting from increases in the consumer price index. Cubans' real wages dropped 37 percent between 1989 and 2000 (falling from 131 to 83 pesos), representing a hardship for the majority of the population, who depend on wages as their most important source of income.

Figure 8.4 Average Monthly Salary: Nominal and Real, 1989–2000

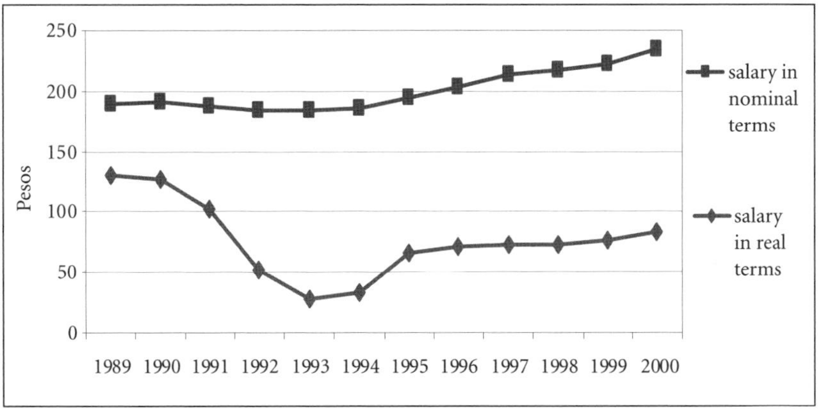

Source: Data compiled by the authors based on statistics from the Ministry of Finance and Prices and the authors' calculations

During this ten-year period, three periods can be discerned: the first between 1990 and 1993 when real wages fell sharply; the second between 1994 and 1995 as wages rose, and the third since 1995 with a slowdown and stagnation of wages. This slowdown seems to result from the erosion of the effectiveness of stabilization measures taken earlier in the decade. Overall, wages have lost relevance as a source of income and the incentive for work has also declined during this period.

In the search for better performance and stimulation of productive capacity, different incentive pay systems have been implemented and are now benefiting some two million workers (Rodríguez 2000). As a consequence, incomes for this proportion of the population have improved with accompanying increased access to consumption, though this has not compensated for the decline in real income. Yet, the sustainability of this practice in the longer run is uncertain as these incentive schemes are an expense that is charged to production as a cost, thereby raising the question of how long this measure can be sustained without affecting the competitiveness of production and the expected effect on workers.

Another important factor for analysis—one that is not the product of national labor, but has tended to substantially increase the monetary resources of a portion of the population—is the amount of remittances received from outside the country. While the amount cannot be precisely determined because most of it does not reach the country through bank transfers, it may be said at the very least that the amount is rising, based on trends of increased sales in shops for the recovery of foreign exchange (TRDs). According to estimates by CEPAL (Comisión Económica para América Latina y el Caribe), remittances amounted to approximately US$3 billion between 1989 and 1996 (CEPAL 1997). Table 8.1 shows that other researchers have estimated the possible amounts of annual remittances between US$300 million and US$1.1 billion between 1998 and 2002.

Table 8.1 Remittance Estimates, 1998–2002

Study	Estimate (US$ millions per year)	Equivalent in Cuban pesos (based on current exchange rate, millions of pesos)
CEPAL (1998)	800	16,800
Aguilar (2001)	300–735	6,900–16,905
Marquetti (2002)	800–1,100	20,800–28,600

Source: Prepared by the authors based on data reported by cited studies

Similarly, other sources of income in U.S. dollars come from providing services to tourists and to Cubans in the self-employed labor market, which also contribute to the increase and recirculation or redistribution of these same benefits to other parts of the population. Between 30 percent and 60 percent of the population is estimated to access earnings in U.S. dollars through these different mechanisms. However, it is well to point out that while the number of persons with access to U.S. dollars has indeed risen, this segment of the population is not homogeneous and is highly concentrated and polarized by means of access and geographical areas. Incomes of self-employed workers are much higher than those of salaried workers. Some incomes in this sector are especially high due to the characteristics of their business, for example, farmers, dealers in the agricultural market and owners of small restaurants.

While the unrestricted circulation and the legalization of U.S. dollar possession has introduced differentiation with respect to access to consumption, this policy measure has also permitted appreciation of the national currency in domestic exchange markets. Figure 8.5 presents data on the informal exchange rate since 1989. The Cuban peso has risen substantially in the foreign exchange market, where its value appreciated from 78 pesos to the U.S. dollar in 1993 to 19.2 in 1996 (lowest figure) and 20 pesos in 1998. After the terrorist attacks against the United States on September 11, 2001, it depreciated to 26 pesos to the U.S. dollar and remained stable throughout 2002. This appreciation has contributed to decreasing, though insufficiently, the gap between population groups with respect to differentiated access to the U.S. dollar.

Figure 8.5 Evolution of Prices in the Cuban Economy, 1989–2002
(1989=100%)

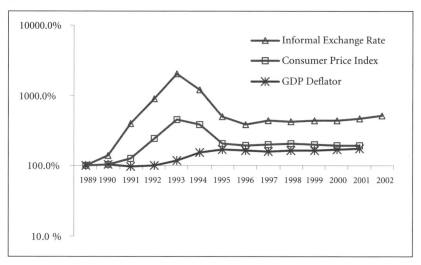

Source: Authors' calculations based on data released by CEPAL (2000) and ONE (2002)

In the subsequent sections of this chapter, data on the principal components of a broad range of consumption categories are presented to show how these have changed as a result of the crisis, as well as to explain how supply sources have changed. As the data will help document, differences in income are translating into differentiated access to consumption.

Food Consumption

Agricultural Production and its Contribution to Consumption

Agricultural products have historically made up half of food consumption demand, and hence their contribution is decisive for improving Cuban nutritional levels. In the two decades preceding the crisis, agricultural farm production grew, but these rates did not always correspond to expectations based on investment and input levels. During the 1990s and as a result of the dependence acquired on foreign earnings in earlier periods, the contribution of domestic agricultural production to consumption contracted sharply. The aggregate value of the sector declined by 54 percent between 1989 and 1994 (Figure 8.6).

Figure 8.6 Agricultural Production, 1985–2000
(in constant 1981 million pesos)

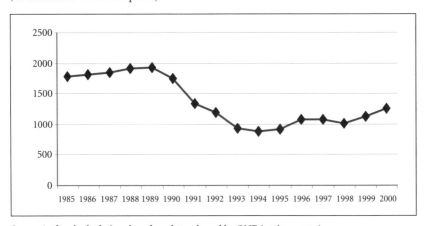

Source: Authors' calculations based on data released by ONE (various years)

As a part of economic adjustment and in seeking to boost agricultural production, a series of policy changes in the production and sale of domestic agricultural production took place in 1993. These processes included transforming large state farms into Basic Cooperative Production Units (UBPC) and opening up agricultural markets. Both actions soon began to reenergize this sector, although results in production still lag far behind what had been achieved by the late 1980s (Figure 8.7 and Table 8.2).[10] Nevertheless, the advances in crop production are sig-

Figure 8.7 Agricultural Production, 1980–2001
(1989 =1.0)

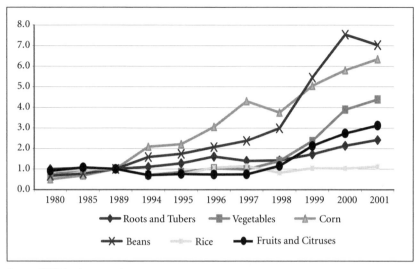

Source: ONE (various years)

Table 8.2 Agricultural Yields, 1990 and 2001
(tons per hectare)

	1990	2001	% change
Tubers and root crops	4.61	7.54	1.6
Bananas	5.83	8.71	1.5
Vegetables	3.85	13.32	3.5
Rice	3.06	3.27	1.1
Corn	0.87	2.33	2.7
Beans	0.27	0.96	3.6
Citrus	8.86	14.76	1.7
Other fruits	4.21	7.96	1.9

Source: Prepared by authors based on ONE (various years)

nificant, particularly because yields are higher than they were in the pre-crisis period. With the sole exception of pork, there has been no recovery of livestock production, because it is more dependent on import of inputs, especially cattle feed.

As Figure 8.8 indicates, imports play a significant role in making up unmet demand because of the relative inelasticity of the supply of farm products. This is especially true of dairy products, beans, and rice, with their unstable world market prices (dairy products have tended to rise), thereby entailing greater outlays of foreign exchange to cover their importation without being able to increase quantity or variety.

Figure 8.8 Contribution of Imports and National Production to Nutrition Consumption (percentage)

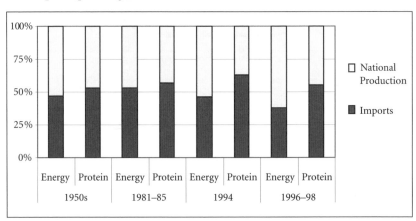

Sources: Marcos (1987), Espinosa (1992) and calculations by the authors

Table 8.3 presents data on agricultural foreign trade since 1989. As this table shows, under agreements with the Socialist Bloc, the traditional specialization of Cuban agriculture in sugar production and the export of this product had guaranteed revenues in foreign exchange. This enabled the country to import foods that it could not produce efficiently and to cover expenses in foreign exchange for purchasing capital goods and current inputs for domestic farm production. With the collapse of this agreement in 1989, this situation changed radically in subsequent years. Presently, the foreign trade balance of the Cuban agricultural sector has fallen significantly and in order to keep producing, it requires foreign exchange subsidies derived from other economic activities.

Table 8.3 Agricultural Trade Balance,* 1989–1998
(US$ million)

	1989	1993	1994	1995	1996	1997	1998
Exports	4372	947	993	1012	1290	1218	1006
Imports	933	497	475	627	733	759	733
Balance	3439	3439	518	385	557	459	373
Imported Inputs	1400	700	800	900	1000	1150	1200
Resulting balance	2039	(250)	(282)	(515)	(443)	(691)	(927)

* Includes Fishing, beverages, and tobacco

Source: Fernández (2002), page 131

Hence, food imports must be replaced, to the degree possible, by seeking efficiency in profitable domestically produced crops. Incentives should be given to make wholesale prices (*acopio*[11]) and existing domestic trade mechanisms more flexible. The current centralization of decision making with respect to supply and current organizational forms and management systems hinder this phase of the process and lead to large losses along the way from producer to consumer. This system runs counter to the dynamism and flexibility required by the products, most of which are perishable; it also lessens the quality and quantity of supply. This structural shift in farm production toward products of vegetable origin is reflected in a larger share of domestic production in providing food energy. It has also brought a change in nutrition patterns and habits of the Cuban population that is beneficial to its health.

The significant drop in domestic food production combined with the impossibility of filling this gap with imports has resulted in an insufficiency in the supply of the minimum necessary food nutrients through the rationed and social consumption markets. As a result, the completion of the basic consumption basket must be realized in liberalized markets where prices are set according to supply and demand. These prices are high, thereby greatly reducing the capacity to satisfy these needs for households at average or below average income levels.[12]

Nutritional Intake

The population has access to a food basket that supplies the nutrients necessary for human development from domestic production and imports. Per capita consumption of food in this basket has varied over time, depending on the country's economic resources. From a nutritional standpoint, there was an improvement in per capita intake that even surpassed the minimum requirements established by FAO in the pre-1989 phase. According to Rodríguez, the establishment of consumption levels through a rationing system has not meant that these standards are the most that could be attained. According to 1978 data, real consumption surpassed the rationing level by the following percentages: meat 15 percent, rice 46 percent, beans 26 percent, shortening 100 percent, potatoes 220 percent, and yams 80 percent (1987: 79–80).

From 1965 to 1994, sugar consumption had declined, as complex carbohydrates became an increased source of energy, thereby improving diet quality. The diversification of farm production and imports toward cereals, vegetables and beans had also indirectly helped bring about this improvement. Consumption of products supplying animal-origin protein increased until 1989, at which point it fell sharply and has not been able to recover to date (Figure 8.9). However, the most critical situation has been the consumption of fats, seriously affected by the decline in consumption of animal-origin products (invisible component) and the sharp drop in imports of vegetable oils and shortening on which the country was over 90 percent dependent.

Figure 8.9 Nutritional Dietary Contribution in Comparison with FAO Recommendations, 1965–2000

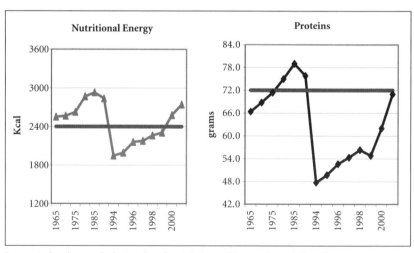

Source: Authors' own calculations based on Ministry of Economics and Planning

As a result of the economic crisis, nutritional intake dropped far below established parameters, jeopardizing secure access to food. By 2000, calorie intake had risen sufficiently to meet basic nutritional needs; the following year, protein intake reached recommended nutritional levels, although sugar products still occupied a high percentage of calorie intake, while fats and animal-derived protein made up an insufficient part of the daily diet. By 1993, fats and essential fatty acids stood at only 80 percent and 74 percent of recommended levels. These figures are very much interconnected because fats allow for the formation of essential fatty acids, as well as acting as a carrier for liposoluble vitamins. Recent evidence suggests that there has been some improvement, however consumption of fats and essential fatty acids still only meet half of the recommended requirement.

The components of vitamin B complex, which are not produced by the body and have to be ingested through fruit and meats, dropped around 39 percent and have not yet recovered sufficiently. Complex B vitamins affect restoration of the nervous system, and vitamin B12 plays a role in the important formation of red blood cells. That is why the government has been concerned and moved to pharmaceutically manufacture B-complex, distributing it free to the population during the worst years of the crisis to compensate for the nutritional deficit. In 1993, intake of vitamin A—essential for growth, vision, and the reproduction and integrity of the immune system—had dropped 59 percent below recommended levels, and by 1998 stood at 54 percent. Children over the age of 7 are the most vulnerable to vitamin A deficiency, and yet this group was not included in the protection provided by the rationed dairy product distribution program. To alleviate this situation, soy yogurt is now allocated for the 8–13 year old group.

A Havana-based study[13] (Lam 2002: 15) showing the coverage offered by the rationed market by age groups, makes it clear that the nutritional contribution of this market surpasses the needs of the population under age 6, except in fats; however, children aged 7–13 only have guaranteed between 53 percent and 64 percent of their nutritional requirements through rationed food sources, without counting oils, which provides only about 20 percent of recommended nutritional requirements. The least covered group is that between 14 and 64 years, who provide the nation's production and reproduction, ensure the advance of the economy, and care for children and the elderly. The most critical case of unmet nutritional needs is for seniors over 65, who have lower incomes and fewer possibilities of seeking other incomes through work, thus basically depending on family aid. This situation is somewhat eased for some participants in school and workplace meal programs, as they receive government distributed food at very low prices.

Table 8.4 Coverage of Nutritional Recommendations Provided by Rationed Products by Age Groups
(percentage of total caloric recommendations)

Nutrients	0–2 years	3–6 years	7–13 years	14–64 years	65 or over
Calories	120.0	115.4	63.7	43.1	61.8
Protein	133.0	132.0	53.3	32.1	55.4
Fat	67.6	67.4	22.4	12.9	17.1

* Recommendations of the National Institute of Nutrition and Food Hygiene in Cuba

Source: Lam (2002)

The rationed market is the main nutrient-providing source for Cuban households, but not the only one. Indeed others supplement it, which at subsidized prices—such as government meal programs, social consumption and household production—or under the laws of free market prices, enable diet to be completed on the basis of household incomes. It is interesting to analyze the contribution of each of these sources in terms of calorie supply and the spending associated with the nutrition obtained from each source.

In 1995, the consumption recorded in Table 8.5 shows that Cubans on average were consuming a food basket with a calorie shortage of 407 kcal, even though 96.7 percent of available energy came from the subsidized price market. Due to the economic restrictions confronting the country and the downward trend of government consumption, this gap had to be satisfied through private consumption purchased at market prices. That meant that the total cost of the minimum consumption basket rose from 73 to 284 pesos and that the largest share of purchases (83 percent) took place under the laws of supply and demand.

The contribution to total caloric intake and the proportions of subsidized versus market-based remained the same in 1998, with the largest share still derived from state sources. There was however, an improvement in the amount of kilocalories from these sources, particularly related to household production and the rationed market. Even so the consumption basket continued to have a calorie shortage, though only 33 percent of its value in 1995. The cost of the 1998 basket was 45 percent less than that of 1995, and hence purchasing was easier for households.

Table 8.5 Contribution to Caloric Intake by Supply Source, 1995 and 1998

		1995			1998	
Source	Kcal	% relative to FAO recommended total kcal	Monthly Estimated Expenditure (pesos)	Kcal	% relative to FAO recommended total kcal	Monthly Estimated Expenditure (pesos)
State-Subsidized Consumption						
State-run retail stores	1,150	48%	23.00	1,166	49%	23.32
Public food programs	223	9%	4.46	170	7%	3.40
Social Consumption	300	13%	6.00	328	14%	6.56
Household production	254	11%	5.08	520	22%	10.40
Market-based Consumption						
Agricultural Markets	32	1%	16.64	31	1%	16.12
Dollar Stores	34	1%	17.68	50	2%	26.00
Total	1,993	83%	72.86	2,265	94%	85.80
Deficit	407	17%	211.64	135	6%	70.20
FAO Recommendation	2,400		284.50	2,400		156.00

Source: Prepared by the authors based on Pérez and Miranda (1997), ONE (1999) and expert opinion

A comparison between expenditures necessary to cover minimum food requirements (156 pesos) and monthly per capita income, which for 1998 was 116 pesos,[14] shows that income was insufficient to cover even basic food needs.[15] But the entire population was not under this limit in its income, and hence it must be determined which segments were most affected in order to establish aid policies targeted to the needs of each population group. At the same time, however, Figure 8.10 and Table 8.5 show that, though the caloric deficit is only 8 percent of total calories, this segment of goods represents 46 percent of the cost of the minimum consumption basket in pesos. Thus, households that only have access to rationed goods (*la libreta*) and lack opportunities to receive supplemental nutrition through worker's lunchrooms or household production are those that face the greatest food deficit.

Moreover, differences between the countryside and the city, the cap-

Figure 8.10 Structure of Consumption by Distribution Source, 1998

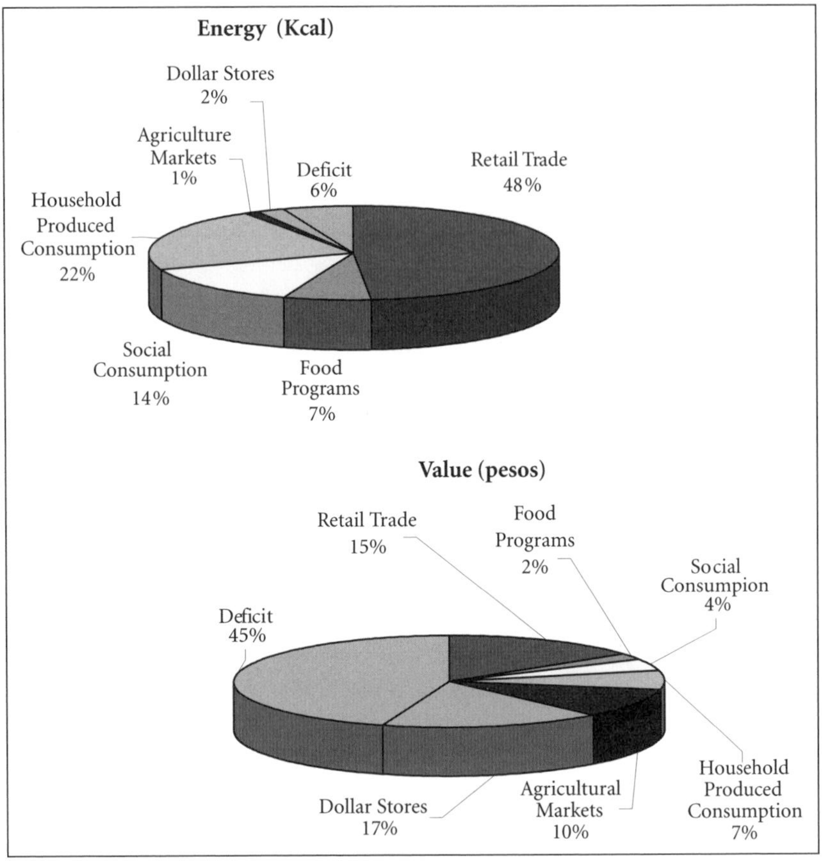

Source: Elaborated by the authors based on data from ONE (1999) and expert opinion

ital, and the rest of the country must be kept in mind, as well as the differences between those who are of working age and those who are over 65, whose primary income is social security. That fact makes their situation worse than that of the population's average. Government po-lices have been designed and funds allocated to seek to lessen the gap through social welfare based food programs. For example, in the city of Havana, lunch and supper is provided for more than 57,000 people over the age of 65. As of 2000, government studies sought to determine which groups most needed aid. These studies began with research focused on minors under the age of 15 and older people, as well as those with dis-abilities. As a result of these studies, special food aid programs have been set up and the lowest pension payments have been increased.

Other Consumer Goods

Production and Import of Other Goods

In historic terms, the contribution of domestic production to the consumption of household durable goods, including electrical appliances and a large portion of other goods, has been marked by strong dependence on imports, initially from the United States and later from the socialist market. It should be pointed out that as a result of the island's insertion into the socialist division of labor and the investment policy pursued by the country in the 1970s, production grew and for the first time the supply of household durables included nationally produced refrigerators and radios.

Total production and importation of consumer goods grew until 1985 and then remained stagnant until the end of the decade, reflecting increased constraints in foreign trade relations and the prelude to the crisis (Table 8.6 and Figure 8.11). Both production and importation then fell sharply between 1989 and 1994. With the crisis, the structure of those imports, which had improved between 1971 and 1989 in favor of non-food imports, underwent a reversal, as food imports were once more given priority. That trend continued until the economy began to recover in the second half of the 1990s.

Table 8.6 Total Domestic Production of Other Consumer Goods, 1963–1989

	1963	1970	1975	1980	1985	1989
Clothing and footwear						
Fabrics (thous. sq. miles)	112.6	78.0	144.2	160.3	205.4	220.03
Underwear (thous. units)	45.7	24.8	42.7	37.1	47.2	44.8
Outerwear (thous. units)	25.8	26.2	47.4	44.1	52.0	54.2
Shoes (thous. pairs)	17.9	10.6	14.0	8.8	14.1	11.9
Cleaning goods (thous. tons)						
Bath soap	34.0	32.9	40.6	37.7	38.9	36.9
Hand soap	11.6	16.7	17.8	14.7	14.8	13.6
Household detergent	13.2	10.0	22.0	23.0	20.0	12.9
Toothpaste	0.9	1.8	3.7	3.7	50.0	6.1
Consumer durables (thous. units)						
Refrigerators	0.0	5.8	50.0	25.0	25.9	9.1
Television sets	0.0	0.0	25.6	40.3	94.1	70.5
Radio sets	0.0	19.1	112.9	200.0	236.3	172.7

Source: Comite Estatal de Estadísticas (various years)

Figure 8.11 Imports of Consumption Goods and Their Structure, 1958–2001

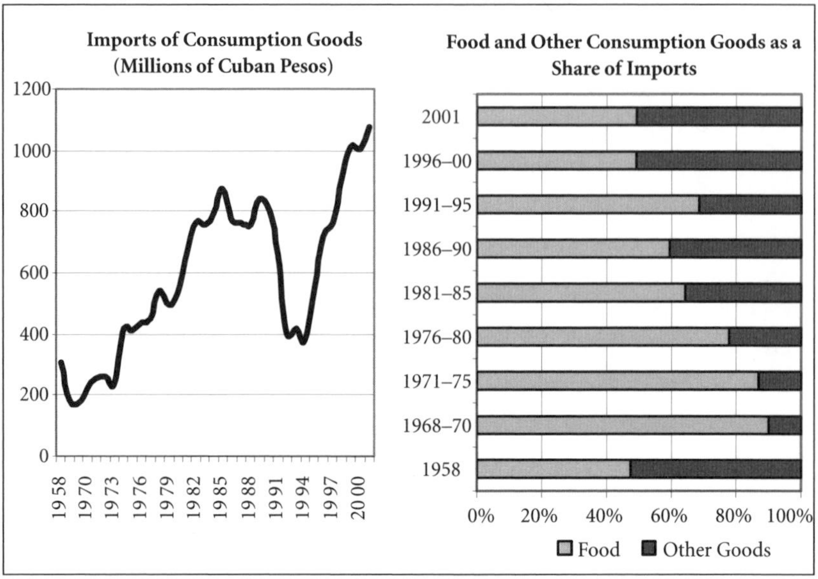

Source: Authors' calculations based on CEE and ONE (various years)

Consumption of Other Goods

One indicator of consumption of durable goods is the sales of such articles through retail trade channels. If sales of clothing and footwear are taken as representative for analysis, Figure 8.12 shows that these indicators dropped due to the contraction of national production and imports until 1970, at which point the trend reversed and per capita sales improved, remaining relatively stable until the late 1980s. It must be noted that a portion of those articles is made available not through the market but distributed free as a portion of social consumption in schools, workplaces and social assistance (uniforms, work clothes and shoes, fabric, etc.) and hence they are not reflected in sales.

Per capita sales of personal hygiene goods remained stable until 1989, with the exception of toothpaste, which rose sharply (Figure 8.13). Between 1989 and 1993 supply—available only through the rationed market—declined significantly. Figure 8.14 presents data on durable household goods sales per thousand inhabitants: these rose significantly between 1975 and 1989 as a result of growth in domestic production and imports, stimulated by the relatively low prices of such articles and of credit terms offered to the population for their purchase.

The results could be seen in the possession of articles of this kind in Cuban homes.

Figure 8.12 Textiles, Clothing and Shoe Retail Sales, 1965–2001
(number of units per person)

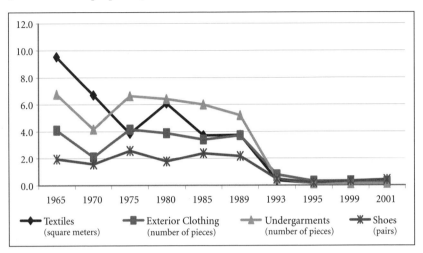

Source: Authors' calculations based on CEE and ONE (various years)

Figure 8.13 Personal Hygiene Retail Sales, 1965–2001
(number of units per person)

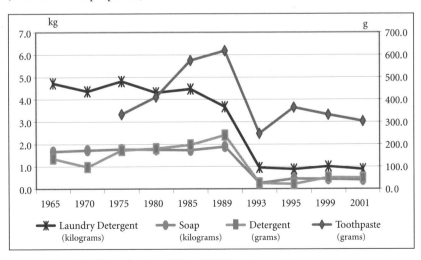

Source: Authors' calculations based on CEE and ONE (various years)

Figure 8.14 Durable Goods, Retail Sales, 1965–2001
(units per thousand inhabitants)

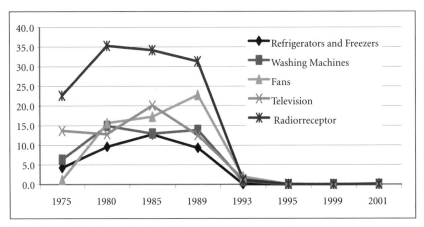

Source: Authors' calculations based on CEE and ONE (various years)

Table 8.7 Ownership of Durable Consumer Goods, 1975–1985
(per 100 households with electricity)

	1975	1980	1985
Television sets	33	74	91
Refrigerators	15	38	50
Washing machines	6	34	59
Radios*	42	105	150

* For every 100 homes without electricity

Source: Rodríguez and Carriazo (1987)

With the crisis, the market for non-food consumer items practically disappeared, although some shops selling school uniforms and footwear, as well as infant clothing for very young children, remained open. It was not until the second half of the 1990s that a small market opened for the sale in national currency of some of these articles such as clothing, shoes, personal hygiene and cleaning items and minor household items. The market in foreign exchange opened in 1993 with a greater variety of selection and quality, but with prices greater than the income range of most of the population, especially for consumer durables, which after ten years were showing signs of physical deterioration and technological obsolescence. Thus, consumption was constrained by financial resources. In short, the model of consumption can be seen to have varied in sources of supply, selection, prices and quality of articles over time, depending on the economic possibilities of the country. In terms of individuals, prior equity and universality has given way to un-equal access.

Market Segmentation

Background

Different market segments, as well as different forms of their access and regulation, can be discerned throughout the entire period analyzed in regards to the distribution of consumer goods. These markets operated until 1989 basically in Cuban pesos. We say "basically" because already from the mid-1980s, the parallel circulation of the U.S. dollar was es-tablished with the beginning of the expansion in tourist activity. This parallel circulation of the U.S. dollar is strengthened with the advent of the crisis in the 1990s.

Box 8.2 Market Segmentation

Period	Existing markets for accessing consumption goods
1976–1989	Rationed market State-run parallel market (food and industrial products) Fairs and artisan markets Farmer's Markets (1980–1986) Black-market
1990–1993	Rationed market Black market Self-employed market
1994–	Rationed market Agricultural Markets (market-based and fixed prices, intensive or-chards, organic (urban gardens and household plots and fairs) Industrial and artisan markets Self-employed market State markets with prices set according to supply and demand Dollar Markets Black Markets

Source: Prepared by the authors

Consumer goods market segments currently operate in different cur-rencies: Cuban pesos, convertible pesos and U.S. dollars; more recently transactions also can be carried out in Euros, although this possibility is still restricted to the tourist area of Varadero. Price setting also dif-fers among market segments. The type of currency used in commercial transactions, as well as their price level, determines who has access to one or another commercial space. Another source of differentiation among market segments is also found in the rules of access for suppliers.

Figure 8.15 presents a measure of the significance of each market in the satisfaction of the needs for consumer goods in physical terms. The sections that follow describe the operation of each market and trends in consumption in each of the major markets (rationed, black or informal, agricultural and U.S. dollar markets) with a focus on access to consumers and its impact on well-being.

Characterization of the Most Important Markets

Regulated or Rationed Market

The rationed or regulated market is a market of products that attempts to guarantee the satisfaction of minimum food, clothing and footwear needs at state-subsidized prices. It is characterized as being universal

Figure 8.15 Consumer Good Market Shares by Market Type, 1975–2002

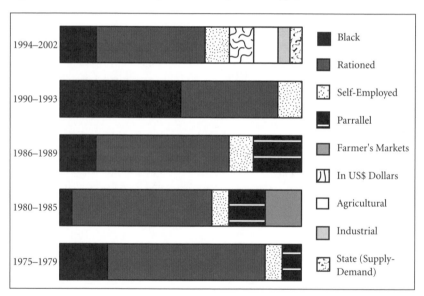

Source: Prepared by the authors based on expert opinion

and equal: that is, all Cubans in the same age group have the right to enjoy equal product assignment, regardless of their income, needs, and preferences. Furthermore, this system includes the granting of special quotas for elderly people, cases of those who suffer from illness or have special dietary needs (for example, diabetics and pregnant women).

The supply of rationed and state-subsidized goods has varied over time, in relation to the country's economic resources. The supply of items such as rice, beans, sugar, salt and, especially, products related to infant feeding has been maintained regardless of national economic circumstances since 1962, when rations were first introduced (Table 8.8). However, the rationed supply of other consumer goods disappeared almost in its entirety with the economic crisis in the early 1990s.

Table 8.8 Articles and Ration Quotas, 1962 and 2002

		March 1962		November 2002	
Articles	*Unit*	*Quantity per person*	*Frequency*	*Quantity per person*	*Frequency*
National					
Lard or oil	lb	2	monthly	0.5	monthly
Rice	lb	6	monthly	6	monthly
Beans	lb	1.5	monthly	1.25	monthly
Raw sugar	lb	3	monthly	2	monthly
Refined sugar	lb	3	monthly	3	monthly
Greater Havana and 25 other cities					
Washing Soap	unit	1	monthly	1	every two months
Detergent		8 ounces (in powder)	monthly	1 liter (per household)	quarterly
Bar of soap	unit	1	monthly	1	every two months
Only in Greater Havana					
Beef	lb	0.75	weekly		
Chicken	lb	2	monthly		
Fish		1 lb(fresh)	monthly	425 g (canned food) or 0.7 lb (fresh)	monthly
Eggs	unit	5	monthly	8	monthly
Milk for children 7 years and younger	liter	1	journal	1	journal
Milk for 5 people over 7 years old[a]	liter	1	journal		
Foods	lb	3.5	weekly	15	monthly
Additional malanga (root vegetable) for children 7 years and younger	lb	2	weekly		
Butter	ounce	2	monthly		
Meat[b]					
Beef	lb			0.5	
Chicken	lb			1	
Minced meat fortified with soybeans	lb			0.5	
Sausages	g			225	

a. This quota could be replaced with 6 tins of 400 grams of condensed or evaporated milk.
b. The frequency of the deliveries of meat products is not stable and depends on availabilities. It involves guaranteeing at least two monthly deliveries.

Source: Díaz (2000) and the authors

In order to guarantee the supply of food and other basic necessities in 2001 through rationed markets, the state spent US$665.3 million in their acquisition (Lam 2002). These products were sold in national currency for the sum of 1103.2 million pesos. Table 8.9 presents the data on the costs and sales by categories, as well as the implied index of peso per U.S. dollar conversion. These estimates do not include food supplement programs that are provided by the state to given segments of the population (the elderly, patients, children and adolescents with low weight) free of charge or with prices equal to those in the rationed market.

Table 8.9 Rationed Market: Costs in US$ and Sales in National Currency, 2001

	Spending in foreign exchange (US$ millions)	Sales to the population (Millions of pesos)	Index of convertibility (pesos per US$)
Total	665.3	1103.2	1.66
Food	542.7	947.8	1.75
Hygiene and Cleaning Supplies	13.1	47.6	3.63
Cooking Oil (Kerosene)	109.5	107.7	0.98

Source: Prepared by the authors based on Lam (2002)

A study by the Centro de Estudios de la Economía Cubana (Togores 1999) reported that the contribution of rationed distribution to per capita food calorie intake was nearly 58 percent of total requirements in 1995. Based on a study of real daily consumption in the City of Havana, rationed sources of food supplied 49 percent of total calorie intake, 40 percent of vegetable-origin protein, 30 percent of animal protein and 19 percent of fats in 1999 (Nova 2002).[17] Between 1999 and 2001, rations in the case of energy remained stable and were increased for proteins and fats. Indeed, the Ministry of Economy assessed that the contributions of rations to consumption have been maintained at these levels covering approximately 45 percent of energy, 43 percent of protein and 37 percent of fats in 2001 (Lam 2002). This trend can be interpreted to indicate that the objectives of supplying consumer goods to the population through this channel are attempting to be maintained, while gradually improving its quality, always within the narrow limits of the external finance situation imposed on Cuba. These results are summarized in Figure 8.16 below.

Figure 8.16 Daily Per Capita Consumption by Market and Energy Source, 1995–2001

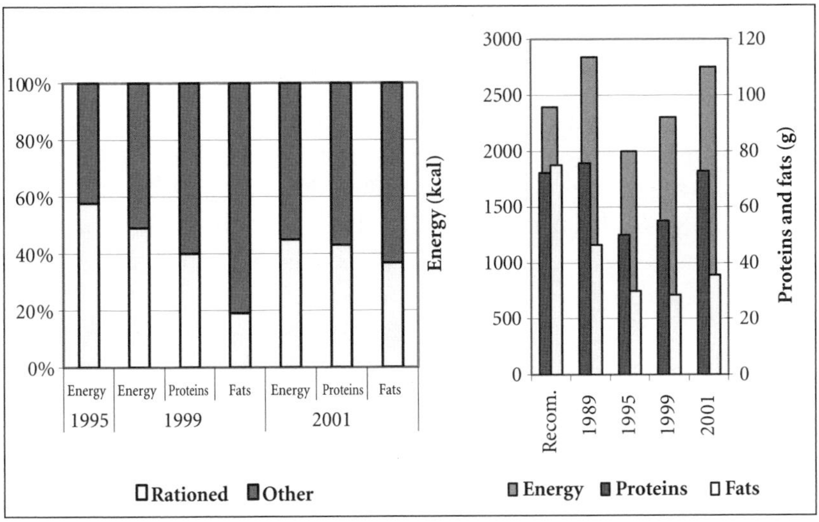

Source: Prepared by the authors based on Togores (1999), Nova (2002), and Lam (2002)

Finally, the rationed market also includes the distribution of non-food products. We already mentioned the products for personal and domestic hygiene, which have continued to be distributed through this modality, although in quantities that have fluctuated depending on foreign currency availability. Currently, approximately half of the ration current until 1989 is distributed. Textile, clothing and footwear, also were part of the quota, and were guaranteed both to children and adults. Currently, the distribution of only a portion of products for the infant population is guaranteed, for example the newborn basket, school uniforms, as well as orthopedic and school footwear.

Informal Markets
In Cuba, as in the rest of the world, the informal sector has always been present, although its characteristics have varied depending on given economic situations and other aspects, among them the sociopolitical, which have conditioned its existence. Until 1989 the informal sector basically focused on fulfilling the deficits of goods not supplied by state supplied markets. During the 1980s, Cuba's internal financial situation was kept relatively balanced, so that the prices in this market were not as elevated, in comparison with official prices, and it is estimated that these purchases represented around 20 percent of the population's income (see González 1995). Following the disappearance of the Socialist

Bloc and the external conditions that permitted the sustainability of the Cuban economy, the country suffered a strong economic contraction with GDP falling abruptly in the 1990s. Consequently, exports, imports and industry were paralyzed, at given moments functioning at between 15 to 20 percent of their capacities. The parallel market as a complement to the rationed market disappeared, and the latter remained as the only legal market, though quite deteriorated and limited in its supply. In unison, monetary liquidity increased. At the same time, the nominal wage gradually experienced small increases, while inflation increased and productivity diminished.

The sum of these factors has had implications for labor markets, translating into an emigration of the formal sector workforce towards new areas where income can be improved or a material counterpart can be obtained. In turn, this has produced two changes with respect to the representative structure of different labor markets: one within the formal sector itself where labor has sought to be employed in companies of the so-called "emerging economy" and another one where workers have migrated toward the informal sector. Both of these movements are comprehensible given changes in average real wages and some indicators, which reflect the balance of labor resources. As income is much higher in the informal, rather than formal, sector, this labor market constitutes a point of attraction for those of the labor force aspiring to maintain or elevate their standard of living. At the same time, the average wage of the Cuban population has exhibited little variation across time, tending to decrease in nominal terms and, with the increase in inflation, deteriorate significantly in real terms, most especially 1991 and 1994. After 1994, this trend shifts and nominal wages begin to increase while inflation slowly diminishes. However, as this pattern has become stagnant, the recovery of the purchasing power of income has been only partial.

Informality, as a process, occurs differently between urban and rural areas, depending on the levels of development reached with regard to urbanization and industrialization. These differences have established contrasts in the type of activities that develop for those who work in the sector, as well as the income levels generated and constitute one of the primary reasons that most informal workers in rural areas or the outskirts of provincial capitals migrate toward urban areas, where markets permit the expansion of their activities. The supply sources for products, equipment, raw materials and capital for the development of different activities in the informal sector draw from rationed products, private producers and state and mixed enterprises. The form of exchange of informal enterprises ranges from bartering to the sale of products of licit origin or not, and of individual production.

Between 1989 and the present, the informal sector[18] has evolved through different stages. Informal market transactions grew exponentially until 1992. This growth was motivated by the drastic reduction of supply in state-run stores and the corresponding accumulation of circulating pesos in the hands of the population. It is estimated that in this period the volume of sales in this market succeeded in being equal to state sales to the population. Between 1993 and mid-1995, the submerged economy reached its greatest volume, corresponding to the years when food scarcity was highest. During this period, informal market transactions surpassed sales in the official economy.

After 1995, transactions in the informal market decreased as a result of policy measures implemented to tidy internal finances, reopen legal markets for the majority of food, open industrial and craft good markets, as well as liberalize self-employment activity. The social recognition of an important part of the submerged market activities resulted in the incorporation of a greater number of these agents into the official economy and a greater supply of goods in legally authorized markets. Along with this increase in supply, the reduced purchasing power of the population led to significant price reductions in official markets (González 1995). Nevertheless, a significant volume of purchases and sales for a given group of articles continues to flow through the informal market, where they are offered at lower prices than those of the only alternative option—the market in foreign exchange. Examples of these types of goods include dairy, beef and eggs.

The prices of the formal sector of the economy, combined with the scarce availability and poor quality of these products, have enabled the informal sector to establish monopoly prices. Thus, income is redistributed to a minority, those who participate as sellers, and access to these goods is limited for the majority of the population due to low wage earnings. The activities that are carried out in the informal sector are varied. They encompass all phases of the productive cycle from production to distribution and include the majority of services. The prices in the informal market, as has already been noted, are much higher than those in the rationed market—on average more than 40 times higher. Over time, prices in the informal market have tended to fall, especially after the opening of agricultural and industrial markets. However, since January 1998, prices have halted their declining trend and are practically stagnant. In order to illustrate this behavior we have taken the average price for a basket of 12 essential articles and we present these findings in Figure 8.17 below.

Figure 8.17 Average Prices in the Informal Market,[a] 1995–2002
(January 1995 = 1.0)

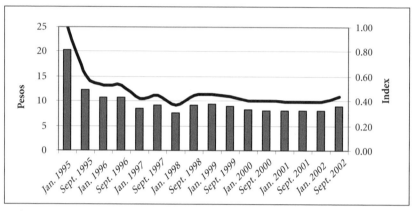

a. The average price index is calculated for a consumption basket that includes a set of essential commodities for the Cuban diet, as well as hygeine products. These products are fresh milk, rice, black beans, bread, pork, sugar and soaps.

Source: Prepared by the authors based on ONE (1995–2002)

Agricultural Markets

Starting in mid-1993, the economic transformations of the 1990s began in Cuban agriculture with the creation of Basic Units of Cooperative Production (UBPC)[19] After this structural change in land administration directed at ownership, changes directed at providing incentive schemes for agricultural production also became necessary. Accordingly, the new opening of agricultural markets in the 1990s was directed at resuscitating agriculture production. Among the needs of the population, that of food is precisely the basis of survival and well-being of the human being. Despite the revolution's achievements with regard to nutrition, which were sustained to a large extent through imports, the black market for food reached such dimensions upon entering the Special Period[20] that the value of these sales was higher than the value of state crop production as a whole. Cuba's new agricultural markets initiated their operations under these conditions in October 1994.

The basic objectives of agricultural reform were to encourage agricultural production; counteract the negative effects of a black market for food; ensure access to products not distributed by the state and to promote surpluses with the aim of achieving self-sufficiency. Agricultural markets were initially created by retail trade companies belonging to the Ministry of Domestic Commerce (Ministerio de Comercio Interior (MINCIN)). The location of such markets was subject to regulation through established by-laws and authorization given by the locality's Administrative Council of the Poder Popular, which could also authorize special regulations when necessary targeted to particular local needs. Starting in 1999, other forms of agricultural markets appeared. However, these were either administered by the Ministry of Agriculture and the Army of the Working Youth (Ejército Juvenil del Trabajo (EJT)), or sale stands belonging to Cooperatives Units of Agricultural Production (UBPC). These new markets complemented the established network of state-run agricultural markets. Finally, as part of the movement of urban agriculture that generated increased activity by the end of the 1990s, urban agriculture crops produced in the periphery's and city's intensive, as well as organoponic, gardens were finally incorporated into retail sales.

Prices in the MINCIN's agricultural markets are set by the laws of supply and demand. Nevertheless, further on we will analyze how the design of this economic system works against that purpose. In the case of the Ministry of Agriculture (MINAG) and EJT's agricultural markets, prices are set by local authorities who use the prices in MINCIN-administered agricultural markets (according to a fixed percent of these) and local conditions. Thus, these markets operate under price caps, which fluctuate between MINCIN agricultural market prices and state-subsidized prices for the ration card. The fundamental principle that governs agricultural markets resides in their adherence to state commitments—only production exceeding that contracted by state entities and non-contracted production can be sold. Prior to 1998, agricultural market sales were concentrated in the non-state sector and within this, with private *campesinos* (or small landholders) who contributed the greatest number of products. Due to limited fuel availability, centralized collective agriculture was not only hard hit by a reduction in production, but also a fall in transportation services that could be provided to farmers by the Ministry of Agriculture at the advent of the Special Period. Consequently, harvesting in the spread-out farm sector began to diminish, as well as the delivery commitments to the state by this sector.

As a result of the introduction of a rule that limited these state entities from entering the agricultural market—stipulating the fulfillment delivery of an assigned share of their production to the state procurement agency—the private sector was favored over the rest of the producers, who were tied by stronger commitments to the state. This regulation, well intentioned in the sense of trying to protect the deliveries of food to the population and other prioritized destinations, became the greatest obstacle for a true resuscitation of agricultural production, both for the benefited and harmed sectors. As already mentioned, new spaces for the marketing of agricultural products were opened in 1999, which attenuate this situation and succeed in improving the state's share in the crop market.

Regulations limit the products that can be sold in agricultural markets—all crops, except for livestock such as of cattle, buffalo and equine animal meat, as well as fresh milk and its derivatives. The sale of crops such as coffee and its derivatives, tobacco, cacao, and its derivatives, and potatoes are also excluded from these markets. We would like to clarify the reasoning behind these prohibitions. The sale of livestock according to market-based prices is prohibited because the supply of animal protein is very deficient; indispensable minimums are not yet being produced. In addition, limitations are designed to avoid the risk of depleting livestock herds (cattle and equine animals), whose biological cycle are longer and more difficult to replace. In the cases of tobacco, of coffee, and of cacao, the rationale is to protect exportable goods that can be sold in foreign markets. Finally, potatoes are heavily subsidized by the state, almost all material inputs are of imported origin, from the seed itself to pesticides and other chemical products and therefore sales of this crop are banned.

Annual sales in value terms contracted between 1995 and 1998 in the agricultural market, while volumes sold increased. Since 1999, with the opening of MINAG's and EJT agricultural markets, as well as numerous sale sites for Agricultural Production Cooperatives (CPA),[21] sales grew and surpassed levels corresponding to the operation of the market in its first year. After 1999, the trend of price declines was maintained, although these decreased at a smaller rate, and the quantities sold continued to grow at even higher rates, which results in an increase in sales in value terms.

Figure 8.18 Agricultural Market Sales and Shares by Supply Source, 1995–2002

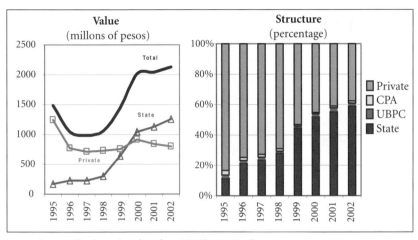

Source: Prepared by the authors based on ONE (1995–2001)

Before 1998, the private sector dominated agricultural sales, with more than 70 percent of total sales in its control. Starting in that year, the sales of the state sector increased, which can be attributed to the impact of the opening of the MINAG and EJT agricultural markets. The decrease in volume weight and relative share of sales of the co-operative sector is remarkable. The UBPC and CPA, but especially the UBPC, face difficulties in shipping products, since they usually do not have access to the necessary means of transportation and state-regulated freight prices turn out to be very high, which increases expenditures and substantially reduces profits. In light of this situation, they have decided to sell harvests, at an agreed-upon price, higher than the price set for the delivery of goods to the state, but much lower than agricultural market prices. The foregoing has also contributed to the increase in the participation of the state in sales, through its collection of production (*acopio*).

Agricultural markets delivered an important blow to the black market, which had reached tremendous proportions and was particularly central in the case of food. With only the opening of agricultural markets operations, prices were significantly reduced, and a progressive and substantial improvement in the food situation of the population was seen. Additionally, throughout the liberalization period and subsequent strengthening of other consumer goods markets, these forces exerted their influence on the fall of additional prices, for example

Figure 8.19 Agricultural Market Sales by Volume and Price,[a] 1994–2002

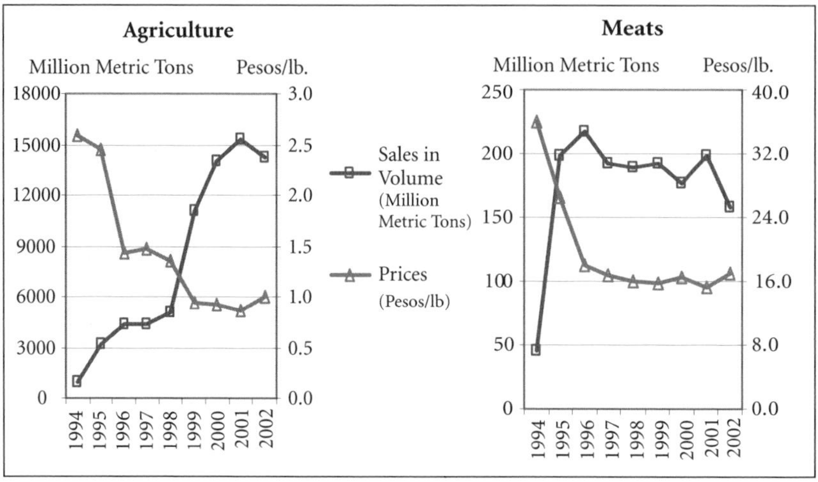

a. Volume of sales is expressed in thousands of hundred weights. A hundred weight amounts to 100 pounds or 46 kilograms.

Source: Prepared by the authors based on ONE (1995-2001)

those in industrial goods. These markets promote an economic space in which the population can spend part of its income, and in fact help to diminish the pressure on food markets and also reduce the proportion of the population's food expenditures.

While the opening of the new markets in 1999 contributed to a substantial improvement in crop sales; this was not so in the case of meat products, whose supply continues to be dominated by the private sector. Meat prices have remained constant, resisting to decline since 1996, while agriculture prices have failed to fall since 1999. During 2002 new forces have pressured prices to increase in these markets, such as the incidence of meteorological phenomena[22] and the growing financial constraints for the acquisition of inputs by the extremely adverse world environment.

It is necessary to point out that agricultural markets are imperfect markets. The private sector, with a minor share of supply (that does not exceed 20 percent of production for many traded products), has managed to extract significant profits, whose magnitude is largely a result of the constraints on its supply. The "barrier to entry," which is the result of the subordination of agricultural markets sales to prior fulfillment of state collection commitments (*acopio*)—since these do not place all potential suppliers with the same market access—as well as other impediments to their participation (for example, the exclusion of cattle and dairy, pig and specialized poultry and specialized rice producers), place the private sector in a privileged situation.

Thus, we can state that agricultural markets are practically cartelized; suppliers act concertedly in order to maintain high prices and limit growth or tend to decrease physical supply, with the negative consequences that this entails for consumer well-being. Therefore, a group of relatively reduced producers and brokers are privileged beneficiaries due to the market's design, and they manage to enrich themselves on the population's account, and even on accounts of those who could be potential rivals. Although the incorporation of the private sector increased competition in MINAG and EJT agricultural markets, the continued policy of fixed prices meant that there has not been a substantial decline in charges to consumers. The change, however, is that the private sector now plays a role in price setting. For these reasons, we underscore that agricultural markets have had a positive effect, but their benefits to consumers could reach greater dimensions in the future. The productive increases triggered up to the present are not sufficient to reach the full satisfaction of dietary needs. In the future, it will be necessary to continue to enhance this reinvigorating mechanism, as well as deepening the rest of the reforms related to the productive food sector.

Market in Foreign Exchange[23]

In the summer of 1993 the Cuban government decided to remove the penalties or to legalize foreign exchange holding, primarily the U.S. dollar, for the population. This has been one of the most controversial measures of the economic transformation program—on the one hand, this decision has played an important role in the evolution of the economic resuscitation processes that started in 1994; but on the other, it has contributed to an increase in the levels of dollarization.[24] The de-penalization of foreign exchange holding responded to a situation in which the circulation of the U.S. dollar had become increasingly regularized during the initial crisis years due to the opening of the Cuban economy, and most specially, the increase in tourist activity. Consequently, the number of transactions carried out in U.S. dollars had increased considerably. Another important source for the origin of foreign exchange in the hands of the population was from remittances received from Cubans residing abroad temporarily or permanently. In fact, some researchers classify the emigration of the 1990s and these transfers to the island as a "family level transnational strategy" (Monreal 2000) in order to cope with the severe process of economic adjustment that was triggered by the loss of Cuba's traditional international incorporation. Though the adjustment process has attempted to keep its impact on households at a minimum, there has been nevertheless a contraction in consumption.

As part of the transformation process of the 1990s, other non-wage income sources were added including: the incentive systems associated with tourism and other business activities related to exports or to import substitution; the opening of self-employment and authorization of earning income from room rental, which can also generate foreign exchange earnings through the delivery of certain services (particularly, rents, gastronomy and personal services); and the opening of a foreign exchange market for the population through the *Casas de Cambio* (exchange bureaus). Thus, the magnitude of the foreign exchange resources in the hands of the population increased significantly after 1989.

One of the principal objectives of the institution of the de-penalization of foreign exchange holding was to guarantee the capturing of a significant share of U.S. dollars in the hands of the population by the state, and to destine these resources toward financing the externally financed trade deficit that had increased following the onset of the economic crisis in the early 1990s. These transfers only would compensate partially the deficit in convertible currencies that was caused by the drop in the income for exports of goods and services since 1991. The necessary complement to the de-penalization of foreign currency holding was the expansion of the already existing network of retail establishments that carried out their sales only in U.S. dollars. These installations, which originally provided their services to the foreign personnel that were in the country (diplomats, tourists, technical collaborators, students, etc.), expanded their sales to Cubans with access to U.S. dollars. Thus, the infrastructure of this segment of the national market has grown steadily in recent years, and by 2000 succeeded in having more than 5,500 establishments operating in U.S. dollars nationwide.

In fact, the de-penalization and the associated expansion in sales in U.S. dollars represented the tacit recognition that the domestic market must play a more active role in the transformation and upturn of the economy.[26] Regardless of the controversy regarding the opening of the domestic market in foreign exchange, this measure has had multiple

Table 8.10 Number and Types of Establishments Operating in US$, 2000

Stores	1,882	Cafeterias	522	Photographic Services	151	Electrical Appliance Workshops	100
Street and other authorized sale sites[a]	1,286	Bars	77	Service centers	117	Auto Rental	53
Restaurants	633	Nightclubs	43	Other Commercial Services	208	Others	448

a. 'Sale sites' (*puntas de venta*) is a term used to refer to either cooperative-based sales of agricultural goods, or dollar store sites.

Source: Ministerio de Comercio Interior (2001)

positive effects. In the first place, guaranteed net income from sales in foreign exchange is allocated primarily towards financing consumption through social consumption funds for distributing rationed goods to the population. In this way, the restitution of a portion of supply and the improvement in quality that has been recently noted can be attributed to the increased stability of the state's income guarantees in foreign exchange. Secondly, and no less important, this U.S. dollar consumer market has also served as a platform for the resuscitation of the country's manufacturing sector through import substitution and helped prevent the subsequent loss of employment in the manufacturing sector of the economy. Those whom access this market have the possibility of improving the quality of their consumption basket and of encountering the most modern trends in these categories.[27] Finally, the existence of this market and the incentives given to workers in some prioritized activities in foreign exchange trigger better job performances and greater productivity.

In order to characterize the evolution of the domestic market in foreign exchange, we now present some statistics on their dynamic. Figure 8.20 also presents data on the share of the three most important retail chains in operation, Cubalse (Cuba al Servicio del Exterior, S.A.), CIMEX (Corporación Importadora y Exportadora, S.A.) and TRD-Caribe (Tiendas de Recuperación de Divisas), which encompasses more than 75 percent of total U.S. dollar sales.

Although retail sales structure in dollar stores has not varied much, the type of products sold in these markets has undergone significant

Figure 8.20 Retail Sales in Foreign Exchange and Their Principal Suppliers, 1994–2001

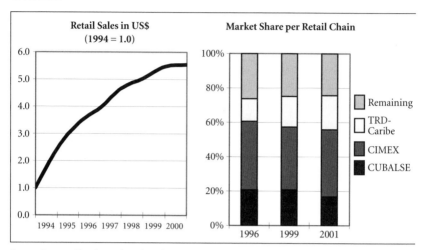

Source: Prepared by the authors based on Marquetti (1998), authors estimates (2001)

change. When retail sales in dollar stores to the population first started, they concentrated on essential articles such as food, clothing, footwear and hygiene and cleaning products. However, the ratio of basic products relative to non-essential consumer goods has shifted towards favoring the latter in recent years (Table 8.11).

Table 8.11 Sales in US$ by Product Type, 1995 and 2000
(percentage)

	1995	2000
Essential goods	46.2	34.3
Food	8.1	7.7
Footwear and clothing	32.3	21.6
Hygiene and cleaning products	5.8	5.0
Other goods	53.8	65.7
Snacks, refreshments, and beer	8.5	10.0
Electro domestic appliances [a]	2.9	7.2
Other products [b]	42.3	48.5

a. This group only includes refrigerators, televisions, kitchens, and fans.
b. In this group we find hardware, electronic products and other electric appliances, jewelry and jewelry stores, cosmetics and perfumery, alcoholic beverages and cigarettes, toys, knits, among others.
Source: Prepared by the authors (2001)

The systematic increase in the ratio of non-essential consumer goods relative to essentials demonstrates that availability of U.S. dollars is concentrated in relatively few hands, despite the argument that the U.S. dollar is accessible to more than 60 percent of the population. Furthermore, the change in the composition of purchases also reflects the fact that the growth of the domestic food market, specifically through agricultural markets and of multiple points of sale by cooperatives and organic (small urban gardens and household plots) farms, has been able to offer goods at competitive prices relative to foods available in U.S. dollar stores. State sales of clothes and footwear in national currency have also expanded, particularly after the opening of currency exchange bureaus.

Sales in the U.S. dollar market are reaching their stabilization point (Figure 8.20). While sales grew very rapidly between 1994 and 1996, this rate has subsequently diminished. This pattern merits some reflections about the important factors concerning U.S. dollar possession by individuals. At the end of 1994, the Centro de Estudios de la Economía Cubana conducted research to determine the potential existing supply of foreign exchange in Cuba. It arrived at the conclusion that the sum total should range between US$310 and US$510 million. The analysis indicated that remittances corresponded to more than 75 percent of the potential market. Other projections in 1996 and 1998 arrived at similar conclusions, although in the latter year tourist-related income such as gratuities, rents and other services, as well as a steady increase in Cuban personnel contracted abroad and in those receiving special stimulus incentives, acquired greater significance. Nevertheless, these trends did not imply essential changes with respect to 1994 proportions, as can be observed in Table 8.12.

Table 8.12 Potential Market in US$, 1994–2001
(US$ million)

Contribution	1994	1998	2001
Remittances	250–400	650–800	790–1050
Special forms of stimulus [a]	30–50	80–110	80–110
Income derived from tourism [b]	20–50	55–130	80–145
Others [c]	5–10	30–55	50–75
Total	305–510	815–1095	1000–1380

a. The expenditures that imply the different stimulation variants are included.
b. It represents the estimated value of the income that the tourism generates for rent of dwellings, of autos, and of the gratuities.
c. Income of foreign-based Cuban personnel (artists, intellectual, athletes, etc.)

Source: Marquetti (2000)

Estimates regarding the total U.S. dollar-denominated domestic market were derived from estimates of specific market segments. In the tourism sector, more than an estimated 90,000 tourists had been lodged in private rooms in 1998, indicating a projected income of more than US$50 million in rents and collateral services alone.[28] Additionally, income from tips in U.S. dollars average between five and ten million dollars per year. The studies in Table 8.12 also took into consideration the increase in banking accounts in U.S. dollars. The reserve margins, spontaneously set by currency holders, were also estimated. One of the reasons for forecasting the latter was to find additional explanations for growth levels experienced by this market segment.

The analyses significantly found that income obtained by the market segment operating in U.S. dollars corresponds to the estimated market potential. In other words, the reported growth reached by this commercial segment is approaching its maximum income levels, given the quality and variety of the existing supply (Marquetti and García 1999).[29] Updated projections through 2002 corroborate the previous assertion and also show that, without an important increase in tourist flows, recorded levels of U.S. dollar circulation in Cuba should fluctuate between US$1.3 and US$1.4 billion dollars in the coming years.

Some observations with regard to the pricing policy applied in this market should also be mentioned. Dollar store prices are set by adding a markup on the price established by the Ministry of Finance and Prices to the book value. The book value in stores includes importation costs, internal transportation expenditures, and tariffs and handling expenditures before retail placement. The commercial surcharges on the book value of items are high (130 percent on average) and, in fact, function as an indirect sales tax. The resulting high prices contribute to the devaluation of income in national currency. In addition, the purchasing power of workers with fixed income also tends to be reduced because other alternative markets (agricultural markets and industrial) function with a pricing structure that utilizes prevailing prices in the foreign exchange market as a reference point. Despite justifications for applying this policy, it acts as a factor that diminishes the purchasing power of wages, while the high commercial surcharges constitute an indirect tax that is systematically paid by workers. In many cases, these consumer expenditures in U.S. dollars go towards essential products that are either not available in other markets or not supplied in sufficient quantity by rationed markets and thus this tax is regressive.

Upon analyzing the challenges of the Cuban economic model, González (1997: 25) presented policy recommendations in anticipation of growing dollarization. He proposed that the bulk of products supplied for popular consumption should be distributed through markets operating in Cuban pesos, leaving only the products of greater variety and more selective quality in dollar stores. In this way, Gonzalez argued that it would be possible "to begin to reverse the dollarization in consumer arena and strengthen the purchasing power of the wage paid in Cuban pesos."

Figure 8.21 Dollarization and Total Monetary Circulation, 1995–2000
(millions of Cuban pesos)

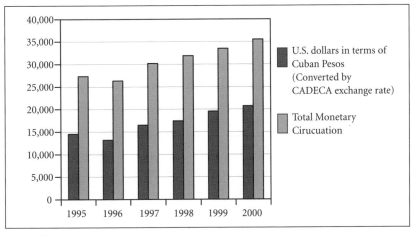

Source: Triana (2001)

However, reversing dollarization requires the creation of various forms of financing and convertibility for domestic activities that do not generate foreign currency income, especially for producers of consumer goods. Although an important part of consumption is financed centrally, the economy's foreign-exchange constraints prevent the full satisfaction of the population's basic needs. An alternate policy option to diminish the dollarization of the economy would be to reduce the surcharges added to products sold in markets operating in U.S. dollars. This, of course, would not affect the magnitude of net income, since it would stimulate sales, speed up monetary circulation and generate a similar net income level, with the great advantage of improving the population's access to this market and, accordingly, consumption.

Conclusion: Market Segmentation—Pro or Con?

Some of the policy measures implemented in order to reignite the economy have further complicated social realities. The free circulation of the U.S. dollar is one such example, as access or the lack of access to hard currency guarantees or limits consumption of a certain number of products. Moreover, as this chapter has underscored, some of these products available only in U.S. dollars are essential goods, which are no longer available in sufficient supply through the rationed market. As a result, these measures have created differences across social strata which were previously nonexistent.

Simultaneously, the reduction in leisure and recreation options, some of which are only accessible in dollars, has increased the strain on the population.

According to Ferriol (2001)

> . . . the "segmented" market has become an instrument of stimulation to production, price regulation and social redistribution . . . If the market for food was not "segmented," given the income of the population and the supply of food products for consumption, prices would be the result of the confrontation between available total income and total supply of food. Under those conditions the prices resulting from the limited availability of products can be very high and exclude groups of the population of lower income from consumption.

Segmentation can direct the still-limited availabilities of food toward given social interest groups. For example, consumption by students and workers can be directed through the network of school and work lunchrooms; agricultural workers and cooperative members can fulfill their needs through the promotion of self-sufficiency in agricultural production; chronic patients can be aided through medical diets. However, the aforementioned advantages do not mean that this form of management can be utilized on an ongoing basis, that "to the extent that the supply is stabilized and equilibrates demand, distribution should take place through the market, which is the most efficient and best expresses the possibilities of adapting to the private demands of every consumer."

In a study on inflation and stabilization, Sánchez (1998) expresses that:

...the phenomenon of segmentation of markets has a decisive role in the real value of the income of state-salaried workers, since as a consequence of this there are two effects of relatively recent appearance that have a significant impact on the perceptions of the effectiveness of the applied policy measures. One of them is the growing transfer of basic consumption toward a market with monopoly prices, the other one is the induction of inflation by means of those same prices. The ever-growing transfer of articles of consumption toward the network of stores in foreign exchange and the agricultural markets equals, in fact, a partial liberalization of prices ... and the generation of induced inflation, forcing the consumer to try to find supplement to wages from other sources, promoting the expansion of the illegal market.[30]

According to microeconomic theory, rationing—depending on its magnitude—can limit individual consumption choices (Varian 1999: 29–30; Echevarría and others 2001: 57–58). However, people who cannot have access to essential goods because of high market prices are not in a position of making choices. Usually, rationed goods are sold at less than market price, thus making it possible for those with insufficient income to have guaranteed access to those items. Thus, rationing directly influences the distribution of consumer goods, preventing them from being distributed to those who can pay more for them. Rationing is an instrument that not only impacts the optimal decision reached by the consumer, but also serves as a mechanism that makes it possible to serve society's basic needs, beyond the limits imposed by the current distribution of income (González 2001: 21).

Despite the protection to the most vulnerable provided by rationing, a set of associated problems should also be mentioned. Universal rationing introduces an excessive egalitarianism and, as a result, consumption stops constituting a lever that induces a greater labor effort and greater productivity. With rationing, low prices are provided to consumers and, in the final analysis, also to producers. This benefit to producers definitively does not trigger greater productivity in the generation of consumer goods. Furthermore, if the determination of the variety of food distributed through rationing does not take into account consumption habits and individual preferences, it can result in large losses of resources.

The opening of the domestic market in U.S. dollars has had multiple positive effects. Net income guaranteed by dollar sales is basically allocated to finance the very consumption of households that rationed goods target. Thus, this source of stable financing has enabled the restitution of supply for some goods and improvement in their distribution. This market has also served as platform for reviving Cuba's manufacturing sector via import substitution and prevented the subsequent job loss in the manufacturing sector. Access to this market makes it possible to improve the quality of the consumer goods basket and exposure with the most modern trends in these categories. The existence of this market and the incentives in U.S. dollars introduced through stimulus packages in some prioritized activities has triggered improved job performance and greater productivity.

In sum, the centralized character of social policy has guaranteed, at the margin of market rules, universal and equitable access to health, education, welfare and social security, as well as certain minimum levels of consumption of specific food items. However, at the same time, these instruments do not only target those who have not managed to adapt to the changes associated with the economic crisis and adjustment process, and thus could yield greater benefits and equity. Greater rationality and focus in public expenditure could enable subsidies to concentrate on people with limited income. Certainly, we agree with the proposals by the U.N. Economic Commission for Latin America (CEPAL) researchers, who, in their study on the Cuban economy in the 1990s, declared:

> It is evident that the multiplicity of rules, forms of operation, and prices in the markets generate serious economic distortions and adversely affect consumption of the population. In the initial stage of the economic adjustment, this policy was justified by the double objective of expanding supply and reducing the excessive monetary liquidity. At present, however, this policy begins to hinder the process of reforms underway in the Cuban economy. Government officials are studying this complex problem.

References

Aguilar Trujillo, José A. 2001. "Las remesas desde el exterior: Un enfoque metodológico-analítico." *Cuba: Investigación económica*, Año 7, No. 3, July–September. Havana: INIE.

Arias, Claudio. 1998. *Consideraciones sobre el desarrollo del mercado agropecuario*. Master's Thesis. Department of Economics. Havana: University of Havana.

Barreiro Pousa, Luis. 2001. *El comercio minorista de bienes en Cuba: Propuesta de perfeccionamiento con enfoque de marketing*. Doctoral Thesis in Economics. Havana: University of Havana.

Brundenius, Claes and Mats Lundahl. 1980. *Development Strategies and Basic Needs in Latin America: Challenges for the 1980s*. Westview Special Studies on Latin America and the Caribbean. Boulder, Colo.: Westview.

CEPAL. 2000. *La economía cubana. Reformas estructurales y desempeño en los 90's*. Mexico: Fondo de Cultura Económica.

CEPAL. 1997. *La economía cubana. Reformas estructurales y desempeño en los 90's. Anexo estadístico*. Mexico: Fondo de Cultura Económica.

Collective of Authors. 2002. *Estructura económica de Cuba*. Havana: Editorial Félix Varela.

Comité Estatal de Estadísticas. 1981. *Cuba, desarrollo económico y social durante el período 1958–1980*.

Comité Estatal de Estadísticas. Various years. *Anuario estadístico de Cuba*. Havana: CEE.

Díaz Vázquez, Julio. 2000. "Consumo y distribución normada de alimentos y otros bienes en Cuba." *La última reforma agraria del siglo*. Caracas: Editorial Nueva Sociedad.

Echevarría, Oscar; Hernández, Alina; Tansini, Ruben and Mario Zejan. 2001. "Crecimiento económico y distribución del ingreso" in *Instrumentos para el análisis económico*. ASDI-INIE-University of Uruguay.

Espinosa, Estela. 1992. *La alimentación en Cuba. Su dimensión social*. Tesis en opción al grado de Doctor en Ciencias Económicas. Havana: University of Havana.

Fernández, Pablo. 2002. "El sector agropecuario en Cuba: evolución y perspectivas" I *Cuba: el sector agropecuario y las políticas agrícolas ante los nuevos retos*. MEP-ASDI-University of Uruguay.

Fernández, Noelvis; Vázquez, Yanaisy; Galeote, Zamirys; López, Erick and Raúl E. Pérez. 2001. *Evolución de las ventas minoristas en divisas*. Havana: University of Havana. Department of Economics.

Ferriol Muruaga, Ángela. 2001. "El modelo social cubano: Una aproximación a tres temáticas en debate." *Cuba: Investigación económica,* Año 7, No. 1, January–March. Havana: INIE.

García Álvarez, Anicia. 1997. "Mercado agropecuario: evolución actual y perspectiva." *Cuba: Investigación económica,* Año 3, Nos. 3–4, July–December. Havana: INIE.

García Álvarez, Anicia. 1998. *Las imperfecciones del mercado y sus consecuencias para el bienestar social.* Havana: CEEC.

González, Alfredo. 1995. "La economía sumergida en Cuba." *Cuba: Investigación económica,* Época II, No. 2, June. Havana: INIE.

González Gutiérrez, Alfredo. 1997. "Economía y sociedad: Los retos del modelo económico." *Cuba: Investigación económica,* Año 3, Nos. 3–4, June–December. Havana: INIE.

González Gutiérrez, Alfredo. 1999. "El nuevo modelo de análisis de las finanzas internas." *Cuba: Investigación económica,* Año 5, No. 2, April–June. Havana: INIE.

González Gutiérrez, Alfredo. 2001. "Aplicación de los conceptos de la macro y la microeconomía en la economía cubana." *Cuba: Investigación económica,* Año 6, No. 4, October–December. Havana: INIE.

Lam, Lorenzo. 2002. *El consumo normado en Cuba.* Ponencia presentada al VIII Forum de la ANEC. Havana: Association of Cuban Economists (ANEC).

Marcos, M. 1987. "Algunos aspectos de las condiciones de vida del cubano antes del triunfo de la Revolución." *Revista Demanda,* 2, Año 9. Havana.

Marquetti Nodarse, Hiram and Nancy Madrigal. 1993. "El comercio internacional: Desafíos para el comercio exterior de Cuba." *Economía internacional,* Vol. I, No.1. Havana.

Marquetti Nodarse, Hiram and Omar Everleny Pérez. 1995. "La economía cubana: actualidad y tendencias." *Economía y desarrollo,* Vol. 1, No.1. Havana: Economics Institute, University of Havana.

Marquetti Nodarse, Hiram. 1998. "La economía del dólar: Balance y perspectivas." Havana: CEEC.

Marquetti Nodarse, Hiram. 2002. "Dolarización de la economía cubana: impacto y perspectivas." *La larga marcha desde el Período Especial hacia la normalidad—un balance de la transformación cubana.* Kieler Geographische Schriften, Band 103. Kiel, Germany: Institute of Geography.

Marquetti Nodarse, Hiram and Anicia García Álvarez. 1999. "Cuba: Proceso de reanimación productiva e industrial. Resultados y problemas." *Balance de la economía cubana a fines de los años noventa.* Havana: CEEC.

Marx, Karl. 1856, 1970. *Contribution to the Critique of Political Economy.* (Translated from the German by S.W. Ryazanskaya ; edited by Maurice Dobb). Moscow: Progress.

Mesa Lago, Carmelo. 2000. *Buscando un modelo económico en América Latina ¿mercado, socialista o mixto? Chile, Cuba y Costa Rica.* Caracas, Venezuela: Editorial Nueva Sociedad.

Ministerio de Finanzas y Precios. Various years. *Balance de ingresos y gastos de la población.* Havana: MFP.

Monreal, Pedro. 2000. *Migraciones y remesas familiares: Notas e hipótesis sobre el caso de Cuba.* Havana: CIEI, University of Havana.

Nova, Armando, Anicia García, Pablo Fernández, et al. 1995. "Mercado agropecuario: ¿apertura o limitación?" *Cuba: Investigación económica,* Época II, No. 4, Diciembre. Havana: INIE.

Nova, Armando. 1996. "Mercado agropecuario: Factores que limitan la oferta." *Cuba: Investigación económica,* Época II, No. 3, Julio. Havana: INIE.

Nova, Armando. 2002. "El mercado interno de los alimentos." *Cuba: Reflexiones sobre su economía* (Omar Everleny Pérez Villanueva, ed.). Havana: University of Havana.

Oficina Nacional de Estadísticas. 1995. *Algunas reflexiones sobre el mercado agropecuario.* Havana: ONE.

ONE. 1995–2001. *Ventas en el mercado agropecuario,* January–December. Havana: ONE.

ONE. 1995–2002. *Sondeo de precios en el sector informal, meses disponibles.* Havana: ONE.

ONE. 1996. *Sondeo de precios en el mercado informal, Mayo.* Havana: ONE.

ONE. Various years. *Anuario Estadístico de Cuba.* Havana: ONE.

Pérez M. and R. Miranda. 1997. *Situación nutricional de la población cubana.* Havana: Association of Cuban Economists (ANEC).

Pérez, Niurka and Cary Torres. 1996. "La apertura de los mercados agropecuarios en Cuba: Impacto y valoraciones." *Unidades Básicas de Producción Cooperativa. Desarrollo rural y participación* (Collective of Authors). Havana: University of Havana.

Rodríguez Castellón, Santiago. 1995. *Las UBPC: Los problemas y el mercado.* Havana: Centro de Estudios de la Economía Cubana (CEEC).

Rodríguez Castellón, Santiago. 1995. "El mercado agropecuario seis meses después." *Economía y desarrollo,* No. 107. Havana: Instituto de Economía, University of Havana.

Rodríguez Castellón, Santiago. 2000. "La comercialización de productos agrícolas" in *Research Project Report University of Havana–University of Hanover.*

Rodríguez García, José Luis and George Carriazo. 1987. *Erradicación de la pobreza en Cuba*. Havana: Editorial Ciencias Sociales.

Rodríguez, José Luis. 2000. "Informe sobre los resultados económicos del 2000 y el plan económico y social para el 2001." Havana: *Granma*, December 23, 2000.

Sánchez Egozcue, Jorge Mario. 1998. *Cuba, inflación y estabilización*. Presentation at the XXI LASA Congress. Chicago, Illinois: LASA.

Togores González, Viviana. 1997. *Consideración sobre el sector informal de la economía: Un estudio de su comportamiento en Cuba*. Mimeo. Havana: CEEC.

Togores González, Viviana. 1999. "Cuba: Los efectos sociales de la crisis y el ajuste económico de los 90's." *Balance de la economía cubana a finales de los 90's*. Havana: CEEC.

Triana Cordoví, Juan. 2001. "La economía cubana en el año 2000." *La economía cubana en el 2000: Desempeño macroeconómico y transformación empresarial*. Havana: CEEC.

Varian, Hal. 1999. *Microeconomía intermedia, un enfoque actual*. 5th Edition. Barcelona: Antoni Bosch.

Notes

1 According to the Comité Estatal de Estadísticas (CEE) report (1981) nominal income of the population grew at an annual average rate of 5 percent between 1958 and 1980.

2 Personal consumption is comprised of those goods and services acquired directly by the population utilizing their personal monetary income received directly in specie. It also includes expenses for housing depreciation. Social consumption is the spending on goods and services by the institutions that serve the population, in other words spending by those organizations that satisfy collective needs. (see CEE 1989 p. 78).

3 In 1959 retail trade was comprised of three major groups. The first one made up of large specialized businesses and joint ventures, for the most part North American, was established in provincial capitals. The second was formed by the specialized businesses spread throughout the country. Finally, there was an underdeveloped network of rural businesses, belonging for the most part to owners of large livestock companies. As a part of the measures taken by the new government and in response to specific economic and political situations, the first group of businesses was nationalized and the Ministry of Domestic Trade was created in order to direct, carry out, and control this activity. The state sector became dominant in this sphere. Nevertheless, many of the small businesses remained in the

hands of the private sector up until 1968.

4 A market that appears in the 1980s, when the availabilities of some articles increased through their production and/or importation, making it possible to sell these goods at prices higher than those in the rationed market.

5 The drop in GDP between 1989 and 1993 is calculated with data based on Oficina Nacional de Estadísticas, *Anuario estadístico de Cuba* (1996).

6 A regulated market was established in 1962 in order to allow equal access by all social strata to essential consumer goods.

7 The data cited in this article is only up to the year 2000. After this year, changes were made in the statistical baseline of prices and there are no series available with comparable prices.

8 Though some transactions took place in the underground economy, these were not as significant during this period. Income provided through wages was sufficient to guarantee sufficient access to consumption for the majority of the population.

9 The real salary is calculated by dividing nominal income by the consumer price index for each respective year in constant 1981 prices.

10 The agriculture sector has still not returned to its former level measured in aggregate value terms.

11 *Acopios* are arrangements whereby cooperatives and UBPCs are required to deliver an assigned share of their production to the state procurement agency at fixed prices.

12 For further information on income groups and changes in income distribution, the reader should review Espina's chapter.

13 The city of Havana is not representative of the rest of the country because it has access to higher quotas through rationing, besides having a higher income level and access to other income-earning possibilities including wage incentives for production, self-employment, services to tourists, and remittances.

14 Calculation by the authors based on per capita monetary income of the Cuban population for 1998, as reported in the *Anuario estadístico de Cuba.*

15 Other needs such as hygiene, clothing, and payment of a set of services—transportation, electric power, drinkable water, cooking fuel—that are absolutely necessary are omitted.

16 In response to increased consumer demand deriving from greater income and with the aim of ensuring greater access, a market with open access and differentiated prices was added to supplement existing distribution channels through ration cards starting in 1971. Initially, this parallel market sold tobacco and alcoholic beverages beyond rationed consumption. As rationed distribution evolved toward becoming focused on the distribu-

tion of basic necessities, consumer and small-scale industrial goods were sold in markets, denoted as "parallel" due to their characteristic as markets operating in co-existence to the ration system. With the collapse of the Socialist Bloc in 1989, this market's supply source—imported goods—disappeared and, without any goods to distribute, this market's role as a source of distribution became trivial.

17 In the rest of the country, state-guaranteed rations are less.

18 According to Cuba's Oficina Nacional de Estadísticas (ONE), the informal sector includes those working *por cuenta propia* (self-employed), be they registered and legal, or not. In addition, the informal sector includes those in the *mercado agropecuario* (agricultural markets).

19 UBPCs were established after 1993 as part of the restructuring of the agricultural sector where large state-owned farms were distributed to the workers employed on these farms, without surcharges for their continued operation and for an indefinite time period. The land continues to be owned by the state and the cooperative contributes investments through bank credits for machinery, pesticides, etc.

20 The term used to denote the period of emergency following the collapse of the Socialist Bloc.

21 Agricultural Production Cooperatives (CPA) are associations of formerly independent farmers who voluntarily joined forces to create cooperative units based on principles of collective ownership and operation. These grew after 1975.

22 In November 2001, Cuba was ravaged by hurricane Michelle; in September 2002, Isidore hit and 11 days later, Lili, struck the island.

23 For the drafting of this section, we have basically relied on the works of Marquetti (1998 and 2000) and García (1998).

24 According to estimates by Triana (2001), culminating in the year 2000 the foreign currencies (basically the United States dollar) represented more than 50 percent of total monetary circulation, which indicates that the said currencies continue to fulfill fundamental functions in the Cuban economy.

25 Sale sites (*puntos de venta*) are a term used to refer to either cooperative-based sales of agricultural goods, or dollar store sites.

26 These ideas are analyzed in greater detail in other works, including Marquetti (1993 and 1995).

27 We can comment, for example, on electric appliances: the stocks in the Cuban homes at the end of the 1980s were very little varied and, even worse, they generated high electricity consumption.

28 This explains, partly, why it was decided to implement a special decree for all those people who derived rents from their real estate to these ends.

29 The evolution of the total sales in the TRD between 1998 and 2000 corroborates this assertion upon being compared with the results that were obtained in a similar indicator between 1993 and 1997.

30 Consider that the wage supplements in foreign exchange or consumption articles are not within everyone's reach, and, although foreign exchange holding now reaches 30–60 percent of the population, the average spending in stores operating in foreign exchange is US$10 per person per month.

Commentary

The End of Egalitarianism? Economic Inequality and the Future of Social Policy in Cuba

by Lorena Barberia, Xavier de Souza Briggs and Miren Uriarte

As Cuba's labored emergence from the economic crisis of the 1990s continues, several chapters in this volume draw attention to important new trends in household consumption and socio-economic mobility on the island. For many households with access to remittances from abroad or earnings in tourism and other sectors of the economy driven by foreign direct investment, the past decade has created new opportunities for income generation and social mobility. Yet for those whose economic fortunes are tied more closely to the cash-strapped state, real income has declined, and mobility prospects appear to have narrowed. As Mayra Espina observes, there is an evolving *spatial* dimension to these divergent fortunes as well: poorer and more economically isolated households tend to concentrate in particular regions, such as the rural eastern areas of the island, and even in particular neighborhoods, such as those on the periphery of metropolitan Havana. Combined with lackluster economic growth and fiscal over-extension for the nation as a whole, these striking new patterns of inequality, represent challenges for Cuba's economic and social policy, for its political life and for the concepts of egalitarianism that Cuba's leaders have employed to defend the socialist state for almost half a century.

In this essay, rather than review the trends that Espina and others have captured so richly, we consider questions of changing poverty, mobility and social policy in Cuba in comparative

perspective. We seek to reconsider Cuban debates on these issues in the context of important international debates about
how to define human well-being, how to both protect public
obligations and leverage private initiative, and how to secure
prosperity and human development as the global economy
changes. We begin by examining how "the problem"—inadequate income or inequality or both—is being defined and
measured in Cuba as trends become more complex. Next,
we explore the implications of these definitions and trends
for social policy design and implementation. Where policy is
concerned, we focus on three issues: first, the sustainability of
the Cuban welfare state in the context of lackluster economic
growth; second, the viability of Cuba's long-standing emphasis
on universalism and relatively standardized public service delivery as the needs of the population diversify; and third, the
specific policy implications of spatial inequality—among other
implications, the option of targeting *places* beyond targeting
particular *demographic groups*. These three issues are global
concerns; the latter two reflect a particularly vexing dilemma
for governments that articulate a high degree of commitment
to human development—whether and how to create favorable
and equal prospects for well-being through *un*equal treatment
that addresses diversity in a society.

Our essay draws on selected chapters in this volume—most
of all, Jorge Domínguez on how weak economic growth and fiscal constraints limit the state's social protection capacity, Mayra
Espina on changing patterns of economic and social inequality,
and Viviana Togores and Anicia García on segmented markets
and household consumption. We also draw on the discussions
and invited papers offered at a two-part international research
roundtable we held in April 2003 at Harvard University and
January 2004 in Havana. The roundtable was jointly organized
by the David Rockefeller Center for Latin American Studies at
Harvard, the Gastón Institute for Latino Community Development and Public Policy at the University of Massachusetts/
Boston, and Oxfam America. Participants represented those institutions, as well as the Massachusetts Institute of Technology,

the World Bank, and several leading research centers in Cuba (the Center for Sociological and Psychological Studies (CIPS), Center for the Study of the Cuban Economy (CEEC), and the National Institute of Economic Studies (INIE)). Finally, we draw on evolving international debates about economic and social development, the measurement of social progress, and links between economic and spatial restructuring—i.e. economy and place.

Mobility, Poverty and Inequality in Cuba: What's the Main Problem?

Several Cuban authors in this volume consider how lower household incomes (or expenditures) and limited social mobility for significant portions of the population have contributed to increased poverty in Cuba since 1989, with "poverty" defined as inability to meet basic needs. Like their counterparts worldwide, some Cuban analysts are focusing on growing inequality and its correlates, while other researchers emphasize indicators of deprivation for those on the bottom. Two key questions are: Which problem definitions and associated *metrics,* or standards of measurement, are most appropriate for a changing society? And, if it turns out that several different metrics are relevant and important, which should drive policy?

We think it important from the outset to underscore the measurement challenges that are much more serious today than they were in 1989. Not only is there a general shortage of publicly available data, but the emergence of diversified survival strategies has complicated data gathering and analysis. The increase in non-official sources of income included in measures of the population's real income and expenditures (GDP, household budget surveys, and macroeconomic wage and income data) all present a challenge to measuring income, poverty, and inequality among Cuban households. Specifically, some analysts warn that official income estimates understate the real level of unmet needs and inequality.

Given these constraints, Togores and García examine the level of access to consumption derived from wage income and restrictions to consumption implicitly imposed by the segmentation of markets. Relative to 1989 levels, the chapter's authors note that consumption fell 31 percent between 1990 and 1993, with a modest (7 percent) decline in social and government spending and a much larger (39 percent) drop in private spending. The researchers find that total expenditures had risen 37 percent by 2000, yet consumption by Cuban households remained 13 percent below the 1989 level. Togores and García conclude that Cuba's recovery in household consumption, but not household income, was largely driven by social and government expenditures, which rose 68 percent over the decade.

Meanwhile, Espina's data indicate an increase in overall income inequality—with a Gini index that increased sharply from 0.24 in 1986 to 0.38 in 2000—plus emerging territorial differences in income and changing social mobility patterns. She argues that the restructuring of the economy has created new pockets of poverty and fewer options for mobility. Recognizing that the exact scope of poverty remains an issue of significant debate, Espina points out that in terms of access to basic needs, the portion of the urban population "at risk" of poverty rose from 6.3 percent in 1985 to 14.7 percent in 1995.[1]

At issue here are whether and to what degree policy-makers should rely on a basic-needs approach to define policy priorities, both in governing the economy and designing appropriate social policies to invest in human welfare and compensate for economic shocks. On one hand, inability to afford a market basket of basic needs constitutes the reigning poverty definition in most nations. Such definitions of poverty emphasize objective material conditions and, assuming adequate metrics, such definitions can highlight extremes of deprivation in which any just society has a compelling interest. On the other hand, these definitions downplay subjective dimensions of hardship, convey little about risk factors affecting future prospects—being cash-poor at the moment but highly educated and "well-connected" socially, for example—and hinge on socially, not scientifically, determined standards of consumption.[2] Basic-needs deprivation standards also tend to downplay inequality within and across borders. As Lant Pritchett notes, by the World Bank's current poverty standard of US$1 per day, 94 percent of the world's population is *not* poor. A lowest-common-standard approach thus dramatically understates what much of the globe considers unacceptably poor, and efforts at "poverty reduction"—again, using the single low standard—effectively discount significant progress to raise incomes for much of that 94 percent.[3]

While health, education, and other social outcomes are highly correlated with incomes worldwide, the importance of these non-pecuniary dimensions and the need to distinguish such dimensions from income and other economic indicators inspired the creation of the United Nations' Human Development Indicators—an index published annually, in which Cuba's decades of investment in education, health, and other social needs have been quite apparent.[4] Meanwhile, in Europe, researchers and policy-makers have vigorously debated a concept of "social exclusion" that likewise emphasizes life prospects, risk factors, and social isolation rather than immediate income adequacy alone.[5]

Within nations, conceptual problems of determining deprivation and need quickly become problems of policy and politics, and these problems often lead not to sweeping, absolutist reforms, but to a patchwork of corrective measures. In the United States, for example, eligibility for many "means-tested" social programs, such as income assistance ("welfare") and food subsidies ("food stamps") track the federal poverty line, which defines income adequate for meeting *some* basic needs in *some* parts of the country (officially, no adjustments are made for enormous geographic variation in costs of living). Yet programs routinely use multiples of the poverty line—125 percent, 150 percent, and even 200 percent—to allocate benefits to households that are, in effect, deemed "needy" as well as deserving. And other programs for rental housing assistance ignore the poverty line entirely, using percentages of area median income (a locally defined measure that rises and falls as incomes, not costs, change) to define "very low income," "low income," and "moderate income" groups. Changes in the official, if rather simplistic, poverty rate absorb most of the attention in public debate—such as it is, in a nation distracted by many other concerns—but social policy programs are engineered to address at least some of the limitations of the basic-needs standard. The politics of social welfare policy in the United States thus tends to revolve around imperfectly measured need, rigged assistance programs that expand on basic-needs standards, and, as veteran policy observers argue, an implicit social consensus about *how much* inequality is acceptable.[6]

Seen in this comparative light, the contributors to this volume each offer a valuable account of change and opportunity in Cuba. Togores and García track consumption in very universal terms and show how the Cuban state adjusted to massive shifts in the ability of households to access goods and services. Meanwhile, Espina reminds us that this broad storyline about shifts and transfers is terribly incomplete without a story about inequality told in income, social mobility and spatial terms. She also underscores the more subtle shifts in ethos, identity and other subjective dimensions of access (or lack of the same)—changes that can reshape the social fabric and the polity over time. These shifts are key considerations as we address the rightful targets and mechanisms of social policy.

Social Policy in Cuba: Linking the Economy and Human Development

Most research and commentary on Cuban social policy has emphasized its achievements and, specifically, Cuba's strong gains in social indicators over the past forty years in spite of its status as a low-income developing country. As Michael Woolcock expressed it at our roundtable, cases of "growth without development" abound in the international debate, but if anything, the long-run trends in Cuba suggest "development without growth." More generously, Cuba is one of a small handful of nations or subnational regions—including Costa Rica, Kerala (India), and China until economic liberalization—that show a consistent commitment to social development even when the opportunity cost in economic growth foregone is, arguably, quite high.[7] As Lant Pritchett observes, this visible outlier status cuts both ways: In plain terms, "look at what we have achieved *without* great wealth," and conversely, "look at how poor we remain in spite of impressive social indicators."[8]

Recent analyses, some in this volume, highlight the importance of additional, closely related considerations, however. First, the shape and sustainability of the Cuban welfare state are in serious question. Cuba spends one-third of its GDP on social programs, the highest investment in Latin America[9], and unlike many neighbors in the region, Cuba did not compromise social welfare when its economy contracted sharply—just the opposite, as we have seen. As Togores and García note in a recent study (not in this volume), real per-capita social spending investments grew at approximately 23 percent annually between 1993 and 2001,[10] but in the same period, as Pérez Villanueva shows in his chapter, GDP growth averaged just 1.6 percent per year. Jorge Domínguez suggests that the lack of economic growth and resulting fiscal limits on the state make current social policies—unreformed pensions most visibly, but other social protection and human investment policies as well—unsustainable.

In the 1990s, the Cuban state countered economic shocks based on a three-pronged strategy: the reallocation of government resources, the adoption of specific social policy innovations to accomplish more with less, and an increase in social expenditures to reinforce a social safety net strained to the breaking point. In the decade ahead, unless economic growth is enhanced, it is unlikely that the Cuban state will be able to fund and provide a variety of social services at current levels. Since the state is the nearly exclusive provider of social programs in Cuba, the stakes are enormous. Individuals have no other options for education, health care and other needs, and the state has few options but to ensure that these needs are met. As Espina argues, the state's legitimacy is closely tied to the conditions of these services.

Second among the key considerations is this classic one:

How should we define "social" as opposed to "economic" policies? In recent research on domestic policies to reduce poverty in Cuba, Ángela Ferriol of the National Institute for Economic Studies reported at our roundtable that among the policies found to be most effective, most important were "those that foment the productivity in the use of labor and capital factors" and those that promote fixed capital investments for export production.[11] Clearly, then, as Tendler reiterates, we should not simply treat policies of social investment as enabling economic performance or, conversely, as constrained by lack of the same.[12] Many economic policies *are* social policies too, for better or worse, and the effects of economic liberalization in many developing countries make clear that the Cuban experience is not so exceptional in this regard.

Both considerations—what kind of welfare state will be sustainable and how economic policies will help meet social needs—provide the context for our final discussion. There is growing evidence that neither human development, nor economic growth in Cuba, is best assured by the one-size-fits-all domestic policies long favored by the Cuban state. Cuba's recent accomplishments and challenges highlight the need for a fundamental re-examination of universalism and targeting.

Universalism and Targeting, People and Place

Large-scale, centrally designed and fairly standardized social initiatives have been the hallmark of Cuban social policy. Particularly in the early years of the socialist state, such initiatives helped the nation swiftly address long-standing social problems such as malnutrition and illiteracy.[13] While recognizing the state's fundamental role as architect and guarantor of social welfare, some question the effectiveness of this strategy as Cuba moves forward to address a more complex economy and a rapidly differentiating population. As income inequality translates into an unequal distribution of social problems, and as a diversity of social assets translates in turn into unequal income prospects, service demands will continue to diversify in such areas as income assistance, preventive medical care, special education and youth development programs, and workforce development (including re-training). Can one-size-fits-all universal programs hope to address the proliferation and diversification of needs?

In their chapter, Togores and García underscore that the centralized character of social policy has ensured access and minimum levels of certain consumption goods, such as food. Espina adds that the public and universal character of services such as health and education created "spaces of equality" missing in many other nations—in effect, progressive social and economic rights of the kind emphasized in many arguments worldwide favoring "rights-based development." As the United Nations Development Programme observes, while "development" articulates goals for human progress and benchmarks to track such progress, it often lacks clearly defined public and private obligations that help determine the nature of progress as well as who benefits.[14]

Notwithstanding the role of social rights in Cuba's development history, however, Espina suggests that centralized planning has proven inflexible vis-à-vis the needs of particular sectors of the population (*groups*) or geographic areas (*places*). She argues that without efforts to target both groups and places, standardized interventions will only succeed in reproducing inequality.

In the last three years, Cuban policy increased investment in universal programs while adding targeted interventions to address selected needs. First education and then health saw rather large investments in 2000, 2001, 2002 and 2003. In education, class sizes were reduced, schools refurbished and outfitted with televisions and computers, and the salaries of teachers increased. In health care, polyclinics and family doctors' offices were refurbished; some policlinics were outfitted with high technology medical equipment, bringing high-tech medicine ever closer to the ground. At the same time, targeted interventions such as the deployment of social workers in vulnerable "barrios" and new workforce training initiatives have been introduced, aiming at addressing the needs of the most vulnerable.[15] And investments have also been directed at targeted social assistance, the means-tested benefit that has traditionally gone to families without adequate economic support such as single mothers with young children, families of deceased workers, and elderly workers who retire without having met the minimal time required for a social security pension in Cuba. According to a recently published joint CEPAL and INIE study on Cuba's social policy, households obtaining social assistance increased by 51 percent between 1997 and 2002, reaching 107,733 households in 2002.[16]

We think there is an important distinction between *universal* (as a matter of scope) and *standardized* (as a matter of character) policies. In any society, the universality of certain social policies, such as free access to quality healthcare, indicates a commitment by society as a whole to ensure basic access for all of its members to a good or service essential to well-being. As we noted above, that commitment must be sustainable for economic as well as political reasons. But universal need not—and perhaps cannot—mean standardized. That is, universality can rarely assume that the same factors will contribute in the same ways to individual, family, or community well-being.

The essential questions, then, are these: how *much* inequality is acceptable; how to define *diversity of need* in the context of non-standardized initiatives (for example, those that target varied services to varied groups, according to special needs); and how to deliver *excellent* services under the new definitions. The first and second questions are for government and, depending on the society, for non-governmental instruments of collective action and deliberation. In some nations, the third may be guided by government—through "steering," in the language of government reinvention, because government sets directions, regulates service provision, and tracks its effectiveness—without government *providing* all services ("rowing").[17]

We find Espina's arguments compelling—that important new economic disparities and differences in mobility prospects are key organizing factors for a fundamentally new Cuban society. The corresponding new challenge is not "doing more of the same with less," according to equality objectives that existed prior to the Special Period,[18] but redefining the acceptable levels of inequality, reorganizing the targets of social policy accordingly to serve varied *groups*, and, where appropriate, reorganizing service provision as well. Over time, this reorganization may include important roles for non-governmental actors. In the near term, the need to experiment with more decentralized public provision will surely continue.

As sharp a contrast as it may seem, the U.S. context offers a useful perspective. A decade ago, sociologist Theda Skocpol offered an incisive analysis of the history of the U.S. welfare state and of the prospects for identifying and securing politically viable protections for the persistently poor. Skocpol argued for "targeting within universalism," which she defined as universal policies offering very obvious benefits to the nonpoor as well as key opportunities for targeting (via special extensions of core benefits and limited redistribution toward the neediest groups).[19] Historically, argued Skocpol, programs that began with a narrow base of beneficiaries rarely expanded and adapted as needed, while those that started broad (universal) were often targeted successfully later on. If the U.S. experience is in any way prologue, even as income inequality grows in Cuba, universalist social policies could be targeted in a variety of ways to make services more responsive to diverse need and—possibly—to redistribute benefits to the most vulnerable as well. Neither will happen, though, through a denial of racial or other differences evident in the new inequality or, for fiscal reasons, through a standardized, do-more-for-everyone approach to social programs.

In this process, as Bane and Mead remind us, a higher level of government is often necessary to ensure fair and effective provision of assistance to the needy.[20] But as Grindle's research on educational reform across Latin America in the 1990s shows, shifts in targeting represent reform proposals that introduce new political dynamics into the process of policy-making and implementation, and the political path to reform can be daunting.[21] Unlike politically popular reforms in the mid-20th century, which aimed at increasing access, quality-enhancing reforms generally involve the potential for lost jobs and lost control over budgets, people, and decisions. Moreover, when reforms succeeded, the emergence of new political actors—states and local governments, schools, school councils, and others—meant that much of the fate of improvement was decided locally.

A second theme in Espina's analysis—the new territorial or *spatial* dimensions of inequality in Cuba—is also compelling, although the analysis is more preliminary and the recommendations (about targeting places) are more challenging to interpret than recommendations about targeting groups. As Espina notes, the socialist state tackled the spatial inequalities of Cuba's pre-revolutionary days head on, encouraging rural development (in general) and making special investments in the poorest communities on the eastern end of the island. Now, spatial inequalities have made themselves felt with considerable force once again. The market-driven investment in tourism and ancillary industries has meant that some areas of the country have obtained great economic benefit while others have lagged behind. The lag is measurable both in different degrees of integration into growth sectors of the economy and in unequal human development indicators that show eastern areas of the island to be the most disadvantaged.

In general, Espina's analysis echoes a large and growing literature on how spatial patterns both reflect and influence patterns of social and economic inequality—i.e., of how space is both part effect and part cause of inequality. On one hand, urban form follows economic function, with specific patterns of urban development heavily shaped by social and political preferences in particular societies at particular points in time.[22] In industrial economies of the nineteenth and early twentieth century, for example, manufacturing cities tended be highly centralized, with worker housing radiating out from large job concentrations such as factories. These city forms were slow to adjust when economic restructuring rapidly shifted jobs out of the city (or region or nation) and a new, more geographically decentralized service economy emerged. Many neighborhoods that had been dominated by worker housing became jobless ghettos with high rates of dependence on public assistance. In the United States, where occupational segregation and residential segregation by race were quite high, these areas became racially identifiable ghettos as well. On the other hand, in most countries the "geography of opportunity" does not only reflect access to nearby jobs or entrepreneurial markets, but access to quality public services, useful social connections, political influence and other arbiters of one's quality of life and life chances as well.[23]

Espina suggests that Cuba's limited re-insertion into international tourism and other economic growth sectors is likewise distributing investment and jobs in distinct territorial patterns. To be sure, around the world, tourism favors certain locational assets—historical treasures, beaches, nature preserves, etc.—that are difficult, slow, and in some cases impossible, to duplicate from one place to the next. Similarly, there is some evidence that access to the other main source of U.S. dollars in Cuba's dual economy—remittances from abroad—also follows a spatial pattern. With higher historic migration from urban areas, particularly Havana, and with geographic mobility very limited on the island since 1959, it is reasonable to expect that receipt of remittance dollars and the consumer networks generated from these flows (detailed in Barberia's chapter) are concentrated in Havana and a small number of other cities. Furthermore, Espina and Eckstein (in separate chapters) show why a racial skew in the population of Cubans abroad makes for unequal remittance income by race on the island. Access to better data, for example, on the residential locations of remittance beneficiaries, would make it possible to study geographies of high and low access to this precious, transnational resource.

But for now, where spatial factors are concerned, Espina does not report any systematic analysis of the relationship between local economic transformations and income, poverty or social outcomes. This is true at the inter-local level, comparing eastern provinces to those in the west, say, but also at the intra-local level, such as within the differentiated local labor market that is the Havana metropolitan area. In Cuba, only the briefest public discussion of such spatial inequalities took place when, in 2002, it was revealed that children in Havana were beginning to show significantly lower educational attainment than children from the Eastern provinces. Although the institutional causes of this—large class sizes and serious disrepair of urban schools—were dealt with quickly, the disparities underscored the fact that risk and vulnerability vary significantly by place of residence.

A closer look at Cuba's principal city—with a population of 2.2 million, Havana is home to one-fifth of the nation's population and is five times larger than Santiago, the next most populous city—is needed, because the usual assumptions about poverty and place are unreliable for this city. The absence of investment in the city's housing and infrastructure reflects decades of development policies that favored the countryside. Yet appearances can be deceiving. The city's physical deterioration, which could lead one to believe that poverty is extremely widespread, must be distinguished from residents' quality of life and economic prospects. In Havana, substandard housing is the norm for doctors and engineers as well as taxi drivers and lower-rank government officials. Likewise, physically deteriorated, cash-poor neighborhoods are home to a level and variety of human capital that would be the envy of many poor urban neighborhoods in the United States.[24] The disjuncture between socioeconomic status and access to quality housing and neighborhoods is, on one hand, a reflection of the social development that universally available education, health care and pensions have allowed, along with policies of non-discrimination in employment and housing. But this disjuncture is also a reflection of housing policies that have, for decades, discouraged the sale of housing and even the use of income to improve housing conditions. The result is that many families "stayed in place" (literally, residentially) although their status and life chances changed substantially.

Thanks to the generous and highly centralized financing

and provision of public services—in contrast, say, to the highly localized, fiscally unequal provision of public education and other basic service in U.S. cities—and to post-revolution policies that redistributed some higher-status homes to very poor Cubans, place of residence was not an important predictor of mobility in socialist Cuba before the Special Period. The questions now are about what role place will play in the context of the new inequality in Cuba and about how policy should respond. As Briggs argues, whether in a black township in South Africa, an Arab enclave in Paris or a low-income Hispanic barrio in Los Angeles, policy-makers usually have a variety of options:[25]

- *Cure strategies* that reduce rates of residential segregation by race, income, or other differences, often by moving more disadvantaged populations out of at-risk areas—whether regions, localities or sublocal areas (neighborhoods)—and, in some instances, attracting higher-status in-movers to bring consumer demand, human capital, and more into these at-risk places. Cure strategies can be slow, costly, and, in some cases highly unpopular—where residential mixing across status lines is taboo—but there is powerful evidence that such interventions can produce positive change; and,

- *Mitigate strategies*, which seek to break the links between place of residence and life prospects, for example by linking people to distant jobs, strengthening schools and other institutions that act as buffers, and upgrading at-risk areas through community and economic development (changing places rather than shifting people among places). Mitigate strategies are often more popular than "cures," and they encourage investments in people and place that are important symbolically as well as substantively, but such investments can distort market signals and, in the worst examples, prop up doomed economic ventures for the sake of currying political favor. Mitigate strategies can also provide political cover for persistent inequalities that "grassroots" development can only affect in limited ways.

Thus far, there have been few spatial analyses of poverty and inequality in Cuba and fewer commentaries on these or other policy options. On the first score, studies continue to categorize neighborhoods according to the quality of the housing—an important, but as we have noted, a very partial and potentially misleading indicator of the actual geography of risk and opportunity within and among Cuban localities. On the second issue, targeted policy interventions have, as we have noted, emphasized special groups of people more than special places. But the visibility of the Havana schools crisis and corresponding state response may be a sign of things to come. International lessons in the field of local economic development, in particular about "turning around" outdated local economies and equipping workers with new skills, will be particularly important on this spatial dimension of domestic policy. One can draw lessons both obtuse and inspired from watching local economies survive or thrive—and both kinds of lessons have been drawn, from the United States to Brazil, from Germany to Japan. Not every locality can be home to a world-class technology cluster—a Silicon Valley, to name the world's wealthiest and most famous—but any place can identify its strategic strengths and liabilities, work to secure a more viable niche in the larger global and national economy, and within the local city-region, build bridges between the most vulnerable neighborhoods and the region's key market sector(s).[26] In Cuba, this process will be shaped in important ways by limits on foreign investment and by the U.S. embargo, of course, but it will also be shaped by the willingness of central and local policy-makers to innovate and work cooperatively with firms.

Discussion

At this critical juncture, Cuba's egalitarian social policies face two closely related challenges—one of sustainability in lieu of economic growth and another from the compelling rationale for more targeted, less one-size-fits-all social programs. Differential access to growth sectors in the economy and to remittances from abroad track important identity group differences that the Cuban state has downplayed for decades now—racial differences being the most prominent example—but they also reflect territorial patterns in economic restructuring and social access that are still poorly understood. The potential policy implications include a re-definition of how much inequality is acceptable in a changing society, more innovation in targeting groups that are particularly vulnerable while ensuring the broadest possible access to basic services—what one astute observer of the politics of social welfare in the United States has referred to as "targeting within universalism"—and newer policies to cure or mitigate spatial inequalities. On all of these fronts, in the community of nations, Cuba is exceptional only in the particulars of its experience and in the ways in which earlier socialist commitments, for example to universal, centrally planned public services, tend to frame the current dilemmas. The dilemmas themselves are urgent worldwide.

The resurgence of interest in understanding poverty and inequality in Cuba makes it possible to assess many of the trends that made the 1990s a special period on the island in many senses of that word. Now a new generation of analyses and policy debates can build on this interest. We hope the new wave will do more and more to consider economic and social change in Cuba in global perspective.

Notes

1   María Carmen Zabala, "Situación de la pobreza en el Caribe: actualidad y perspectivas de Cuba en el contexto caribeño," Manuscript presented at Seminario Internacional de Estrategias Para La Eliminación De La Pobreza, sponsored by CLACSO-CROP, 2002.

2   For an in-depth discussion of the poverty standard in the United States, as well as the roles of social research and cultural values in framing the policy debates over poverty, see Alice O'Connor, *Pov-*

erty Knowledge: Social Science, Social Policy and the Poor in Twentieth Century U.S. History (Princeton, NJ: Princeton University Press, 2001).

3 Lant Pritchett, "Who is *not* Poor?: Proposing a Higher International Standard for Poverty," Unpublished manuscript, Kennedy School of Government, Harvard University, October 2003.

4 See United Nations Development Programme, *Human Development Report 2003* (New York: Oxford, 2003).

5 See John Hills, editor, *Understanding Social Exclusion* (London: Oxford, 2002).

6 On the latter, see Gary Burtless and Christopher Jencks, "American Inequality and Its Consequences," in *Agenda for the Nation*, edited by Henry J. Aaron, James M. Lindsay, and Pietro S. Nivola (Washington, D.C.: Brookings Institution, 2003), pp.61–108.

7 See Patrick Heller, *The Labor of Development* (Ithaca, NY: Cornell, 1999) and Dani Rodrik, editor, *In Search of Prosperity* (Princeton, NJ: Princeton, 2003).

8 Lant Pritchett, Personal communication with the author, October 12, 2003.

9 Comisión Económica para América Latina y el Caribe (CEPAL), *Panorama Social de América Latina 2000–2001*, Santiago, 2001.

10 Viviana Togores González and Anicia García Álvarez, "Access to Consumption in the 1990s," Paper presented at Poverty and Social Policy in Cuba: Addressing the Challenges of Social and Economic Change Faculty Roundtable, Harvard University, Cambridge, Massachusetts, April 2003.

11 Ángela Ferriol Muruaga, "Approaches to the Study of Poverty in Cuba," Paper presented at Poverty and Social Policy in Cuba: Addressing the Challenges of Social and Economic Change Faculty Roundtable, Harvard University, Cambridge, Massachusetts, April 2003.

12 See Judith Tendler, *Why Social Policy is Condemmed to a Residual Category of Safety Nets and What to Do about It (Geneva: UNRISD, 2002).*

13 See Miren Uriarte, *Cuba: Social Policy at the Crossroads* (Boston: Oxfam America, 2002); and Susan E. Eckstein, *Back from the Future: Cuba Under Castro* (Princeton, NJ: Princeton, 1994).

14 UNDP, *Human Rights and Human Development: Human Development Report 2000* (New York: Oxford, 2001).

15 Uriarte (2002).

16 Comisión Económica para América Latina y el Caribe (CEPAL) and National Institute for Economic Research (INIE), *Política social y reformas estructurales: Cuba a principios del siglo XXI* (Mexico City: CEPAL and INIE, 2004).

17 David Osborne and Ted Gaebler, *Reinventing Government: How the Entrepreneurial Spirit is Transforming the Public Sector* (New York: Plume, 1992).

18 "Special Period" is a term coined by Fidel Castro in a speech given in 1990. It is used in Cuba to refer to the adjustments triggered by the collapse of heavily subsidized trade with the Soviet Union. As Castro explained it, Cuba was entering a "special period in times of peace." He called for austerity and sacrifice—as the functional equivalent of national wartime mobilization—and justified certain changes in what Domínguez terms "foundation stones" of Cuban socialism, e.g., bans on foreign direct investment and private business ownership by Cubans.

19 Theda Skocpol, "Targeting Within Universalism: Politically Viable Policies to Combat Policies in the United States," in *The Urban Underclass*, edited by Christopher Jencks and Paul Peterson (Washington, D.C.: Brookings, 1991), pp. 411–436.

20 Mary Jo Bane and Lawrence M. Mead, *Lifting Up the Poor: A Dialogue on Religion, Poverty and Welfare Reform* (Washington, D.C.: Brookings, 2003).

21 Merilee Grindle, *Despite the Odds: The Contentious Politics of Education Reform* (Princeton: Princeton University Press, 2004).

22 Allen J. Scott, *Metropolis: From the Division of Labor to Urban Form* (Berkeley: University of California, 1988); Allen J. Scott, editor, *Global City-Regions* (New York: Oxford, 2001).

23 Manuel Pastor, "Geography and Opportunity," in *America Becoming: Racial Trends and Their Consequences, Volume I*, edited by Neil J. Smelser, William Julius Wilson, and Faith Mitchell (Washington, D.C.: National Academy Press, 2001), pp. 435–467; and Xavier de Souza Briggs, "Re-Shaping the Geography of Opportunity: Place Effects in Global Perspective," *Housing Studies* 28, 2003.

24 Mario Coyula and Jill Hamberg, "Havana City Report," Un-

published manuscript, September 2003. And see Roberto Segre, Mario Coyula, and Joseph Scarpaci, *Havana: Two Faces of the Antillean Metropolis* (Chapel Hill : University of North Carolina Press, 2002).

25 Briggs (2003).

26 See Hank V. Savitch and Paul Kantor, *Cities in the International Marketplace: The Political Economy of Urban Development in North America and Western Europe* (Princeton, NJ: Princeton, 2003).

PART
IV

Transnational Networks and Government Responses

9

Transnational Networks and Norms, Remittances, and the Transformation of Cuba

by Susan Eckstein

Against all odds, Cuba's Communist regime survived the domino collapse of the Soviet bloc and then the Soviet Union. It survived even though its economy contracted by about a third as a result of the lost trade and aid. And it survived even though the government did not embrace large-scale market reforms and, unlike the Communist governments in China and Vietnam, did not experience renewed economic and diplomatic ties with the United States, the remaining world hegemone.

How is the resilience and resistance of the Castro-led regime explained? Economists, like many in this volume, point to specific policies that helped the economy partially rebound from its 1993 nadir. Political scientists typically point to formal regime characteristics. Those sympathetic to the regime point to certain democratizing processes that made the government more responsive to, and representative of, the populace. They point to several examples: the Party's greater inclusiveness in opening membership to religious believers; new local level mechanisms of governance such as Popular Councils; a generational shift in "who rules," the Castro brothers aside, and—until the spring 2003 crackdown—increased tolerance of dissident activity. On the other hand, analysts critical of the regime point to instruments of repression under Castro's autocratic rule, a strong state obstructing civil society's ability to assert its will and way.

Left undocumented and unexplained are the ways that ordinary Cubans have transformed Cuba since 1990. While formal institutions suggest that Cuba remains frozen in a Marxist-Leninist state socialist economy, I will show from a societal vantage point that Cuba, de facto, bears ever less resemblance to the Soviet era. Social, cultural, and economic life has been transnationalized, initially despite the state and despite constraints imposed from the U.S. side of the Florida Straits. Changes brought about by ordinary people have been so dramatic that they have induced institutional changes, at the local and national level, and in the United States as well as in Cuba. A full understanding of Cuba in the post Soviet era rests on an analysis of these transformations.

When survival became tenuous, as the island economy plunged into deep recession, Cubans defied laws, norms, and social pressures standing in the way and reached out to family in the diaspora. I seek to examine how islanders' quests for assistance from family abroad—in the form of remittances—have transformed Cuba, including in ways remittance recipients never envisioned or intended. I conclude with a discussion of theoretical lessons that can be abstracted from the Cuban experience.

My analysis draws on statistical data, as well as news and relevant secondary source materials. However, it mainly draws on information combed from semi-structured interviews with 130 rank-and-file and well-placed persons in the two historically most important U.S. Cuban-American settlements, Greater Miami Dade County (Florida) and Greater Union City, Hudson County (New Jersey), mainly between 2000 and 2003.[1] The leadership sample includes businessmen, clergy, government officials, politicians, and heads of nonprofit organizations that service the Cuban-American community. These individuals served as key informants about the communities and emergent informal cross-border ties. In addition, they were queried, as were the rank-and-file émigrés, about their personal background, reasons for emigration, their transnational ties, and how, when, and why their ties changed. Both sets of interviewees, in turn, were asked for names of others to interview, for snowball sampling purposes.[2] Some 80 Cubans in Havana were interviewed in a similar manner. A select sample was interviewed in-depth.

Where relevant, I compare the Cuban with the Dominican experience since the Dominican Republic has a fairly similar sized but differently based political economy. Data on the Dominican Republic and the Dominican diaspora derive, however, entirely from secondary sources.

Barriers to Transnational Ties, 1959–1989

State and community structures, norms, and informal social pressures all conspired to keep transnational ties minimal. These ties were considered a negative asset during Castro's first three decades of rule, and both the United States and Cuban governments set up formidable barriers to bonding across borders.

Government-Imposed Barriers

Both the U.S. and Cuban governments established institutional barriers to informal cross-border contact.

Washington restrictions began with the embargo, instituted in 1962. The embargo restricted Cuban-American rights to freely travel to their homeland. President Carter, under whose administration U.S.–Cuban relations briefly thawed, lifted the travel ban, but President Reagan reimposed it. In addition, the embargo prohibited Cuban-American (and all U.S.) investment in Cuba. Remittance-sending was minimal at the time, so Washington advanced no specific measures to regulate cross-border people-to-people income transfers. Meanwhile, the U.S., along with the Cuban government, made mail and telephone communications difficult.

The Cuban government imposed yet more barriers. In its efforts to keep Cubans who rejected the revolution from influencing on-island folk it stigmatized émigrés, portraying them as *gusanos*, worms. Good revolutionaries were not to have contact with the "undesirables" abroad. To minimize ties the government, in addition, permitted only selective exile visits, and only under circumscribed conditions. It also penalized economically and politically islanders known to maintain contact with Cubans who joined the diaspora. During the Carter years, however, Havana authorities made an exception. They allowed some 150,000 Cuban-Americans to visit. But after the visits fueled a mass exodus of approximately 125,000 islanders, from the port of Mariel, the government clamped down again on travel. As few as 5,200 Cuban-Americans gained entry to the island in the mid-1980s (Eckstein and Barberia 2002: 804, 814). When the Cuban government did allow visits, it required Cuban-Americans to stay at state-run hotels, rather than with their families, with a maximum two-week stay. With dollar possession illegal and Cubans having little reason to want dollars, cross-border economic ties were minimal.

Informal Constraints

Both in Cuban and in Cuban-American neighborhoods informal dynamics further contained transnational social and economic ties. Normative pressures, as well as internalized values, minimized bonding across the Florida Straits.

Islanders, on their part, distanced themselves for a combination of psychological, principled and pragmatic reasons from family who had fled. For one, they resented when their mothers and fathers, sisters and brothers, put politics above family and emigrated. Psychological wounds were deep, and stood in the way of cross-border bonding. Second, the Cuban government and ruling party instilled values that discouraged bonding with those who fled the revolution. Third, authorities led the populace to understand that ties with exiles were a liability. Job advancement and Party membership were reserved for islanders without diasporic contacts. Thus, either because islanders internalized the revolution's principles or because they feared the personal consequences of defying officially sanctioned rules, they had incentive to break with family abroad. Minimally, they saw reason to keep covert any ties they maintained, and in so doing they did not publicly challenge state sanctioned norms.

Cubans interviewed spoke of how embittered they were when parents and other close family abandoned them for the United States, but also of how their political conviction and economic ambition led them to cut contact with kin who left. The experience of Lourdes (a pseudonym, as are all other interviewee names), a 40 year-old unemployed single mother, is telling. When she was a teenager, her mother abandoned her, fleeing to Miami. She could not forgive her mother for leaving. But professionally ambitious and a committed revolutionary, Lourdes also worried that any contact with her *gusano* mother would jeopardize her career. Not wanting her mother's defection to stand in her way, she broke off direct contact. They communicated only indirectly and infrequently, through other relatives.

The experience of Pablo, a 48-year old cinematographer, reveals, in turn, how Communist Party loyalists were socialized to reject not merely ties with family who fled but also the materialism their exiled family embraced. Consumerism took on symbolic political significance. Pablo remembers receiving packages from his family who left in 1960.[3] "When the packages started arriving . . . I remember thinking, 'who do they think we are?' They sent packages with the most basic items, such as Colgate toothpaste and brand-name shampoo. I was outraged by their lack of understanding. It seemed like an attempt to colonize those of us who remained in Cuba. We didn't fight a revolution for Colgate toothpaste! We fought for more important rights." In this manner transnational gift-giving soured transnational social relations. "Good revolutionaries" rejected both gifts and the bonding in which presents were embedded.

The impersonal manner in which family in the diaspora occasionally sent goods and sometimes money (hidden in packages and letters, since, as noted, dollar possession then was illegal), further strained cross-border relations. Islanders were miffed when items arrived without notes. The cinematographer, for example, resented that his aunts in the United States "would never send personal letters telling us about their lives or asking us about ours." He could not help but question their motives. "Did they want to impress me with how much better off they were in Miami?" He similarly resented when a cousin never wrote back. "He just sent money. I was appalled." Cuban-Americans often omitted notes because they did not want their island relatives to get into trouble. But however considerate their motives, they violated islander gift-giving norms, embedded in Cuban, not specifically revolutionary, culture. How one gave gifts, as well as the gifts given, became contentious, and drove a wedge between families on the two sides of the Florida Straits.

Informal social pressures further kept Cubans from bonding with friends and family who fled. Islanders not won over by the official ethos felt informal constraints to conform at work and in their neighborhood. Thus, islanders kept whatever cross-border contacts they retained covert, concealing gifts received. The cost of overtly not conforming was high. Neighbors, along with Party and mass organization activists, disapproved. "You didn't want to show that you had clothing from abroad or signs of American influence," a Catholic agency employee remembers. People receiving gifts "were very careful when and where they used them." Social pressure accordingly minimized transnational cross-border social and material ties even when Cubans privately coveted them.

Punishment for defiance of regime rules also discouraged cross-border bonding. Cubans putting family above politics sometimes paid the price. University-educated José is a case in point. He always maintained contact with his many Miami relatives. While he never denied the communication, when interviewed, he confided that he used to understate how extensive his ties were. Even the ties he admitted deprived him of Party membership.

The émigré community similarly opposed cross-border bonding. Exiles ostracized, stigmatized, penalized economically, and sometimes attacked violently (or threatened to attack) fellow Cuban-Americans who dared not observe a personal embargo of Cuba. Ordinary émigrés, businesspeople and institutional leaders who did not conform paid a price. One Miami businessman interviewed noted, "If you don't comply with the 'politically correct' way, they hurt your business. They call your customers and pester you on the phone." And a Miami school director explained that you can get penalized for not merely what you do but what you say. "They accuse you of being a Communist if you don't say what's mainstream. You can get fired if they don't like what you say."

At times retribution for defying the community-sanctioned personal embargo took a violent turn. For example, a Miami travel agency booking the scarce air traffic between the two countries at the time was bombed on several occasions. Even clergy who favored cross-border engagement paid a price. A New Jersey priest, for example, who traveled to Cuba in the late 1970s to negotiate the release of political prisoners and to engage in a Cuban government sponsored dialogue with the diaspora, experienced bomb threats and church disruptions when he returned. The abuse was such that he had to be reassigned to a parish in a non-Cuban-American community.

To discourage cross-border gift-giving, along with interpersonal bonding, militant exiles sent packages containing bombs to the island. This led the Cuban government to confiscate packages, which in turn discouraged émigrés from sending gifts to island family.

Accordingly, informal social dynamics, along with formal institutional practices and regulations, both in Cuba and in the United States, kept cross-border bonding minimal and covert. Yet, with family among the deepest held Cuban values, politics proved to strain but rarely to rupture entirely cross-border kinship contact and commitment. Many of those whose close families were divided by the revolution quietly defied pressures to sever ties, but they had contact only intermittently and rarely face-to-face.

The Economic Crisis of the 1990s and the Breakdown of Informal Cross-Border Barriers

Cubans experienced a subsistence crisis following the demise of Soviet aid and trade. Between 1989 and 1993 average caloric intake contracted nearly 30 percent (see Eckstein 1994: 226). Islanders suffered hunger and malnourishment. The government referred to the crisis as the Special Period, and implied it would be temporary, until the economy was reorganized.

Contributing to the crisis, the government received little foreign investment, financing, and aid from Western governments and businesses to offset the Soviet pull-out. Weak export earnings further limited government import and investment possibilities. The government more successfully developed tourism, to the point that it became the most vibrant economic sector and principal source of foreign exchange. However, by the turn of the century the economy had yet to rebound to the pre-1990 level (see ECLAC 2000; Mesa-Lago 2000; LeoGrande and Thomas 2002; Eckstein 2003: 10–11).

Comparisons with trends in the Dominican Republic during the same time period highlight Cuba's woes. The Dominican Republic received over three times as much official aid, and substantially more multilateral aid. Dominican exports, about half Cuba's in 1990, rose to over three times Cuba's at the turn of the new century. And by the turn of the century Dominican tourist earnings also exceeded Cuba's, although the differential in revenue raised in the two countries declined in the 1990s (cf. Eckstein 2003: 11).

Despite the crisis, the government sought to maintain its decades-old cradle-to-grave welfare state, on which its legitimacy had rested. Given scarcities, the government withdrew most non-essentials from stores. It focused on meeting subsistence needs. To ensure "equality of sacrifice" it expanded the ration system that it had been phasing out in the 1980s. But rationed items, priced affordably, covered no more than half family monthly needs. Peso-dependent Cubans no longer could afford prices of food not rationed. Scarcities fueled a black market in which one chicken or a pound of cheese, for example, sold for one-third to one-fourth the average worker's monthly income.

Nonetheless, Cubans with access to dollars managed, since the black market in dollars drove the official exchange rate from 1 US$ to 1 Cuban peso to an informal "street rate" of 1 US$ to 130 Cuban pesos in 1993.

In the context of the crisis Cubans reached out to family abroad for dollars and other help, the taboo on ties across the Straits notwithstanding. Remittances—people-to-people cross-border economic transfers—became Cubans' main, though not only, dollar source.[4] Total remittances rose from an estimated US$50 million in 1990 to more than US$700 million at the decade's end, and possibly to US$1 billion in the early 2000s (see Eckstein 2003: Table 2).[5] In the decade of the 1990s the diaspora pumped more money into the economy through remittances than foreign governments, banks, and other businesses infused in the form of aid, investments and loans. Cubans on both sides of the Straits prioritized personal needs and family values over political principles.

In Cuba, as elsewhere, remittances first and foremost finance basic needs (see Massey et al 1998; EIU *Latin American Country Briefing*, October 23, 2001). According to countrywide estimates, 96 percent of remittances to Cuba financed family consumption around the turn of the century (*Economist* October 23, 2001: 23).

Cubans receiving remittances sufficient to cover more than basic needs purchased consumer durables, initially almost exclusively on the black market since the government had withdrawn most non-essentials from the official distribution system. To a lesser extent, Cubans used remittances to finance home purchases and home improvements. Although the government guaranteed that no one paid more than 10 percent of their income on housing (and most spent less), by the 1990s housing had fallen into severe disrepair. With dollars islanders could informally upgrade their housing. And with dollars islanders could finance renovations through a black market in construction supplies. As in the case of food, housing subsidies no longer addressed people's needs.

Some in the diaspora also financed island family-run businesses, despite the embargo and Cuban government restrictions on entrepreneurship. These ventures supplemented or substituted for state jobs that no longer paid a living wage. The de facto devaluation of the peso, as the dollar gained in strength, dramatically weakened the purchasing power of official earnings (even after the peso's value partially rebounded in the mid-1990s). Cuban law, however, restricted profit opportunities. It required private businesses to be owner-operated, to employ only family members, and to pay high (and regressive) taxes, including in hard currency, thus imposing severe hurdles to capital accumulation. Indeed, the restrictions on entrepreneurial enrichment gave Cubans reason to sustain, deepen, and expand, when possible, their transnational networks.

The Reenvisioning and Broadening of Transnational Networks in the Special Period

Cross-border transfers rested on a transformation of family ties across borders. The change began on the Cuban side of the Straits, but subsequently involved changes on the U.S. side as well. The impetus for the changes initially came from the Cuban side, although changes on the U.S. side soon followed suit.

The Cuban Side

In the context of the crisis, islanders came to view transnational ties as an asset, no longer as a liability. They pragmatically began to cultivate contacts with relatives they previously kept at bay, unashamedly made transparent ties they previously sustained covertly, and cultivated new transnational networks by sending family members abroad and by marrying foreigners.

Interviews reveal how quickly the crisis broke down informal barriers that had kept cross-border families socially apart, even when formal barriers remained. Reflecting on the crisis-induced change, a child psychiatrist on the island noted that "During the moments of most extreme hardship in the Special Period it was really remarkable . . . how the Cuban-American community responded so quickly and generously to the needs of family members here. People couldn't eat. They even were eating worms and grass. There was a feeling of desperation and a striking feeling of being rescued by those abroad." The psychiatrist remembers the flood of "rescue packages" that arrived suddenly in the neighborhoods. "People received money and packages including from people they had not previously met. This is when," he added, "there was a sudden change in perceptions of and relations with family abroad." Even as a Party activist "raised by the revolution," he was taken by the outpouring of generosity. His Miami relatives, including young cousins he never had met, "went out of their way to be generous and express their solidarity."

This material assistance led Cubans to change their views both about family abroad and their gift-giving. Lourdes' experience here too is telling. The timing of the crisis could not have been worse for her. Just when the economy went into deep recession she, with a six year old child, divorced her husband, an adulterous alcoholic. To make matters worse, she had quit her job to take care of her sick aunt and uncle. She made some money as a masseuse, illicitly in that she refused to pay self-employment license fees and taxes. However, she did not earn enough to support her family. She managed only because her relationship with her mother in Miami then improved. Her mother sent medicines and clothing as well as money. Lourdes' feelings towards her mother suddenly changed, although deep down she remained resentful that her mother had left her. Material bonding concealed unhealed psychological wounds.

Ordinary Cubans deliberately began to *cultivate* overseas contacts, even if with ambivalence, to just get by. In soliciting help from once-defined *gusanos*, islanders tacitly acknowledged the revolution's failure to meet the most basic of needs and the wisdom of those who left. Reflecting on how psychologically difficult it was to reach out to family the revolution had divided politically, a city planner in his mid-40s spoke of how "Many families who had cut contact with their relatives had to swallow their pride and initiate contact . . . It was the only way to survive the crisis."

The new outreach to the diaspora became a subject of jokes. Noted for their humor, Cubans generated jokes throughout Castro's rule that spread like wildflowers, by word of mouth. Jokes help lighten tense times while reflecting conditions from which they emanate. During Special Period desperation, humor reflected reenvisioned relations across borders. As views toward the diaspora turned topsy-turvy, islanders joked of having *fe,* Spanish for faith but a shorthand for *familia en el exterior,* family abroad.

With the crisis, of course, transnational kinship ties were no laughing matter. Indeed, islanders without an overseas family pipeline developed strategies to send members with the most income-earning potential abroad. That is, they sought to *create* transnational networks, transnational social ties that they hoped would become an economic asset. Cubans began to emigrate as part of a *family* project, *un proyecto de familia,* even when going overseas individually. Cubans came to envision emigration as a way to help island kin, not, as during the first three decades of Castro's rule, a break with homeland family.

Cubans also married, or tried to marry, foreigners for money—if not love—to improve their lot and that of their family. Upon moving abroad they could send remittances home. An informal foreign marriage market emerged in Havana around embassies. In early 2002, I was told that the "going rate" for a Spaniard was US$4,000 to US$5,000, for a Costa Rican US$1,000, and for a Panamanian US$500. The differences reflect the perceived economic worth of marriage to someone from the respective countries. Cubans also advertised marriageability abroad through personal profiles posted on an electronic website. Talk of instrumental foreign marriages, moreover, became acceptable, even though it defied longstanding valuation of marriage for love. Marriage sometimes became so instrumental that previously divorced couples, separated by the Florida Straits, sometimes remarried for convenience, to help ex-spouses move to the United States. Washington gave immigration preference to family reunification. A *Marielito* (an informal term for émigrés who fled in the 1980 mass exodus from the port of Mariel), interviewed in Miami, for example, acknowledged that he remarried his island wife to help her emigrate.

Cubans came to view emigration as an alternative to remittance dependence. As of the 1990s, even once-fervent revolutionaries, such as Lourdes, saw their future more in migration than change at home. During the Special Period, Lourdes had become disillusioned with the revolution. She continued to admire its ideals but was distressed living in poverty and with hardship. "Everyone who leaves is able to send money to Cuba while those who stay have no hope of overcoming the crisis," she bemoaned.

In principle, as more Cubans seek refuge abroad, new transnational networks and chains of remittance-sending are formed. But the United States limits entry to 20,000 Cubans a year.

The Cuban government, in turn, contributed to the broadening of islander overseas networks and to bonding of potential economic worth. It, for one, allowed Cubans to take temporary jobs abroad without forfeiting domestic rights. Workers overseas could earn hard currency that they and their family could draw on in Cuba.

The government shifted its stance toward the diaspora in ways that deepened bonds between those who left and who stayed. In this vein, the Cuban government relaxed visitation restrictions. It eased visa requirements, and it permitted a broader range of émigrés to visit and for longer than in the past. Second, the government modified its public stance toward the diaspora. Émigrés were no longer considered *gusanos*, but were redefined as the "Cuban community abroad," following a growing trend among Third World governments to reclaim their immigrant populations (Glick-Schiller 1999: 94–119). Visiting members of the "community abroad" would bring dollars, which the government, in principle, could appropriate (in ways detailed below) for its own institutional use. The government was desperate for dollars, for all imports in the post-Soviet era had to be purchased with hard currency, and export earnings, as noted, had nosedived. Also, it needed the currency to address its mounting hard currency debt, the origins of which dated back to the Soviet era. However, the shift in stance toward the diaspora was politically risky.

Visits on a large scale during the Carter era had fueled the mass migration from the port of Mariel. Given its desperation for dollars, the government took the political risk.

The U.S. Side

Cuban-Americans exhibited varied responses to Cuban efforts to build bridges and bury political differences. The leadership reacted one way, and ordinary people in another.

By the 1990s Cuban-Americans had become powerful in Union City and especially in Miami, and they used their clout to influence Washington's Cuba policy. The Cuban-Americans who came to dominate in diverse institutional domains almost without exception had emigrated in the 1960s, or were children of families who had emigrated then. They projected their values on to the community and dominated public discourse. Vehemently anti-Castro, they advocated a U.S. foreign policy consistent with their political formation. They deftly lobbied for a tightening of travel and remittance prerogatives. They became one of the most effective ethnic lobbyists: well-networked, well-organized political campaign contributors. And they were concentrated in Florida, a swing state with the fourth largest number of electoral votes. To win the Cuban-American vote both political parties, especially in election years, addressed their demands.

Aiming to "squeeze" Castro's regime economically to cause its collapse, the leadership sought to subvert income-sharing across the Straits. In the 1990s their lobbying efforts resulted in legislation that limited direct travel to Cuba for family visits to once a year and remittance-sending to a maximum of US$300 quarterly, at a time when the archetypal Latin American immigrant remitted close to US$200 monthly (MIF/IDF February 2002). And for three years in the 1990s they succeeded in getting Washington to ban direct travel and remittance-sending altogether. Then, at the eve of the 2004 election George W. Bush, with his eye on the Florida vote, announced new restrictions on visits and remittance-sending. The most conservative faction of the émigré leadership strongly supported the new measures, Congressman Lincoln Diaz-Balart among them. The 2004 measures restricted Cuban-American family visits to once every three years, restricted package-sending except of basics, and lowered the cap of cash émigrés could take with them on island visits. The Bush administration, moreover, restricted visitation and remittance rights to immediate family, parents and children.

For cross-border bonding to pick up against this backdrop, Cuban-Americans had to defy both leadership pressures and Washington regulations. Indeed, the number of Cuban-Americans who annually visited the island surged from 7,000 in 1990 to some 100,000 ten years later (see Eckstein and Barberia 2002: 814). By the turn of the century an average of 1 in 10 Cuban-Americans visited yearly. The number visiting picked up even during the years when Washington prohibited direct travel (by entering via third countries). Interviews suggest that Cuban-Americans began to visit with increased frequency, with shorter intervals between trips. New Cuban government permissiveness was essential for the step-up in visiting, but so too was a change of heart among émigrés.

On the U.S. side, changes within the émigré pool spearheaded the rise in travel. The composition of the Cuban-American community changed in the 1980s, but especially in the 1990s. As the Cuban economy caved, islanders increasingly sought refuge abroad for economic reasons. Unlike earlier émigrés, they typically did not have political principles that stood in the way of bonding with family they left behind. And with little time lapse since emigration, they tended to have family on the island they wanted to see.

But even earlier émigrés, increasingly pessimistic of a regime change in their lifetime, in growing numbers nostalgically sought to reconnect with their roots. In the case of devout Catholics, Pope John Paul II's call on his 1998 Cuba trip for international openness towards Cuba (cf. Eckstein and Barberia 2002) was also influential. Meanwhile, as visitors reported no negative experiences when visiting or retribution in their neighborhoods and places of work upon return, travel had a contagion effect. Reflecting the changing viewpoint, surveys of Miami Cuban-Americans show that the percent who endorse travel negotiations for island family visits jumped from 40 percent in 1991 to 70 percent six years later (FIU-IPOR 2000, 2004).[6] And in 2004 nearly half of all Miami Cuban-Americans felt unrestricted travel should be allowed.

Cubans who emigrated in different years and under different circumstances, however, differed in their stance toward travel. In 2004, the visits of recent émigrés to Cuba was double the number of visits by early émigrés, for example.

The new Cuban immigrants who defied the leadership's advocacy of a personal embargo to parallel the state-level embargo did so quietly, covertly, and sometimes illegally. They did not publicly challenge the leadership. They did not partly because they lack the organizational skills of earlier émigrés. Having grown up in Castro's Cuba, they have no experience in civil society engagement, and they developed a distaste for politics there. But they also remain publicly voiceless because they have been silenced by older exiles—including through the media. Some who tried to publicize their point of view report having encountered resistance. They claim that local newspapers refused to publish their articles and letters-to-the-editor, and that radio talk show hosts refused to accept their call-ins. Consequently, the impetus for change in cross-border networking on the U.S. as well as the Cuban side of the Florida Straits initially arose at the informal "grass roots" level. Changes at the people-to-people level, together with the failure of U.S. policy to bring the Castro regime to heel, however, led to a split within the Cuban-American leadership. The exiles' failure to convince both Washington and the American people of their reasoning to allow six year old Elián González to remain in the United States fueled the split. Elián's mother, who had sought refuge in the United States, died at sea, while he was washed ashore. When U.S. authorities returned Elián to his father in Cuba, influential Cuban-Americans felt they had been misunderstood. Rethinking their stance, key members of the Cuban-American National Foundation, the community's main lobbying group, and a group of wealthy businessmen, began to advocate cross-border engagement over isolation. A nascent human rights movement in Cuba, moreover, convinced them that Cubans themselves might bring about a regime change. "Hardliners," who remained opposed to cross-border collaboration, very publicly withdrew from the Foundation's directorate. The faction favoring transnational engagement, however, was too influential to be openly silenced.

Against the backdrop of division among the community's leadership, Washington in 2003 briefly broadened the definition of family qualifying for Cuba visitation rights and increased the amount of money Cuban-Americans could legally take with them on trips to Cuba, to US$3,000. As a chief officer of the Foundation acknowledged to me, "foreign policy ends when your grandmother is hungry." The turnabout in its stance toward cross-border ties was in sync with the transnational bonding sought by ordinary Cubans and increasing numbers of ordinary Cuban-Americans, especially the post-1990 arrivals. However, as the 2004 election approached, Bush sided with the more hard-line leadership faction, on the assumption that they could better deliver the Cuban-American vote: mainly long-term émigrés with high citizenship rates (cf. Eckstein 2004). To curry their favor, Bush withdrew travel and remittance rights he had extended just the year before.

The Remaking of Cuban Norms and Values in the Special Period

As the crisis induced more active, overt cross-border bonding, island norms and values changed. Cubans began to embrace, and openly so, the material lifestyle the United States epitomized and their overseas relatives personified. No longer did islanders have to uproot themselves and seek refuge abroad to be acquisitive. Cubans embraced the imported lifestyle to the point that previous stigma of it disappeared. Dollars earned informally and at times illegally through tourism, black marketeering, and even state jobs, also contributed to the cultural transformation. However, remittances alone were embedded in cross-border people-to-people ties and transnationally induced normative changes.

Overseas relatives and their remittances ushered in a mimicking of Miami materialism that led islanders to yearn for dollars for far more than basic subsistence. Cubans came to welcome not just Colgate toothpaste that such "good revolutionaries" as the previously mentioned cinematographer had found so repugnant, but soap, shampoo, detergent, and soon thereafter electric fans, televisions, VCRs, brand-name clothing and shoes and other consumer goods made possible by their family abroad. By the early 2000s Cuban awareness of U.S. brand-names had become among the highest in any non-English speaking country (*New York Times* Section 3 May 26, 2002: 4) Any remaining residue of "Che" Guevara's utopian vision of the "new man," who worked for the good of society, was relegated to the dustbin of history. Working for the good of society, rather than individual gain, had captured the Cuban imagination especially during the first decade of the revolution; now illusions focused on individual and family access to consumer goods. Differences between families on the two sides of the Florida Straits came to hinge more on their pocketbooks than their values.

The taboo on American-style consumerism broke down to the point that Cubans proudly flaunted materialism in their everyday life. Kids began to show off their Nikes and Adidas. "The Miami Cuban culture promotes Lycra (spandex), puffy hair, lots of make-up, and gold," bemused a man who, with remittances from a sister who left during Mariel and another who left in 1998, lives in a freshly painted house that he fenced in and furnishes with a TV, VCR, CD player, stereo, computer, wireless phone and beautiful artwork. "Class distinctions have become more noticeable, but in a strange way," he added.

His home renovations reflected a new desire not merely to be materialist but conspicuously so. To the dismay of Pedro, the previously mentioned city planner, "between 1960 and 1990 families who could fixed up the interior of their homes, but they left the exteriors untouched. Now (though) people put up fences and paint the outsides. They want to show that they are living better. They're into conspicuous consumption. . . . It used to be taboo to show that you were living better than others."

The government somewhat reluctantly became party to the new materialism. The government tacitly encouraged consumerism through reforms designed to capture and profit from dollars Cubans informally acquired. The government increased consumer opportunities. It opened dollar stores previously restricted to foreigners to anyone holding American currency, and it expanded the number of such stores and their stock. It also legalized dollar possession, enabling islanders to more easily and openly acquire and spend the foreign currency.

The government further fomented the new materialism by introducing a debit-type card that enabled islanders to purchase goods for which their overseas family paid. In this vein, a 60-year old Havana woman proudly paraded around her neighborhood showing off her newly acquired Transcard debit-like card. She boasted of how she could spend hundreds of dollars with the card, with her daughter, who emigrated after marrying an American in the late 1990s, responsible for the bill. The government also extended debit-like card privileges to selective workers as a work incentive. Workers could make purchases with the cards at specified state stores. In addition, the government introduced a so-called convertible currency, with hard currency value, although only within Cuba. Cubans awarded a portion of their salary in the new currency as a work incentive could purchase goods unavailable and unaffordable with their peso earnings.

The new consumer oriented government even supported the commodification of the religiosity it increasingly tolerated in the 1990s. In conjunction with Pope John Paul II's 1998 island visit, the government officially agreed to allow islanders to celebrate Christmas once again. It did not take long before state stores capitalized on the commemoration of Christ's birth by adding extensive stock for the occasion (cf. *New York Times* December 25, 2002: 8).

Paradoxically, the once anti-materialist government came to promote consumerism more directly, and to depend more on it fiscally, than governments in market economies. In the process, the government also inadvertently fueled a black market on a scale rarely found in market economies. Cubans who illegally offered goods for less than state stores charged created a market for their wares. The desire to take advantage of black market opportunities led Cubans to pilfer supplies from their jobs, also on a scale rare in market economies and without precedent in Castro's Cuba.

Authorities, however, remained ambivalent about the consumerism for several reasons, including the corruption it induced. Difficult to regulate, informally circulating dollars posed challenges to state socialist planning. Authorities also recognized that cross-border income transfers were embedded in networks and norms, defying revolutionary principles. The Party leadership spoke of dollars as ideologically contaminating, encouraging individualism as well as materialism (Leo-Grande and Thomas 2002: 325–64). And remittances were inconsonant with the official socialist reward system, linked to work contribution, a reward system that for decades had been legitimated in terms of Marxian philosophical thought (cf. Marx, in Feuer [ed.] 1959). Remittances depended on who you knew, on the generosity of overseas networks, not on work skills and effort. But moral and ideological principles became a luxury the government no longer could either afford or effectively impose. Remittances became Cuba's second most important source of hard currency.

The Transnationalization of the Cuban-American Community Economic Base

Economic changes in the Cuban-American community, above all in the municipalities of Miami-Dade County where new Cuban immigrants are concentrated, such as Hialeah, are providing a bedrock for the new cross-border bonding and the materialism to which it has given rise. Entrepreneurial Cuban-Americans are capitalizing on, as well as fueling, the new island materialism.

Enclave businesses are transnationalizing their economic base. Whatever entrepreneurs' private political views toward the Cuban revolution, they are taking advantage of new market opportunities grounded in the thickening transnational ties. The economic transnationalization includes Cuban-Americans who directly engage in work across borders, what Portes, Guaranizo and Landolt (1999) refer to as transnational entrepreneurs. However, it also includes inwardly oriented enclave businesses that now also target the Cuban market.

Changes have occurred especially at the informal level. A new occupation has evolved, premised entirely on cross-border ties and trust. So-called *mulas*, a name borrowed from the drug trade, make a business of carrying money and goods from the United States to the island. In Cuba they sometimes offer home delivery services through a network of Cuba-based *mulas* they know, some of whom make deliveries by motorcycle. In lesser numbers émigrés have set up new informal "mini-banks." Such "bankers" take deposits from fellow Cuban-Americans that island kin can withdraw almost immediately, from island "bank" partners. Both the *mulas* and "bankers" *created* niches for their services by underpricing formal remittance transmitting services and by building on and deepening cross-border trust that previously was non-existent, and by imposing no bureaucratic procedures or legal requirements. In the changed milieu, local neighborhood-based travel agencies that specialize in U.S.–Cuba bookings, once the target of exile bombs, have diversified their activity to include courier services, tapping into the new demand for cross-border economic transfers. These travel agencies themselves employ *mulas* to carry money and goods routinely to the island.

Yet other entrepreneurial Cuban-Americans have developed informal businesses that build on the emergent transnational bonding, businesses that similarly circumvent laws that stand in the way and that similarly build on informal cross-border trust. Illustrative of such ventures, one émigré, unable to make use of his island medical training, operates an "informal 1-800-Flowers for Cuba." People in Miami pay him for funeral arrangements for island family. The doctor-turned-businessman arranges through a Cuban network for the provisioning of flowers and food. Also illustrative, a *mula* operates a cross-border island food distribution business. The *mula's* family in Cuba purchases food from farmers with money the *mula* collects in Miami, and distributes to islanders goods ordered and paid by Cuban-American customers. Community pressure in the old Cuban-American areas of settlement would have made such transnationally rooted ethnic entrepreneurship near-impossible in the past.

Stores increasingly also cater to island clientele, and now very publicly so. Neighborhood pharmacies and shipping companies offer island delivery services. Stores targeting the Cuban market pre-date the 1990s, but they have expanded dramatically in scale and scope since the Special Period. Mega-discount stores now also cater heavily to nascent Cuban consumer yearnings, advertising that they have *todo para Cuba*, everything for Cuba. Such advertising encourages Cuban-Americans to purchase goods for island family as well as for themselves. Indicative of how the stepped-up cross-border bonding is becoming a base for transnational retailing, an owner of one of Miami's main mega-discount stores acknowledged in 2000 that most of the US$1.2 million worth of goods he sells yearly end up on the island (www.miamiherald.com August 10, 2000: 3). Inexpensive so-called privately owned dollar stores in Miami, like the government dollar stores in Cuba, increasingly cater to island consumers, though the former at bargain prices, the latter at high mark-ups.[6] Cuban-Americans who visit the island rarely go empty-handed, and their island family can sell for dollars in the black market items they prefer not to keep.

Non-Cuban-American owned businesses have also fueled the informal dollarization of Cuba and the consumerism it makes possible. This is especially true of multinational wire service companies such as Western Union and, to a lesser extent, MoneyGram, that operate in Cuban-American neighborhoods, These companies appeal to Cuban-Americans who wish to comply with U.S. law and who believe the regulated businesses to be more trustworthy than the informal transfer services. But they typically charge higher service fees, and more for transfers to Cuba than to other countries in the Caribbean and Central America (cf. Orozco 2002a, 2002b). Moreover, they require remitters to fill out affidavits, in accordance with the embargo, making senders as well as island recipients accountable for income transfers. Both because of the charges and legal requirements, formal agencies only capture an estimated 25 to 40 percent of the money the diaspora remits to Cuba. The remainder is transferred informally, on visits as well as through *mulas* and mini-banks. The explosion of U.S.-to-Cuba remittance-sending accordingly hinges more on the strengthening of cross-border bonding and trust than on technical breakthroughs in wire transfer services. Paradoxically, a much higher portion of remittances to Cuba than to less regulated, market economies in the region enters informally,[7] the net effect of which is to reinforce if not deepen transnational people-to-people bonding.

Thus, formal and informal businesses on the U.S. side of the Florida Straits are fueling island material consumption and a consumer culture that strengthens U.S.-to-Cuba monetary and in-kind transfers. And so too are they fostering the ties in which economic activity is embedded.

The Transnationalization and Transformation of Cuba's Socialist System of Stratification

Economic transfers of money and goods in-kind flow in one direction, from the United States to Cuba. However, they impact on bases of stratification that span the Florida Straits.

With nothing material to offer, Cuban remittance recipients reciprocate symbolically. The symbolic reciprocity transpires especially among families transnationalized in the post-Soviet era. These families not only visit most frequently and are most inclined to income-share, but they also are most appreciative of the symbolic rewards nonmigrants have to offer.

Transnational income-sharing raises migrant social status within the homeland context. Cubans who previously stigmatized migrants as outcasts, *gusanos*, as authorities had taught them to do, are re-envisioning those who leave as heroes. However, new migrant attained cultural capital is conditional on remaining abroad, retaining homeland ties, and sharing economic assets. The new cultural capital is a by-product of and reward for immigrant sacrificing of earnings, of decapitalizing economically.

New cultural capital also includes new respect. In this vein, a woman who recounted how she experienced "almost a civil war" by neighbors and co-workers when her family fled in the 1960s and how she had eggs thrown at her when joining the Mariel exodus in 1980, marveled how Cuban attitudes changed in the 1990s. When she visited during the Special Period the same people treated her, in her words, "like a *señora*." Similarly, the previously mentioned child psychiatrist, who had not permanently emigrated but taken temporary work in Europe, felt his family respected him more once he went abroad to work.

The new cultural capital includes deference and authority as well. By way of illustration, an unemployed woman estranged from her mother who moved to Miami in 1980 re-envisioned her mother in the 1990s as "the matriarch." The change came when her mother became the primary caretaker and source of income for the family remaining on the island.

Emigration has become so status-enhancing in the transnationalized context that esteem is not contingent on how migrants make a living. The previously noted city planner mentioned in dismay that Cubans now see those living abroad as superior regardless of their source of income. "They could be trash collectors! (No matter), Cubans feel they are part of the elite." Comparable status is not bestowed on Cubans engaged in similar low skilled work in their homeland or in the context of the communities in the United States where they resettled. It is grounded specifically in the cross-border context. Low-skilled work did not itself gain stature. Rather, the relevance of the work, in the minds of people back home, became irrelevant. Migrant generosity and migrant demeanor on visits mattered instead.

The new status, however, came with new expectations of migrants: to both stay abroad and share earnings with non-migrants. The child psychiatrist understood the situation well. "Once you leave Cuba," he noted, "you inevitably become an outsider in your country. . . . You no longer are viewed as an exile, as a *gusano*, but as an outsider with an almost superhero aura. Even your family now sees you differently . . . Return migration isn't possible because family, neighborhood, and society don't accept that you want to return," he added with dismay. Having taken temporary work abroad, he felt "permanently exiled." He sensed that his network of friends and co-workers as well as family would otherwise consider him an economic failure and remiss in his moral economic commitment to them. The social pressure was such that he even felt it would be difficult to return to his job in Havana's premier pediatric hospital and reintegrate professionally. Informal social dynamics now pressure islanders to go and remain abroad to sustain economic benefit-generating transnational networks. Migrants as a result feel unwelcome at home not, as before, for leaving but for returning!

The new cross-border material-symbolic exchanges, and bases of stratification to which they have given rise, were not exclusively voluntarily sustained. In particular, migrants felt pressed to meet and maintain status enhancing home country kinship expectations. Therefore, they sometimes behaved on visits in disingenuous ways to seek validation and reinforcement of their newly acquired migrant-linked status. "Some may be in debt, with mortgages and car payments, but they come here and act as if they are wealthy and without problems," the cinematographer interviewed explained. Another informant added, "You feel you must even dress and act a certain way when you come back, flaunting prosperity. Society and your family need to see that you can succeed and are in a superior position to them because you migrated . . . " Income-sharing, in addition, came to be seen as a duty. Reflecting on the transnational moral obligation that evolved, the psychiatrist noted how migrants feel pressure to make sacrifices. "It is very difficult for those who leave now, as the pressure on you is tremendous. . . . There is a strong implicit social contract between a migrant and his family," a 'contract' that, in his view, was 'almost a religion.' "You are pressured to succeed and solve all your family's problems. You need to visit to fulfill an obligation to your family."

A 'social contract' implies negative sanctions when expectations are not fulfilled. Castigation of migrants who fail to comply with the new home country norms reinforces the likelihood that remittances will continue to be forthcoming. The psychiatrist who took temporary work in Scandinavia returned without money. His family did not question him, but he felt pressure from friends and neighbors who demanded to know why he had not returned with cash to share. He passed on gifts of clothing that his European friends had given him, to his siblings and parents, because he had nothing else for them. He found the experience humiliating as well as alienating. His Cuban friends turned their backs on him when they realized he returned without money. Some even were angered when he tried to explain how difficult it was to live abroad. Instead of cross-border gift-giving being frowned upon as in the past, non-gift-giving now is stigmatized.

The transnationally rooted basis of status is eroding the preexisting domestically grounded stratification schema. The most educated

Cubans with the formerly most prestigious state jobs cannot afford the same material lifestyle on their official salary as remittance-receiving people. Status on the island has come to rest increasingly less on skill level than on dollar access and in-kind gifts obtained through who you know abroad. The island recipient, as well as the overseas gift-giver, acquires status in the process. A Cuban interviewed astutely noted that there is now a "new class . . . and a new contradiction. . . . Many of those who (recently) migrated and their island families are lower class with limited education. But they have access to a lifestyle inaccessible to the professional class loyal to the revolution."

Remittances undermined Cuba's socialist hierarchy because their value was unrelated to the status of the Cuban recipient and because even humble laborers abroad transferred more money than previously high status islanders earned as a result of years of professional training and hard work. Indicative of the new stratification schema, Cubans began to calculate their peso paychecks in dollars, with once prestigious doctors, for example, commanding the equivalent of US$20 a month. Accordingly, those who stayed in Cuba and worked their way up the socialist bureaucracy, the socialist system of stratification, experienced *de facto* downward mobility.

The devaluation of formerly prestigious peso-based jobs, combined with declining opportunities in the peso economy, contributed to a drop-off in Cuban commitment to higher education. The proportion of the relevant school-aged population enrolled in post-secondary studies leveled off. It was merely one percentage point higher, 19 percent, in 1998 than in 1980. In contrast, during the 17 year interim the comparable level enrollment rate in the Dominican Republic rose from 18 to 23 percent (cf. World Bank 2001: 86 and World Bank 2002: 90–92; www.worldbank.org/education/pdf/tertiary).[8] The leveling off in Cuba partly resulted from a cut-back in government-controlled university admissions once the depressed economy offered fewer professional opportunities (cf. Eckstein 1994: 99). But in the course of the 1990s it resulted increasingly also from youth dismay with the economic pay-off of school-linked credentials.[9] In the Dominican Republic the worth of the local currency had not declined as much as in Cuba, and the private sector offered more opportunities. Consequently, Dominicans continued to have incentive to acquire upper levels of schooling, human capital, a springboard for economic and cultural capital accumulation.

In Cuba, the adult labor force, as well as youth, became disillusioned.

Peso-dependent skilled state workers lost interest in their jobs. Rates of absenteeism have risen, and professionals without access to remittances have been leaving state jobs for low-skilled work providing informal access to dollars.[10] They have gravitated particularly toward tourism, which in the 1990s became the second most important source of informally attained dollars. But tourism generated its own "contradictions." Cubans without dollar access resented so-called tourist apartheid, the privileged lifestyle visiting foreigners enjoyed while they struggled to survive. And the island became a destination for sex tourism. Some university-educated women who in the past would never have dreamed of selling their bodies for sex took up prostitution.

Yet, Cubans do not have equal access to transnational networks of economic worth. Indeed, as Espina Prieto notes in her chapter, remittances reinforce other bases of inequality in the new Cuba. Families who remained loyal to the revolution have been particularly disadvantaged. They were less likely to have transnationalized, leaving them without access to income-sharing networks. Regime loyalty worked particularly against Afro-Cubans. In the early years, Castro's government very publicly sought to redress pre-revolutionary racial inequities. Benefiting from the revolution, few Afro-Cubans emigrated, especially before the 1980 Mariel exodus but even through the Special Period. In 2000, 84 percent of Cuban-Americans (including U.S.-born) identified themselves as white (cf. census analysis in Eckstein 2004). Against this backdrop, a study in Cuba not surprisingly found that only 5 to 10 percent of Afro-Cubans receive remittances, compared to 30 to 40 percent of whites (cf. Economist Intelligence Unit, *Cuba Country Report* February 2003: 12; see also de la Fuente 1998). The study also found Afro-Cubans to have attained fewer tourist jobs that provide informal dollar access domestically. Afro-Cubans without dollar access became Cuba's new poor.

Unequal regional access to remittance-generating transnational networks also drove a wedge into the socialist government's effort to reduce historical inequities between the city and the countryside (cf. Eckstein 1994: chapter 6). Havana, with 20 percent of the country's population, receives an estimated 60 percent of all remittances (UCTEC March 17, 2002: 11,12). A rural/urban social divide, accordingly, is also on the rise.

The "dollar apartheid," rooted first and foremost in differential access to remittances and secondarily to informal tourist earnings, has, in turn, undermined the government's longstanding general commitment to equality. The Gini index is estimated to have risen from 0.22 to 0.41 between 1986 and 1999 (Brundenius 2002). While the ratio between the highest and lowest income earners in the state economy had been 5 to 1, as of the 1990s some Cubans informally attained several hundred times more income than others. Consumption also became more income-contingent than in the past.

Popular culture, in turn, reflected and reinforced the new transnationalized social hierarchy. Cuba's Los Van Van, a favorite music group among the younger generation of Cubans on both sides of the Florida Straits, sing about the "migrant hero." In contrast, musicians in the past sung of migration in negative terms. So too do telenovelas and films capture the social and cultural seachange. A taxi driver, saddened by how the obsession with consumerism had eroded moral values, felt the film *Paradise under the Stars* captured the erosion. The film depicts an immigrant who returns from Spain during a funeral. "The Cubans are so excited about the gifts he brings that they forget about the funeral!"

Limits to Transnational Family-Based Networks, Norms, and Remittance-Giving

Despite the dramatic growth in cross-border income transfers, Cubans abroad at the turn of the new century remitted, according to available estimates, substantially less money than Dominicans. Cubans, in principle, had access to a somewhat larger overseas network than Dominicans, since a higher percentage of first-generation Cubans than Dominicans resided in the United States (where most émigrés from both countries settled). Nevertheless, Dominicans in the United States sent on average more than twice as much money home as Cuban-Americans and remitted about three times as much per home-country resident (cf. Eckstein 2003: Tables 2 and 3, pp. 13 and 23).

Both individual and institutional factors account for Cuban and Dominican differences in scale of remittance-sending. At the individual level, more Dominicans have attributes associated with cross-border income-sharing: recent and economically motivated migration (cf. Díaz-Briquets and Pérez-López 1997). Émigrés with such attributes are likely to have family remaining in their homeland they want to see and help, and no political reluctance to infuse money into the home country economy.

But the country differences are not entirely explicable at the individual level. Although cross-national studies also show remittance-sending to vary with migrant income, on average Cuban-Americans remit less than Dominicans even though they earn more.[11] This was especially true of Cuban émigrés prior to the 1990s. Though many are well-to-do by immigrant standards, politically they typically honored the personal embargo of the Castro regime.

Institutional differences also are at play. Both at the state and community levels, and in the United States as well as home country, institutional forces encourage Dominicans to bond across borders, and few obstacles stand in the way. Washington, for one, imposes no homeland travel, remittance-sending, or investment restrictions on Dominican (or other non-Cuban Latin American) émigrés, at least not on those in the United States legally. Two, the Dominican government encourages cross-border involvements more than the Cuban government, and also faces fewer obstacles from Washington. The Dominican government promotes hometown associations and programs in the United States that encourage diaspora remittance-sending and investment, homeland political involvements, and homeland identity (cf. Orozco 2002a, 2002b; Grasmuck and Pessar 1996).[12] Three, the Dominican diaspora leadership actively encourages transnational social, cultural, economic and political activity (cf. Grasmuck and Pessar 1996; Levitt 2001). In contrast, the Cuban-American community leadership discouraged such involvements for decades and some influential leaders continue to do so (cf. *New York Times* April 17, 2003: 6; *Wall Street Journal* April 29, 2003, posted on http://www.ciponline.org.nxlkhost.com/cuba/cu-ainthenews/newsarticles/wsj042903).

A "hard-line" minority, called "radical exiles" by disapproving Cuban-Americans, aggressively still oppose cross-border ties. The great majority of Cuban-American media remain firmly opposed to such ties, and "radical exiles" have gone so far as to launch a culture war. They violently protested, for example, a Miami concert by Cuba's Los Van Van, a musical group popular both among the new immigrants and the younger generation on the island. Protesters hurled objects and shouted epithets angrily and loudly at ticket-holders. Fearful of retribution, some concert-attending émigrés dressed up in costumes to disguise their identity, while other émigrés said they stayed away out of fear. Meanwhile, the 2002 Latin Grammys were moved to Los Angeles because the threats of violence made the venture too risky. While some of the more moderate Cuban-American leadership wished Miami to host the awards ceremony because of the money and prestige it would bring the city, "radical exiles" did not want Cuban performers to set foot in the city, much less win prizes. They sought to obstruct cross-border bonding at the symbolic as well as social and economic levels.

Lingering effects of earlier hostilities at the people-to-people level also stand in the way of unfettered cross-border income-sharing among families transnationalized prior to the 1990s. Some families by the time of the crisis had been divided beyond repair. In such instances Cubans found themselves without cross-border networks that could be activated. María, a divorced journalist who at age 15 unexpectedly was left in the hands of her grandmother on the island, is a case in point. Without a good-bye, her mother, like Lourdes', fled to Miami. "Initially my mother and I corresponded by letter, but there was so much conflict between us. She was very critical of the revolution and her letters attacked everything I believed in and worked for." María added that her mother "was more concerned about her political beliefs than about how I was feeling. She gave me no emotional support. I was bitter and aggressive. Finally, the letters became so painful that I asked her to stop writing. I said 'it would be better not to write because the day the Americans invaded we would be on opposite sides killing each other. . . . (W)e would never agree.' We never wrote to each other again. I don't know if my mother is dead or alive. We have not spoken in over thirty years . . ." Although desperate for assistance, María felt it would be hypocritical to start looking for her mother.

Meanwhile, some émigrés can not forgive family who remained loyal to the revolution. They therefore send money only sparingly, if at all. Some 1960s émigrés reported reluctantly sending money beginning in the 1990s, but just enough so that their island relatives "would not die." Others "maintained their distance" and refused to send money when asked.

Independent of politics, ambiguity about new yet-to-be routinized transnational norms and conflicting views about appropriate usages of remittances among Cubans on both sides of the Florida Straits occasionally limited émigré generosity. Some émigrés resented when island kin asked for more than they wanted to give or used remittances for purposes they had not intended. Some Cuban-Americans complained that island family wanted emigration assistance, a responsibility they did not want to take on. A New Jersey woman, for example, conveyed how angry she was when her elderly sister in Havana asked for help to move to the United States. "This was impossible," said she. "The visit wasn't about taking someone to the U.S." The Jersey woman told her sister that she was "retired and couldn't support her, pay for her Medicare, and provide spending money." Yet other émigrés resented when dollars intended to be shared among island relatives were hoarded by the person through whom the funds were funneled. Misuse disinclined kin abroad from sharing additional earnings. Such was the case of a Miami woman who left US$1,000 with her Cuban niece, Marguerita, on a visit, "for family emergencies." Marguerita used the dollars to redo her apartment for a start-up black market room rental business. The aunt, upset both that Marguerita hoarded the money and that she used it for purposes other than intended, did not want to send more money.

Conclusion

Experiences of ordinary Cubans in the post-Soviet era have several theoretical implications. And comparisons between Cuban and Dominican experiences highlight ways that the Cuban experience is and is not unique.

For one, the Cuban experience suggests that nominally strong states are not necessarily able to impose their will and way when out of sync with what their citizens want. Neither the U.S. nor the Cuban government, strong states for different reasons, succeeded in keeping cross-border bonding and remittance-sending at bay once coveted by ordinary people. The governments mainly shaped whether the ties were overt or covert, formal or informal, legal or illegal. Similarly, powerful immigrant leadership and lobbyists were unable to keep at bay cross-border involvements ordinary Cubans wanted.

Two, informal transnational ties rooted in intra-family yearnings may unintentionally in the aggregate induce macro economic, social, cultural, and political changes. The Cuban case illustrates that family ties across borders may transnationalize norms and values, transnationalize the economic base of immigrant enclaves and home country economies, and erode the influence and authority of once entrenched political leadership. And so too may they transform kinship life, inducing families to take on new economic and status-conferring functions. Society, the normative order, and economic life all were transformed in the process of families transnationalizing. Cross-border kinship ties had the unintended effect of undermining the state socialist economy, the socialist system of stratification, and the socialist normative order.

In the process transnationalized families also unwittingly generated new societal contradictions and problems, such as race-based and regional inequities, crime and corruption.

Three, transnational bonding is conducive to a new form of social capital formation, transnational social capital. Cubans activated, cultivated and created transnational networks that previously were non-existent or covert. They transformed these networks into benefit generating relations sustained by new norms and new cross-border trust. The characteristics, correlates and consequences of the transnationally grounded social capital differ from those of nationally grounded social capital. In post-industrial countries social, human, cultural and financial capital are known to be mutually interchangeable and reinforcing, and rooted predominantly in "weak social ties."[13] In Cuba the new form of social capital is family-based, across borders, and "bundled" differently. Overseas ties are valued independently of the skills network members have. And Cubans abroad are rewarded with cultural capital, with esteem, respect, and admiration, when decapitalizing economically, that is, when remitting income to homeland family. Remittance-senders are rewarded for their generosity with new social status specifically in the context of the cross-border field their network ties have created, status low-skilled émigrés neither enjoyed before emigrating nor enjoy as humble folk in the United States.

While continued institutional barriers on both sides of the Florida Straits may obstruct unfettered transnational social capital build-up, increasingly Cubans are typifying cross-border bonding and sharing of economic assets that has become characteristic of other new immigrant groups. Differences have become more of degree than kind, and the differences in degree are diminishing. Among other immigrant populations where social, cultural, economic and political cross-border barriers were minimal a severe economic crisis of the likes of Cuba's was not a precondition for the informal asset generating transnational field to evolve.

Ordinary Cubans, like other Latin Americans, in essence are increasingly taking history into their own hands. However modest and instrumental the ambitions of Cubans who have reached out to family in the diaspora, the net effect of their involvements has been to transform Cuban socialism as we knew it. The full long-term effects remain to be seen.

References

Boswell, Thomas. 2002. *A Demographic Profile of Cuban-Americans*. Miami: Cuban-American National Council.

Bourdieu, Pierre 1986. "The Forms of Capital." In J.G. Richardson (ed.), *Handbook of Theory and Research for the Sociology of Education*. New York: Greenwood Press, pp. 241–58.

Brundenius, Claes. 2002. "Whither the Cuban Economy after Recovery? The Reform Process, Upgrading Strategies and the Question of Transition." *Journal of Latin American Studies* 34 part 2 (May 2002): 365–96.

Celent Communications. 2002. *Global Money Transfers: Exploring the Remittance Gold Mine*. New York: Celent Communications.

Coleman, James S. 1988. "Social Capital in the Creation of Human Capital." *American Journal of Sociology*. Supplement. S95–120.

———. 1993. "The Rational Reconstruction of Society." *American Sociological Review* 58 (February): 1–15.

Díaz-Briquets, Sergio and Jorge Pérez-López. 1997. "Refugee Remittances: Conceptual Issues and the Cuban and Nicaraguan Experiences." *International Migration Review* 31 no. 2 (Spring): 411–37.

Eckstein, Susan. *Back from the Future: Cuba under Castro*. Princeton: Princeton University Press, 1994.

———. 2003. *Diasporas and Dollars: Transnational Ties and the Transformation of Cuba*. Cambridge: Massachusetts Institute of Technology, Center for International Studies, Rosemarie Rogers Working Papers Series #16

———. 2004. *On Deconstructing Immigrant Generations: Cohorts and the Cuban Émigré Experience*. San Diego, CA: Center for Comparative Immigration Studies, Working Paper 97, University of California-San Diego (April).

Eckstein, Susan and Lorena Barberia. 2002. "Grounding Immigrant Generations in History: Cuban-Americans and Their Transnational Ties." *International Migration Review* (Fall).

Economic Commission on Latin America and the Caribbean (ECLAC). 2000. *La Economía Cubana*. Mexico, D.F.: Fondo de Cultura Económica.

Economist Intelligence Unit (EIU). 2001. *Cuba Country Report*. (February).

Florida International University (FIU), Institute for Public Opinion Research (IPOR). 2000. *FIU/Cuba Poll*. Miami: FIU-IPOR.

Glick-Schiller, Nina. 1999. "Transmigrants and the Nation-States: Something Old and Something New in the U.S. Immigrant Experience." Pp. 94–119 in *The Handbook of International Migration: The American Experience*, edited by Charles Hirschman, Philip Kasinitz, and Josh DeWind. New York: Russell Sage Foundation.

Granovetter, Mark. 1974. *Getting A Job.* Cambridge: Harvard University Press.

LeoGrande, William and Julie Thomas. 2002. "Cuba's Quests for Economic Independence." *Journal of Latin American Studies* vol. 34 part 2 (May): 325–64.

Levitt, Peggy. 2001. *Transnational Villagers.* Berkeley: University of California Press.

Marx, Karl. 1959. "Critique of the Gotha Programme." In *Marx & Engels: Basic Writings in Politics and Philosophy,* edited by Lewis S. Feuer. Garden City, NY: Anchor Books.

Massey, Douglas et al. 1987. *Return to Aztlan.* Berkeley: University of California Press.

———. 1998. *Worlds in Motion: Understanding International Immigration at the End of the Millennium.* Oxford: Clarendon Press.

McHugh, Kevin, Ines Miyares, and Emily Skop. 1997. "The Magnetism of Miami: Segmented Paths in Cuban Migration." *Geographical Review* 87 no. 4: 504–19.

Multilateral Investment Fund (MIF)/Inter-American Development Bank (IDB). 2002. "Remittances to Latin America and the Caribbean. Washington: MIF/IDB (February).

———. 2002a. "Money, Markets and Costs." Washington D.C.: Inter-American Development Bank-International Monetary Fund. http://www.thedialogue.org/publications.html.

———. 2002b. "Globalization and Migration: The Impact of Family Remittances to Latin America," *Latin American Politics and Society* (Summer).

Portes, Alejandro, William Haller, and Luis Guarnizo. 2002."Transnational Entrepreneurs: An Alternative Form of Immigrant Economic Adaptation. *American Sociological Review* 67 (April): 278–98.

United States Bureau of the Census (USBC). 1981 to 2000. *Statistical Abstract of the U.S.* Washington, D.C: Bureau of the Census, U.S. Department of Commerce, Economics and Statistics Administration.

United States Department of Justice (USDJ), Immigration and Naturalization Service (INS). 1999 and 2000. *Statistical Yearbook of the Immigrant and Naturalization Service.* Washington, D.C.: INS.

U.S.–Cuba Trade and Economic Council (UCTEC). 2002. "Economic Eye on Cuba." March 17. http://www.cubatrade.org.

World Bank. 2001, 2002. *World Development Indicators 2001* and *World Development Indicators 2002*. Washington, D.C.: World Bank.

————. 1997. *World Development Report*. New York: Oxford University Press.

Acknowledgments

My thanks to Lorena Barberia for research assistance on this project, and to the Committee for Cuban Democracy, the Mellon-MIT Inter-University Program on Non-Governmental Organizations and Forced Migration, and the American Council of Learned Societies for funding of the project. And my thanks to Jorge Domínguez for comments on an earlier version of this chapter. I also wish to thank June Carolyn Erlick for editorial assistance.

Notes

1   By the 1990s, however, migration to New Jersey tapered off while migration to Florida mushroomed. Reflecting the shift in trend, in 1998 over 14,000 Cubans noted intention to settle in Florida while less than 500 planned to settle in New Jersey (cf. USDJ 2000: 71) . Nonetheless, Cubans remained the largest as well as the most important ethnic group politically, economically, and socially in both communities.

2   For more information about the survey and methodology, see Eckstein and Barberia 2002. Material analyzed in this essay forms part of a larger study of Cuban-American/Cuban transnational ties and the transformation of Cuba. For this reason, I draw only selectively on field work material here.

3   Under the Carter administration émigrés could more easily send packages to Cuba. However, it was expensive, cumbersome and perceived as risky. Cuban-Americans never knew whether packages would arrive, whether they would be opened, and whether island family would be penalized for receiving gifts. And émigrés received no community moral support for sending packages. Any contact with Cuba defied the personal embargo the community advocated.

4   At the turn of the century remittances were estimated to account for 70 percent of the dollars Cubans informally accessed. U.S.–Cuba Trades and Economic Council (UCTEC), "Economic Eye on Cuba" (March17, 2002, p. 12. http://www.cubatrade.org).

5   For a discussion of the range of remittance estimates and estimating difficulties, see Eckstein (2003: 12, 13) and the references therein.

6   Authorities justified what they claimed to be an ideal mark-up, 140 percent, on equity grounds: a hidden tax on dollar consumers to support programs benefiting people without dollars. Accordingly, an item costing US$100 to

produce or import, with a 140 percent tax, would sell for US$240.

7   In 2000, 70 percent of the funds Mexicans received in remittances from the United States were sent electronically. The percentage was so high in good part because the Mexican government had made a concerted effort to reduce sending costs. In general, only 17 percent of all Latinos in the United States send remittances through people travelling to their country of origin (Celent 2002: 10, 11, 20, 21).

8   According to the World Bank online source, the Cuban post-secondary school enrollment rate in 1997 had dipped to 12 percent.

9   Concerned about declining teen-age commitment to higher education, in the early 2000s Castro launched a campaign to encourage large-scale enrollments in social work/social inquiry studies.

10 Absenteeism and quit rates rose, for example, to the point that there were teacher shortages in key subjects. Illustrative, in Cienfuegos 9 percent of all teachers abandoned their job in 1993 (*Cuba Business* September 1994: 6).

11 Forty-three percent of Cubans but only 26 percent of the general Hispanic population (which included but was not limited to Dominicans), for example, earned US$50,000 or more in 1998. UCBC 2000: 10, 146.

12 Hometown associations are important among Mexicans as well. They were encouraged by the Vicente Fox government (2000–2006) to promote community along with family remittances.

13 See Bourdieu (1986) and Coleman (1988, 1993) for original theorizing about the relationship between social and other forms of capital in the post-industrial country context, and Granovetter (1974) for initial theorizing about the "strength of weak social ties."

10

Remittances to Cuba: An Evaluation of Cuban and U.S. Government Policy Measures

by Lorena Barberia

Until the last decade, remittances had a limited economic impact for Cuba. Comprehensive changes in policy regulating the receipt and use of U.S. dollars in Cuba took place in the 1990s. As a result, the number of émigrés sending money to their friends and family on the island surged. Since the 1990s, these remittance flows have become quite significant, comprising one of Cuba's largest sources of foreign currency earnings. Indeed, by the turn of the 21st century they are as important as the country's export income and tourism revenues and greater than foreign direct investment.

In absolute terms, remittances (the transfer of private income to other households) are as important for Cuba's economy as they are for other countries in the Caribbean, roughly equivalent to those received by the Dominican Republic and twice as high as those received by Haiti. The source of these transfers is primarily from Cuban émigrés residing in the United States. The propensity to send transfers to family and friends by Cuban émigrés in the U.S., where the vast majority settled over the last four decades, also seems to be on par to that of other Latin American and Caribbean immigrants. Indeed, a 1998 survey of Latin American immigrants' remittance behavior found that the percentage of Cuban-Americans sending remittances is higher than Mexican-Americans and lower than Dominican-Americans.[1] Moreover, the available evidence indicates that a strong majority of Cuban-Americans send remittances. Indeed, 67 percent of Cuban respondents living in the United States confirmed they send monies to their families in Cuba in a November 2001 Inter-American Development Bank survey (Orozco 2002).

In a 2000 study on remittances and markets, Manuel Orozco argues that government actors play as crucial a role as do senders and recipients—the players most commonly studied. Orozco's work draws attention to the importance of systematically studying the effect of government policy on remittance behavior. In the case of Cuba, both the migrant-sending and receiving governments have repeatedly attempted to influence remittance flows since the commencement of hostilities in the early 1960s. Both governments initially blocked remittances. From the early 1960s until 1993, Cuba prohibited the circulation of foreign currency and limited receipt of remittances to in-kind transfers. The United States has periodically prohibited direct financial transfers to Cuba since imposing an embargo on Cuba in 1962. Over time both governments have relaxed their restrictions. Beginning in 1978 and more dramatically since U.S. dollar legalization in 1993, the Cuban government has embarked upon a strategy to increase the flow of dollars sent by émigrés via official channels. The United States, which first legalized remittances in 1978, has since then attempted to cap the amount of private funds sent to the island and, from 1994 to 1998, it banned the sending of private family transfers altogether.

Following early work to establish a conceptual framework for this study of remittances in the case of Cuba by Monreal (2000) and efforts to document U.S. and Cuban government policy by Díaz Briquets and Pérez-López (1997), this chapter seeks to contribute to the remittance literature, addressing the questions raised by case study evidence by undertaking a retrospective assessment of Cuban and U.S. government policy on remittances from 1959 to the present. The second part of the chapter reviews the literature on the interaction between government policy and remittances. The third section tracks the policy measures introduced by the Cuban government—first to attract remittances, then to influence their domestic uses—and assesses their effectiveness. Finally, the chapter maps and evaluates the efficacy of the policies implemented by the United States governing remittance flows to Cuba.

The research material for this chapter is based on both primary and secondary sources. Primary data are drawn from the author's interviews in the United States and Cuba from 2000 to 2003. As part of a collaborative research project on transnational ties, the author conducted interviews on a nonrandom snowball sample of 77 residents in Greater Miami Dade County, Florida and Greater Union City, Hudson County, New Jersey and 28 residents in Havana, Cuba.[2] In Havana, the author also interviewed 28 government officials, researchers, church officials and industry-related representatives. In addition, follow-up interviews were conducted with remittance firms in the United States, Canada,

Spain and the Caribbean in 2002 and 2003. The field interviews with Cuban families on both sides of the Florida Straits, and in particular their references to the Cuban and U.S. governments, provided the initial impetus for this chapter. Many respondents expressed distrust and fear about whether these interviews would go to "the government." Similarly, the interviews highlighted the difference between the private behavior of Cuban families and the practices officially permitted by both governments and how these both changed over time. Finally, secondary information spanning the period between 1959 and 2004, including Cuban and U.S. government documents, statistical data, as well as studies on migration, remittances, and the Cuban economy were analyzed.

Notwithstanding evidence presented by primary and secondary sources, quantitative research on remittances to Cuba should be interpreted with caution. First, as this chapter attempts to explain, several factors have contributed to a pattern whereby the majority of resources are transferred through non-official means. This trend—confirmed by the author's interviews—creates problems for quantitative estimates of the overall amount of remittances sent to the island. Second, in terms of measurement and reporting by official sources, international balance of payments statistics include remittances in estimates of net current transfers. Cuba follows a similar methodology, reporting remittances in its balance of payments statistics. Net current transfers include estimates on the overall volume of remittances derived from "the turnover of dollar shops minus dollar earnings accounted for by official payment of dollars (mainly through incentive schemes)" (Morris 2000). These figures are only rough estimates and should be interpreted with caution, particularly since they assume that the majority of remittances are spent by consumers in the state-run dollar stores, and do not take into account other venues such as black market transactions. Nevertheless, this chapter uses official data as a benchmark, noting the aforementioned measurement problems and biases. Throughout the study, remittances and private transfers are referred to interchangeably.

Utilizing both primary and secondary data, this study argues that (1) the aggregate flow of remittances and their uses are highly sensitive to macroeconomic, political and institutional factors in Cuba, the receiving country, and are less sensitive to the policies imposed by the sending country, the United States; (2) Cuban government policy has been successful in attracting remittances and partially successful in channeling these flows toward the state-controlled economy; and (3)

Cuban government policies are encouraging use of these flows for consumption and less so for savings and direct investment.

A Review of the Literature on Government Policy Directed at Remittances

Most policy analysis studies on remittances thus far have concentrated on government-adopted measures to attract remittances to the home country (country of origin). Notable progress has been made in an important area of research—how effective "migrant-specific" schemes are in attracting remittance flows through official channels such as the formal banking sector.[3] European governments have concentrated their attempts to attract remittances on specific incentives such as repatriable foreign currency accounts and foreign currency-denominated bonds. For example, Yugoslavia, Greece and Turkey have all instituted foreign currency account schemes (Russell 1986). Governments in developing countries have also adopted measures aimed at maximizing remittance flows through official channels by means of repatriable foreign currency accounts and foreign currency-denominated bonds.[4] In some cases, governments have also instituted mandatory remittance policies.[5]

Yet, studies aimed at evaluating such policy measures find weak evidence regarding their ability to attract remittances. In assessing the impact of Greek, Turkish and Yugoslav government schemes, Swamy (1981) reports that these policy measures had no significant impact on the total flow of remittances.[6] Birks and Sinclair (1979) report similar findings with respect to Arab governments' policy efforts. In his review of remittances in seven Asian economies, Athukorala (1993) found that migrant-specific incentive schemes to attract remittance flows through official channels were less successful when the macroeconomic fundamentals remained distorted and when institutional deficiencies remained unrectified.[7] Consequently, the two countries with the most distorted policy environments, Philippines and Pakistan, had the highest rates of remittances flowing through unofficial channels relative to the other five countries examined, India, Bangladesh, South Korea, Sri Lanka and Thailand. Moreover, as Russell (1986: 691) writes, "there is also a question as to whether or not the volume of remittances which can be influenced by policy measures warrants the administrative and political costs."

Fewer studies have examined how governments have attempted to channel the *uses* of remittances in the home country and the extent to which they are directed toward *socially optimal ends*. This lack of research results in part from the fact that governments, until recently, were less concerned with channeling the uses of remittances within the domestic economy. As Puri and Ritzema (1999: 10) write of governments in Asian labor-exporting countries "despite a keen interest to develop policies to attract remittances, they have given much less attention to policies aimed at influencing the pattern of utilization of remittances." An alternate explanation for the lack of government policy on the *uses* of remittances is that it is difficult for government policy to mandate the uses of these private family transfers. Since households primarily spend these resources on basic needs, housing and social protection, remittances are already channeled toward *socially optimal ends*. For example, DeSipio (2000) recounts that Mexican migrants report that nearly three-quarters of these funds will be used for health care.

Those studies that have begun to examine the impact of government policy on the uses of these flows have thus far concentrated their attention on the sub-national level. Torres (2001) traces a series of Latin American state government policy measures adopted in the late 1990s and aimed at directing these flows toward productive investment. In cases such as the Mexican state of Guanajuato, Torres concludes that state governments have been partially successful in luring substantial flows of remittances toward small-scale entrepreneurial activity and local community development projects. Research on how national policies impact the uses of remittances, however, has remained limited.

In contrast to research on home country remittance policy, the impact of host government policy on remittance flows has been less studied. This is due in part to the fact that few host countries have implemented policies imposing restrictions on the monies that can be sent home by migrants. As a result, the majority of studies in this area have been directed at analyzing the impact of *indirect* host country policies on remittance flows. For example, there has been significant attention to analyzing the interaction between public transfers and private remittances.[8] In the transnational sphere, Taylor's (2000) work examining whether public transfers influence remittances from U.S. households to Mexico is seminal, reporting that U.S. households' remittance expenditures increase when they receive non-needs-tested income, such as unemployment insurance and social security.

This chapter seeks to improve understanding of how national policies in both the migrant-sending and receiving countries impact the overall flows and uses of remittances. It seeks to do this by presenting a case study of the policy changes taken in Cuba and in the United States and how these contributed to the response of these flows to Cuba over the last four decades. In order to illustrate how reactive remittances have been to government incentives and disincentives, it utilizes distinct historical periods with significant policy shifts during the last four decades. The study also seeks to analyze the responsiveness of remittance flows toward specific policies, whether directed at inducing investment or at consumption for recipients, by tracing the broad range of policies adopted by the Cuban government.

Cuban Remittance Policy: From Prohibition to Leveraging

Over the last four decades, the Cuban government shifted its initial policy of tight control on remittance flows and their domestic uses to the current policy, which attempts to attract and leverage remittances through official channels. The characteristics of Cuban remittance policy during the post-revolutionary period can be separated into three stages. In each stage, there has been a significant policy shift with respect to both monetary and migratory policy that translated into a shift in remittance flows over time. The first and most prohibitive stage transpired from 1959 to 1979; an intermediate stage took place between 1980 and 1992 with partial liberalization; and the third stage characterized by successful absorption of remittances into the official economy occurred after the legalization of the U.S. dollar in 1993.

Prohibition

The first stage, from 1959 to 1979, can be characterized as the most prohibitive. During this stage, Cuban government policies deterred remittances, and foreign currency remittance flows to the island were virtually non-existent. Following the 1959 triumph of the revolution and the successive reforms and nationalizations of the 1960s, there was a mass exodus of Cuba's political, economic, and social elites to the United States during the 1960s and early 1970s. The Cuban government permitted migration, but began to tightly control departure through a series of measures. Stipulations for migration required: (1) permanent exit from the island without the possibility of return, even for temporary visits; (2) relinquishment of émigrés' rights as citizens, although not their status as Cuban citizens; and (3) confiscation of émigrés' property and assets (Martín and Pérez 1997: 86).

Migration produced not only a physical separation of families, but also in many cases a severance in the relations between those who stayed and those who left. The revolutionary government and its supporters saw those who left as traitors to the Cuban revolution and its goals. Implicitly and explicitly vis-à-vis the Cuban state's migration policy, Cubans who left understood that they were also choosing to sever their economic and social ties with Cuba. Under the circumstances, those leaving were given little incentive to remit funds to their relatives.

In addition, the government instituted economic policy measures limiting private family transfers. In the midst of failed counterrevolutionary uprisings in the Escambray mountains in the early 1960s and the April 1961 Bay of Pigs invasion by invading brigades of Cuban exiles, and as the massive exodus of Cuba's upper classes accelerated, the Cuban government undertook a series of nationalizations and monetary policy reforms as a political move to wrest control and power from counterrevolutionary foes.[9] As part of this strategy, the Cuban government moved to increase its control over the economy's assets and financial flows by nationalizing farms, foreign-owned and Cuban-owned large and medium-scale enterprises, as well as petroleum refineries. In terms of financial assets, U.S.-owned banks were nationalized on September 17, 1960 and Cuban-owned banks were nationalized on October 13, 1960.

In August 1961, the government announced the creation of a new Cuban peso. Heads of households were allowed to exchange a maximum of 10,000 old pesos in circulation; bank deposits were automatically converted, but the remaining old pesos outside the banking system were lost. Cuba's National Bank declared that the new official exchange rate would be one new peso per one U.S. dollar, although the value of the peso was worth fractionally less in world capital markets (Domínguez 1978: 228). Households that had been hoarding pesos outside the official banking system and those holding their savings in U.S. dollars lost significant portions of their wealth.[10] As a result of these measures and the regulations imposed by the U.S. embargo in 1962, direct correspondent banking services between the United States and Cuba were interrupted and effectively shut down.

In subsequent years, the government introduced reforms aimed at transforming Cuba's economy into a centrally planned economy. With the socialization of the means of production, the Cuban state replaced market-based distribution with the allocation of goods and services through centrally fixed prices (Mesa Lago 1981: 16). With the introduction of price controls and rationing to guarantee distribution of consumer goods, the value and significance of money in the domestic economy lost much of its importance. Indeed, those with surplus pesos had difficulty spending them in the centrally planned and progressively more rationed economy.[11]

For the next two decades, the Cuban government strongly discouraged contact between island families and their *gusano* émigré relatives.[12] Visits by Cuban émigrés, a common channel for unofficial remittance transfers, were prohibited. Thus, the state only sanctioned remittances of in-kind transfers—small packages containing clothing, medicines, food and other consumer goods. In-kind transfers surged primarily during the period between 1968 and 1975, when the Cuban economy underwent a period of contraction and bilateral tensions ebbed. Agencies were established in the United States, with packages sent on flights between the United States and Cuba. Yet, these practices continued to be stigmatized and discouraged as this quote from one of the interviewees for this study testifies:

> Prior to our return, family ties and contact were forbidden by members of the Communist Party. There was basically no communication between my cousin, a university professor, and us [my family in the U.S.] for over 20 years. When I went back to Cuba [in 1979], he opened up a closet filled with the packages my mother had sent with clothing and medicines for the family [during the late 60s and early 70s]. He said, "please tell her [your mother] not to send any more of these clothes, because we don't want them and we can't wear them." As university professor, he couldn't wear any of the clothing because it would arouse suspicion and could get him in trouble as evidence of having contact with his family abroad.

In sum, émigrés wanting to help their relatives on the island had limited options for the first two decades after 1960. Direct banking and financial transactions between the United States and Cuba were non-existent. The primary channel for sending remittances to the island was through packages containing in-kind and cash transfers. The migration of Cubans with no possibility of return to their homeland, combined with the transformation of Cuba's monetary system and the subsequent collapse in financial transactions between the United States and Cuba, contributed to the limitations on remittances. Even in cases in which private family transfers managed to get through the barriers, island recipients were reluctant to accept these items. Although no official statistics or studies reporting transfers for this period were found, it is estimated that remittance flows were minimal.

Rapprochement

From 1979 to the early 1990s, the Cuban government initiated a strategy to re-establish relations with the émigré community, and government policy toward remittances also shifted. Cuba's policy stance toward remittances during this period can be characterized as more receptive, but still highly restrictive. During this second stage, significant policy reforms encouraged remittance flows, including a liberalization of émigré travel policies, the opening of foreign currency stores and introduction of financial transfers. Most importantly, Cuba instituted policies in a way that would attract remittances and ensure that they would be channeled toward the official economy.

Table 10.1 Cuba's Domestic and Migrant Population, 1941–2000

Decade	Population in Cuba[a]	Cuban citizens legally admitted to the U.S. by the INS[b]	Cuban-born Population in the U.S.[c]	Cuban-origin population in the U.S.[d]	Ratio of Cuban Migrants in U.S. to Domestic Population in Cuba	Ratio of Cuban origin population in U.S. to Domestic population in Cuba
1941–50	5,876,052	26,313	—	—	—	—
1951–60	7,077,190	78,948	79,150	—	1.1%	—
1961–70	8,603,165	208,536	439,048	—	5.1%	—
1971–80	9,365,972	264,863	607,814	—	6.5%	—
1981–90	10,694,465	144,578	736,971	1,053,197	6.9%	9.8%
1991–2000	11,217,100	169,322	784,910	1,236,511	7.0%	11.0%

a. Population estimates are for the last year in the decade as reported by ONE (2002).
b. Cuban citizens legally admitted to the U.S. by the INS as summarized in the *Statistical Yearbook* 2002.
c. Cuban-born population recorded according to U.S. Census data.
d. Cuban-origin population recorded by U.S. Census data.

Sources: ONE, *Anuario estadístico de Cuba 2001;* United States Office of Immigration Statistics, Office of Management, Department of Homeland Security (DHS), *2002 Yearbook of Immigration Statistics,* Table 2; Bureau of the Census, Historical Census Statistics on the Foreign-Born Population of the U.S.: 1850-1990; Table 3 Region and Country or Area of Birth of the Foreign-Born Population: 1960 to 1990; and Bureau of Census, *Foreign-Born Population by Country of Origin and Citizenship Status, 2000.*

By 1980, Table 10.1 shows that the number of Cubans residing in the United States had reached more than 600,000, or approximately 6.5 percent of the island's domestic population. Cuban government officials, including President Fidel Castro, now referred in speeches to Cubans living in the United States as members of the "community," rather than stigmatizing them as *gusanos* (Martín and Pérez 1997: 89). Political discourse not only shifted; so did government policy.

The Cuban government removed its categorical prohibition on family visits during the December 1978 Dialogue talks between the Cuban government and Cuban émigrés.[13] For the first time, émigrés were allowed to visit their families for two-week periods, provided they stay in state-run hotels charged in U.S. dollars. From 1979 to 1982, an estimated 150,000 Cuban-Americans made the journey (Marazul 2000). Despite moves to improve relations with Cubans living abroad, Cuba's migration policy remained unchanged—migration continued to be considered permanent.

Following this policy change, family visits became a primary vehicle for channeling private financial transfers to families. However, remittances were mostly in-kind. Emigrés were permitted to bring goods such as televisions, stereos and other appliances with them as part of their luggage. A 1979 *Miami Herald* article estimates that more than US$150 million were transferred by April 1979 (García 1996: 52). During their stay, Cuban émigrés also brought cash remittances for their families. With U.S. dollar transactions illegal for Cuban domestic residents, recipient households had limited options for spending these resources themselves. Visiting émigrés, however, were allowed to purchase both luxuries and necessities for their island families in Cuban foreign currency stores during their visits.[14] These stores, known as *diplotiendas* and *tecnotiendas,* had first been opened to sell foreign diplomats a wide range of imported goods, as well as fresh and canned foods. Ordinary Cuban citizens were rarely authorized to purchase commodities in these stores.[15] Thus, visiting émigrés converted their U.S. dollars in *diplotiendas.*

As a part of normalization of émigré relations, mechanisms for receiving cash transfers from abroad were also introduced. Through the *Banco Nacional de Cuba* (BNC), Cuban citizens were allowed to receive foreign currency transfers from private parties abroad. The only restriction on receipts was that remittances had to be converted into Cuban pesos at the official one Cuban peso per US$ exchange rate (Pérez-

López 1995: 50). When a relative received a transfer from abroad, the BNC issued the recipient a transfer certificate that could be used only for purchases at state-operated foreign currency stores.

Despite significant policy shifts, the flow of remittances to Cuba from 1979 to the early 1990s remained limited for five reasons. First, regulations prohibiting the circulation of dollars deterred cash transfers to Cuban families on the island. While the Cuban government relaxed its restrictions on family visits, it tightened the penalties associated with holding foreign currency by codifying the penalties associated with these operations into the nation's criminal code. In 1978, the National Assembly approved a comprehensive criminal code that became effective on November 1, 1979.[16] Section 1 of Article 282 in the Cuban penal code prohibited the exporting of foreign currency, obtaining foreign currency balances in excess of needs, the selling, transferring or buying of foreign currencies, travelers checks, money orders or other instruments denominated in foreign currencies.[17] Individuals violating these laws were subject to incarceration for between one to eight years. Section 2 of article 282 prohibited the holding of foreign currencies or securities and the engagement in financial transactions outside Cuba either personally or through an intermediary. Individuals found to be holding U.S. dollars could be incarcerated for between six months and three years, as well as fined between 200 and 500 pesos.

Second, remittance sending depended primarily on those traveling to the island. The proportion of Cuban émigrés returning to visit their families diminished significantly as a result of the re-introduction of travel restrictions by both the U.S. and Cuban governments in the early 1980s. Cuban government officials charged that the massive return of émigrés in 1979 incited the unrest that led over 10,000 Cubans to occupy the Peruvian embassy and eventually steered Castro into opening the Mariel port to 125,000 Cubans who left the island. It was Cuban-American/Cuban contact and gifts for recipient families, Cuban officials rationalized, that stirred islander discontent. Scholars also articulated this hypothesis, explaining that the incursion of émigré culture and U.S. goods contributed to Cuba's "Blue Jean Revolution" (Martín and Pérez 1997: 52). In response, Havana limited émigré entry, in terms of visitation and correspondence, to prevent "another Mariel." In 1985 Castro suspended family visits altogether until 1986 in retaliation for propagandistic Radio Martí broadcasts. When émigré visits were once again allowed, Cuba capped the number of visitors at

2,500 per year until 1987 and then 5,000 per year until the early 1990s (Marazul 2000).

Third, after two decades of separation, Cubans on both sides of the Florida Straits had mixed reactions to the exchange of cash and goods. The case of a Havana resident interviewed for this study by the author is illustrative of the ideological conflicts experienced during these re-encounters and the struggle some felt when faced by their returning family's in-kind and cash gifts. Pablo was an eight-year old boy from a middle-class family in the Vedado neighborhood when Fidel Castro took power on January 1, 1960. In the subsequent decades, Pablo rose to become a loyal Communist Party member with a prominent government position that included travel to foreign countries. Pablo remembers receiving packages from his aunts and his nanny, both of whom had left Cuba in 1960 and established themselves in Miami by the late 1970s:

> When the packages started arriving, I was in my late 20s. I remember thinking "Who do they think we are?" My aunts did not come to visit, even though we had not seen them in nearly 20 years. Instead, they sent packages with the most basic items such as Colgate toothpaste and brand-name shampoo to my mother and their sister, a middle-class housewife with no formal affiliation to the Communist Party or the neighborhood mass organization unit. I was outraged by their lack of understanding. It seemed like an attempt to "colonize" those of us who had remained in Cuba. We didn't fight a revolution for Colgate toothpaste; we fought for more important rights. Moreover, they would never send personal letters telling us about their lives or asking us about ours in Cuba. Eventually, we lost ties with these family members and our relations never warmed.

Fourth, Cuban families' basic needs were largely satisfied, and private investment opportunities were limited to the black market. Cuba had experienced an economic boom with 8.2 percent annual average per capita growth rates between 1970 and 1974 (Madrid-Aris 1997: 217). Although a short-term recession and the foreign debt crisis that hit the island's economy in 1976 when world market sugar prices plummeted produced a slow down, the Cuban economy continued to remain dynamic in terms of its macroeconomic indicators.[19] For example, industrial and agricultural output improved, leading Cuba to experience 5.1 percent annual average per capita growth rates from 1980 to 1984 (ibid). The Cuban government had also initiated several market opening reforms, including the implementation of major wage reform in 1980 (the first since 1963) and the liberalization of private economic activity in the agricultural and state sectors of the economy. As a result, recipient families were not experiencing the type of shortages caused later by a severe economic contraction in the early 1990s.

The fifth reason for low remittance volumes—further developed in the fourth section of this chapter—is related to U.S. policy. Since the U.S. embargo prohibited direct commerce between U.S. and Cuban banking institutions, Cuban-American émigrés who wanted to send remittances had to utilize cumbersome and costly third country remittance system routes. In the late 1970s and early 1980s the most common mechanisms for third country transfers were via money orders and money transmissions through non-bank financial institutions, mechanisms that Cuba had developed with other Western economies.

Thus, remittance activity increased moderately during the second stage from 1979 to 1992. Funds were either carried directly by visiting émigrés or sent with those who were traveling to the island. However, private family transfers remained minimal in the 1980s. The illegality of dollar possession and the limited channels for converting or spending these resources resulted in minimal transfer of currency and goods by migrants to their island relatives.

Courting Remittances

In the 1990s, Cuba comprehensively shifted its policies to increase and channel the flow of remittances into the official economy. Spurred by a severe contraction in the Cuban economy caused by the abrupt collapse of Soviet aid and trade in 1989, this third stage would prove to be the most far-reaching. The fundamental shift in policy aimed at attracting remittances is best understood within the context of the factors that contributed to the economy's collapse and the constraints faced by the Cuban government, which limited the government's policy options.

The onset of the crisis was sparked by the collapse of Cuba's external trade, which by the late 1980s had become concentrated with its trade partners in the Soviet Union, Eastern Europe and China. By 1989, more than 80 percent of Cuba's trade was with its COMECON partners. Cuba had become highly dependent on imports for basic necessities and primary inputs in industrial production such as food and fuel. Moreover, with the collapse of Soviet aid, international financing for these expensive imports was limited to short-term, costly international borrowing options. Exports decreased from nearly US$6 billion in 1989 to less than US$2 billion by 1993—a 67 percent decrease in three years. In the same period, Cuba's imports decreased by 73 percent. As a result of this precipitous shock, the Cuban economy's gross national product shrank by more than 32 percent between 1990 and 1993. The crisis then magnified and reverberated in the domestic economy.

In the face of continuous declines in production and supply, the prices of dollars and goods in the black market, as well as excess peso circulation, all surged. The black market peso-dollar exchange rate depreciated at an accelerating rate. At the start of the crisis in 1989, the black market rate was seven Cuban pesos per U.S. dollar. By June 1993, Cuban consumers were exchanging 165 pesos for one U.S. dollar (CEPAL 1997: 127). Household consumption declined by 33 percent between 1989 and 1993 (CEPAL 2000: 44). As the crisis intensified, dollars and in-kind transfers from émigrés flowed into the economy illegally and unofficially. CEPAL (2000) estimates that roughly US$311 million in net transfers entered Cuba between 1990 and 1993.

Recognizing that Cuba had entered a "special period," the Cuban government adopted stabilization measures to restore fiscal and external balances. Based on an export and foreign direct investment-driven growth strategy, the government sought to promote traditional primary commodity exports, such as sugar, nickel, and tobacco, as well as a new found source of foreign currency earnings—international tourism. As part of its macroeconomic stabilization strategy, the government initiated a series of reforms. Beginning with the legalization of the U.S. dollar in 1993, Cuba then developed a plan to maximize the state's capture of these resources, the majority of which derived from tourism and remittances.[20] Indeed, from the onset, President Fidel Castro explained that the intent was not only to "legitimize, but to ensure that [the Cuban government] captures a percentage, through commerce, of these dollars, so that as [Vice President] Lage explained, they can be used to benefit the population as a whole."[21]

During the 1990s, the change in Cuba's remittance policy took place in three phases, with each wave of reforms furthering the state's channeling of these resources into the official economy. Significant shifts were first undertaken in monetary policy. These policies were expanded with a second wave of reforms targeted at increasing the flow of remittances through official channels by the augmentation of consumer spending and investment options in the economy. In a third wave, official remittance transfers schemes were introduced, and return migration was permitted for the first time.

Development of a New Financial Architecture

The legalization of U.S. dollar circulation and operation in the domestic economy was the first step in Cuba's monetary policy reform.[22] Fidel Castro announced the de-penalization of foreign currency possession during his July 26, 1993 speech celebrating the anniversary of the Moncada Barracks uprising. During his speech, Fidel Castro specifically cited the government's desire to increase the flow of remittances as a critical component in its decision to de-penalize foreign currency operations:

> We must increase our income in convertible foreign exchange . . . Transfers or remittances of money from abroad is (sic) an extremely important source of convertible currency in the country, one of the sources that exist in the country and it circulates in the country—or, to say it better, it is in the people's hands. A system was established for some time: money could be spent in foreign currency and it was collected in dollars in Cuba, but in a special period situation . . . the peso loses a lot of its value and then no one sends foreign currency to be exchanged for pesos. Other means are sought to send them [dollars]. They enter the country practically in a clandestine way . . .[23] This is a source of foreign exchange . . . the idea is that it is no longer a crime to hold foreign currency, to exchange currency that is held, or even to open accounts in foreign currency.[24]

The legalization of the U.S. dollar was an important first step because it sanctioned significant flows that had spontaneously begun to increase in response to the crisis. After Fidel Castro's July 1993 announcement, both the Cuban peso and the U.S. dollar were allowed to circulate freely in the domestic Cuban economy.[25] Cubans could utilize dollars for their purchases in the state's *diplotiendas* and in the black market.

Table 10.2 GDP, Earnings and Obligations, 1993–2003
(in thousands of pesos and thousands of US$)

	1993	1994	1995	1996	1997	1998	1999	2000	2001	2002	2003
GDP[a,b] (current pesos)	—	19,198,300	21,737,100	22,814,700	22,951,800	23,900,800	25,503,600	27,634,700	29,570,000	30,680,000[b]	31,600,000[b]
GDP (constant pesos)	—	20,582,950	21,088,720	22,741,810	23,308,680	23,599,310	25,071,330	26,482,100	27,273,700	27,573,600	—
Earnings (in US$)											
Merchandise exports	1,000,000	1,385,000	1,600,000	2,015,000	1,812,000	1,512,000	1,496,000	1,760,000	1,762,000	1,500,000	—
International tourism receipts	636,000	763,000	977,000	1,185,000	1,326,000	1,571,000	1,695,000	1,737,000	1,692,000	1,633,000	—
Foreign Direct Investment[d]	54,000	563,000	5,000	82,000	442,000	207,000	178,000	448,000	39,000	—	—
Net current transfers from abroad (including remittances)[b]	—	309,900	646,200	743,700	791,700	813,000	798,900	842,400	813,000[b]	820,000[b]	915,000[b]
Remittances[b,c]	—	262,820	582,630	686,490	726,360	732,910	740,370	798,390	759,400[b]	758,980[b]	—
Official Development Assistance	43,870	47,080	63,570	57,210	65,340	80,090	585,300	44,010	53,600	61,020	—
Obligations (US$)											
Merchandise Imports	1,500,000	2,055,000	2,825,000	3,205,000	398,700	4,197,000	4,365,000	4,877,000	4,838,000	4,161,000	—
Foreign debt[d]	8,785	9,083	10,504	10,465	10,146	11,209	11,078	10,961	10,893	10,900	11,000
Trade Deficit (US$)	500,000	670,000	1,225,000	1,190,000	2,175,000	2,685,000	2,869,000	3,117,000	3,076,000	2,661,000	—

a. The World Bank reports GDP in current nominal local currency units. Data only reported from 1994–2000. Comparable GDP data in US$ using pesos converted into US$ by the average unofficial exchange rate or official exchange rate in respective year is not compatible with the above referenced data. The official exchange rate for one Cuban peso is one US$.

b. GDP; net current transfers, remittance estimates in current pesos for 2001-2003 is calculated based on data reported by CEPAL (2004).

c. Remittances are computed as the difference between net current transfers and official development assistance.

d. Foreign debt is defined as non-Soviet debt. Data on foreign debt and foreign direct investment are from CEPAL (1997, 2001 and 2004).

Sources: Foreign debt and foreign investment data is from CEPAL (1997, 2001 and 2004). Data for all other indicators is from *World Development Indicators* (2004)

Table 10.2 summarizes Cuba's foreign currency earnings and obligations between 1993 and 2003 based on data published by the World Bank in its *World Development Indicators 2004* report and the UN Economic Commission for Latin America (CEPAL) in its annual review of the Cuban economy. The available data for the previous year, 1992, based on economic data released by Cuba's Central Bank and Ministry of Finance, estimate remittances at US$43 million (CEPAL 1997). Net current transfers, which are almost exclusively remittances, appear to have surged with dollar legalization increasing to US$309 million in 1994, the year after the dollar's legalization. Indeed, CEPAL estimates that roughly US$3 million in remittances entered Cuba between 1989 and 1996—the majority after the 1993 legalization of the U.S. dollar and most particularly in 1995 and 1996 after the introduction of the convertible peso (1997: 124).

While effective in legitimizing and attracting remittance flows to the island, the legalization of dollar holding and circulation soon began to undermine the government's ability to effectively manage its monetary policy and its distribution of resources. Because the state paid all wages and salaries for the overwhelming majority of the population in Cuban pesos, exchange rate stabilization was crucial to giving peso earners greater buying power in the unofficial economy. Yet, the government had limited control over the unofficial black market exchange rate. Furthermore, the primary mechanism through which the government could appreciate the Cuban peso's unofficial exchange rate was by selling dollars in the domestic black market. However, as the government itself was trying to obtain dollars for international purchases, this alternative ran counter to its external balancing needs. The Cuban government therefore had to reconcile domestic needs with its ability to finance the trade deficit and foreign borrowing.

The Convertible Peso and the Exchange Rate

By 1995, the Cuban government introduced a solution to these countervailing pressures. The government created domestic convertibility through the introduction of an extra-official exchange rate between Cuban pesos and U.S. dollars and a domestically "convertible peso" that would replace the need for the dollar in commercial transactions. [26] At the same time, the Cuban government opened U.S. dollar exchange bureaus, Casas de Cambio S.A. (CADECA), where U.S. dollars could be exchanged for convertible pesos at a one to one exchange rate and Cuban pesos at a fluctuating exchange rate. [27]

The Central Bank of Cuba issued "convertible pesos," promissory notes fully backed by foreign currency reserves and equivalent to legal tender for domestic transactions in U.S. dollars. CADECAs also introduced an extra-official exchange rate to allow dollars to be sold for Cuban pesos. Both these measures gave the Cuban government an enhanced ability to collect scarce dollars in circulation by exchanging them for legal notes and Cuban pesos. The reverse transactions, whereby Cubans would be allowed to purchase U.S. dollars with their Cuban pesos, were initially not allowed and when the policy was liberalized in the late 1990s, a cap of US$100 was established.

The 1995 monetary reforms were confidence-building measures designed to increase consumer confidence in the value of the Cuban peso and its use in domestic transactions, while permitting the government to capture foreign currency in circulation. By December 1995, the Cuban government had opened 16 exchange offices. The number of CADECA money exchanges operating throughout the island grew to 88 houses in 1999 and reached 291 agencies by 2002 (Banco Central de Cuba 2004). According to estimates by the Centro para el Estudio de la Economía Cubana (1997), CADECA collected US$10 million emitting a portion of convertible pesos and Cuban pesos equivalent to 225 million pesos in 1996. CEPAL (2000: 170) estimates that CADECA was exchanging an average of US$20 million annually by 2000.

In analyzing these flows, it is important to note that dollar earnings from sectors such as tourism and small-scale enterprise economic activity might be the sources for a portion of these exchange volumes.[28] Nevertheless, a significant portion of this total derives from remittance recipients. With these qualifications in mind, the evidence suggests that in comparison to net transfers, the policy of introducing exchange bureaus has provided the state with a partially effective means for capturing a relatively minor portion of remittance flows.

In addition, the state extracted additional earnings from these monetary reforms through seigniorage, commonly defined as the gains derived from the issuing of new monies.[29] The convertible peso was an effective means for the government to increase its borrowing capabilities, exchanging foreign currency for Cuban government paper with a promise that the paper had value equivalent to that of the dollars being collected. Based on these foreign currency earnings, the Central Bank engaged in seigniorage by making short-term loans to government enterprises and private borrowers with interest rates based on LIBOR[30] points at 90-day terms; CEPAL (1997: 132) estimates that through this mechanism, the Cuban government is able to gain 1 percent on dollar circulation.

The introduction of domestic peso convertibility also contributed to exchange-rate stabilization. As Table 10.3 below shows, the Cuban peso had depreciated in value in the initial years of following the collapse of the Soviet Union, moving from 5 pesos to the U.S. dollar in 1989 to an average 95 pesos per U.S. dollar in 1994 (and a peak value of 1552 pesos in 1993). Once monetary reforms were implemented, this trend was reversed and the variance in the Cuban pesos exchange rate also decreased considerably. After a 66 percent appreciation in 1995 and a 40 percent appreciation the following year, the Cuban peso has fluctuated within the range of 20 to 26 pesos per U.S. dollar from 1997 to 2003 for an average appreciation of 5 percent during the period. The exchange rate has been held constant at 26 pesos in 2002 and 2003. In a January 1999 interview Cuban Minister of Economics and Planning José Luis Rodríguez attested to the positive effect remittance flows had on the extra official exchange rate. When questioned about the size and magnitude of these flows in 1998, Rodríguez responded that he believed the decrease in the exchange rate from 25 to 20 pesos to the U.S. dollar was the most effective proof that remittances had not declined during the year in question (IPS 1999).

Banking Reforms
Complementing monetary policy reforms and the de-penalization of dollar holding, the government reformed the Cuban banking system to attract remittance flows by diversifying financial banking instruments and improving transnational transfer mechanisms. The net effect of these reforms has been to improve the banking and financial infrastructure to ensure that foreign currency transactions, including remittances, are rapid and transparent.

First, Cubans were permitted to open U.S. dollar-denominated checking and interest-bearing savings accounts. By December 1995, 2,508 savings accounts had been opened and total deposits were equivalent to US$4.4 million.[31] One year later, the number of interest-bearing U.S. dollar savings accounts had grown to 4,500, and total deposits equaled US$9.5 million. Two years later, the number of accounts had grown five-fold. According to the U.S.–Cuba Trade and Economic Council, Inc. (2000a), personal U.S. dollar-denominated deposits were estimated at US$50 million in 1998. Confirming this trend, Francisco

Table 10.3 Exchange Rates, Inflation, Monetary Overhang, Seignorage and Interest Rates, 1989–2003

	1989	1990	1991	1992	1993	1994	1995	1996	1997	1998	1999	2000	2001	2002	2003
Official Exchange Rate	1	1	1	1	1	1	1	1	1	1	1	1	1	1	1
Extra-official Exchange rate (annual average)	5	7	20	35	78	95	32	19.2	23	21	20	21	22	26	26
Informal Market Exchange Rate	100	—	—	—	1552	1396	739.6	554.7	—	—	—	—	—	—	—
GDP Deflator (1981=100)	—	—	95.3	98.7	115.9	149.2	164.9	160.5	157.5	162.0	162.7	166.9	—	—	—
GDP Deflator (1997=100)	—	—	—	—	—	—	—	—	100.0	101.3	104.8	106.5	108.4	110.8	111.2
Monetary Liquidity (% GDP)[a]	20	23.9	37.4	51	66.5	48.8	40.2	38.9	38.3	37.5	35.9	37.3	41.8	44.5	38.4
Seignorage (% GDP)[b]	2.5	3.9	9.0	11.0	16.1	-5.4	-3	1.2	-0.4	1.0	—	—	—	—	—
Interest rate for dollar-denominated savings accounts[c] (12 month deposit)									4.5	—			2.0	2.0	2.0
Interest rate for convertible-peso denominated savings account (12 month deposit)										—			4.0	4.0	4.0
Interest rate for peso-denominated savings accounts (12 month deposit)									4.0	—			4.5	5.5	6.00

a. Cumulative excess money in circulation and bank deposits (M1/GDP).
b. Data reported by CEPAL (2000) page 126. The command over societal resources, or the purchasing power obtained by issuing new money, is known as seigniorage. The reduction in value to holders of existing money balances due to the issuance of new money is termed the inflation tax. The sum of the inflation tax and seigniorage is equal to the real (i.e., inflation-adjusted) change in monetary holdings, or real balances. The relationship between them is:

Real Balances = Seigniorage + Inflation Tax.

c. Dollar-denominated accounts were first allowed in 1995.

Source: All indicators are based on data reported by CEPAL (1997, 2000, 2001, 2003 and 2004).

Soberón, president of the Central Bank of the Republic of Cuba, reported at the end of 1999 that greater confidence in the banking system had resulted in a 57 percent increase in U.S. dollar-denominated deposits during that calendar year (U.S.–Cuba Trade and Economic Council, Inc. 2000a). As is the case with CADECA, however, the proportion of dollars brought in through this mechanism remained relatively minor.

Second, the state diversified its banking system by creating new state-owned banks and permitting foreign banks to open branches in Cuba. The Banco Nacional de Cuba had been the only banking entity allowed to operate from 1960 to 1984. In the late 1980s, Cuba opened its banking sector and allowed newly created state-owned commercial banks to enter the financial market.[32] By 1998, at least three new Cuban banks entered the financial market—the Banco Internacional de Comercio created in 1994, the Banco Metropolitano S.A. created in 1996, and Banco de Crédito y Comercio created in 1997. These banks, licensed to operate in Cuban pesos and convertible currencies, seek to increase and modernize banking services for Cubans and foreigners operating commercial transactions in U.S. dollars. Moreover, state-owned banks have modernized themselves, installing ATMs and introducing debit cards to promote foreign currency deposits.

In addition, foreign-owned banks such as the Dutch-owned ING Barings and the Spanish-owned Banco de Sabadell have representative offices in Havana, and Caja Madrid, a Spanish savings bank, has opened a non-bank financial institution joint-venture with Cuba's Banco Popular de Ahorro (Robinson 2002). In May 1997, the government undertook further reform through Law 172 by dividing the Banco Nacional de Cuba (BNC). The Banco Nacional de Cuba was split into a regulatory central bank, the Banco Central de Cuba (BCC), and a commercial bank, which retained the bank's original name, BNC. A regulatory structure for commercial banks and non-bank financial institutions was adopted with Law 173. The banking and financial system continued to grow and reached a size of 8 commercial banks, 18 non-banking financial institutions, 13 foreign-owned bank representation offices and 4 foreign-owned non-banking financial institutions by 2002 (Banco Central de Cuba 2004).

Third, Cuba undertook reforms to link its banking and financial institutions directly to international capital markets. In 1990, Cuba joined S.W.I.F.T., a global bank-owned cooperative supplying secure messaging services and interface software that links 6,766 financial institutions (banks, brokers, investment managers, securities depositories and clearing organizations, and stock exchanges) in 189 countries, including the United States.[33, 34] Since then, the government has also authorized new entities to use S.W.I.F.T. For example, the eight state-owned Cuban banks, the Banco Central de Cuba, Banco Financiero Internacional, S.A., Banco Internacional de Comercio S.A., Banco de Crédito y Comercio, Banco Popular de Ahorro, Banco Metropolitano S.A., Banco Nacional de Cuba, and Banco Exterior de Cuba, all use S.W.I.F.T. for commercial banking transactions.[35]

The Liberalization of the Consumer Market

The development of financial architecture was a necessary and effective first step toward ensuring that private family transfers from abroad would be funneled into the formal economy. Following these efforts, Cuba developed a second wave of reforms targeting consumers. Measures included the creation of spending and investment options at the consumer or household level. Since 1994, the state has developed so-called "dollar stores" and agricultural markets where families can purchase food and household goods. Similarly, the opening of private sector self-employment and housing provides new, albeit limited, investment options for remittance recipients. Cuban tax policy has also been modified to indirectly extract earnings from remittance flows. When the government introduced the first post-revolutionary income tax system in 1994, remittances were the only untaxed dollar earnings. Ad valorem duties in dollar stores and agriculture markets have proven to be effective instruments for indirectly taxing remittance recipients. These policies leverage remittances, while avoiding direct policies that would be disincentives to senders and recipients.

Consumer Spending: Dollar Stores and Agriculture Markets

Following the 1993 U.S. dollar legalization, Cuba revamped foreign currency stores, which had been in operation since the late 1970s, opening them to Cuban consumers. It did so by increasing the number state enterprises operating dollar stores, by diversifying the types of stores, by increasing the stock of Cuban household goods and by linking these stores to the new financial architecture that was being developed.

As these stores operate in dollars, the majority of their customers are primarily remittance recipients and also those employed in tourism-related activities. Cuba diversified ownership and expanded store operation nationwide through various Cuban state enterprises, including firms such as CIMEX, TRD-Caribe, Cubalse and Caracol, each of which owns a particular U.S. dollar store chain. For example, the Tiendas de

Recuperación de Divisas (TRD) stores are owned by TRD Caribe, part of the Ministry of the Revolutionary Armed Forces' (MINFAR's) Financial Division. By 2000, this chain had opened more than 400 TRD stores throughout the island.[36] In total, Ross and Mayo (2003: 10) estimate that there were 300 retail dollar stores in Havana and a total of approximately 1000 nation-wide in 2003.

In addition, the stock of goods has changed to better meet consumer needs and preferences.[37] Whereas initially, dollar stores were targeted to foreign tourists and contained luxury items, today they contain a vast array of basic food items, such as eggs, proteins, milk and coffee—goods that are no longer available in sufficient quantity through the state-rationed *libreta*. These well-supplied stores also sell processed foods, such as tomato paste, cooking oil, and fruit juice—goods that are available only in these stores. Finally, some stores also contain sections with clothing, consumer electronics—fans, televisions, air-conditioners—and beauty supplies.

Table 10.4 State-Enterprise Dollar Sales to Cuban Consumers and Tourists, 1993–2003

	Annual Gross Revenue in "dollar stores" (US$ million)	Sales from Domestic Suppliers in "dollar stores" (percentage)
1993	263	—
1994	220	—
1995	580	18%
1996	640	27%
1997	700	43%
1998	870	46%
1999	—	47%[a]
2000	1,250	48%
2001	1,100	55%
2002	—	—
2003	1,300	—

a. *Granma.* 12 December 1999. "En los resultados de 1999 se aprecia una mejoría, ante todo, en los indicadores de eficiencia económica"

Source: The data for 1993 to 1998 is from Marquetti Nodarse and García Álvarez (1998:49). The data from 2000 to 2003 is based on EIU Cuba Country Reports (February 2001: 22 and February 2002: 21) and EIU Country Profile Reports (2002: 31 and 2003: 39)

Part of the strategy to cater to consumers has included shifting toward more efficient local suppliers. State enterprises have increased the proportion of domestically produced goods sold in dollar stores. Table 10.4 presents a summary of total annual dollar store sales from 1993 to 2003, as well as the proportion of these sales that can be attributed to domestic production. Whereas only 18 percent of goods sold by dollar stores were manufactured in Cuba in 1995, the percentage had reached 55 percent in 2001. Cuban food processing and light manufacturing industries, for example, grossed US$137 million and US$200 million respectively by 2000 (EIU 2001: 22).

Dollar stores have introduced modernized payment systems, facilitating the link between receiving remittances and consumer spending. Cuban consumers visiting some dollar stores can conveniently use their Transcard electronic debit cards. Western Union has also located its offices in CIMEX-operated dollar stores. Consumers can pick up remittances sent by a relative at the Western Union desk and seamlessly proceed to purchase a range of commodities from basic household items to nonessentials.

Liberalized in 1994, agricultural markets seek to increase the supply, diversity and availability of food for Cuban households. By 1999, food spending in these markets represented approximately 10 percent of household expenditures (Peters 2000: 13). The majority of sales in agricultural markets go to private farmers, cooperatives, state farms, and intermediaries. However, here too, the state has introduced measures to capture earnings. Similar to the strategy of locating Western Union and CADECA bureaus within or alongside dollar stores, CADECA bureaus have been conveniently located within agricultural markets. However, unlike dollar stores, agricultural markets are required to operate in Cuban pesos.

While exchange bureaus placed in agricultural markets have been only partially successful in attracting dollars, the strategy to encourage remittance flows through dollar stores, on the other hand, has proven highly successful in several terms. Dollar stores are sources of state financing. State enterprises operating dollar stores sell imported goods at an average 240 percent markup and domestically produced goods at a 170 percent markup. A small proportion of this markup is reinvested within the state enterprise to finance production and operations. The majority of revenue extracted from dollar store markups is directed toward the state budget. The magnitude of dollar store sales relative to Cuba's balance of payments is also considerable. By 2003, gross annual sales in dollar stores were US$1.3 billion in comparison to US$915 million in net current transfers. Finally, the shift to domestic, and mostly state-owned, suppliers has reduced the state's need to finance costly imports, which have to be paid in foreign currency.

Investment Options: Formal and Informal Assets

Whereas Cuban government policy has liberalized options for consumer saving and spending that indirectly tap into remittance flows, policies to liberalize small-scale private business activity and housing, two common uses of remittances cited in the international literature, have remained limited. The restrictions on private investment are consistent with the state's strategy to limit the productive uses of remittances outside the state sphere of the economy.

Starting in 1993, the Cuban government authorized self-employment and liberalized the small-scale transportation and service sectors of the economy, which require comparatively lower start-up costs and levels of investment.[38] Since then, roughly 3 percent of the Cuban labor force has obtained licenses to work as *cuenta propistas*, or self-employed workers with private businesses in 170 different occupations. Small-scale private business activities in university-trained professions and in the manufacturing and industrial spheres of the economy were not liberalized.

Several policies have been introduced to limit the growth of the self-employed sector. Workers in these mostly service sector firms must be family members. Self-employed business operators are required to obtain their supplies from state distributors or to prove that the goods were obtained from officially registered, tax paying suppliers. Despite these restrictions, there are reasons to presume that remittance flows have entered the private sphere of the economy. Many of these activities, such as *paladares* or family restaurants, require significant start-up capital and continued investments. These capital requirements far exceed the income available to Cubans through formal jobs. Moreover, the lack of credit markets and sustained economic contraction make it difficult to conceive that these investments are being made exclusively with domestic capital. As Duany (2000) suggests, "anecdotal information indicates that many *cuenta propia* workers frequently receive dollars per remittances."

Housing has been cited as the most significant unmet need of Cubans during the 1990s, with significant expenditures required for rehabilitation and repair. Most of these costs surpass the salaries of peso earners, yet according to Hamberg (2001: 6), 85 percent of Cubans own their own homes and between two-thirds to three-quarters of all units created since 1959 are "self-built." While scarce and costly food needs took precedence over housing repair for most Cuban consumers, self-building and rehabilitation continued throughout the decade of the crisis. It is likely that remittances financed these expenditures, as in other countries, where private family transfers have been used to purchase and finance homes. In the case of Cuba, government policy has tightly constrained investments in housing and real estate property exchanges since 1959. Non-transferable property rights have been reinforced by stiff regulations and penalties for illegal housing sales, as well as for self-building in the 1990s. Those choosing to undertake self-building are subject to heavy fines.

Fiscal Policy: Income and Sales Taxes

In August 1994, the Cuban government introduced a personal income tax system as part of a larger tax reform. For the first time since 1959, progressive taxes ranging from 5 percent to 50 percent on personal income earned through wages, salaries, interest, dividends and income derived from currency exchange were collected from Cuban households. In the income tax law, remittances were not considered income and therefore were excluded from income taxes.

However, as income taxes impose duties on all earnings of productive economic activities in the dollar-based economy, remittances targeted toward these areas are indirectly taxed. Recipients depositing their dollars in savings accounts pay taxes on the interest earned. Recipients investing in private self-employment pay income taxes on their profits, as the tax code obliges businesses to pay taxes in the same currency as their earnings. Therefore, self-employed businesses with sales in U.S. dollars must pay taxes in the same currency. Nuñez Moreno (1998: 8) estimates that *cuentrapropistas* paid income taxes equivalent to 1 percent of the total state budget in 1998.[39] The earnings of those in the self-employed sector, such as *paladares* and room rentals, comprised two-thirds of total income tax earnings in 2001 (CEPAL 2001: 68).

Other indirect mechanisms for taxing remittances have been introduced with value-added taxes on final sales conducted in U.S. dollars. These taxes, for example, have been instituted at artisan handicrafts markets where light manufacturing products, such as shoes, are sold. Luxury taxes have also been instituted on items such as tobacco. Taxes on dollar store purchases are also a significant source of revenue. Although data on the proportion of fiscal revenues collected in U.S. dollars are not available, total indirect taxes amounted to 60.6 percent of fiscal revenue in 2003 (CEPAL and INIE 2004).

The Official Remittance Transfer System

Whereas the first and second wave of policy reforms focused on monetary policy reform and the augmentation of consumer and investment infrastructure, the third wave of reforms has focused on developing Cuba's infrastructure by establishing official remittance channels and strengthening relationships with the Cuban émigré community vis-à-vis migration policy. Strategically, Cuba first developed a domestic strategy and shifted toward remittance and migration policy only after in-country channels were in operation and policy makers had had a chance to test their effectiveness in attracting and directing ongoing private flows toward the official economy.

Cuba has created a wide variety of options for remittances to be sent through bank and non-bank channels, primarily through subsidiaries of the government-owned CIMEX Corporation. Because U.S. policy restricts the amounts and channels for sending remittances through banks, money transmitter companies, and postal services that can be sent by U.S. residents, as will be explained further on in this chapter, a variety of transfer instruments accessible from the United States via third countries have been created as well.[40] These six channels, which comprise the official remittance transfer system operating in Cuba as of 2004, are described below.

First, funds can be wired through banks in many European, North American, and Latin American countries, including Italy, Mexico, Venezuela, and Spain, which have established cooperation agreements with the banking system (see Table 10.5). The bank emitting the transfer charges a fee to the sender and the Cuban bank charges a commission to the recipient. For example, cash transfers can be sent from Caja de Ahorros y Monte de Piedad de Madrid in Spain to recipients' accounts in the Banco Popular de Ahorro in Cuba with average wire fees split by both banks. Senders pay a 4.5 percent commission in Spain and recipients pay a 5 percent commission in Cuba. By 2003, Banco Popular de Ahorro had set up agreements with more than 48 banks in Europe, Latin America and Canada (BDA 2003).

Table 10.5 The Cuban Remittance Transfer System: Banking Institutions

Foreign Firms[a]	Annual Amount	Transfer Fee (percent)	Cuban Partner
ARGENTARIA, Caja Postal y Banco Hipotecario S.A. (Spain)	n.a.	2.5–5.0%	Banco Financiero Internacional (BFI)
Havana International Bank Ltd (UK)	n.a.	n.a.	Cuban Banks
Ing Barings (Holland)	n.a.	n.a.	Cuban Banks
Netherlands Caribbean Bank N.V. (Dutch Antilles)	n.a.	n.a.	Cuban Banks
National Bank Of Canada (Canada)	n.a.	10%+	Cuban Banks
Banco Bilbao Vizcaya (Spain)	n.a.	n.a.	Cuban Banks
Banco Sabadell (Spain)	n.a.	n.a.	Cuban Banks
Fransabank Sal (Lebanon)	n.a.	n.a.	Cuban Banks
Banco Nacional De Comercio Exterior Snc (Bancomext) (Mexico)	n.a.	n.a.	Cuban Banks
Caribbean Finance Investments Ltd (UK)	n.a.	n.a.	Cuban Banks
Caja de Ahorros y Monte de Piedad de Madrid (Caja Madrid–CM— (Spain)	n.a.	5% (BPA) + 4.5% (CM)	Banco Popular de Ahorro (BPA— Corporación Financiera Habana (CFH)
Fincomex Ltd. (UK)	n.a.	n.a.	Cuban Banks

a. These are examples and not a complete list.

Source: Publicly available information from commerical banks and author's interviews

Second, remittances can be sent via a direct money transfer service through money transmitters or remittance forwarders (see Table 10.6). On July 8, 1999, the Cuban government-operated Fincimex S.A., a subsidiary of Corporación CIMEX S.A., in cooperation with Western Union Financial Services International began a direct cash remittance

Table 10.6 The Cuban Remittance Transfer System: Remittance Forwarders

Foreign Firms[a]	Annual Amount	Transfer Fee (percent)	Cuban Partner
Western Union	US$250,000,000(2001)[c]	10–30%	CIMEX
MoneyGram[b]	n.a.	9–22%	CIMEX
Caribe Express	n.a.	10–18%	Banco Financiero Inter- nacional (BFI), Banco de Credito y Comercio (Bandec), Transcard and OceanCard.
One Money Transfers	n.a.	8.6–26%	CIMEX
El Español	n.a.	n.a.	n.a.
Ria Financial Ser- vices (U.S.)	n.a.	n.a.	n.a.
Duales (Canada)	n.a.	10–15%	n.a.
Cash2Cuba (Canada)	US$320,000 (2002)[d]	10–22%	CIMEX
Antillas Express	n.a.	8–7%	CIMEX

a. These are examples and not a complete list.
b. MoneyGram began transfers to Cuba in 2000 and entered into a joint venture agreement with Transcard in 2001.
c. Author's calculations. In a summary table, Orozco (2002: 4) cites 2001 IDB/MIF survey data of a representative sample of migrants in the U.S. showing that 32.1 percent of all Cuban émigrés reported sending transfers through Western Union. Based on this ratio and the total World Bank estimated flows of net current transfers in 2001 of US$813 million, the estimated market size for Western Union would be approximately equal to the figures reported in this table.
d. Cash2Cuba has been in operation since 1997, it transfers funds through Transcard or a money order. Figures are for December 2002. Cash2Cuba reported it had registered 10,000 users in its first month of online operation.

Source: Author's calculations, author's confidential interviews with industry reprsentatives, as well as publicly available information released by Antillas Express, Caribe Express, ICC Corporation and Moneygram.

service between Cuba and the United States. Western Union has opened offices throughout Cuba in CIMEX-operated dollar stores, where Cuban recipients can pick up their transfers in U.S. dollars. Western Union requires cash payment and charges US$29 per transaction regardless of whether the amount is US$25 or US$300.[41] Transaction fees, ranging from 10 to 30 percent, are charged to senders and split between both firms, with the Cuban firm receiving a proportionately larger share of the total.

The growth in money transmitter companies servicing Cuba has been remarkable. As of June 2002, there were 100 Western Union-CIMEX offices in Havana and 14 provincial offices operating in Cuba. In addition, there are several other money transmitters that wire cash to Cuba throughout Canada, Latin America, and the United States. MoneyGram, the second-largest money-transmitting company in the United States, opened its operations to Cuba in December 2000. The growth in the amount of remittances transferred through money transmitters has also risen. For example, Panagea, a firm which led Western Union's marketing campaign on the launching of the new service, reported that "for the year 2000, actual sales volume and revenue [for Western Union] exceeded goals by 65 percent, and incrementally grew by triple digits versus the prior year. (2003)"

Third, remittances can be sent to a debit card held by individual Cuban recipients. The debit card, Transcard, began operations in Cuba in 1998. Similar to a check card with respect to appearance and usage, senders from anywhere in the world (including the United States) remit funds via a money order, bank wire, or electronic fund to a specified recipient account number in Canada. Transcard Canada then transfers these funds to a debit account in Cuba within three working days. The Cuban government-operated Fincimex S.A., a subsidiary of Corporación CIMEX S.A., in cooperation with TransCard, issued by Canada-based TransCard Canada Limited, jointly manages the Transcard remittance service. The revenue derived from the service fee, which ranges between 5.0 and 5.5 percent, is shared between the two firms.

Cuban consumers receive the equivalent U.S. dollar sum as a prepaid credit. Consumers can carry an unlimited amount of funds on a single card that can be used for purchases in a wide variety of stores on the island. As Table 10.7 shows, Transcard reported 100,000 cardholders in Cuba in 2000, equivalent to 1.5 percent of the working age population. In 2004, a new debit card was introduced by the Empresa de Telecomunicaciones de Cuba S.A. (ETECSA), a Cuban-Italian joint venture, which permits electronic transfers from Italy and Spain to Cuba via its subsidiary, SerCuba.

The volume of remittances transferred through this debit card has posted positive results, although the overall volumes are lower than money transmitter volumes reported by Western Union and others. According to Fincimex, US$11.5 million were debited to Cuban cardholders in 1998.[42] One year later, the sum tripled, with Transcard Canada Limited reporting that "over US$33 million were transferred to Cuba from fund capturing agents in Florida in 1999."[43] In October 2000, Transcard Canada modified its remittance forwarding service to comply with U.S. regulations. Prior to this date, remitters in the United States could send an unlimited amount of funds to Cuba via Canada. The new reforms require U.S. remittance senders to use a pre-authorized, U.S. based agent or merchant for deposits. In the United States, Transcard has expanded its operations by entering into agency agreements in place with competitors including, Va Cuba Inc. and Money-Gram Payment Services Inc.[44]

Fourth, private family transfers can be sent via couriers. Courier companies, such as DHL and A.I.S. (American International Service), operate door-to-door service from the United States to Cuba. DHL, which has operated in Cuba since 1990, sent 80,000 packages to Cuba in 1998 for US$81 per pound (U.S.–Cuba Trade and Economic Council 1999). While other courier firms have more competitive prices, this channel remains the most expensive in comparison to the other five options available to remittance senders.

Fifth, relatives living abroad can authorize their families in Cuba to utilize credit cards on which they agree to pay balances. Credit cards accepted in Cuba include Visa credit cards, issued by Visa International's Mexico subsidiary Banco Confia, and MasterCard credit cards, issued by MasterCard International. In addition, remittance senders can use credit cards issued by Cuba's Banco Financiero Internacional, Argentina's CabalCard and Mexico's Banamex credit card.[45] According to the U.S.–Cuba Trade and Economic Council (2000a), "the Office of Foreign Assets Control (OFAC) of the United States Department of the Treasury in Washington, D.C., permits individuals not subject to United States law to use Visa credit cards and MasterCard credit cards for transactions within the Republic of Cuba provided that the Visa and MasterCard credit cards are not issued by United States-based financial institutions."

Sixth, Cuba has entered agreements to facilitate transfers via postal money orders in Latin America and the Caribbean, as well as Europe. In June 1999, Correos de Costa Rica, S.A. signed an agreement with Correos de Cuba to transfer remittances electronically between the two countries. A maximum of US$500 can be transferred per day; a 9 percent commission fee is split between the companies. According to an interview reported in the press, the Costa Rican Postal Services director cited the significantly higher commissions charged by other services in the Cuban remittance market as a primary motivation for becoming involved in this business venture. According to Director Ricardo Toledo, "Costa Rica views this as a labor on humanitarian grounds (*La Prensa* 11 June 1999)." Table 10.7 summarizes the Cuban firms and foreign partners involved in remittance transfers through debit cards, couriers, credit cards and postal services.

Relative to the total amount of remittances transferred from abroad, the amounts sent via official channels have increased since the introduction of financial channels. For example, Fincimex (2003) reported that between October 1995 and December 1998, US$43 million were transferred through banks and home delivery services prior to the introduction of services such as Western Union and the Transcard debit system. Based on the World Bank data on net current transfers for the same period, this would be equivalent to less than 2 percent of all remittances received by Cuban recipient families in the same period. By 2001, based on the author's calculations and presented in Tables 10.6 and 10.7, an estimated minimum of US$283,650 million had been sent through two of the official channels (Western Union and Transcard). Based on World Bank published estimates of current transfers in the same year, the data suggests that roughly 35 percent of the total volume of remittances were sent through two of these official channels.

Although data on total official flows were not available for all six channels, it is reasonable to expect that the majority of official remittances are sent either through money transmitters or debit cards. The quantity and value of the remaining channels, which include banks, courier, credit cards, and postal service transactions, can be expected to be at relatively low levels within Cuba, as the majority of transactions are in specie, rather than financial instruments. This assumption is also corroborated in survey data on Cuban émigré patterns. In a summary table, Orozco (2002: 4) cites 2001 IDB/MIF survey data of a representative sample of migrants in the United States showing that 32.1 percent of all Cuban émigrés reported sending transfers through Western Union, 3.6 percent used courier services and 10.7 percent sent funds through credit unions. Yet, the figures presented in this study also indicate that large shares of remittances are clearly being transferred through non-official channels. This too is corroborated by Oro-

Table 10.7 The Cuban Remittance Transfer System: Debit Cards, Couriers, Credit Cards and Postal Services

Type of Institution	Foreign Firms[a]	Annual Amount	Transfer Fee (percent)	Cuban Partner
Debit cards[b]	Trans$card (Canada)	US$33,000,000 (1999)[e]	5.5–5.0%	Fincimex
	QuickCash	US$650,000(2001)[f]	10–20%	Cuba Express and Banco Popular de Ahorro (BPA)
	SerCuba[d]	n.a.	3.6–13%	Empresa de Telecomunicaciones de Cuba S.A. (ETECSA)
Couriers[c]	American International Service, S.A.	n.a.	4–10%	CIMEX
	DHL	n.a.	US$80.40/ 1lb	UTISA[g]
Credit cards	BFI Card	n.a.	n.a.	Banco Financiero Internacional (BFI)
	Banamex	n.a.	n.a.	n.a.
Postal Service	Correos de Costa Rica, S.A.	n.a.	9%	Correos de Cuba, S.A.
	ICC Corporation Giro Postal[h]	n.a.	60%–17%	Correos de Cuba, S.A.

a. These are examples and not a complete list.
b. Deposits can be sent via internet.
c. Couriers perform cash delivery service to residents in Cuba.
d. This service started in 2004.
e. Fincimex reported that US$11.5 millon were transferred using TRAN$CARD in 1998 and Transcard reported that U$33,000,000 were transferred in 1999. According to Transcard, there were an estimated 98,000 cardholders in Cuba in 1999 and 100,000 by 2002. Fincimiex reports 82,289 users in 2001. As of 2003, Transcard reports that it is accepted at over 6000 point of sale locations and at financial institution locations throughout Cuba where funds can be withdrawn as cash.
f. QuickCash data are for 2001; the comparable figure for 1998 was US$220,000.
g. UTISA is a Panama-based Cuban firm.
h. Money order amounts are limited to between US$15 and US$100.

Source: Author's calculations, author's confidential interviews with industry reprsentatives, as well as publicly available information released by Camara de Comercio de Cuba (2002), CEPAL (2000), Quickcash, ETECSA and Transcard.

zco (2002: 4) who reports that, on average, senders transmitted 46.4 percent of remittances to Cuba with friends traveling to Cuba.

Migration Policy

With a worsening economic crisis during the 1990s, Cuban émigrés increasingly left for economic reasons, rather than as part of a political exodus, as had occurred during the early years of the revolution. Indeed, a 1993 University of Havana study of 188 rafters whom the Cuban government intercepted at sea found 83 percent to be seeking refuge in the United States to help island family in need. (Martínez, Martín, Morejon, et al. 1996). Recognizing a shift from political to economically-driven migration among émigrés, especially those who left the island after 1980, Cuba undertook significant policy reform to improve relations with émigrés and, for the first time in five decades, to facilitate temporary migration.

Since 1994, the Ministry of Foreign Relations has maintained a special office, Dirección de Asuntos de Cubanos Residentes en el Exterior (DACRE), dedicated to émigrés relations. The office sponsored two conferences on the Nation and Migration in 1995 and 1995, and began publishing a quarterly magazine. Travel policies for émigrés returning to visit their families have eased as well. Although Cuban émigrés are considered Cuban citizens, those who emigrated after 1970 were required to enter the country with both a Cuban passport and visa. In 1996, the Cuban government introduced a multiple-entry permit and, for the first time, permitted repatriation of any émigré over the age of 60. In October 2003, these measures were furthered with the announcement that effective April 2004 Cuban residents living abroad with an authorized passport would be able to enter the country without a visa in prepration for the third conference on the Nation and Migration in May 2004. As previously mentioned, political discourse has also advanced, with senior government officials referring to émigrés as members of the "community," as well as "compatriots living in the United States" (Martín and Pérez 1997: 114).

Policies have also been instituted to expand citizenship rights for émigrés. For example, the Cuban government has even extended investment and bank account privileges to émigrés. Émigrés, according to the 1993 Foreign Investment Law, enjoy private property and investment rights denied to remaining islanders (although the U.S. embargo prohibits Cuban-Americans from taking advantage of the government opening). They also may now open U.S. dollar bank accounts in Cuba.

Meanwhile, during the second Nation and Migration Conference in Cuba, Cuban-Americans gave testimony to the National Assembly on the effect of a new citizenship law, making recommendations on how changes could be incorporated to address émigrés "trans-national" character.

Finally, Cubans who legally leave the island are no longer considered permanent migrants. The government has gradually lowered the age for those seeking to visit their relatives abroad, a common exit route for migration. Previously only men over the age of 55 and women over the age of 50 were allowed to visit their relatives abroad, but by 1994 any Cuban over the age of 18 could apply for an exit permit (Martín and Pérez 1997: 4). For the first time, the Cuban government also liberalized migration policy to permit temporary departure. Those who obtain legal permission (*permisos de residencia en el exterior*) may reside outside of Cuba for up to 11 months with full citizenship rights and privileges, as long as they pay a fee for each additional month after the first month they reside abroad. Fees vary across countries by income level. Whereas émigrés living in the United States or Europe pay US$175 per month, those living in Mexico or the Dominican Republic pay US$30 per month.[46] Migration scholars estimate that 10,000 such permits have been granted.[47] Those who choose to leave illegally, such as the estimated 45,000 Cubans who left between 1990 and 1994 during the *balsero* crisis, are excluded from these terms.[48]

A Synopsis of Cuba's Strategy

In sum, private family transfers to Cuba from abroad, mainly from U.S.-based senders, surged dramatically in the 1990s. The legalization of the U.S. dollar in 1993 was a critical first step, but the development of a domestic and external financial architecture for remittances has been crucial in establishing a long-term strategy to sustain their continued flow. In 2003, net current transfers were reported to have increased to US$915 million, US$606 million more per year than in 1994. Indeed, official data show that remittances grew at an average rate of 16 percent per year over the ten-year period from 1994 to 2003 and exceeded foreign direct investment by over US$3 billion dollars.

The evidence presented in this section suggests that the Cuban government strategy has been moderately successful in attracting remittance flows via official channels through the wide-ranging set of financial instruments developed in the 1990s. This strategy has been less successful in increasing the rate of growth of remittances. Official data show that growth rates declined from the peak rates in the early 1990s immediately following dollar legalization and even decreased slightly in 2001 and 2002. Nonetheless, despite being an important source for financing Cuba's balance of payments obligations in foreign currency, remittances have been insufficient to cover Cuba's trade deficit (in goods only), which stood at US$2.6 billion in 2002.

U.S. Policy: From Prohibition to Control

Having examined the impact of Cuban government strategies with respect to the sending and use of remittances by recipient families, this chapter now turns to examining U.S. policy toward the sending of remittances to Cuba. Since 1963, U.S. law has imposed tight restrictions on the transfer of remittances, as well as on direct travel to Cuba and visitor expenditures on the island. Prohibitions and controls on private transfers to island relatives resulted from an overall U.S. strategy to restrict Cuba's access to dollars as a means of fomenting economic hardship and island discontent with the Castro regime. These policies were briefly loosened between 1978 and 1982, when the United States first permitted remittances to be sent to Cuba. Since then, U.S. policy has attempted to tighten controls by issuing regulations, restrictions, and caps on the amount of remittances that can be sent to Cubans on the island and for a brief four-year period, between 1994 in 1998, discontinued official transfers altogether. In 2003, the United States partially shifted its policy by maintaining restrictions, but significantly increasing maximum amounts. This policy was reversed in 2004 when restrictions were again tightened. This section on U.S. policy towards Cuba seeks to focus on understanding how host countries attempt to affect the flow of remittances and the degree to which restrictive host country policies can be effective.

Prohibition

Following the successful overthrow of the U.S.-backed Batista dictatorship in 1959, relations between the United States and Cuba's revolutionary government gradually eroded. As Washington's fears of the populist, and possibly Communist, ideological orientation of the Cuban government increased, U.S. policy makers began to employ overt and covert tactics to destabilize the emerging anti-capitalist regime in the economic, as well as political, sphere. In the following decade, Washington established a global economic blockade strategy toward export-dependent Cuba. This tactic aimed to block Cuba's access to foreign currency by severing its own economic ties with the island, as well as those of Cuba's major trading and borrowing partners in the West.[49] On the international front, the United States pressured its allies into following similar policies by cutting off ties between Cuban and international banking institutions.[50]

Although reliable estimates are not available, remittances were sent back to the island by Cuban arrivals to the United States in the early 1960s, but these were primarily sent to facilitate migration (García 1996: 17). Dollars were transferred via postal money orders, the primary channel for sending funds to Cuba at that time. When direct mail between Cuba and the United States was suspended in 1962, this channel ceased to be an option (Sullivan and Morales 2002: 10).

As part of its strategy to issue comprehensive sanctions, the U.S. Treasury Department's Office of Foreign Assets Control (OFAC) issued the Cuban Assets Control Regulations (CACR) on July 8, 1963 under the authority of the Trading with the Enemy Act, codifying and further tightening the trade embargo that had been issued by President Kennedy in 1962.[51,52] Under the original regulations, any transfer of property, including cash and other specie, were prohibited. Section 515.201 of the 1963 CACR regulations prohibited U.S. citizens, residents, and corporations from engaging in "(1) all transfers of credit and all payments…; (2) all transactions in foreign exchange by any person within the United States; and, (3) the exportation or withdrawal from the United States of gold or silver coin or bullion, currency or securities by any person within the United States " with Cuba and its nationals.

From 1963 to 1978, U.S. policy outlawing transfers reinforced Cuba's de facto policies inhibiting family ties and remittance flows. Since direct commercial bank transfers were prohibited by U.S. law and strictly regulated by OFAC, any currency or in-kind transfers that took place during this period required a triangular payment system through a third country.

Partial Lifting on the Sending of Remittances

Under President Carter, the United States sought to achieve the normalization of diplomatic and economic relations with Cuba. Easing travel and remittances were top items on the administration's agenda. In March 1977, the Carter administration announced several modifications to the CACR designed to liberalize travel and remittances from the United States to Cuba. Section 515.563 of the CACR amended the original regulations to provide for "a general authorization for family remittances for the support of close relatives in Cuba." Under the new regulations, family remittances were not to exceed a maximum US$500 per quarter to close relatives in Cuba (Kaplowitz 1998: 97).

In 1978, the Office of Foreign Assets Control implemented revised CACR instructions permitting remittances to be transferred to Cuba through licensed family remittance forwarders or U.S. banks. Since U.S. policy continued to prohibit direct financial transfers, there were two alternate routes for getting funds to families in Cuba. Transfers either had to be hand-carried by remittance forwarding institutions from the United States to Cuba in specie, or the authorized entity in the United States was required to transfer funds to a third-country financial institution from which the Cuban-based entities would then obtain the funds. Thus, although transfers were permitted, regulations imposed significant transaction costs on companies engaged in sending remittances to Cuba.

Thus, Carter administration policy allowed legally authorized remittances for the first time since the 1962 prohibition of financial transactions and travel put an end to officially sanctioned flows. The explanation for the policy shift on Cuban remittances can best be understood as part of U.S. immigration policy toward Cuba in the context of the Cold War. Since 1959, U.S. policy was based on the premise that migration was caused by a political exodus of Cubans fleeing from communism. Upon arrival in the United States, Cuban exiles were given preferential treatment, with benefits including automatic qualification for citizenship after one year and one day of residency in the United States and the possibility to participate in re-settlement programs (Eckstein and Barberia 2001: 3).

By allowing private remittances to flow to families, President Carter sought to support those Cubans remaining on the island, who were viewed as victims of communism. An additional feature of the Carter administration's policy on remittances corroborates this proposition. In addition to allowing US$500 in remittances to be sent to families on the island per quarter, the new 1978 CACR regulations added an additional US$500 remittance that could be sent for relatives who were emigrating to the United States (Kaplowitz 1998: 97). Interestingly, despite the numerous revisions to the CACR, the amount and clause on the sending of funds to assist those trying to leave the island has remained intact since 1978.

Moreover, the Carter administration pursued this strategy not only by liberalizing remittance flows, but also by entering into secret negotiations with the Cuban government aimed at securing the release of 3,000 political prisoners to the United States and the improvement of relations with émigrés through the relaxation of Cuban government restrictions on travel, remittances, and migration. Although inter-governmental negotiations were publicly replaced by the first negotiations between the Cuban government and a small group of 75 émigrés in the 1978 National Dialogue talks, the Carter administration is recognized as having been the "architect" behind the scenes and in line with its human rights promotion agenda (García 1996: 48).

Attempts to Control and Cap Remittance Flows

The U.S. liberalization of remittances to Cuba initiated in 1978 lasted until 1980. However, in 1980, actions by both governments abruptly closed the gateway that had been opened regularizing family ties. Cuba, partly in reaction to the 1980 Mariel Boatlift exodus of more than 125,000 Cubans from the island, limited émigré family visits. The Reagan administration set out to return to the U.S.'s traditional approach of a comprehensive embargo on Cuba. In 1982, the Reagan administration announced the revocation of general travel authorization, but maintained the modifications introduced by the Carter administration allowing émigrés to return to the island to visit close relatives under the rubric of the general license (Kaplowitz 1998: 123).

The sending of remittances, left untouched in the CACR's revisions conducted in 1982, were restricted four years later in 1986 (Kaplowitz 1998: 124). Further tightening occurred in 1988 when OFAC announced the institution of a licensing system for travel service providers and remittance forwarding agencies involved in Cuba-related transactions. Specifically, a new paragraph was introduced to Section 515.563 of the CACR regulations requiring that:

> Persons subject to U.S. jurisdiction, including persons who provide payment forwarding services and non-commercial organizations acting on behalf of donors, who wish to provide services in connection with the collection or forwarding of *remittances* authorized pursuant to this section must obtain a specific license from the Office of Foreign Assets Control (OFAC 1988).

By 1992, over 31 remittance forwarders had received OFAC approval for sending transfers to Cuba, 24 of which were located in the Miami-Dade County (OFAC 1992).

As the economic impact of the collapse of trade and aid with the Soviet Union hit Cuba, U.S. policy sought to reinforce these impacts by furthering economic sanctions to speed Castro's demise. The United States pursued a similar policy with respect to remittances. First, official remittance flows were reduced. In 1991 OFAC announced an amendment to Section 515.563 whereby the limits of US$500 per quarter would be reduced to US$300 per quarter, reducing the annual amount of remittances that could be sent to the island by US$800 or 40 percent (OFAC 1991). Although remittances for island families were reduced, the clause permitting a onetime US$500 remittance allowance for migration, as stipulated since 1978, was left intact.

Three years later, President Clinton went one step further, banning family remittances altogether—except under extreme humanitarian emergencies—from August 1994 until 1998. When massive numbers of Cuban rafters arrived on U.S. shores during the August 1994 *balsero* crisis, Clinton decided to revert U.S. policy to standards established in the early 1960s at the onset of the breakdown in bilateral relations. Reacting to the huge exodus and Cuba's shattered economy, President Clinton revoked the general license clause in the CACR and announced that OFAC would require case-by-case specific licensing for family remittances. Under the new instructions, close relatives in the United States could send remittances to Cuba for severe medical emergencies and/or terminal illness. For those fortunate enough to receive permission to migrate officially, the onetime US$500 remittance benefit could still be sent (OFAC 1995: 7).

This decision to ban remittances reflected a shift in U.S. migration policy toward Cuba. For the first time, the United States reversed its policy of granting preferential treatment to refugees from Cuba, a policy that had been in place for more than 30 years. Instead of receiving the automatic asylum granted to Cuban refugees by the United States since 1959, more than 25,000 rafters were detained at the U.S.-operated Guantánamo Naval Base. Denouncing the *balsero* crisis, President Clinton justified U.S. policy on the following grounds: "The real problem is the stubborn refusal of the Castro regime to have an open democracy and an open economy, and I think the policies we are following will hasten the day when that occurs" (Smith 1996: 302). This shift in U.S.

policy had been loudly advocated by the militantly anti-Castro Cuban-American National Foundation (CANF), which was convinced that starvation and deprivation were the most effective means of toppling the regime. Cuban-American academic Lisandro Pérez reports that in meetings that took place with President Clinton in the aftermath of the *balsero* crisis, CANF President Jorge Mas Canosa "insisted that the President [Clinton] stop remittances entirely. The President agreed to do it" (cited in Azcri 2000: 11).

During the mid-1990s, the U.S. Congress enacted legislation calling for the executive branch to implement further controls on remittance flows to the island. Indeed, both key pieces of U.S. legislation passed in the 1990s focused on tightening sanctions and included a section on "restricted" family remittances to Cuba. The 1992 Cuban Democracy Act—commonly referred to as the Torricelli Act—also called for tightening remittances, although its principal aim was to strengthen sanctions by banning U.S. subsidiary trade with Cuba and deterring shipping trade to Cuban ports. Section 1706 of Title XVII of the Act states that "the President shall establish strict limits on remittances to Cuba by United States persons for the purpose of financing the travel of Cubans to the United States, in order to ensure that such remittances reflect only the reasonable costs associated with such travel, and are not used by the government of Cuba as a means of gaining access to United States currency."

Similarly, Title I, Section 112 of the Cuban Liberty and Democratic Solidarity Act of 1996, commonly referred to as Helms Burton, directs that the President of the United States should,

> before considering the reinstitution of general licenses for family remittances to Cuba, insist that, prior to such reinstitution, the Cuban government permit the unfettered operation of small businesses fully empowered with the right to hire others to whom they may pay wages and to buy materials necessary in the operation of the businesses, and with such other authority and freedom as are required to foster the operation of small businesses throughout Cuba; and (b) if licenses described in subparagraph (a) are reinstituted, require a specific license for remittances described in subparagraph (a) in amounts of more than US$500; and (2) before considering the reinstitution of general licenses for travel to Cuba by individual residents in

the United States who are family members of Cuban nationals who are resident in Cuba, insist on such actions by the Cuban government as abrogation of the sanction for departure from Cuba by refugees, release of political prisoners, recognition of the right of association, and other fundamental freedoms.

Towards the end of the decade, U.S. policy moved once again toward legalizing remittance flows, although maintaining tight controls on transfers. In 1998, the Clinton administration lifted its four-year ban on the transfer of remittances to Cuba. In March 1998, the president announced resumption of family remittances to Cuba at pre-August 1994 levels. Following Pope John Paul II's visit to Cuba in January 1998, OFAC re-authorized individuals subject to United States law with relatives in Cuba to send up to US$300 every four months, or US$1,200 annually, under a general license (OFAC 1998).

Following the resumption of remittances in 1998, Cuban émigrés began sending private money to their families using licensed OFAC remittance agencies in the United States. Cuban-American relatives sending money to the island had to provide data about themselves and the Cuban recipient household, as well as sign a remittance affidavit certifying their knowledge about U.S. remittance policy. Although the decision to re-authorize remittances represented a step toward loosening restrictions on official transfers, the requirement of a remittance affidavit for Cuban remittances sent an alternative message to Cuban émigrés. Given the historical context and political environment in the Cuban-American community with respect to transborder family ties, OFAC licensing requirements represented a significant deterrent. Hardline opponents in the Cuban-American community viewed travel and the sending of remittances as treasonous acts in support of the Castro regime that had forced their exile. Bombings and threats to remittance service providers and travel agencies engaged in "trade with the enemy" had been common occurrences during the late 1970s and early 1980s when Cuban travel agencies and remittance businesses were first opened. Since OFAC regulations required "going public," they provided a disincentive for remittance senders to use official channels for sending private transfers to their families in Cuba.[53]

Remittance policy was liberalized further in January 1999 when President Clinton announced his decision to expand legal remittances by permitting non-governmental organizations and all U.S. citizens, regardless of whether or not they had close Cuban family members on the island, to send cash remittances to Cuba (OFAC 1999). The only limits on such transfers stipulated by the regulations were that funds not go to finance senior-level officials of the Communist Party or senior-level officials of the Cuban government. Non-governmental organizations would be licensed, on a case-by-case basis, to send larger remittances to independent non-governmental entities in Cuba. It is important to note, however, that the United States did not choose to liberalize flows completely. Instead, caps on amounts were maintained and individuals sending remittances were still required to sign remittance affidavits.

While the Clinton administration loosened restrictions on the sending of remittances to Cuba, it cited a similar rationale and motivations used to justify previous decisions on migration and remittance policy towards the island. The purpose of expanding the sending of remittances to Cuban families on the island, a senior official in the State Department explained, was "intended to strengthen support for the Cuban people," to allow them "some elbow room" and "some modicum of independence" (*New York Times*: January 5, 1999). Thus, U.S. government officials presented the relaxation of U.S. policy on remittances as part of Washington's consistent and long-standing "pressure cooker" approach to Cuba policy.[54]

Despite controls and regulation, the number of U.S. firms engaged in transactions increased significantly in the 1990s as result of the re-authorization of travel, remittance and package delivery services to Cuba. Table 10.8 presents a summary of the number of licenses authorizing travel, carrier and remittance forwarding services for transactions with Cuba in 2004, based on data released by the Office of Foreign Assets Control and reported by the U.S. Treasury Department's Office of Foreign Asset Control (2004a). By 2004, OFAC had issued 406 travel-related and service-related licenses to 115 United States-based companies including American Airlines, Western Union Financial Services, and Moneygram Payment Systems. The number of remittance forwarders rose from 31 in 1992 to 126 by 2004. With the majority of these companies located in the Miami-Dade County, there were 90 remittance forwarders authorized to send cash transfers to Cuba in Florida, or roughly two-thirds of the total number of companies sending money to Cuba. The number of couriers who could take in-kind packages totaled 47 and nearly 60 percent of these couriers based in Florida.

Table 10.8 Number of OFAC Licenses by U.S. State and Service Type, 2004

State	Travel Service Providers	Courier Service Providers	Remittance Forwarders	Total
California	23	2	14	39
Arkansas	1	1	1	3
Colorado			1	1
Florida	152	27	90	269
Georgia		1		1
Idaho	1			1
Illinois	3	1	1	5
Indianna	1	1		2
Louisiana	3	2	2	7
Massachusetts	5			5
Minnesota	1	1		2
Nevada	3	1	1	5
New Jersey	11	3	8	22
New York	11	3	4	18
Oregon	2			2
Puerto Rico	5	2	3	10
Tennessee	1			1
Texas	3	1		4
Virginia	1			1
Washington	2			2
Washington, D.C.	4	1	1	6
Total	233	47	126	406

Source: Calculated by the author based on data reported by U.S. Department of the Treasury, Office of Foreign Assets Control (2004)

Since taking office in 2000, the George W. Bush administration has strengthened efforts to limit the flow of U.S. dollars to Cuba, thus pressuring the Cuban government by upholding and strengthening U.S. policy in effect since 1999. Although the administration slightly loosened restrictions in 2003, it quickly overturned and further tightened restrictions by 2004. In March 2003, OFAC regulations were issued that loosened minor restrictions by eliminating the long-standing requirement that there be a "demonstrated humanitarian need"[55] in Cuban-American visits to relatives in Cuba and allowing Cuban-Americans to transport up to US$3,000 in relative remittances when traveling to

Cuba. The 2003 regulations also retained the limit of US$300 in re-mittances per household per quarter.[56] Simultaneously, the Bush ad-ministration committed itself to increased controls on these flows by charging the newly created Department of Homeland Security with en-hancing OFAC's regulations to further curtail illegal transport of goods and funds to Cuba (U.S. Department of Homeland Security 2003).

On June 16, 2004, OFAC enacted amendments to the Cuban As-sets and Control Regulations following the recommendations of the President's Commission for Assistance to a Free Cuba, headed by U.S. Secretary of State General Colin L. Powell. The recent amendments limit travel by émigrés to the island by reducing the number of trips to once every three years (previously émigrés were permitted once per year). The 2004 regulations also eliminate general licenses for home-land travel by Cuban-Americans, requiring Cuban émigrés to apply for a specific OFAC license (OFAC 2004b). After, July 2004 relatives could receive authorization to visit "immediate family" once every three years and to carry a total of US$300 in remittances for family members in Cuba, drastically less than the US$3,000 maximum previously allowed under OFAC regulations.

By 2002, the Commission estimated that 50,650 parcels worth ap-proximately US$243 million were being sent monthly (Commission for Assistance to a Free Cuba 2004: 73). The new amendments restricted the sending of "gift parcels," to a cap of US$200 worth of food, vita-mins, seeds, medicines, medical supplies, clothing which could be sent per month. Non-food parcels could be sent to household recipients no more than once a month. Under the new restrictions, only immediate relatives, a spouse, child, grandchild, parent, grandparent, or sibling, in Cuba could receive cash remittances, though the overall amount that could be sent (US$300 per quarter or US$1,200) remained the same. Thus, the new 2004 OFAC amendments put a tighter cap on the send-ing of unofficial transfers to Cuba by traveler's and in-kind gift parcels and narrowed cash remittances to immediate relatives, but the overall amount of the latter were left unchanged.

A Synopsis of the U.S. Strategy

After decades of prohibition during the early 1960s and 1970s, the United States partially liberalized the sending of monies and gifts to Cuba between 1978 and 1980. Since then, U.S. policy has attempted to control and tighten restrictions on the sending of remittances to Cuba, banning them altogether for four years between 1994 and 1998. The United States has "regulated" remittances as a punitive measure and as an instrument of its foreign policy toward the island. Yet, officially reported flows suggest that these measures were not as successful as intended. In the period from 1994 to 1998 when the United States banned remittances altogether, reported private family transfers to Cuba continued to rise, although at a slower rate. Following U.S. re-authorization in 1998, net transfers increased, but by only 5 percent in 1999. Remittances did decrease in 2001 and 2002 following the worldwide recession and September 11 attacks on the United States, but not as a result of any change in U.S. policy. Thus, neither the tightening, nor the loosening of U.S. policy, appears to have had significant impact on the overall volume of official remittance flows to Cuba.

Conclusion

Since the commencement of hostilities between Cuba and the United States in the early 1960s, both governments have repeatedly attempted to influence private family transfers. Initially, both governments tightly controlled these transactions. In the case of Cuba, restrictive policies were primarily restricted through tight control of monetary policy. In the case of the U.S., policies targeted restrictions on bilateral financial transactions. However, as economic and political dynamics evolved, Cuba's policy shifted more radically from overall prohibition to leveraging remittances. The United States, on the other hand, has largely continued its initial policy approach of limiting remittance flows, despite a relative loosening of earlier regulations governing the amounts and channels Cuban émigrés could use to send funds to their families.

This chapter has attempted to show that Cuba has been partially successful in attracting and channeling remittances toward the state-controlled economy. In the case of the sending country, the analysis of the case of Cuba's reforms suggests that the aggregate flow of remittances and their uses are highly sensitive to macroeconomic, political, and institutional factors. Remittances remained at minimal levels during periods when the Cuban government actively discouraged contact with the Cuban émigré community. In macroeconomic terms, dollar legalization in 1993 was a critical first step in shifting remittance patterns from the émigré community residing abroad. Furthermore, institutional factors were decisive in ensuring that a significant majority of the resources flowed through official channels, both directly, through development of a dollarized financial architecture and indirectly, through the creation of consumer dollar stores.

However, not all policy tools utilized by Cuba to encourage remittance flows through official channels have been effective. Only a small proportion of net transfers have been channeled to interest-bearing U.S. dollar checking and saving accounts or exchanged into domestic currency through exchange bureaus. In contrast, the Cuba government has been largely successful in two areas: official transfer mechanisms and consumer spending. The opening of state-run consumer markets for food and other goods has proven to be an effective means of attracting remittance flows to the official economy. In terms of magnitude, annual dollar sales have surpassed official remittance flows. Based on official data, a higher proportion of remittances are also being sent through official channels, reaching at least 40 percent of total officially reported flows by 2002.

Nearly a decade after reforms were initiated, however, a sizable portion of remittances are still sent through non-official channels and circulate in the extra-official economy. Based on the Cuban government's own reporting of the amount of net transfers, more than half of these total flows continue to be sent through unofficial channels. Similarly, significant flows are not being spent in the state-run economy. Finally, once these resources enter the domestic economy they create impacts, many of which are unanticipated or exert countervailing pressures to the policy goals targeted by the government. A case in point is Cuba's extra-official exchange rate with the convertible peso. As Cuba moves toward a unified exchange rate, the appreciation pressures exerted by remittance flows run counter to the country's export and tourism-oriented development strategy.

U.S. policy toward private family transfers to Cuban relatives on the island has shifted from prohibition of these transactions to capped allowances under tightly regulated procedures. Since the early 1960s, U.S. policy has continued to maintain Cuba's international economic isolation, but has become less effective over time. Cuba has expanded its trade and monetary relations with Western and Latin American countries, allowing it to develop direct financial transactions mechanisms that provide viable third country channels for émigrés in the United States to send funds. In light of the crisis sparked by the collapse of the Soviet Union, tightening measures instituted by the United States have been largely ineffective in limiting the flow of remittances to Cuba. Indeed, during the U.S. ban on remittances from 1994 to 1998, such flows continued and even grew.

In analyzing the effectiveness of Cuban and U.S. government policies on the pattern of remittance flows to Cuba, this chapter presents evidence that migrant-sending governments can be quite effective at enhancing the development role of remittances, even in cases where flows are restricted by the receiving country government, the United States. However, the case of remittances to Cuba also draws attention to the limits faced by governments in attracting flows. The evidence presented in this chapter strongly shows that the majority of net current transfers appear to be largely channeled towards consumption and not productive investment. In addition, the Cuban government has had to incur significant costs in order to increase these flows. The long-term sustainability and effectiveness of this strategy is a question which is only now beginning to be examined.

References

Antillas Express, Inc. (Online) "Envíos de Dinero a Cuba." http://www.antillas-express.com/ (cited July 16, 2001).

Athukorala, Premachandra. 1993. *Enhancing Developmental Impact of Migrant Remittances: A Review of Asian Experiences.* New Delhi: International Labour Organisation, Asian Regional Team for Employment Promotion.

Azicri, Max. 2000. *Cuba Today and Tomorrow: Reinventing Socialism.* Gainesville: University Press of Florida.

Banco Central de Cuba. (Online) 2004. http://www.bc.gov.cu. (cited August 8, 2004).

Banco Nacional de Cuba. 1996. *Informe económico 1995.* Havana: BNC.

Banco Popular de Ahorro. (Online). 2003. http://www.bancopopulardeahorro.com. (cited 20 August 20, 2003).

Barberia, Lorena; Johnson, Simon and Daniel Kaufmann. 1997. "Social Networks in Transition." Davidson Discussion Paper No. 102, University of Michigan Business School, October 1997.

Birks, J.S. and C.A. Sinclair. 1979. "Migration and Development: The Changing Perspective of the Poor Arab Countries." *Journal of International Affairs,* 33:2: 285–309.

Camara de Comércio de Cuba. (Online) http://www.camaracuba.cubaweb.cu/. (cited August 10, 2002).

Caribe Express. (Online) http://www.caribeexpress.com/ (cited August 10, 2002).

Castro, Fidel Ruz. 1993. "Castro Gives Speech at Moncada Barracks Anniversary." Latin American Network Information Center (LANIC) Castro Speech Database. (Online database) http://lanic.utexas.edu/la/cb/cuba/castro.html. (cited June 22, 2000).

Centro para el Estudio de la Economía Cubana. 1997. *Balance de la Economía Cubana a finales de los 90s.* Havana, Cuba: Universidad de La Habana.

Comisión Económica para América Latina y el Caribe (CEPAL). (1997) 2000. *La Economía Cubana: Reformas Estructurales y Desempeño en los '90s.* Mexico D.F.: Fondo de Cultura Económica.

———. 2001. "Cuba: Evolución Económica durante 2000." LC/MEX/L.465. Mexico: CEPAL.

———. 2003. "Cuba: Evolución Económica durante 2002 y perspectivas para 2003." LC/MEX/L.566. Mexico: CEPAL.

———. and Instituto Nacional de Investigaciones Económicas. 2004. "Política social y reformas estructurales: Cuba a principios del siglo XXI." LC/MEX/G.7 LC/L.2091. Mexico: CEPAL.

Cox, Donald and Emmanuel Jimenez. 1990. "Social Objectives: through Private Transfers: a Review." *The World Bank Research Observer.* 5:205–218.

Cox, Donald, Zekeriya Eser and Emmanuel Jimenez. 1998. "Family Safety Nets during Economic Transition: the Study of Family Transfers in Russia." in *Poverty, Policy and Responses: the Russian Federation in Transition* edited by Jeni Klugman. Washington D.C.: World Bank.

CUBAPOLIDATA Gateway to Cuba's Political and Military Data. "*Cuban Armed Forces Review.*" (Online) http://cubapolidata.com/cafr/cafr_business_activities.html. (cited July 12, 2002).

De Sipio, Louis. 2000. "Sending Money Home . . . For Now: Remittances and Immigrant Adaptation in the United States." Washington D.C.: InterAmerican Dialogue and The Tomás Rivera Policy Institute.

Díaz Briquets, Sergio and Jorge Pérez-López. 1997. "Refugee Remittances: Conceptual Issues and the Cuban and Nicaraguan Experiences." *International Migration Review* 31:2: 411–37.

Domínguez, Jorge I. 1978. *Cuba: Order and Revolution.* Cambridge: Harvard University Press.

Duany, Jorge. 2000. "Redes, Remesas y Paladares: La Diáspora Cubana desde una Perspectiva Transnacional." Paper presented at Taller sobre Redes Económicas y Sociales, auspiciado por el Grupo de Trabajo sobre Cuba del Consejo de Investigación en Ciencias Sociales en Nueva York.

Eckstein, Susan and Lorena Barberia. 2001. "Cuban-American Cuba Visits: Public Policy, Private Practices." A Report of the Mellon-MIT Inter-University Program on Non-Governmental Organizations (NGOs) and

Forced Migration. Cambridge, MA: MIT, Center for International Studies, Inter-University Program on Non-Governmental Organizations (NGOs) and Forced Migration.

————. 2002. "Grounding Immigrant Generations in History: Cuban-Americans and Their Transnational Ties." *International Migration Review.* 36(3):799–837.

Economist Intelligence Unit (EIU). 2001. *Cuba Country Report February 2001.*

————. 2002. *Cuba Country Report February 2002.*

————. 2002. *Cuba Country Profile Report 2003.*

————. 2003. *Cuba Country Profile Report 2003.*

Elbadawi, Ibrahim A. and Roberto Rocha. 1992. "Determinants of Expatriate Workers' Remittances in North Africa and Europe." Policy Research WPS #1038. Washington D.C.: The World Bank.

El Economista de Cuba. 2000. "La Espiral de la Recuperación." (Online) *El Economista de Cuba ONLINE: Dossier 2000.* http://www.eleconomista. cubaweb.cu/2000/nro45/45_157.html. (cited July 16, 2002).

Empresa de Telecomunicaciones de Cuba S.A. (ETECSA). 2004. (Online) http://www.sercuba.com/default.aspx (cited August 20, 2004).

Financiera CIMEX S.A. 2003. (Online) http://www.cubagob.cu/des_eco/ banco/espanol/sistema_bancario/fincimex.htm. (cited August 20, 2003).

García, Maria Cristina. 1996. *Havana USA: Cuban Exiles and Cuban-Americans in South Florida, 1959–1994.* Berkeley: University of California Press.

Granma. December 12, 1999. "En los resultados de 1999 se aprecia una mejoría, ante todo, en los indicadores de eficiencia económica."

Hamberg, Jill. 2001. "The Worst of Times and the Best of Times: Cuban Housing Policy since 1990." Mimeo.

ICC Corporation. 2002. "Cash 2 Cuba." (Online) http://www.cash2cuba.com/ remittance.do (cited July 16, 2002).

————. 2001. "Preciosfijos.com." (Online) http://www.preciosfijos.com/ (cited July 16, 2002).

Inter Press Service (IPS). January 15, 1999. No. 18.

Jatar-Hausmann, Ana Julia. 1999. *The Cuban Way: Capitalism, Communism and Confrontation.* West Hartford, Conn: Kumarian Press.

Jensen, Robert T. 1998. "Public Transfers, Private Transfers and the 'Crowding Out' Hypothesis: Evidence from South Africa." Faculty Research Working Paper R98-08, John F. Kennedy School of Government, Harvard University.

Kaplowitz, Donna Rich. 1998. *Anatomy of a Failed Embargo: U.S. Sanctions against Cuba.* Boulder: Lynne Rienner Publishers, Inc.

La Despenalización del dolar, trabajo por cuenta propia y cooperativización de granjas estatales en Cuba : documentos y comentarios: Cuba en el mes. Dossier; No. 3. 1993. Rodríguez, Caridad and Nelson P. Valdés (editors and compilers). Albuquerque, New Mexico: Latin American Institute; Havana: Centro de Estudios sobre América, Sección de Información.

La Prensa. June 11, 1999. "Costa Rica será centro de transferencia de remesas familiares a Cuba." (Online). http://www.laprensahn.com/caarc/9906/c11003.html. (cited June 22, 2000).

Madrid-Aris, Manuel. 1997. "Growth and Technological Change in Cuba." *Cuba in Transition* (Vol. 7:216–228). Association for the Study of the Cuban Economy.

Marquetti, Hiram Nodarse and Anicia García Alvarez. 1998. "Proceso de reanimación del sector industrial: principales resultados y problemas." In Centro de Estudios para la Economía Cubana (CEEC) (Eds.), *Balance de la Economía Cubana a finales de los 90s (pp.19–60).* Havana, Cuba: Universidad de La Habana.

Marazul Tours. "Memories: the History and Philosophy of Marazul Tours." (Online) http://www.marazultours.com/. (cited June 22, 2000).

Martín, Consuelo and Guadalupe Pérez. 1997. *Familia, Emigración y Vida Cotidiana en Cuba.* Havana: Editora Política.

Martínez, Milagros, Magaly Martín, Blanca Morejón, Guillermo Milán, Invalis Rodríguez, Lourdes Urrutia, Consuelo Martín, Antonio Aja and Marta Díaz. 1996. *Los Balseros Cubanos: Un estudio a partir de las salidas ilegales.* Havana, Editorial de Ciencas Sociales.

Mesa-Lago, Carmelo. 1981. *The Economy of Socialist Cuba: a Two-Decade Appraisal.* Albuquerque: University of New Mexico Press.

MoneyGram. 2002. (Online): http://www.moneygram.com/consumer/. (cited May 15, 2002).

Monreal, Pedro. 2000. "Migraciones y Remesas Familiares: Notas e Hipótesis sobre el Caso de Cuba." Mimeo.

Morley, Morris H. 1987. *Imperial State and Revolution: The United States and Cuba, 1952–86.* Cambridge: Cambridge University Press.

Morris, Emily. 2000. "Interpreting Cuba's External Accounts." *Cuba in Transition* (Vol. 9:145–148). Association for the Study of the Cuban Economy.

New York Times. January 5, 1999. "U.S. Ready to Ease Some Restrictions in Policy on Cuba."

Nuñez Moreno, Lilia. 1998. "Impactos del Sector Informal en la Estructura Social Cubana" Presented at the XXI Latin American Studies Association Meeting. Chicago, IL.

Oficina Nacional de Estadísticas. 2001. *Anuario estadístico de Cuba 2001.* Havana: ONE.

Orozco, Manuel. 2000. "Remittances and Markets: New Players and Practices." Washington D.C.: InterAmerican Dialogue and the Tomás Rivera Policy Institute.

———. 2002. "Challenging and opportunities of marketing remittances to Cuba." Washington D.C.: InterAmerican Dialogue.

Panagea. 2003. (Online). http://www.pangeapartners.com/. (cited August 20, 2003).

Pérez-López, Jorge. 1995. *Cuba's Second Economy: From behind the Scenes to Center Stage.* New Brunswick: Transaction Publishers.

Peters, Phillip. 2000. *The Farmer's Market: Crossroads of Cuba's New Economy.* Arlington, VA: Lexington Institute.

Puri, Shivani and Tineke Ritzema. 1999. "Migrant Worker Remittances, Micro-Finance and the Informal Economy: Prospects and Issues." International Labor Organization Working Paper 21. Washington, D.C.: ILO.

QuickCash. (Online) http://quickcash.cubaweb.cu/esp/login.asp. (cited June 22, 2000).

Republic of Cuba. Ministry of Foreign Relations (MINREX). 2002. "Servicios Consulares." (Online) http://www.cubaminrex.cu/consulares/serv_consintro.htm. (cited July 16, 2002).

Robinson, Karina. 2002. "Fortress Cuba?" (Online) *The Banker*, August 2002. http://www.thebanker.com/art3jun02.htm. (cited July 16, 2002)

Ross, James E. and María Fernández Mayo. 2003. "Cuba's Food Market and U.S. Exports." USDA Gain Market Report C13010.

Russell, Sharon Stanton. 1986. "Remittances from International Migration: A Review in Perspective." *World Development* 14:6: 677–696.

Sánchez Egozcue, Jorge Mario. 2000. "Cuba: Estabilización y Tipo de Cambio. *Comercio Exterior 50:1:* 38–54.

Smith, Peter. 1996. *Talons of the Eagle: Dynamics of U.S.-Latin American Relations.* New York: Oxford University Press.

Sullivan, Mark P. and Maureen Taft-Morales. 2002. "Cuba: Issues for the 107th Congress." Report for Congress. Order Code: RL 30806. Washington D.C.: Library of Congress Congressional Research Service.

Swamy, Gurushri. 1981. "International Migrant Workers Remittances: Issues and Prospects." World Bank Staff Working Paper No. 481. Washington D.C.: World Bank.

Taylor, Edward J. 2000. "Do Government Programs 'Crowd In' Remittances?" Washington D.C.: InterAmerican Dialogue and The Tomás Rivera Policy Institute.

Torres, Federico. 2001. "Migrants' Capital for Small-Scale Infrastructure and Small Enterprise Development in Mexico." Presented as a draft on October 9. 2001. Washington D.C.:World Bank.

Transcard Canada Limited. "Financial Growth." (Online) Transcard Canada Limited http://www.transcardinter.com/investors/financial_growth.html. (cited June 22, 2000).

United Status Bureau of the Census. (Online) 2003. American FactFinder. http://factfinder.census.gov/servlet/BasicFactsServlet (cited August 22, 2003).

United States Department of Homeland Security, Office of Immigration Statistics. (Online) *2002 Yearbook of Immigration Statistics.* http://www.immigration.gov/graphics/shared/aboutus/statistics/ (cited August 22, 2003).

————. 2003. "Enhancing Enforcement of Travel Restrictions to Cuba" DHS Press Release on October 10, 2003.

United States Department of Justice, Immigration and Naturalization Service (INS).(Online) Statistical Yearbook 1998. http://www.ins.usdoj.gov/graphics/aboutins/statistics/. (cited November 22, 2000).

U.S. Congress. 1992. Title XVII—Cuban Democracy Act Of 1992. (Online) U.S. State Department Cuba Archive. Available: http://www.state.gov/www/regions/wha/cuba/democ_act_1992.html. (Cited June 28. 2000).

————. 1996. Cuban Liberty and Democratic Solidarity Act of 1996. (Online) U.S. State Department Cuba Archive. Available: http://www.state.gov/www/regions/wha/cuba/helms-burton-act.html. (Cited June 28, 2000).

U.S. Department of the Treasury, Office of Foreign Assets Control (OFAC). 1963. "Cuba Assets Control: Regulations and Related Documents." *Title 31 Code of Federal Regulations Chapter V Part 515—Cuban Assets Control Regulations.* Pages 1–13. Washington D.C.: Treasury Department.

————. 1988. "31 CFR Part 515 Cuban Assets Control Regulations 53 FR 47526." Issued: November 23, 1988. ACTION: Final Rule (Online). Available: http://www.lexisnexis.com/universe. (cited June 28, 2000).

————. 1989. Cuban Assets and Control Regulations: 31 CFR Part 515. 54 FR 24282. Issued: June 6, 1989 (Online) ACTION: Notice (Online) Available: http://www.lexisnexis.com/universe. (Cited June 28, 2000).

————. 1989. "Federal Register Vol. 60, No. .203." (Online) Available: http://www.lexisnexis.com/universe. (Cited June 28, 2000).

————. 1991. Cuban Assets and Control Regulations: 31 CFR Part 515. 56 FR 49846. Issued: October 2, 1991 ACTION: Notice (Online) Available: http://www.lexisnexis.com/universe. (Cited June 28, 2000).

————. 1992. Cuban Assets Control Regulations, Fitness and Qualifications of Applicants: 57 FR 2624. Issued: January 22nd, 1992. Notice (Online) Available: http://www.lexisnexis.com/universe. (Cited June 28, 2000).

————. 1994. "31 CFR Part 515 Cuban Assets Control Regulations; Restric-

tions on Remittances and Travel Transactions: Part VII 59 FR 44884"
Issued: August 30, 1994 ACTION: Final rule; amendments. (Online) Available: http://www.lexisnexis.com/universe. (Cited June 28, 2000).

———. 1995. "Cuban Assets and Control Regulations: 31 CFR Part 515 Federal Register Vol. 60, No. .203 ". (Online) Available: http://www.lexisnexis.com/universe. (Cited June 28, 2000).

———. 1998. Cuban Assets Control Regulations: 31 CFR Part 515. Part II 63 FR 27348 Issued: May 18, 1998. ACTION: Final rule; amendments. (Online) Available: http://www.lexisnexis.com/universe. (cited July 24, 2002).

———. 13 July 1999. (Online) "An Overview of the Cuban Assets Control Regulations." http://www.treas.gov/ofac/. (Cited June 28, 2000).

———. 2004a. Authorized Providers of Air, Travel and Remittance Forwarding Service to Cuba. Washington D.C.: Treasury Department. http://www.treas.gov/ofac/. (Cited August 7, 2004).

———. 2004b. (Online) "Cuban Assets Control Regulations: Interim Final Rule." http://www.treas.gov/ofac/. (Cited June 28, 2004).

U.S. Department of State, Commission for Assistance to a Free Cuba. 2004. (Online) Report to the President. May 2004. http://www.state.gov/. (Cited June 1, 2004).

U.S.–Cuba Trade and Economic Council, Inc. 1999. (Online) "ECONOMIC EYE ON CUBA© March 1, 1999 to March 7, 1999." http://www.cubatrade.org/eyeonz27.html. (Cited November 22, 2000).

———. 2000a. (Online) "ECONOMIC EYE ON CUBA© January 3, 2000 to January 9, 2000." http://www.cubatrade.org/eyeon2000a.html. (Cited November 22, 2000).

———. 2000b. (Online) "ECONOMIC EYE ON CUBA© May 22, 2000 to May 28, 2000" http://www.cubatrade.org/eyeon2000a.html. (Cited November 22 2000).

———. 2001. (Online) "Realities of MarketCuba©." http://www.cubatrade.org/market.html. (Cited July 24, 2002).

Wahba, Sadek. 1991. "What Determines Workers Remittances? A Framework for Examining Flows from Migrant Workers, with a Focus on Egypt's Experience in the 1980s." *Finance and Development*, 28:4:41–44.

World Bank. 2004. *2004 World Development Indicators*. Washington, D.C.

Acknowledgments

The author wishes to thank the Mellon-MIT Inter-University Program on Non-Governmental Organizations and Forced Migration for funding a 1998 grant for "The Uses of Remittances and Their Effects on Informal Economic Activity in Cuba" and a 2001 grant for "The Ties That Bind: the Role of Refugees in Building Trans-National Family and Bilateral Relations" (the latter received with Susan Eckstein as principal investigator) as well as NGO sponsorship from Jeff Crisp, Head Evaluation and Policy Analysis Unit at UNHCR. This research would not have been possible without the generosity of those who agreed to be interviewed by the author and the support of innumerous scholars and institutions in Cuba including the Center for the Study of the United States (CESEU), the Center for the Study of the Cuban Economy (CEEC), the Center for the Study of International Migration (CEMI), Center for the Study of the International Economy (CIEI) and the Center for Psychological and Sociological Studies (CIPS). The author is also indebted to Sharon Stanton Russell and Ana Julia Jatar Hausmann for comments on the manuscript.

Notes

1   Based on a survey of Latinos on Latino Television Portrayals, DeSipio (2000) reports that 40.4 percent of Cuban émigrés reported sending remittances to their homeland, an average higher than Mexicans, Puerto Ricans and South Americans and below rates reported for the highest groups in Central America and the Dominican Republic. These probability ratios were further confirmed by logistic regression analysis.

2   The author conducted these interviews as part of joint research project with Susan Eckstein as principal investigator aimed at examining social and economic transnational ties. For more information about other aspects of these ties, see Eckstein and Barberia (2001).

3   In her extensive review of remittance research, Russell (1986) points out that policy measures by European labor-sending governments aimed at affecting migrant decisions to maximize the flow of remittances back home have been relatively well documented and evaluated.

4   Foreign currency-denominated bonds allow migrants to invest in their home country using their labor earnings without losses due to foreign exchange differentials.

5   Most mandatory schemes have been unsuccessful; the exception is South Korea (Puris and Ritzema 1999).

6   Using data from 1962 to 1979, Swamy (1981) found that the number of migrant workers abroad and their wages together explained over 90 percent of the variation in the flow of remittances. Neither the relative rates of return on savings in the host or home countries, nor incentive schemes, had a significant impact on total flows.

7   A wider body of research has examined the effects of indirect determinants such as the political, economic, and institutional environment in the homeland country on remittance flows. Researchers have argued that

government policies in the sending country, which affect political and economic conditions in the homeland, may alter a migrant's propensity to remit. For example, Elbadawi and Rocha (1992) and Wahba (1991) argue that government macroeconomic policies that stimulate foreign direct investment flows, such as low black market exchange rate premiums and low rates of inflation, also lead to an increase in remittances.

8   Most of the literature aimed at examining private family income transfers in the context of developing countries has been limited to examining interactions that take place between families within a country without reference to their immigrant status. For more work in this area, see Cox and Jimenez (1990); Cox, Eser, and Jimenez (1998); Jensen (1998); and Barberia, Johnson, and Kaufmann (1997). Taylor (2000) provides an overview and assessment of the impact of this research on the role of transnational remittances.

9   As Jorge I. Domínguez states, "Cuban entrepreneurs had close connections with the United States and because by this time they could certainly be presumed to oppose government policies, the survival of the revolutionary government required that the management of Cuban enterprises be passed to loyal revolutionaries, however bureaucratically incompetent (1978: 147)."

10 The total amount of money in circulation in August 1961 was 1,187 million pesos. A total of 497.6 million pesos or 42 percent was confiscated (Domínguez 1978: 229).

11 According to Mesa-Lago (1981: 47), "the monetary surplus steadily increased in the 1960s and in 1970 reached a peak of 86 percent over the population income; in other words, the total income of the population exceeded by almost twofold the value of available supply."

12 *Gusano*, which means worm in Spanish, is a pejorative term.

13 For further discussion on U.S.–Cuba travel policies and émigré visits see Eckstein and Barberia (2002).

14 For more on the introduction of these stores, see Pérez-López (1995).

15 Eventually a select group of Cuban nationals, such as diplomats and artists who earned foreign currency abroad, were also allowed to purchase commodities in these stores. Through *Oro* stores, Cubans could sell their gold jewelry to the state and receive receipts to use for consumption in state dollar stores.

16 The 1979 Cuban Penal Code replaced the Social Defense Code of 1936. For a detailed discussion, see Pérez-López (1995).

17 The penal code was revised in 1987, but no alterations were made to prohibitions on the holding of foreign currencies.

18 This is a pseudonym. This interview was conducted in Cuba and published in Barberia (2002) with the pseudonym Pedro.

19 During the late 1970s and early 1980s, consumer demand exceeded supply creating a situation of excess liquidity or monetary surplus, but these trends were showing signs of moderate improvement. According to Pérez-Lopez (1995: 115), "excess liquidity was equivalent to 35-36 percent of population income in the mid-1970s and declined to about 29-30 percent by the mid-1980s."

20 Initially, these reforms were aimed primarily at short-term stabilization policy responses. Over time, the reform package was consolidated. It should be underscored that the policy measures were primarily stabilization measures. However, this study argues that the secondary aim of these policy measures was to further channel remittance flows into the official economy.

21 Based on an interview with President Fidel Castro and Vice President Carlos Lage, reproduced in *La Despenalización del dólar* (1993) p.15.

22 The Cuban government gradually de-penalized the holding of foreign currency in 1993. In June, the government permitted workers employed in the tourist industries to retain their tips earned in foreign currency. Resolution 153 issued by the National Bank of Cuba (BNC) defined ten categories of Cuban citizens that were allowed to own foreign currencies; these included government officials, artists, and athletes who were traveling abroad, airline and fishing vessel crews, as well as international workers posted abroad.

23 Other portions of the speech are noteworthy as well. Fidel Castro explains, "but forwarding money is something that is done everywhere. There are many countries in the world where most of the income in convertible foreign exchange is money remittances from abroad. Mexicans, for example, send billions back to their country. Dominicans send plenty as well—another group who migrated for economic reasons… We—precisely due to our conflicts with the United States and conflicts with the worst elements of that emigration, those who used to be politicians—had been very strict regarding all this matter of transferal of money, although it was not prohibited and it was carried out in a normal fashion in specific amounts through the banks."

24 This excerpt is based on the speech published by LANIC's "Castro Speech" database which contains the full text of English translations of speeches, interviews, and press conferences by Fidel Castro, based upon the records of the Foreign Broadcast Information Service (FBIS), a U.S. government agency.

25 Resolution 140 passed by the National Assembly in August 1993 officially modified Article 235 of Cuba's Penal Code to permit foreign currency pos-

session, exchange and payments in foreign currencies. The official international fixed exchange rate of one Cuban peso to one U.S. dollar, in effect for more than thirty years, remained unchanged and continued to be used in international trade.

26 For an excellent review of Cuba's dual monetary policy in the 1990s, see Sánchez Egozcue (2000).

27 Banks had been authorized to conduct currency exchange operations, but had yet to implement these services.

28 The Ministry of Economics and Planning estimates that Cubans exchange one-fifth of their overall earnings in dollars, however it is not clear if these earnings also include remittances (Instituto Nacional de Investigaciones Económicas (INIE): 1999).

29 The command over societal resources, or the purchasing power obtained by issuing new money, is known as *seigniorage*. The reduction in value to holders of existing money balances due to the issuance of new money is termed the *inflation tax*. The sum of the inflation tax and seigniorage is equal to the real (i.e., inflation-adjusted) change in monetary holdings, or *real balances*. The relationship between them is: Real Balances = Seigniorage + Inflation Tax.

30 LIBOR (London Interbank Offered Rate) is the rate of interest at which banks borrow funds from other banks in the London interbank market. It is also a widely used benchmark reference rate for short-term interest rates.

31 See Banco Nacional de Cuba's *Informe Económico 1995*, p.4.

32 One such bank is the *Banco Popular de Ahorro* (BPA), which was created in 1983 and has 510 branches throughout Cuba. The *Banco Financiero Internacional* (BFI) is a private bank created in 1984. Both allowed savings deposits in dollars in 1995.

33 S.W.I.F.T. is a worldwide community with more than 7,000 financial institutions in 197 countries connected to one another through a proprietary software system. The network provides a mechanism to execute payments, securities, treasury, and trade services among members. According to the U.S.–Cuba Trade and Economic Council, Inc. (2000b), Cuba joined S.W.I.F.T. in 1990, after the government-operated National Bank of Cuba (BNC) obtained approval from S.W.I.F.T. to use computer software compatible with S.W.I.F.T., as the S.W.I.F.T. ST-2OO computer operating system used at the time was manufactured within the United States.

34 As will be elaborated in the fourth section, direct commercial bank transfers are prohibited by U.S. law and strictly regulated by the Office of Foreign Assets Control (OFAC) of the United States Department of the Treasury in Washington, D.C.

35 For further details, see U.S.–Cuba Trade and Economic Council, Inc. (2000b).

36 For further information about MINFAR, see CUBAPOLIDATA's "*Cuban Armed Forces Review.*"

37 This was confirmed by interviews conducted by the author with senior representatives working as managers in dollar stores in Havana.

38 For a more detailed discussion, see Ana Julia Jatar Hausmann (1999).

39 Nuñez Moreno (1998: 8) details that income taxes paid by 177,436 officially registered self-employed individuals contributed 1 percent of the 1998 state budget, which totaled 12,502 million pesos (CEPAL 2000). On average, this represents 700 pesos per officially registered self-employed individual in 1998.

40 In addition, these mechanisms also ease the transfer of remittances from the growing numbers of Cubans who have migrated to Europe and Latin America over the last decade.

41 As will be detailed in the fourth section, U.S. regulations limited remittances sent from the United States to Cuba to US$300 per quarter from 1998 to 2003.

42 For more on Fincimex's operations, see http://www.cubagob.cu/des_eco/banco/espanol/sistema_bancario/fincimex.htm.

43 Information published in Transcard Canada Limited "Financial Growth" webpage: http://www.transcardinter.com.

44 MoneyGram is owned by Minneapolis-based Travelers Express Company, Inc.

45 For more details, see http://www.cubatrade.org/2000hlights.html.

46 Confirmed by Ministry of Foreign Relation's (2002) website, see section on "Servicios Consulares" for further discussion.

47 Confidential interview conducted by the author.

48 The Cuban Penal Code still makes "illegal exit" a crime punishable by up to three years' imprisonment, if the attempt to leave is non-violent, or up to eight years if it involves violence or intimidation.

49 Following the nationalization of U.S.-owned banks on September 17th, 1960 and Cuban-owned banks on October 13th, 1960, President Eisenhower issued a comprehensive embargo on Cuban exports under the general authority of the 1949 Export Control Act on October 20 (Morley 1987: 121). According to Morley, the decision to invoke this act, rather than the Trading with the Enemy Act that would be invoked in 1962, allowed overseas subsidiaries of U.S. multinationals to escape compliance with U.S. policy.

50 For example, the Eisenhower administration was involved in a campaign to prevent Cuba from receiving loans and credits from Western and Canadian institutions (Morley 1987: 88).

51 For more detailed information, see Code of Federal Regulations, Title 31, Chapter V, Part 515 (OFAC 1963).

52 Under authorization from the Trading with the Enemy Act of 1917, the president of the United States has the power to prohibit financial transactions in time of war. The Cuban Import Regulations of February 1962, which banned the importation of Cuban-origin goods, allowed U.S. subsidiaries to continue to trade with Cuba. The Cuban Assets Control Regulations strengthened the blockade by supplanting the 1962 Cuban Import Regulations with a categoric prohibition on all trade with Cuba by U.S. entities.

53 As mentioned in the introduction, the issue of "going public" and government knowledge about private activity was repeatedly raised as an issue of concern during the interviews with Cuban émigrés conducted for this study.

54 With the death of Jorge Mas Canosa in 1997, the Cuban-American National Foundation also supported these policy changes. As quoted in the *New York Times*: "Reacting to the news in Miami, the Cuban-American National Foundation, a conservative exile group, issued a statement on Monday saying that most of the measures to be announced are consistent with current policy and praised the administration for refusing to re-evaluate U.S. policy toward Cuba (cited in Azcri 2000: 11)."

55 See 31 CFR §515.561(a).

56 Concomitant with this trend, pressures calling for the removal of restrictions on remittances in the U.S. continued and in 2002 and 2003 calling for the abolishing of restrictions on the sending of remittances to Cuban families passed as amendments to legislation under consideration in the U.S. House of Representatives. In 2002, Representative Flake's amendment to H.R.5120 lifting the US$1,200 cap on what Cuban-Americans are allowed to remit to their families passed by a 251–177 vote in the House. In 2003, Representative Delahunt's amendment to H.R.2989 prohibiting the use of funds in the bill to enforce any restrictions on remittances from the U.S. to nationals of Cuba or Cuban households passed by 222–196. In both years, amendments passed with considerable margins in the U.S. House of Representatives, though failing to advance beyond this stage.

INDEX